388.122
ERL   Erlichman, Howard
         J.

       Camino del Norte

DUE DATE

Camino del Norte

Number 105:
Centennial Series of the Association of Former Students,
Texas A&M University

Camino del Norte

How a Series of
Watering Holes, Fords,
and Dirt Trails Evolved
into Interstate 35
in Texas

Howard J. Erlichman

Texas A&M University Press
College Station

The paper used in this book meets the minimum requirements of the American National
Standard for Permanence of Paper for Printed Library Materials, Z39.48–1984.
Binding materials have been chosen for durability.
∞

Library of Congress Cataloging-in-Publication Data
Erlichman, Howard J., 1953–
Camino del Norte : how a series of watering holes, fords, and dirt trails evolved into
Interstate 35 in Texas / Howard J. Erlichman.—1st ed.
p. cm. — (Centennial series of the Association of Former Students,
Texas A&M University ; no. 105)
Includes index.
ISBN 1-58544-473-1 (cloth : alk. paper)
1. Interstate 35—History.   2. Roads—Texas—History.   3. Trade routes—Texas—
History.   4. Express highways—Texas—History.   5. Texas—History, Local.   6. Texas—
Commerce—History.   7. Transportation, Automotive—Texas—History.   8. Roads—
Texas—Design and construction—History.   I. Title.   II. Series.
HE356.U55E75   2006
388.1′22′09764—dc22
2005022855

The photo on the title page and front cover is courtesy of the Texas Department
of Transportation.

Contents

Maps

Acknowledgments

Virtually all of the facts, figures, and events presented in this history were assembled—inevitably and unapologetically—from secondary sources during 2000 and 2001. This book would simply not exist without the often spectacular research contributions made by hundreds of historians, scholars, observers, and government archivists over the decades (and even centuries).

Fortunately, virtually all of these research materials were readily available at the libraries of the University of Texas at Austin—an awesome group of archives that include the Benson Latin American Collection, the Center for American History, Perry-Castaneda and the specialty libraries of the Engineering, Geology, Architecture and Planning, Law, and Public Affairs departments. Other important materials were derived from the excellent holdings of the Texas Department of Transportation (TXDOT) Travel Division Library, Texas State Library and Archives, Texas General Land Office, Texas A&M University at College Station, Texas State University at San Marcos, The Laredo Planning Department, Universidad Autónoma de Zacatecas, Austin Public Library, San Antonio Public Library, Laredo Public Library, and the Morton Museum of Cooke County.

Many thanks to the highly professional and consistently helpful staffpersons employed at each of these library sites. I would also like to single out Miguel A. Pavon's deft cartography, Sally E. Antrobus's copyediting skills, and Anne L. Cook's stewardship of TXDOT archives and lore; their talents have helped to improve the quality of this book greatly. Last but not least, I would like to thank the Erlichman family for their unflagging encouragement throughout.

Careful readers will discover that ample doses of existing scholarship have been interwoven in an attempt to achieve greater accuracy or to enhance narrative flow. To reflect a process through which published research has been blended with the author's own interpretation and analysis, many of the source notes should probably be viewed more as bibliographical sources than as independent references to specific facts and figures. The collection, occasional revision, and repackaging of existing information is the sole responsibility of the author; any errors are inadvertent and will, I hope, be corrected in later editions.

Introduction

The subject matter of this book started out as an interest. Then it developed into a hobby. Eventually, the historical puzzle of Interstate 35 in Texas became nearly an obsession. I discovered that the central question—how and why did the magnificent I-35 Corridor develop as (and where) it did?—could be answered only with investigation and research. Fortunately, thousands of excellent books and articles on Texas and North American history would provide the critical foundation for this effort. Unfortunately, most of the existing scholarship had either ignored the subject entirely or offered detailed slices of history too specific, too disjointed, or too local to ease my path. Layer upon layer of centuries-spanning history would have to be uncovered, dissected, prioritized, and repackaged to chronicle the developments that led to I-35.

The physical highway itself, approved as a U.S. interstate in 1947 and largely completed by 1970, would be of little help. Nor would much illumination come from the glittering skylines of San Antonio, Austin, Dallas, and Fort Worth, the technology parks, warehouses, frontage roads, parking lots, strip malls, apartment complexes, and pasture lands that blanket the roadscape between Laredo and the Red River crossing in Cooke County. Yet the towering achievement of I-35, the string of metropolises that it connects, and the nearly 8 million people residing along its path had not just happened on its own. If the puzzle were to be solved—at least for myself—I would have to write my own book.

That I-35 connects relatively recent settlements in Texas with the ancient communities of Mexico added greatly to my interest. The North American Free Trade Agreement (NAFTA) has placed I-35 and Mexico in the headlines since 1994. But how could regional, cross-border trade (and trade trails) not have developed over the preceding centuries, or even millennia? Since the Rio Grande appears significantly wider on most maps than it does in reality, why would this arbitrary political boundary present a greater obstacle to trade flows (and the development of long-distance trails) than does any other principal river in North America?

My modest knowledge of Mexican history and geography indicated that fantastic civilizations had been created in Central America and the Valley of Mexico a thousand years before Cortés's arrival in 1519 near what is now Veracruz. I also recalled that the Spanish conquest of Mexico had extracted massive quantities of silver, decimated native peoples, and created European towns as far north as Santa Fe and Saltillo. These modern communities were established before the first English settlers had arrived at Jamestown and Plymouth Rock. When I discovered that a prosperous network of Indian agricultural and trading communities had existed in West Texas and East Texas for many centuries—but virtually none in the vast, mineral-poor region of Central Texas—I became hooked on the puzzle of I-35.

The questions began to multiply. If European civilization had reached Saltillo in 1578, why had it taken nearly two hundred years to settle the future I-35 gateway at Laredo (1755), less than two hundred miles away? Why had more than a hundred years elapsed between the founding of San Antonio (1718) and the establishment of Austin (1839), less than eighty miles up the trail?

There was more. If the French had explored the upper Red River nearly to present-day Lake Texoma by 1720, and Waco (Indian) Village had been visited by the Spanish in 1721, why had it taken so long for Dallas (1841), Waco (1845), and Fort Worth (1849) to be settled by white people? Why had the I-35 towns of Laredo and San Antonio evolved into major cities while other eighteenth-century communities like Presidio del Rio Grande, San Saba, La Bahía (Goliad), and Nacogdoches have remained familiar only to local residents and historians? Why had the future due-northerly route of I-35—our Camino del Norte—eclipsed the venerable northeasterly Camino Real as Texas' principal highway between the Rio Grande and the Red River?

Since the future route of I-35 developed symbiotically with major metropolises—Laredo, San Antonio, Austin, Dallas, and Fort Worth—the histories of these towns are critical to the story of I-35 itself. But while I have attempted to chronicle the early development of these and other communities, I have ignored most of their later (and greater) fame. Similarly, only two chapters are devoted to the post-1940 period when I-35 and the U.S. interstate highway system were planned, constructed, and improved. I am less interested in the physical highway itself than in the forces that shaped its routing and development. It is suggested that the associated survey, engineering, funding, and construction efforts have been extraordinary for many centuries and that recent efforts to widen, improve, and reroute sections of I-35 are part of a never-ending process.

Since the completion of the bulk of the research for this book in 2001, there has been an explosion of new highway projects and funding schemes to address the dramatic expansion of I-35 traffic generated by population growth, business enterprise, and NAFTA. New highway projects like Texas 130 and the proposed Trans-Texas Corridor are also part of a continuum, falling within the same chronology of events that converted a series of watering holes, fords, and dirt trails into Texas I-35. As will be seen, the predecessor pathways of our focus were developed over a number of centuries by buffalo herds, stone age cultures, Indian tribes, European explorers, hunters, traders, missionaries, soldiers, empresarios, slaves, rangers, pioneers, cattle drivers, freighters, stagecoaches, railroad magnates, cotton farmers, early automobile owners, and military planners. NAFTA and the explosive growth of Central Texas' population are just the latest factors in this long-running adventure.

Therefore, this chronicle is less about the physical placement of I-35 than about the circumstances that led to its creation. The principal circumstances involve the founding of posts and villages and the early development of important towns between the Rio Grande and Red River. Without towns, there would be no roads. Other key aspects are of the indirect variety, occasionally wandering off into areas that would not appear to have much impact on I-35. I would argue, however, that indirect factors—such as pre-Columbian cultures, Mexican silver mining, road- and bridge-building technologies, Indian tribes, railroad developments, military affairs, and "car culture"—are just as important to the history of I-35 as are exploration, settlement, and federal funding.

If recent events, state and local politics, the inevitable role of special interests, and the otherwise intriguing history of communities lying outside the I-35 Corridor (most notably Houston) have been deemphasized, the occasional wanderings into indirect subject matter should be considered as colorful "off" and "on" ramps to the history of I-35.

Camino del Norte

Digging into the Highway's Past

*S*LIGHTLY north of San Antonio International Airport in Bexar County lie the remains of ancient prehistoric peoples. Like most archaeological finds today, the remains were discovered during a series of modern construction projects. In one case, the catalyst was a new middle school, St. Mary's Hall. The prehistoric remains revealed at the St. Mary's site—mainly Folsom and Plainview projectile points dating from the Paleo-Indian period (9200–6000 B.C.)—were found to be consistent with other archaeological sites situated along the northern banks of Salado Creek.[1]

Salado Creek is part of a regional drainage system that has generated hundreds of archaeological sites in Bexar County. Back in 1962, highway construction crews along future Loop I-410 discovered three ancient burial mounds near the Salado crossing of the Old San Antonio Road, a predecessor to US 81 and I-35 northeast of downtown San Antonio. With schedules to meet, a team of archaeologists from San Antonio's Witte Museum was given only two weeks to investigate the site. But two weeks were better than none. The burial mounds were found to be thousands of years younger than the St. Mary's site (possibly dating from 4000 B.C.) and contained a more advanced collection of projectile points, cutting and scraping tools, flint knives, and shell ornaments.[2]

About one hundred miles to the north, the Inner Space Caverns (south of Georgetown) were discovered by Interstate 35 construction crews in 1963. The limestone caverns, among many underground reservoirs associated with the

Edwards Aquifer system, were found to hold the remains of Ice Age mastodons, mammoths, and wolves that were possibly ten thousand years older than the remains at St. Mary's. Southwest of Georgetown along Brushy Creek, the skeleton of a woman (the "Leanderthal Lady") dating back 7,000–9,000 years was uncovered with various artifacts during a 1982 construction project along FM 1431 in Leander. A more recent group of hunters and gatherers have left stone tools, cutting blades, and spear points dating possibly from 2000 B.C. along Walnut Creek in East Austin.[3]

Moving north, Archaic period (Carrollton Focus) projectile points, knives, tools, and hearths have been discovered at the confluence of the three forks of the Trinity River in Dallas County, and 7,500-year-old Scottsbluff points and reworked Clovis points have been found along the Trinity's banks in southeastern Dallas. A variety of artifacts has been unearthed along the Elm Fork of the Trinity in Denton and Cooke counties. In Denton County, the fourteen underground stone hearths discovered near Lewisville revealed ancient campfire sites, flint spear points, and the remains of prehistoric animals. At Moss Lake, northwest of Gainesville on the Red River, a seven-thousand-year-old site was discovered in the mid-1960s. In addition to Archaic period hearths, dart points, and tools, the site included artifacts (pottery, bows and arrows, tools) from a much later Kadohadacho (Caddo) Indian culture of A.D. 850–1000.[4]

Unfortunately, next to nothing is known about the peoples who inhabited these ancient Texas sites. It is not known who they were, how long they occupied a certain living place, whence they had come, or where they were going. One probably has no business trying to link their unknown travel patterns with a history of Interstate 35. But in an attempt to write a chronology of events that led to the development of I-35, one cannot completely ignore ten thousand years of prehistory simply because it is somewhat speculative. In short, if the Salado Creek people lived at roughly the same time (around 8000–6000 B.C.) as peoples residing in a string of prehistoric sites located in future I-35 counties— for example, Comal (Landa Park), Hays (Aquarena Springs), Travis (McKinney Falls), Williamson (Wilson-Leonard), Bell (Kell Branch), Hill (Kyle Rockshelter), Dallas (Three Forks), Denton (Lewisville), and Cooke (Moss Lake)—they may have traded with one another.[5]

It is known that people have lived in North and South America for possibly thirty thousand years. It is also known that the Pleistocene Ice Age ended between 8000 and 7000 B.C. and that mammoths, mastodons, and other large animals became extinct. Surviving humans lived mainly as nomadic hunters, fishermen, and gatherers until the end of the Archaic period (around 1800 B.C.), when the first indications of village life and pottery making were established. Experts believe that these nomadic peoples typically traveled in groups of fifty to a hundred and lived on wild plants, wild game, and local water supplies. These peoples lived in caves and rock shelters and left physical evidence such as open hearths, storage pits, trenches, bones, and skulls. Stone tools, knives, axes, picks, beads, and pipes began to appear after 5000 B.C. Eventually, as the Archaic period drew to a close, the nomads began to dabble in agriculture. Corn was probably introduced by peoples in Central America and has been dated to as early as 2500 B.C. in places as far north as New Mexico and Tamaulipas, Mexico. Pottery vessels and bows and arrows did not appear until around 1 A.D.[6]

Since hunting meant survival, the development of hunting weapons and cutting tools was a technological advance comparable to the invention of the steam engine or microprocessor. Indeed, the most important archaeological object in the research and dating of prehistory is the projectile point: the business end of a spear, dart, or arrow. The projectile point could be a stable technology for centuries or even millennia. But when the technology advanced, as in the case of the Clovis point (used to hunt mammoths) in 9000 B.C. and the Folsom point (used to hunt bison) in 8500 B.C., civilization advanced too.[7]

If this much is known, we may at least speculate that nomadic peoples wandered around the Americas over some kind of primitive trail system until around 1800 B.C. The trails were probably created by migrating animal herds, especially buffalo, in search of grazing lands and water. Buffalo traveled hundreds of miles in seasonal migrations. They learned the best river crossings and found hidden passes through mountain areas. As hunters followed the herds, the buffalo trails became more permanent. Thereafter, as villages emerged, the primitive trail system evolved into increasingly sophisticated trails and trading networks over a period of more than three thousand years.[8]

None of these ancient highways and byways can be linked to I-35, but the trails created a foundation of trade and travel that can and should be linked to modern affairs. Most American history books start with the European explorers (typically Columbus in North America, Cortés in Mexico, and Cabeza de Vaca in Texas), the introduction of maps, and the first recorded itineraries of people and places. However, the intrepid Europeans did not land on vacant terrain. North America had seen at least ten thousand years of prehistoric human occupation, of which the three thousand years from 1500 B.C. to 1500 A.D. might be described as relatively modern. Incredibly, Central Texas—located in the middle of some of the oldest migration paths—somehow managed to escape the civilizing influences that occurred during this three-thousand-year core period. The future development of Central Texas would be shaped by events occurring to the south, west, and northeast.

With thousands of riverbanks like Salado Creek waiting to be investigated in North America—each possibly with its own special treasure trove of prehistoric remains buried under layers of accumulated earth and needing only some new construction project to catalyze its discovery—the implication is that some form of ancient trail system existed thousands of years before European explorers set foot on the continent. We can only guess at whether any of these ancient pathways were utilized by indigenous peoples such as the Coahuiltecans, Karankawas, Tonkawas, Caddos and Jumanos in Texas, or the Mississippian mound builders of Cahokia, Illinois, the Pueblo peoples of New Mexico, or the Olmecs on the Mexican Gulf Coast. However, the later Spanish Caminos Reales (royal highways) almost certainly followed an existing network of prehistoric trailways that had been established over the millennia. Why not speculate that a few of these ancient trails ran through Central Texas, quite possibly linking the Rio Grande Valley with a string of settlements (if not villages) stretching northward to the Red and Arkansas rivers?

So what happened to these ancient trails? First, the geology and climate of North America may appear to be constant during a century or two, but over a period of thousands of years, things change. Who is to say how many heavily trodden dirt paths now lie beneath many feet of topsoil or became part of an adjacent riverbed? Climate experts believe that the arid South Texas plains were once relatively verdant grasslands with a wide variety of wildlife. The Spanish explorers reported surprisingly cold weather with heavy frosts and snows during the 1600s. The course of the meandering Mississippi River, where a sophisticated Indian civilization flourished after 500 A.D., has been a moving target for centuries. Villages are problematic too. How many Coahuiltecan habitats lie buried beneath a parking lot in Laredo, San Antonio, or San Marcos? The great Aztec city of Tenochtitlán lies under modern Mexico City.

As already indicated, many of the ancient trails were blazed by animals long before they were formalized by prehistoric human hunting parties. However, evidence suggests that North American bison herds—the most important source of food, clothing, and materials for several peoples—disappeared and reappeared in cyclical periods comprising many centuries. These cycles were probably due to climatic change. Archaeologists have yet to find any bison remains in Texas, northeastern Mexico, or the Great Plains during two distinct periods—5500–2500 B.C. and 500–1250 A.D. If these estimated gaps are correct, it is probable that Indian hunters simply followed the bison to wherever the herds had migrated.[9]

Some of the Indian migration paths may not have been conventional footpaths at all. The ancient "trails" that guided people from place to place may have been formalized as broad stretches of open land, marked by visible landmarks such as rivers, trees, hills, rocks or positions of the sun, moon, and stars. For example, much of the arclike Balcones Escarpment "trail" between Del Rio and the hills west of Waco was eventually utilized by Spanish explorers. Visible features like the Balcones would provide rough but critical guidance to people— ancient and modern—whose principal concern was finding a new hunting ground, water, better weather, or eventually the location of a friendly trading village.

Water was paramount. It is no accident that a chain of communities developed along the plentiful springs of the Balcones Escarpment. San Felipe Springs (Del Rio), San Pedro and Olmos Springs (San Antonio), Comal Springs (New Braunfels), Aquarena Springs (San Marcos), Barton Springs (Austin), and Waco Springs all lie along the Balcones. Each of these sites is located near future modern cities and shows evidence of a human presence of over ten thousand years. Clovis points and the ancient remains of mastodons, mammoth, and bison have been found at Aquarena Springs. Points, shell beads, and pottery from the Late Archaic period (500 A.D.) have been discovered at Smith Rockshelter overlooking McKinney Falls in Travis County. The Clovis-era Lewisville Site in Denton County is miles away from the Balcones, but the site was near water and currently lies beneath the Garza–Little Elm Reservoir.[10]

Whether the ancient trails of Central Texas were marked by springs, landmarks, or more conventional footpaths, we may speculate that they were linked to a wider interregional system. Possible interregional trade routes are suggested by the discovery of tools, weapons, and ornaments made from shell, bone, and stone that originated from one particular region but were uncovered in hundreds of different locales. The La Calsada archaeological site, discovered thirty-four miles south of Monterrey in 1965, contains artifacts dating from 7500– 5000 B.C. that resemble objects found in central Mexico, six hundred miles to the south, and items unearthed near the junction of the Pecos River and the Rio Grande (Val Verde County, Texas). Similar types of sea shells (dating from 8500–7500 B.C.) have been found both in Central Texas and in archaeological sites north of the Arkansas River in Arkansas. If antiquities found along the

Balcones Escarpment can be linked to remains found at La Calsada, in Val Verde County, or in Arkansas, it may be speculated that a primitive trade route (river and land) stretching from Arkansas to central Mexico may have existed even in Archaic times.[11]

Unfortunately, the development of Archaic period routes and possible interregional trading systems seems to have stalled for around seven thousand years. Climatic changes and relocation of bison herds help to explain human migrations during a span in which the technological sophistication of artifacts developed in 8000 B.C., whether they were from Salado Creek or Central America, was much the same as that of artifacts dating from 1200 B.C. The people who produced these artifacts were nomadic hunters and gatherers, and projectile point technology appears to have been their only area of cultural advancement.

It was not until around 1200 B.C., when the Olmecs arose in the southeastern coastal region of Mexico, south of Veracruz, that the first great civilization in the Americas came into being (map 1). Of course, the Olmecs had precursors. Ancient Mexican cultures flourished much earlier at El Cedral in San Luis Potosí (30,000 B.C.), Puebla (20,000 B.C.), and the Tehuacán Valley southeast of Puebla (10,000 B.C.). The cultivation of corn is believed to have originated in the Tehuacán Valley in around 5000 B.C., spreading as far north as the Río Pánuco by 2000 B.C. Between 1200 and 600 B.C., agriculture and other developments enabled the Olmecs to establish La Venta, a coastal city with around eighteen thousand inhabitants, and to extend trading routes between Central America and central Mexico. Trade goods were usually small, lightweight objects like jade, obsidian, sea shells, mica, and stingray spines. Olmec maps included the depiction of trading routes with a hieroglyphic footprint.[12]

The rise of the Olmecs solidified the position of Mexican and Central American culture as the driving force of hemispheric development and trade over the next 2,700 years. If any pre-Columbian travel and trade made its way to Texas, it would have been directly or indirectly influenced by the Olmecs and their successors. The Olmec Empire mysteriously disappeared in around 600 B.C., and some five hundred years elapsed before new empires were established by contemporaneous but culturally distinct peoples: the Teotihuacanos in central Mexico, the Classic Maya on the southeastern Gulf Coast, and the Zapotecs at Monte Albán (near present-day Oaxaca). Each borrowed heavily from economic structures originated by the Olmecs and these peoples, with the later Toltecs and Aztecs, would dominate prehistoric trading systems

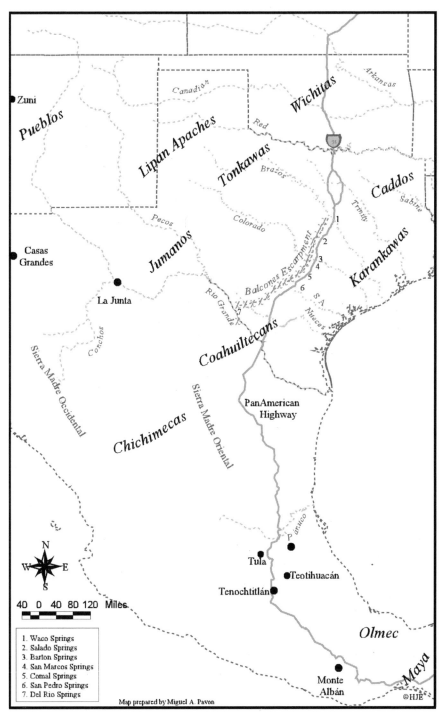

Map 1. Pre-Columbian Civilizations.

until 1519. Native cultures in what would become the United States advanced during the centuries as well but never to the extent of the great Mexican civilizations.[13]

The trading networks established by the Olmecs, and extended by their successors, operated along similar lines. Local trade trails connected one Indian tribe or village to the next village, water supply, or hunting ground. These local trade trails, in turn, were connected to a major interregional trade trail. Since the wheel and draft animals were not introduced to the Americas until the Spanish arrived, it may be assumed that interregional trails, like local trails, remained narrow, winding affairs suitable for human porters (*tlamemes*) and domesticated dogs. From Olmec times to the Aztecs, long-distance trade goods were restricted to prized lightweight items like maize, obsidian, knives, sea shells, and tobacco. Pottery (too bulky) and water (too heavy) were rarely carried over great distances. Trade trails usually followed rivers or led from one watering hole to the next. Most of the hemisphere's major trading centers were located at river confluences or at sites adjacent to topographical change (e.g., mountains and escarpments).

As civilizations advanced, humble trails were upgraded into roadways. The Classic Maya (200 B.C.–900 A.D.) built scores of stone-paved roads called *sacbe* throughout the Yucatán to link their religious sites and temples. One sixty-mile-long sacbe between Coba and Yaxuna, built around 625 A.D., is perfectly straight, nearly fifteen feet wide, and elevated from two to eight feet with stone sides. The roadbed itself, constructed with a series of layers that would have impressed the Romans, comprised a foundation of large stones, a layer of smaller stones, and a whitish limestone cement topping. The translation of sacbe is "white road." Without a wheel, Mayan road engineers used a roller device pushed by fifteen men (usually slaves) to flatten their limestone surfaces. Merchants were responsible for identifying, building, and maintaining trade routes and local rest stops.[14]

Teotihuacán (150 B.C.–700 A.D.), an imperial city of one hundred thousand located twenty-five miles northeast of Mexico City, extended the Olmec-Maya trading networks north to Durango and even traded (for turquoise) with the Pueblo peoples of Arizona and New Mexico. The later Toltecs (800–1300 A.D.) extended this network dramatically. The Toltecs settled no farther north than the traditional east-west "Chichimeca line" between present-day Guadalajara and Tampico—where the river valleys ended and the arid regions began—but their influence was nearly everywhere. Artifacts from all over North America have been uncovered in the Toltec capital at Tula, fifty miles north of Mexico

City, while Toltec objects have been found in Mississippi Valley burial mounds. The Toltecs even formalized the "Turquoise Trail" initiated by the Teotihuacanos. Turquoise nuggets were mined by the Pueblo peoples, then carried via marked Pueblo roads (like those in Chaco Canyon, New Mexico) to warehouses in Casas Grandes in Chihuahua, shipped south to Alta Vista in Zacatecas for processing, and delivered to Tula for final distribution.[15]

The later Aztecs (1300–1519) refined these vast trading networks by improving linkages between their capital city of Tenochtitlán ("prickly pear tree") and the principal tribute-paying regions. Aztec roads had many different names and were categorized as good, swept, straight, winding, small, and old, among other things. Outside the capital, local authorities were usually responsible for maintaining roads, inns, and rest stops. The Aztecs built bridges and elevated causeways, supported by wooden columns and large stones, but do not appear to have utilized any road-building or civil engineering techniques from either the Maya or the contemporaneous Inca (1200–1532). Inca roads were pedestrian-oriented and unpaved, but many of the fourteen thousand miles of highway built between Quito, Ecuador, and Santiago, Chile, included retaining walls and drainage systems. Inca engineers also built thousands of bridges and causeways, many cantilevered, and designed spectacular rope suspension bridges across mountainous gorges.[16]

It is unclear whether the Incas, the Aztecs, or some other culture, past or present, represented the most advanced civilization in American history when the Spanish arrived. It is also unclear whether the Aztec capital of Tenochtitlán was any more sophisticated than Teotihuacán or the Toltec capital at Tula; it just happens that Tenochtitlán's splendor was recorded by Spanish visitors. An awed Bernal Díaz del Castillo (with Cortés in 1519) compared Tenochtitlán favorably with Constantinople, Rome, and Naples. If the demise of the pre-Aztec empires is a mystery, there is clarity concerning the Spanish conquest of the Aztec empire and its decimation by European diseases. The population of central Mexico, estimated at around 25 million in 1519, plummeted to fewer than 1 million by 1600. Losses in warfare were compounded by smallpox, measles, typhus, plague, malaria, and yellow fever, devastating the native populations. Smallpox alone cut Tenochtitlán's population in half within two years of Cortés's arrival.[17]

One may ask what the Olmecs, Mayas, Teotihuacanos, Toltecs, and Aztecs have to do with a history of Interstate 35. Directly, nothing—archaeologists have yet to find any Olmec or later Mexican artifacts in Central Texas. Indirectly, however, the great Mexican civilizations created a foundation of economic development, including trade routes and roads that were adopted and extended by the Spanish and French and that were utilized by the first Anglo-American colonists. I would submit that the roots of I-35 actually started in La Venta in around 1000 B.C., spreading north through central Mexico and catalyzing great (if temporary) trading centers like Alta Vista and Casas Grandes. After Cortés's arrival in 1519, the Aztec network was co-opted by Spaniards, extended to Saltillo by 1578 and eventually to Laredo, San Antonio, and San Marcos.

Saltillo would remain a northeastern Spanish outpost for well over a century. The Coahuiltecans were in the way. Compared to the great civilizations of Mexico and most other Indian cultures in North America, the Coahuiltecans of northeastern Mexico and south-central Texas represented a quasi-stone-age world in 1500. Except for irregular trade with the Caddos to the northeast and the Jumanos to the west, historians have found no apparent connection between the Coahuiltecans (or their coastal cousins, the Karankawas) and the rest of pre-Columbian civilization. The Aztecs, like their predecessors, had declined to extend their empire north of the Chichimeca line but continued to trade with the northern Chichimeca periphery. While evidence of this trade is seen clearly in the upper Rio Grande Valley in New Mexico and all over the Mississippi River Valley, it somehow had little or no influence on south-central Texas.

This is not to say, however, that the region's principal inhabitants, the Coahuiltecans and Karankawas with their simpler cultures, were struggling. Evidence suggests that wildlife remained plentiful for centuries in Coahuiltecan territories located as far south as Río Pánuco. If these regions were inhospitable to agriculture, local tribes simply adapted to local conditions. Like their prehistoric ancestors, bands of fifty or so Coahuiltecans lived on deer, turkey, freshwater fish, and regional specialties like pecans, walnuts, plums, grapes, roots, and berries.[18]

Some anthropologists believe that Coahuiltecan culture may have peaked during the period 200–500 A.D. but then declined through the remaining thousand years of pre-Columbian history. This suggests that the people of south-central Texas lived largely in cultural isolation, hundreds of miles distant from the Mississippi tribes to the east, the Pueblos to the west, and central Mexico to the south. W. W. Newcomb Jr. observes: "The hypothesis that a migration passed through Texas, pipeline fashion, from Mexico to the southeastern section of what is now the United States, leaving no imprint whatsoever on the traversed region, is unbelievable."[19] Yet it seems to have been the case.

In short, for a thousand years the vast territories of south-central Texas and northeastern Mexico escaped the technological advances and sociocultural complexities of the surrounding cultures. When Cortés arrived in 1519, the Coahuiltecans and Tenochtitlán were worlds apart. The rare cultural influences that did intrude upon the Coahuiltecans from the south probably arrived circuitously from the north. This assumes that the Pueblo peoples traded with West Texas Jumanos, who traded with Great Plains Indians, who traded with Mississippi Valley tribes, who traded with East Texas Caddos. If the Caddos declined to trade with the quasi-stone-age Coahuiltecans and Karankawas, the latter tribes would truly have been isolated cultures.

The Coahuiltecans had most of Central Texas to themselves until the mid-1600s, when buffalo-hunting plains tribes like the Tonkawas, Lipan Apaches, Kiowas, and Wichitas began to appear. Nomadic Comanches, a federation more than a unified tribe, did not arrive until around 1700. But when they did, horse-mounted Comanche warriors wreaked havoc on everybody. In the meantime, everything was relative. The Coahuiltecans and Karankawas were less sophisticated than the Caddos, Jumanos, and the more famous plains tribes (Apache, Wichitas). The Caddos and Jumanos were, in turn, less advanced than the peoples of the Mississippi River Valley and New Mexico. The Mississippi and New Mexican civilizations, in turn, paled in significance next to the sophisticated civilizations of central Mexico, Central America, and Peru. These great cultures, in turn, were conquered by Europeans.

Ancient trade routes guided the Spanish conquest, and ancient trails guided the wanderings of Cortés, De Vaca, Coronado, De Soto, Moscoso, and others between 1519 and 1542. Cabeza de Vaca, the first European trader in North America in 1528, learned to conduct business with people accustomed to barter and sign language. De Vaca traded goods like sea shells, bone and stone beads, feathers, textiles, clothing, foodstuffs, medicines, weapons, gourds, and dried bison meat, items that had been traded across networks covering thousands of miles and thousands of years. Later, Europeans added superior technology to the mix, but in the same way that the Aztecs had usurped networks developed by their predecessors, the Spanish and to some extent the Anglo-Americans did essentially the same thing. The Aztecs had ignored Texas, but their trade network made it much easier for the Spanish to extend their own empire northward.

While it would take some time after its founding in 1718 for San Antonio to reach even half the level of commerce of colonial Saltillo (1578), the development of San Antonio was made possible by trade routes through Saltillo, linking Central Texas to the southern civilized world. Texas remained on the far periphery of New Spain, but trading patterns established in the preceding millennia—including primitive trail networks utilized by the Coahuiltecans and Karankawas—helped shape its development. Many of these trading patterns would have bearing on the ultimate shape of Interstate 35.

2

In Quest of Silver, 1519–1776

*W*ITHIN ten years of Hernán Cortés's first visit to Tenochtitlán, Álvar Nuñez Cabeza de Vaca and three other survivors of the Pánfilo de Narváez expedition of 1528 found themselves wandering through southern Texas and northern Mexico. Having knowledge of the sophisticated Aztec empire and the wonders of Tenochtitlán, an island city that had been destroyed and rebuilt by Cortés as Mexico City, the De Vaca party must have found the simple lives of the Karankawas and Coahuiltecans quite a shock. After some time as captives, the foursome traveled as explorers, traders, and occasional guests of various Indian tribes on their circuitous route from the Texas Gulf Coast via the Rio Grande Valley and western Mexico to Mexico City.

No one has been able to pinpoint the exact route of De Vaca's wanderings; if any of his travels evolved into Caminos Reales, one is hard-pressed to confirm them. His rough itineraries, recorded from memory after his return to European civilization in 1536, omitted any mention of trails, whether Indian or buffalo. This omission does not imply that there were no trails, but it does not help. Yet if De Vaca and his three comrades typically had little sense of their whereabouts, they must have followed at least some Indian trails used by the more than twenty different tribes they encountered in Texas and Mexico.[1]

De Vaca's wanderings are not directly related to the eventual development of Interstate 35, but the foursome crossed south-central Texas brush country that is very familiar to residents of present-day Cotulla and Laredo (map 2).

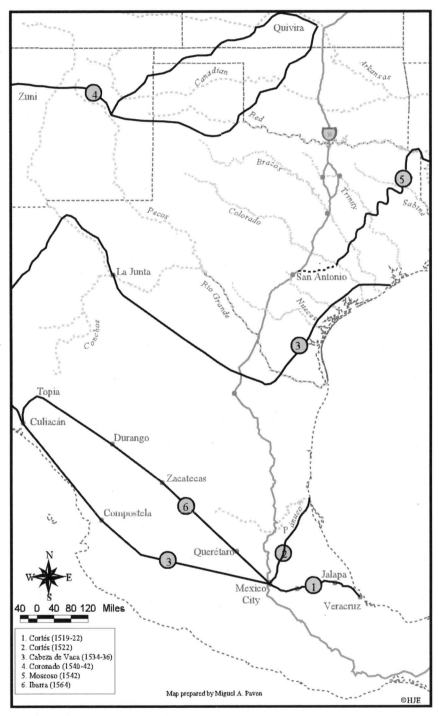

Map 2. The First Europeans: Selected Routes, 1519–1564.

The party's final escape from captivity in the fall of 1534 was achieved by a pre-arranged rendezvous (at a site possibly south of San Antonio) determined by tribal movements, prickly pear season, and moon positions. De Vaca's astonishing firsthand observations about pre-Columbian life in Texas are priceless and include at least one prediction of note: "Throughout the country are extensive and beautiful plains with good pasturage; and I think it would be a very fruitful region were it worked and inhabited by civilized men."[2]

De Vaca's adventures represent one of the greatest and most courageous journeys in North American history. However, his arrival in this unknown part of the world had been deliberate and the motivation was purely mercenary. The Narváez expedition had not been about trade and making friends with the local tribes; it was about potential mineral wealth and plunder. Following Cortés's spectacular conquest of Tenochtitlán in 1521, the Spanish Crown and the explorers and conquistadors contracted to it had developed a keen appetite for additional treasure.

Spain's treasure hunts would have a direct impact on routes that evolved into Interstate 35. Like the actions of the Olmecs, Maya, Teotihuacanos, Toltecs, and Aztecs before them, Spanish exploration, conquest, and colonization activities between 1500 and 1800 created a necessary foundation. In search of treasure, routes and highways were established as far north as New Mexico and Saltillo by 1600. If Texas was a wild and barren land when Moses Austin arrived in 1820, a long and substantial economic history was nevertheless in place to greet him. This was a history of usurpation. The Aztecs had usurped the dominions of their predecessor civilizations, the Spanish had usurped Aztec power, and 350 years later, it would be the Anglo-Americans' turn. Since San Antonio, Laredo, and San Marcos were all established near the end of the Spanish period, they form a colonial bridge between prehistoric Texas and I-35.

Cortés's conquest of Tenochtitlán had been achieved with some one thousand Spaniards, fifty thousand Indian allies, and a conclusive eighty-five-day siege ending in August 1521. As Cortés attempted to extend his control to the far reaches of the Aztec empire, he also built roads. In search of treasure, he slogged through Honduras between 1524 and 1526 and organized a road-building effort to link Mexico City via Oaxaca with San Cristóbal de las Casas, founded in Chiapas in 1528. Díaz del Castillo described efforts by Spanish soldiers and Indians to carve out roads in Chiapas where ancient trails were supposed to be. In the face of occasional Indian attacks, hundreds of miles of jungle brush were cleared and scores of bridges were built. A one-thousand-beam structure was reportedly built across the San Pedro River in western Campeche in four days. Many of these roads and bridges evolved into segments of the Pan American Highway.[3]

Having had enough of the mineral-poor jungles of Central America, Cortés returned empty-handed via Veracruz to Mexico City. His attention shifted to the new capital and the consolidation of his fledgling (and brief) empire, established as New Spain in 1523. Flush with treasure and tribute revenues, Cortés had constructed New Spain's capital city on the ruins of Tenochtitlán in 1522. As many as four hundred thousand Indian laborers had been "enlisted" for the massive urban-renewal project, supplemented by two major European innovations: the wheeled cart and mules. Aztec roads were improved, and many of the island city's canals were filled and converted into avenues. If the streets of the new city followed much of the old Aztec plan, Spanish Mexico City was constructed along a uniform colonial grid-system design that had been introduced at Santo Domingo in 1502. This system was eventually applied to all Spanish town designs in the Western Hemisphere, including Santa Fe, Albuquerque, El Paso, San Antonio, and Laredo.[4]

Plans were afoot by 1522 to link Veracruz, the site of Cortés's landing in 1519, with Mexico City via Tlaxcala, Perote, and Jalapa. The new east-west highway, parallel to Cortés's invasion path, would be North America's first Camino Real. A second (lower) route would follow the old Aztec highway through Puebla and Orizaba. The initial road plans are undocumented, but records indicate that a licensed highway inn was founded in Perote in 1527. It is possible that the location of the first Spanish inns determined the routing of the highway itself—not the other way around. The extent to which the new Spanish roads utilized or upgraded sections of earlier Aztec roads is likewise unclear. But with ample amounts of plunder capital at their disposal and a clear need to transport goods (and more plunder) between the seaport and the capital, Cortés and the Spanish Crown had every reason to ensure that good quality roadways were in place.[5]

The Spanish Crown had maintained a few Caminos Reales in Spain, mainly palace-to-palace affairs, but Spanish and other European roads had been woeful for at least ten centuries. No European highway in 1500 matched the former glory of the Appian Way (Via Appia), a surfaced 130-mile route between Rome and Capua that was commissioned by Appius Claudius Crassus in 312 B.C. The multilayered foundation and drainage system of the Appian Way created a model for the fifty-three thousand miles of Roman highways that followed, including roads built to Roman Spain's copper mines at Río Tinto and her silver mines in the Sierra Morena. The great Roman highways gradually disintegrated. Other than pilgrimage highways and roads linking a royal palace or two, few medieval governments built, maintained, or policed long-distance highways. Medieval travel was so dangerous that local merchants often organized militias to protect their cargo-laden wagons from robbers ("highwaymen"). London, Paris, and other trading centers attempted to institute a toll system in the mid-fourteenth century to fund road maintenance, but the measures were usually ineffective.[6]

The extent to which Roman, Spanish, or Inca road-engineering concepts were applied in the Spanish Americas is unclear. It appears that the Camino Real between Mexico City and Veracruz was marked only by stones, with occasional Aztec-style wooden bridges built across the more difficult streams. Otherwise, little is known about the actual construction of the Caminos Reales—a term that applied to any Spanish road that was supported by funds from the royal treasury. Even with next-to-free Indian labor, road construction was probably viewed as expensive, and Spain was initially after plunder, not long-term infrastructural investment. The Caminos Reales were developed to link the capital city with the new farms, mining districts, missions, and military posts and to implement a system of tribute even more onerous than that of the Aztecs (map 3).

Construction along the often mountainous route between Veracruz and Mexico City began as early as 1524–25, and a government-funded *carro* (wagon) road was in place by 1531. As traffic increased, the lower second road was added. A southern highway between Mexico City and the Pacific port of Huatulco, via Oaxaca, was begun in 1529 but was replaced in the 1540s after a much shorter route was formalized to Acapulco. Founded in 1530, Acapulco prospered in the second half of the sixteenth century from the Pacific trade with Peru and the Philippines—ships from Manila arrived every six months. Before the Camino Real was completed to Acapulco, the journey by human porters (*tlamemes*) to and from Mexico City took about a month. Once the new highway was built, the trip was reduced to less than ten days.[7]

As New Spain was being organized, competitive rivalries and hyperbolic reports of fantastic silver cities—for example, the mythic Seven Cities of Cibola—provoked exploration in the vast uncharted territories of North America. The notorious Nuño Beltrán de Guzmán and his lieutenants conquered a string of northwestern Mexican territories by 1529, helping to found Santiago de Compostela and San Miguel de Culiacán in 1529, Guadalajara in 1532, San Luis

Potosí in 1533, Querétaro in 1537, and Guanajuato (by missionaries) in 1542. Another conquistador, Francisco Vásquez de Coronado, ventured even farther north between 1540 and 1542. From a staging area at Compostela, Coronado traveled through present-day Sonora, eastern Arizona, New Mexico, and the Texas Panhandle before halting at the Wichita villages (Quivira) in central Kansas. There were no Cibolas for Coronado, but a survivor of his ill-fated missionary party, Andres Do Campo, is believed to have returned separately to Mexico City between late 1543 and March 1547, in an adventure that nearly rivals De Vaca's legendary travels.[8]

If the somewhat murky legend is true, Do Campo was the first European to travel north-south between the Red River and the Rio Grande—a distinction he would hold for more than two hundred years. Like De Vaca, Do Campo was captured and enslaved by Indians for possibly one year but either managed to escape or was released. Once freed, Do Campo is claimed to have blazed an unbelievable trail from the Arkansas River in Kansas to the mouth of the Río Pánuco (present-day Tampico). The northern half of Do Campo's journey may have benefited from notes made from Coronado's own possible travels to the North Concho River in west-central Texas. The southern half may have benefited from notes made by De Vaca's comrade, the Moroccan slave Estevanico, or the recent travels of Luis de Moscoso.[9]

Since Do Campo's real or imagined exploits were eventually published in 1552 by one of Cortés's colleagues, Francisco López de Gómara, his adventures became well-known. Do Campo's southern route, parallel to but well to the west of US 281 and I-35, may have passed through southwestern Oklahoma, crossing the Red River near Vernon, Texas, then going due south near the future towns of Abilene and San Saba (Menard County) and crossing the Rio Grande near Eagle Pass. From the Rio Grande, Do Campo may have traveled southeasterly near the future sites of Monclova and Saltillo en route to Pánuco. From Pánuco, Do Campo apparently headed southwest to Mexico City, possibly via the future route of the Pan American Highway.[10]

Coronado returned to Mexico City empty-handed and demoted. Another would-be plunderer, Hernando de Soto, fared even worse. Having already acquired great wealth with the Pizarros in Peru, De Soto landed near Tampa Bay in May 1539, with six hundred men and more than two hundred horses. He then proceeded through what are now Florida, Georgia, South Carolina, Tennessee, and much of Alabama before heading northwest to the Mississippi River. After rafting across the Mississippi into eastern Arkansas in the spring of 1541, De Soto followed the Arkansas River up to the future site of Little Rock, then veered back southeast to the Mississippi opposite present-day Natchez. At this point, De Soto was stricken with fever, and he died in May 1542. His successor, Luis de Moscoso, continued the expedition westward through Louisiana and southwestern Arkansas.[11]

Moscoso apparently crossed the Red River into the northeast corner of Texas at a site near present-day Texarkana. From there, he followed Caddo trade trails throughout, traveling southwesterly through the future site of Nacogdoches and points west. Moscoso ended his mineral quest as far west as the Guadalupe River (or another stream) in early October 1542, possibly reaching the future I-35 site of New Braunfels. After retracing his route back to the west bank of the Mississippi River, Moscoso and his 310 men crafted seven homemade boats and managed to sail down the Mississippi in July 1543. The party eventually reached Río Pánuco in September before making an overland journey to Mexico City, possibly leaving a trail for the intrepid Do Campo.[12]

If the northern territories of Florida, Texas, New Mexico, Arizona, and California proved to be a disappointment to the Spanish Crown, a series of silver strikes in the wild Chichimeca territory north of the traditional settlement line would change everything. In fact, without the discovery of the first northern silver mine in Zacatecas in 1546, new Camino Reales would have been delayed or halted, and Texas history would have unfolded very differently. Without Zacatecas, the Spanish probably would have held to the traditional settlement line that ran from Pánuco on the Gulf Coast through Querétaro in the central highlands to Compostela on the west coast. This was the same Chichimeca line that had marked the northern boundary of the great preceding civilizations—the Teotihuacanos, Toltecs, and Aztecs—for centuries. Without minerals to extract, anything north of this line would have been regarded as hostile and dangerous territory.

The silver ore that would alter the course of Texas history was discovered in Zacatecas by complete accident. Minor silver and gold strikes had been made in Sultepec (1530) and Taxco (1534), southwest of Mexico City, and in northwesterly Guadalajara in 1542. In September 1546, however, the biggest prize of all was uncovered by a crafty frontiersmen, Juan de Tolosa. Tolosa observed that the local Zacatecan Indians apparently possessed enough silver ore to trade the mineral in routine barter exchanges. When the ore was linked to deposits in and around Cerro de la Bufa, a massive silver rush was unleashed in the previously off-limits province of Zacatecas. This silver strike dwarfed anything found in North America to date and triggered an exploration boom in Zacatecas and the adjacent Chichimeca territories. The eight-thousand-foot-high city of Zacatecas, established in 1548, almost immediately became the second largest city in New Spain. The classic boom town featured more than thirty-four companies, sixty mines and smelters, and an expanding population of imported, reasonably well-paid Indian laborers (*naboros*) and black slaves.[13]

The key to the longer-term success of Zacatecas was a new refining technique: amalgamation. Pilot-tested in Pachuca in the early 1550s, the mercury-intensive amalgamation (patio- or courtyard-mixed) process allowed increasingly large volumes of low-quality silver-bearing ores to be refined economically. Zacatecas was less prolific than Potosí (Bolivia), but the district produced more silver in 1562 than all of the other mines of New Spain combined. Fortunately for Philip II, who succeeded his spendthrift father Charles V in 1556 and continued the Habsburg practice of squandering vast mineral treasures on inconsequential military campaigns, this was only the beginning. Including regular boom-and-bust cycles, Zacatecas produced an average of 1.2 to 1.5 million pesos of silver per year between 1559 and 1763 and set new production records in the early 1800s. While New Spain's silver mining industry ebbed and flowed with general economic conditions, labor availability, foreign competition, tax policies, and the royal monopoly on mercury (quicksilver), an estimated sixty thousand tons of silver were extracted from Mexican mines during the Spanish Colonial period.[14]

New highways were critical to New Spain's emerging silver industry. The narrow trails that had served long-distance Indian traders (*pochteca*) for thousands of years proved woefully deficient for mining operations as well as for future military, hacienda, and mission-building activities. Although many of the old trails were still utilized by traditional human porters, the tlamemes were a dying profession. The future was represented by New Spain's evolving (but always chaotic) highway network. Viceroy Antonio de Mendoza, who extended the Camino Real system that Cortés had launched in the 1520s, reported in 1547 that east-west Caminos Reales had been completed between Veracruz and Acapulco, via Mexico City, and that north-south Camino Reales ran from Querétaro via Mexico City to Oaxaca.[15]

The new highways were planned by the viceroy but were usually built and funded by silver magnates and merchants. Businessmen had the most to gain from their completion. The actual details of Spain's road building and road improvement activities are somewhat vague. One can assume that Spanish surveyors and highway engineers combined low-budget European techniques with local conditions. If any Inca techniques were transferred north to New Spain,

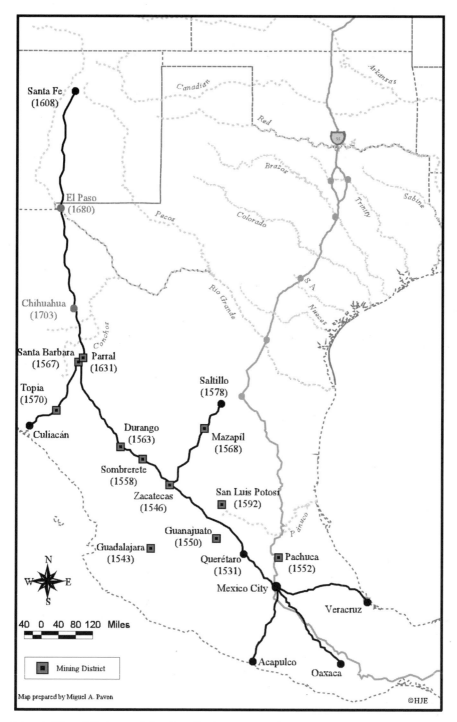

Map 3. Silver Mining and Caminos Reales, 1519–1608.

especially the Incas' remarkable retaining walls, drainage systems, and can-tilevered bridges, there is no record of it. Inexpensive draft (*requerimiento*) Indian labor was employed on most major highway projects, supplemented by Spanish troops.

The quest for silver pushed the Camino Reales north. A 140-mile highway (based on Indian trails) had been completed to the northern outpost of Queré-taro in the 1530s in order to serve a steady stream of merchants, government officials, cattlemen, and livestock. From Querétaro, a northwesterly route was eventually extended to Guadalajara in the early 1540s. This road supplied Zacatecas with provisions and labor on a temporary basis after 1546. When a direct route between Querétaro and Zacatecas became necessary, the Camino Real was extended 240 miles to the north between 1550 and 1555. Fortunately for budget-conscious officials, the flat terrain provided a much easier task than the mountainous road projects between Mexico City and the two coasts. During the next twenty years, the northern route was extended to Durango and Santa Barbara and northeasterly to Saltillo.[16]

Once the northern road was completed between Querétaro and Zacatecas, Zacatecas silver was connected directly to the royal Casa de Contratación (House of Trade) in Seville. The inbound cargo ships from Seville, via the Canary Islands and the West Indies, typically took two to three months to reach Veracruz. Another month was required for the overland journey to Mexico City and another month to reach Zacatecas. Zacatecas immediately became the continent's second most important trade center, after Mexico City. A prestigious royal treasury office (royal *caja*) was established to stamp the Zacatecas silver and coordinate its shipment down to the royal mint in Mexico City. Minted silver was then hauled to Veracruz, shipped to Seville, and distributed throughout Europe.[17]

To accommodate the large iron-wheeled carros and their precious cargo—inbound lead, mercury, and equipment for mining, smelting, and refining and, of course, outbound processed silver—roads in New Spain had to be stronger and wider than those in Spain. Carros were often organized into eighty-wagon convoys driven by teams of oxen, mules, and horses. The carro itself was designed especially for the long-distance trade between Zacatecas, Mexico City, and Veracruz. The wagons had four times the carrying capacity (4,000 lb.) of smaller *carretas* (1,000 lb.) and were fortified to defend against hostile Indian attacks. Unlike mule trains, carros did not have to be loaded and unloaded every day.[18]

Large cargo shipments were also carried by mule trains, cumbersome as they were. Trains were typically arranged in packs of twelve to thirty mules driven by licensed Indian or mestizo drivers (*arrieros*). Many arrieros built sizable freighting businesses in the late 1500s, and more than a few diversified into real estate and other ventures. While Mexico had ample grazing lands for both mules and oxen, mules had their advantages. They could carry up to four hundred pounds of cargo, travel five to six hours without rest, and negotiate narrow, winding trails. Oxen could carry larger loads but they tended to wear out faster and weaken on diets of short, dry grass. Still, common two-wheeled carretas—constructed with wooden pegs, rawhide ropes, and a cottonwood trunk—were more likely to be drawn by oxen than by mules.[19]

Given the economics of silver production, processing, and shipment, military improvements to and protection of the Caminos Reales became increasingly important. By 1555, the new road to Zacatecas could handle all types of vehicles, and a chain of walled garrisons was planned to protect the convoys from hostile Indian attacks. Missionaries often followed the garrisons, and the viceroy issued generous land grants as incentives to military officials. These improvements, in turn, catalyzed the development of feeder roads into the hinterland communities. Long-distance trade followed. Foodstuffs from distant regions like Michoacán began to end up on dinner tables in Zacatecas.[20]

An evolving merchant class, mainly made up of Indians and mestizos, developed freighting businesses, general stores, and regulated inns (*ventas*). Querétaro, the wagon and freighting center of New Spain, would have a thousand inhabitants in 1590 and five thousand by 1630. In addition to mining-related goods and foodstuffs, all kinds of merchandise was freighted north to Zacatecas. A list of licensed goods, mainly from Spain, included silks, cotton, cloth, shoes, slippers, sandals, tools, kettles, dishes, machetes, almonds, figs, and sardines—to name a few. Many of these goods were distributed to licensed inns to minimize possible contacts with hostile Indians. Often fortified, inns were located every fifteen to twenty miles along the Caminos Reales. Viceregal grants and royal licenses were unusually democratic. Most inns were operated by allied Indians or missionaries and some by an occasional aristocrat—the enterprising Cristóbal Oñate apparently received a license to own and operate an inn along the new Zacatecas highway in 1550.[21]

Grants, licenses, and the day-to-day operations of the Caminos Reales were managed at the viceregal and provincial levels. Detailed regulations were established by the Spanish Crown. According to historian John W. Clark Jr., the Crown's Recopilación de Leyes de los Reinos de las Indias addressed a host of possible issues, including price gouging by inn keepers and/or their suppliers (May 1558); the funding and deployment of bridge projects, repairs, and Indian work crews (August 1563); the promotion of new shortcut routes (November 1568); and recommended load weights, determined in arrobas (December 1614).[22]

All of this modernization, including the relentless spread of disease, was bound to create tensions with the local Zacatecans, people of a Chichimeca hunting and gathering culture, who must have been shocked to find their ancient ways so disrupted. Most Indian tribes took slaves as spoils of war, but the Spanish mining system involved a completely new type of servitude—paid labor or not. Since the Spanish recruited thousands of newly Christianized Indians from the south as paid laborers, it was inevitable that hostilities would break out between these Indians, the traditional Zacatecans, and the Spanish.[23]

With an enormous North and South American empire to manage, and its own challenges in Europe, the cash-strapped and perpetually overextended Spanish Crown had insufficient resources to support New Spain's economic development and military defense. These functions were left mainly to private enterprise. Most of the developments, improvements, and defenses occurring along the Caminos Reales were typically structured as reward/risk incentives. The Crown had little capital but much power. It could grant licenses, concessions, land, and inns to entrepreneurs who believed that the business development opportunity outweighed the short-term risk. Common soldiers were often paid with livestock, land, and slaves to provide protection. When a pacification policy was determined to be more successful than military campaigns, licensed stores were established to distribute food, clothing, and shelter to local Indians.

The Zacatecas strike encouraged exploration activity all over Mexico. Silver was discovered in Pachuca (northeast of Mexico City) in 1552, in Guanajuato in 1558, and in San Luis Potosí in 1592. New discoveries were even made in the untapped hills of urban Zacatecas—Mina El Eden, still working today, was opened in 1586. Francisco de Ibarra, nephew of one of the leading Zacatecas silver magnates, led expeditions to San Martín, 115 miles northwest of Zacatecas, and found major silver and lead deposits at nearby Sombrerete in 1558. Ibarra also established the cities of Durango (1563) and Santa Barbara (1567), staging areas for a major silver strike at Parral in 1631. Modest silver deposits were uncovered in Mazapíl, 140 miles northeast of Zacatecas, in 1569.[24]

Following Ibarra's death in 1575, Luis de Carvajal managed to claim Ibarra's territories as his own and moved aggressively to consolidate his empire.

Carvajal established Saltillo ninety miles northeast of Mazapíl in 1578 and added a new capital at present-day Cerralvo (between the future site of Monterrey and the Rio Grande). He also crossed into South Texas at a ford that had possibly been utilized by De Vaca. The Spanish Crown was so impressed with these efforts that Carvajal was granted the massive domain of Nuevo León in 1579. Nuevo León stretched from the Río Pánuco to as far west as Durango and as far north as the San Antonio River—almost precisely the confines of the Coahuiltecans. But Carvajal's empire was short-lived. Ibarra's unhappy heirs induced the Holy Office of Inquisition to arrest Carvajal (a descendant of Portuguese Jews) for heresy in 1590. Carvajal died in prison in 1591.[25]

Most of the northern mining enterprises were constrained by labor shortages. The drastic depopulation of Mexico as native people succumbed to disease and warfare is a fact, although the numbers are controversial. A study by S. F. Cook and W. Borah estimated the preconquest (1519) population of central Mexico at 25 million. Others have presented estimates ranging from 3.2 million to 37.5 million. According to Cook and Borah, Mexico's native population was reduced by nearly 8 million (to 17.4 million) between 1519 and 1523. From there, things only got worse, the numbers dropping to 6 million in 1548, 3 million in 1568, 2 million in 1580, and a low of 750,000 natives in 1630. The census of 1650 indicated New Spain's total population at around 1.2 million, mainly because of Spanish immigrants, black slaves, and other non-Indians. Even if the figure of 25 million is inflated, there is no doubt that Mexico's native population came close to being destroyed between 1519 and 1630.[26]

Not only were the new mines located in sparsely populated areas; the local Indians who had managed to survive the European diseases were typically hostile to Spanish initiatives. In response to this hostility and the general labor shortages, slave-hunting parties were organized out of Santa Barbara and other northern outposts. Since many of these slave hunts were directed at the Río Conchos area, they moved New Spain ever closer to New Mexico and West Texas. Silver exploration activities continued to fan out in a northerly direction. Saltillo was mineral poor, but it provided the most northeasterly outpost of Spanish control.

With silver to produce and transport, the Caminos Reales and an associated chain of garrisons, villages, and stores were extended north to Santa Barbara, Mazapíl, and then Saltillo. In addition to mining, Ibarra had spearheaded the development of another major economic activity: cattle ranching. Andalusian-bred cattle had been introduced to Hispaniola by Columbus, and after a few years of cross-breeding in Cuba, they were transported to the mainland by

Cortés, Narváez, Coronado, De Soto, and their successors. Unlike the silver industry, which required aristocratic connections, cattle ranching was a middle-class affair. The profession was open to almost any small entrepreneur (including missionaries) with energy and commitment. It was encouraged by the Crown to stimulate settlement, support defense, and spread Christianity. Many of the Chichimeca territories were found to have excellent grazing lands, and since the silver industry needed beef, leather, and tallow, the economics were logical. Land grants as large as four thousand acres were issued to committed individuals, and some haciendas boasted cattle herds of more than a hundred thousand head. Cattle ranching led to the establishment of Saltillo, located 230 miles northeast of Zacatecas, and then Monterrey and Villa de Almadén (Monclova).[27]

Of course, New Spain was modeled on Spain, and Spain was still locked into a feudal-style, agriculture-based economic system that had been developed in the early Middle Ages. Funded by silver, the objective in New Spain was to establish large agricultural estates, missions, and presidios (forts) through which Spanish political and religious control could be institutionalized—just as in Spain. While the missionary component of this program was probably well intended, New Spain's Indian population was viewed mainly as a potential labor supply. In the words of José Carlos Maríategui, "the Spaniard brought to America the effects and methods of an already declining spirit and economy that belonged to the past." Spain's proven (if increasingly obsolete) system was transferred, with few revisions, to the Americas. It was managed by an age-old understanding among the Spanish Crown, the Catholic Church, the military, and the large agricultural landowners.[28]

The far northern outposts of Saltillo (1578), Monterrey (1596), and Santa Fe (1608) were established according to pattern. Saltillo, located 610 miles northeast of Mexico City and less than 200 miles southwest of present-day Laredo, eclipsed Cerralvo and Monterrey as the region's most significant cattle town and staging area. Saltillo's fortunes greatly impacted the future development of Monterrey, Monclova, Laredo, and San Antonio, but northeasterly exploration activities were delayed by a lack of silver deposits and by possible concerns about territorial rights—given the fate of Carvajal. Juan de Oñate, son of a Zacatecas silver magnate, was licensed in 1598 to lead 130 colonists, 83 wagons, and 7,000 head of livestock due north from Santa Barbara through the future site of Chihuahua (not founded until 1703) and a Rio Grande ford at El Paso del Norte. While the upriver town of Santa Fe was eventually established in 1608

as the northern terminus of a fifteen-hundred-mile Camino Real from Mexico
City, there would be no Seven Cities of Cibola in New Mexico.[29]

Spaniards had extended the Caminos Reales from Veracruz via Mexico City
to distant Saltillo in less than sixty years, between 1519 and 1578. But many
decades elapsed before the northern side of the Rio Grande—Texas—was investigated. This left Saltillo as the Crown's northeasternmost settlement for
more than a hundred years. Other than a brief interest in Matagorda Bay,
which was discovered, renamed San Francisco, and claimed for the Spanish
Crown in 1558, serious European forays into Texas had been extremely rare
and uneventful. Explorers and slave hunters occasionally wandered into the region, but these visits were always temporary. Meanwhile, the viceregal treasury
was crippled by a cyclical decline in silver production between 1630 and 1670.
With limited funds available for colonization, the vast mineral-poor territory
of Texas was left to the Coahuiltecans, Karankawas, Tonkawas, and Caddos. In
1665, one venturesome group of Spaniards nearly reached the Nueces River before being turned back by hostile natives. Exploration continued, irregularly
and unprofitably, for the next ten years.[30]

But the insignificant territory north of the Rio Grande was about to become
significant. The jolt occurred when French explorer René-Robert Cavelier,
Sieur de la Salle, stumbled into Lavaca Bay, Texas, in January 1685. La Salle had
reached the Mississippi River and claimed "Louisiana" for the French king
Louis XIV during his voyage of 1682, an action that split Spain's Gulf Coast
empire in two and moved France closer to Spain's silver holdings. However, La
Salle's expedition of 1685 somehow missed the mouth of the Mississippi River
by four hundred miles. Whether this was the result of navigational errors or
not, La Salle sited the new French colony of Fort Saint Louis to the north of
Lavaca Bay and apparently established relations with Tejas Indian villages located east of the Trinity River. Unfortunately for France, the colony floundered,
and La Salle paid for his strategic errors with his own life—he was killed east of
the Brazos River by two of his own men in March 1687. Fort Saint Louis was
eventually abandoned and then destroyed by Karankawas in December 1688.[31]

La Salle's attempted foray into Spanish territory was a call to action. Alonso
de León, a Coahuila-based explorer and trader and the newly appointed governor of Nuevo León, made two expeditions into the wilds of South Texas in
1687 and 1688 in search of La Salle's rumored colony. In 1687, he traveled
from Monterrey to Baffin Bay, southeast of present-day Kingsville on the Gulf
of Mexico, but came up empty. The following year, De León forded the Rio

Grande at or near the so-called Paseo de Francia (south of present-day Eagle Pass), upriver from where the ill-fated 1665 party had crossed into Texas. This expedition was also turned back before reaching the Nueces River, but De León at least managed to capture Jean Gery, a wily French frontiersman who had been living among the natives near the ford and who probably had a good idea about the whereabouts of the French colony.[32]

Undaunted by De León's failures to date, Viceroy Conde de Galve commissioned De León for a third expedition in 1689. This entrada would make history. De León's task was to find and destroy the French colony, find and retake a captured Spanish vessel, and establish a Spanish mission in the vicinity. Aided by Gery's intelligence, the party of a hundred soldiers, priests, mule drivers, and allied Indians set out in late March 1689, from Monclova, located north of Saltillo and 120 miles south of Paseo de Francia. Monclova had been named for former governor Conde de Monclova after his transfer to Peru. De León's entrada included over 700 horses, 200 head of cattle and pack mules carrying 80 loads of flour, 500 pounds of chocolate, and 3 loads of tobacco. These supplies and gifts had been provided by the royal treasury office in Zacatecas.[33]

Assisted by Indian guides and Jean Gery, De León blazed the first of a series of northeastern trails between Saltillo and the lower Red River in Louisiana (map 4). He traveled south of the future site of San Antonio, but eastern and western segments of his routes would evolve into Texas' first Camino Real, later known as the San Antonio Road to Nacogdoches. De León typically followed Indian trails marked by inscriptions and rock piles, probably segments of ancient trade trails. Such trails had linked East Texas Caddo (Tejas) tribes with West Texas Jumanos for centuries. While Coahuiltecans and Karankawas traded only occasionally, important Indian trading centers were located at the future sites of San Marcos and La Grange—each at the junction of a major trail and a major river.[34]

De León's expedition of 1689 followed what would be known as the Lower Presidio or La Bahía Road of the main Camino Real. The Lower Presidio Road started from the future site of Presidio, also known as Guerrero or San Juan Bautista (in honor of a future mission). Presidio was on the Mexican side of the Rio Grande, thirty miles south of Piedras Negras/Eagle Pass. From Presidio, De León crossed the Rio Grande at Paseo de Francia, located around two leagues (or 5.2 miles) to the south, and continued eastward to the Nueces River, crossing west of Carrizo Springs. He was now in unknown territory. Continuing east from the Nueces, he probably crossed the San Antonio River northwest of the future site of Goliad (La Bahía) and crossed the lower Guadalupe River near present-day Victoria en route to Lavaca Bay. In late April 1689, De León managed to locate the ruins of La Salle's Fort Saint Louis, and he returned to Monclova in May.[35]

On a follow-up trip with Franciscan father Damian Mazanet of Querétaro in 1690, De León retraced the 1689 route to the Guadalupe River. From there, however, he added a new northeast extension, from the La Grange crossing of the Colorado River to a site within fifty miles of present-day Nacogdoches. Much of this route had been utilized by Indians for centuries, only to be discovered in 1686 and 1687 by La Salle and his lieutenants en route to the Tejas villages located east of the Trinity River. De León subsequently established Mission San Francisco de Los Tejas between the Trinity and Neches rivers in April 1690. The local Tejas tribe was a Caddo culture with an early interest in Christianity; Tejas means "friends," but the friendship would not last long. Possibly influenced by the untamed spread of European diseases since 1500, a process that had reduced the Caddo population from possibly two hundred thousand in 1519 to less than ten thousand in 1690, Spanish missionary activity in East Texas would be an on-again, off-again affair for decades.[36]

De León managed to chart most of his journeys through Texas. The Spanish Crown had required that diaries be kept, but the quality of these records varied considerably. There is no record of De León's return trip to Coahuila, but most historians believe that one or both of his expeditions are the first representations of the northeastern extension of the Caminos Reales into Texas. From Saltillo, capital of Coahuila, via Monclova and the Paseo de Francia crossing at Presidio, the extension eventually connected Mexico City with Spain's future northeastern outposts at Natchitoches and Los Adaes, Louisiana. While none of De León's east-west trails are predecessors to Interstate 35, they created a foundation for routes that would be.[37]

As with Cabeza de Vaca some 160 years earlier, De León and the earlier cartographers had trouble with names; the same name was often inadvertently given to different rivers and landmarks. For example, Texas' string of major north-south rivers are confused, misnamed, or rearranged in the records of many of the early colonial expeditions. More precise itineraries have only recently been untangled by modern historians. Thus the exact route of "the" San Antonio Road or "the" Camino Real is inevitably unknown. But since De León left a physical record of his expedition in the form of missions, there is little doubt that he traversed most of the state of Texas. Even if he never passed through the site that would become San Antonio, the future hub of the Texas

Caminos, De León must still be considered the father of Texas' Caminos Reales.

After De León's death in 1691, a succession of Spanish officials and missionaries began to refine and extend the route to East Texas. Domingo Terán de los Ríos, the first governor of the Texas province, made the journey with Father Mazanet that same year. The trip was chronicled by Mazanet, whose remarkable journal provided Coahuiltecan or Spanish names for most of the rivers, streams, and landmarks between Monclova and East Texas. As a result of this diary, it is known that Terán blazed a more northerly route than De León. This route would gain fame as the Upper Presidio Road, the Camino Real, the Camino de los Tejas, and the San Antonio Road.[38]

Terán passed through and named the future site of San Antonio on June 13, 1691, observed an Indian trade fair in San Marcos, and reached the southeastern edge of Travis County, camping out on Onion Creek and crossing the Colorado River southeast of Austin. This eighty-mile stretch of trail between present-day San Antonio and South Austin became a segment of Interstate 35. The Terán party then continued northeast through the future towns of Cameron, Calvert, and Crockett, reaching the Mission de Los Tejas in August, and then blazing a new trail to the future sites of Nacogdoches and Los Adaes, Louisiana. Terán's journey between Presidio and Los Adaes represented the first European crossing of Texas between the Rio Grande and the lower Red River.[39]

Trailblazers like De León, Terán, and their immediate successors, such as Governor Gregorio de Salinas Varona in 1693, never referred to their routes as Camino Reales, however, and their road-building or improvement techniques are somewhat of a mystery. Based on Harry W. Crosby's description of concurrent (1697) Camino Real projects in California, it is likely that De León's efforts and those of his successors were based on simple, standard methods. All highways were routed to water supplies, and most water supplies were already connected by preexisting Indian trails. The task, then, was to improve, widen, and smooth out the preexisting trail. Survey teams, often including missionaries, military personnel, and craftsmen, laid out the new road or marked the existing one by placing stakes along the suggested line of sight. Soldiers and Indian workers removed loose and partly buried stones, often with the help of iron tools, and placed the rocks at the roadway's edge to create a border. Holes were filled in, and then the surface was smoothed out. Excess rocks and rubble were applied as a foundation to slopes and turns that needed additional support.[40]

Texas' Camino Real remained a work in progress for decades. De León's gateway at Presidio was solidified by the establishment of Mission San Juan

Bautista (1700), a presidio at nearby Guerrero (1703), and a series of improvements by 1707. From this complex, Father Isidro Felix de Espinosa made a number of roundabout journeys to East Texas between 1709 and 1719 and founded three new missions. On his 1709 trip, Espinosa is believed to have named San Pedro Springs on the site of San Antonio and recommended that the Upper Presidio Road be routed through this site and extended to the north. Espinosa's route continued through the future towns of New Braunfels and San Marcos and the Colorado River ford in southeast Austin. Most of this region was inhabited by Indians. While all of the Spanish expeditions had focused on East Texas, Espinosa was the first European to highlight San Antonio as an attractive way station.[41]

Spain's renewed interest in Texas and Louisiana was directed at France. Encouraged by the ascension of a Bourbon, Philip V, to the Spanish throne in 1701, French traders had extended their exploration activities from the Missouri River to the Arkansas River and later the Red River. These activities were directed at possible routes to Santa Fe and Mexican silver. Investments in silver enterprises had revived (after decades of neglect) under Philip V, and a strike at Santa Eulalia (Chihuahua) in 1703 helped to launch another cyclical boom through the 1730s. Chihuahua did not match the bonanzas of Zacatecas, Guanajuato, Durango, and San Luis Potosí, but it had important ramifications for Texas and the path of I-35.[42]

With silver in mind, the French began to develop trading relationships with local Indian tribes, typically exchanging guns and ammunition for buffalo robes and skins. Mineral-poor Louisiana emerged as an area of interest. In 1712, a Red River trading monopoly was issued to Antoine Croyat, and the governorship of Louisiana was handed to Antoine de la Mothe Cadillac. In that same year, Cadillac, in turn, commissioned Louis Juchereau St. Denis, a prominent Quebecois who had explored segments of the Red River in 1697, to leave his command at Biloxi to start a Red River trading post at Natchitoches. Spain countered in 1716 by establishing the far eastern post of San Miguel de Linares de los Adaes (twenty-one miles west of Natchitoches) as the capital of Spanish Texas. In the meantime, St. Denis's mandate was to develop trade with Indians and Spaniards as far south as the Rio Grande.[43]

St. Denis left Natchitoches in 1714, apparently taking segments of roads blazed earlier by Terán, Espinosa, and De León, en route to San Juan Bautista. St. Denis had talent. He charted his entire route between the Red River and the Rio Grande, gained his release after being captured and tried by suspicious

Spaniards, and was familiar with a number of Indian languages. He even married into the family of Captain Domingo Ramón, becoming a Spanish subject in the process. When Spain decided in 1715 to reestablish the East Texas missions, abandoned since 1693, St. Denis guided an entrada up the Camino Real and extended Espinosa's Upper Road to as far north as the San Gabriel River—northeast of present-day Taylor—before turning east. By 1716, six new Spanish missions and a fort were established in and around future Nacogdoches County.[44]

In 1718, another entrada was organized by Viceroy Marqués de Valero and Martín de Alarcón, the new governor of Texas, to monitor the French. This expedition consisted of seventy-two men, including Francisco Alvarez Barreiro of the recently formed Royal Corps of Engineers (1711), 548 horses, and great numbers of mules and livestock. Since the water supplies at San Pedro Springs had provided a convenient stopping-off area and potential supply station between San Juan Bautista and East Texas, a new presidio and mission—San Antonio de Valero (in honor of the new viceroy)—was established at the springs. San Antonio was spawned with a few mud and straw shacks and a handful of Indians.[45]

Despite this humble introduction, San Antonio was on the map. As indicated, the ancient site of San Antonio had been occupied, if irregularly, by humans at least since the Salado Creek people of 8,000 B.C. Native peoples had recognized the significance of a site located along the Balcones Escarpment and enjoying ample supplies of water. While there is considerable debate over the actual routes taken by the first European explorers, San Pedro Springs, not fixed to any itinerary or map until after 1718, had provided a way station for cross-Texas Indian travelers for centuries. By selecting the ancient site as their own convenient way station between Saltillo and East Texas, the Spanish were simply reaffirming the site's obvious appeal.

Spain's Texas initiatives unraveled in 1719 when France invaded East Texas successfully, with the help of local Indians, and a fifty-man party under Jean Baptiste Bernard de la Harpe established a Red River trading post at Nassoni, northwest of Natchitoches (near the future site of Texarkana). La Harpe was a subordinate to St. Denis and one of many unfortunate participants in John Law's Company of the West investment scam; the great Louisiana Bubble of 1717 had collapsed spectacularly by 1720. From Nassoni Post, La Harpe sent a twenty-man survey team under Sieur du Rivage to explore the Red River to the west, possibly reaching the future site of Cooke County in the late summer of 1719. If so, La Harpe was the first European to locate an area that would serve as Texas' northern gateway for Interstate 35. By 1722, La Harpe had explored sections of the Canadian and Arkansas rivers to the north and had established relationships with local Wichitas, Taovayas, Tawakonis, and Tonkawas.[46]

The French had managed to capture Los Adaes by June 1719, forcing Spain to evacuate her East Texas mission activities once again. Operations were transferred back to San Antonio, where a new mission, San José, was founded in 1720. In that same year, the French defiantly relocated Natchitoches to the west side of the Red River to reaffirm their tenuous claim that the Red was the proper boundary between New Spain and Louisiana. New Orleans was founded in 1717. In response to these incursions, Viceroy Marqués de Valero appointed Don Joseph de Azlor y Virto de Vera, Second Marqués de Aguayo, as the new governor of an enlarged Coahuila y Texas in December 1719. The two provinces were combined to impress the French. Aguayo would launch the greatest entrada to date, revitalizing Spanish power in Texas and solidifying the Crown's territorial claims.[47]

The aristocratic Aguayo left Monclova in November of 1720 with the intention of fortifying San Antonio and retaking East Texas. His party was substantial: 500 men, including the intrepid Fray Espinosa, 2,800 horses, 4,800 cattle, and thousands of sheep and goats. Aguayo's beeves helped to jump-start the cattle-ranching industry in Texas, but few of the horses and mules survived the round-trip journey between the Rio Grande and Los Adaes. For the first time, the recent but well-traveled route between San Juan Bautista and San Antonio was referred to as a Camino Real. Aguayo was also the first European to reach the future site of Waco on a side trip.[48]

Fortunately, Aguayo's journey of 1721 was recorded by one of his colleagues, Father Juan Antonio de la Pena. While De La Pena's diary is somewhat controversial because there are apparently five different versions of it, his record provides a fascinating view of the expedition and of an old Indian trail that would develop into Interstate 35 between San Antonio and Waco. Due to high water (which made it difficult to distinguish important rivers from insignificant creeks), Aguayo was forced to follow the Upper Road segment of the Camino Real taken by Espinosa in 1709 and by St. Denis in 1716. After establishing a new presidio in San Antonio and sending scouts down to Matagorda Bay, Aguayo followed the Upper Road through the future sites of New Braunfels and San Marcos, reaching McKinney Falls of Onion Creek (in Austin) on May 23, 1721.[49]

From there, the party approached and forded the seasonally high Colorado River. They observed a variety of trees, including large mulberries and blackberry bushes, on both banks. After the crossing, fifty soldiers were dispatched to find some buffalo and ordered to make peace with Apaches if any were encountered. The expedition ventured north to the San Gabriel River (near the future site of Georgetown) and reached the Little River (near the future site of Belton) on May 31. Another group of soldiers was sent out to scout the uncharted territory and to determine the extent of French relationships with local tribes. Moving north, they found the main Brazos River (Los Brazos de Dios) on June 18 with a "luxurious and superior forest [along] its banks," and a ford was eventually located at what is now Waco. The expedition crossed the Brazos easily, but the fear of Indian attacks, with or without French assistance, prompted Aguayo to shift back to the southeast to rejoin the Camino Real en route to East Texas.[50]

Aguayo's visit to the future site of Waco marked the most northerly Spanish penetration of Texas to date. But because France was believed to be well entrenched along the upper Red River, Waco would be ignored for decades. South and East Texas remained the centers of Spanish attention. To spite the French, Aguayo constructed a new mission, La Bahía de Guadalupe, on the very site of La Salle's Fort Saint Louis on Matagorda Bay. Mission La Bahía was eventually transferred to Goliad in 1749, revitalizing De León's old Lower (La Bahía) Road in the process. Aguayo turned out to be one of the most successful builders in colonial Texas. He established ten missions and four presidios between 1719 and 1722, including a new (relocated) presidio in Military Plaza in San Antonio and a major investment in Los Adaes. After returning to Monclova in May of 1522, Aguayo resigned his governorship at the height of his fame.[51]

With twenty Spanish presidios in northern Mexico and the French threat under control, Spanish budget cutters saw opportunities to shut down and consolidate some of the weaker (corrupt) operations. San Antonio was regarded as one of the better managed presidios and was sited near the Medina River borderline that separated Texas and Coahuila, so the tiny village was singled out for fresh investments and immigration. San Antonio was laid out according to Laws of the Indies regulations, with a new church and a system of acequias—irrigation ditches, canals, and aqueducts—under construction between 1718 and 1745. In addition, three East Texas missions were transferred to San Antonio in 1731 (after the missionaries enjoyed a temporary layover at Barton Springs in Austin in 1730).[52]

By 1740, most of San Antonio's thousand or so inhabitants were Indians affiliated with the five missions. Less than two hundred were Spanish soldiers, missionaries, and colonists. Aguayo had hoped to colonize Bexar with Spaniards, but the region was viewed as remote and dangerous. In February 1729, the Spanish Crown had ordered and agreed to finance the settlement of as many as four hundred families from the Canary Islands to boost local agricultural activities. The project was reduced substantially, however; less than sixty Canary Islanders arrived in San Antonio (via Havana, Veracruz, and La Bahía) in March 1731. Since 1718, colonists had been issued all kinds of incentives, including cash, land, livestock, and supplies, to settle the town and serve as a bulwark against Apache raiding parties. As compensation for their risk taking, each Canary Islander family received five breeding cows and a bull, plus five mares and a stallion.[53]

San Antonio was intended to serve as a military, religious, and commercial center between San Juan Bautista and the on-again, off-again positions in East Texas. The Canary Islanders planted maize, oats, cotton, melons, and peppers, but with the possible exception of maize, none of these crops ever developed into a major enterprise. Wheat had to be imported from Coahuila. The missionaries had been raising cattle since the expeditions of the 1690s. But despite economics built on relatively vast mission lands and a supply of cheap Indian labor, the five San Antonio missions managed only 5,115 head of cattle and 3,325 sheep and goats in 1745. These operations were tiny compared with the massive haciendas in northern Mexico.[54]

San Antonio's first commercial ranches were established in the 1750s. Trade with Saltillo (initially through San Juan Bautista, but eventually through Laredo) centered on cattle, by-products, corn, and the commercial needs of the two presidios. Bexar's balance of trade was negative. Mule trains from Saltillo carried high-priced luxury items north and returned south with low-priced cattle by-products like tallow and hides. While New Spain's silver industry continued to generate demand for live cattle, Bexar's cattle and commercial industries were starved for investment capital. Without a silver magnate or hacienda owner to provide backing, San Antonio's cattle industry remained decidedly small-scale for decades. Cattle drives to the Rio Grande typically involved roundups of wild, unbranded stock.[55]

Modest construction projects, fledgling agriculture, and the expanding traffic along the Camino Real began to attract attention from some of San Antonio's neighbors, mainly the Apaches. The Apaches had met Coronado in the Texas Panhandle in 1541, and eastern affiliates of the tribe (Lipans and Kiowas) had gradually pushed their way into Central Texas after 1600. By 1700, they, in turn, had been pushed farther south by invading Comanches and French-assisted Wichitas. When the French arranged an alliance between the Comanches and the Wichitas in 1747—two tribes with very different histories—the Apaches and the Spanish would have a real problem.

Wary of the French and the Apaches, Spain decided to move farther into Central Texas. In the late 1740s, with budget cutters out of power, new missions were established in the largely unexplored regions north of the Camino Real. San Francisco de Xavier was founded in 1746 on the San Gabriel River at Brushy Creek, some forty-five miles east of Georgetown, a spot highlighted by its irrigation opportunities, wild game, and nearby forests. Two more San Gabriel missions and a presidio were financed by the Spanish Crown in 1747.[56]

Unfortunately for Spain, the San Gabriel missions were a disaster almost from the start. Not only were the Apaches uncooperative; Spain's military commanders made blunder after blunder. The missions were eventually transferred to an unidentified site near San Marcos for two years and then to another ill-fated mission project on the San Saba River, 130 miles northwest of Bexar in present-day Menard County. Mission Santa Cruz de San Saba was founded in 1753 to defend and convert local Apaches and to develop nearby mineral deposits along the Llano River. Although the Apaches refused to cooperate, the San Saba complex was eventually destroyed by their enemies. On March 16, 1758, an allied force of two thousand Comanches, Wichitas, and Taovayas sacked the San Saba mission and left the northernmost position in Spanish Texas in a precarious position.[57]

In response to these humiliations, Viceroy Marques de las Amarillas decided to give the San Saba presidio an opportunity to redeem itself. This was a mistake. Spain had not ventured north of Waco, but the Spanish should have known that Comanches had started to appear in larger numbers, that Wichitas and Taovayas had migrated up the Arkansas and Red rivers from Louisiana, and that Paul and Pierre Mallett's discovery in 1739–40 of a river-based route (along the Arkansas and Canadian) between the Mississippi River and Santa Fe had altered the regional landscape. Not only had trading relationships expanded with the Wichitas, but French traders had managed to arrange an alliance between the Wichitas and the Comanches in 1747. This alliance was strengthened in the mid-1750s when the Taovayas arrived in what are now Montague County, Texas, and Jefferson County, Oklahoma.[58]

In short, Spain should have known that powerful French-assisted Indian tribes had assembled along the upper Red River. Colonel Don Diego Ortiz Parrilla, a former governor of Sinaloa and Sonora and the first commandant of the San Saba presidio (in April 1757), had to know that the Comanche and Wichita raiders of 1758 had been armed with French guns. Even French traders had warned the viceroy against attacking the Indian "Nations of the North" (Norteños). Nevertheless, in August of 1759, Parrilla led an expedition force of around 400 Spanish soldiers and 176 allied Apaches, accompanied by priests and some 1,600 cattle, horses, and mules, on a 245-mile trek from San Saba to the north. The plan, if there was one, was to attack Tonkawa villages along the Clear Fork of the Brazos River (Young and/or Stephens counties) and then head northeast to the rumored Wichita and Taovaya villages on the Red River. Arriving in early October, the expedition fared well in its Tonkawa campaign. Parrilla's men killed 55 natives (including five women and five children), recovered 100 presidio horses, and took 149 prisoners as guides to the unknown Red River valley. Parrilla should have halted then and there. The Norteños were entrenched within a north-side Red River fortress, somehow dubbed Spanish Fort, located northeast of Ringgold.[59]

Using French military tactics effectively, small groups of armed Taovayas were dispatched to harass Parrilla's approaching army in the field. Unlike the Spanish, the French had treated Indians as partners, not children or slaves, and many French traders had actually lived within the tribal villages. As a result, the French were happy to share military strategies and muskets, and the Norteños were happy to accept them. When Parrilla arrived on October 7, he must have been shocked by the reception. Faced with a series of mounted sorties, a formidable stockade, a moat, and an adjacent camp of allied Comanches, Parrilla at least had the good sense to retreat after two separate assaults were thwarted. He would have been slaughtered. Still, nineteen of his men lay dead, fourteen were wounded, and many others had already fled. Two Spanish cannons were abandoned during the retreat.[60]

Humiliated but still alive, Parrilla returned to San Saba on October 25, 1759, and delivered his version of events in San Antonio on November 18 and in Mexico City in August 1760. The San Saba strategy was essentially over. A few fearless Spanish missionaries attempted to move the San Saba complex north to the Red River in 1760, a move that would have altered the course of history dramatically. However, the proposal was rejected and Parrilla was reassigned to the governorships of Pensacola, Florida, and Coahuila (in 1764). Spain's weakness, and that of the Apaches, induced affiliate tribes of the Wichitas—the Wacos and Tawakonis—to relocate farther south to the upper Brazos and Trinity rivers. This movement placed added pressure on the reeling

Apaches. While the transfer of the Louisiana Territory to Spain in 1763 would alter the landscape once again, the Wichita tribes would live relatively peacefully until the 1840s.[61]

As Spain was being introduced to the upper Red River Valley, the future northern gateway of Interstate 35, activities along the lower Rio Grande, I-35's future southern gateway, had been stepped up. The momentum was initiated by José de Escandon y Elguera, the entrepreneurial new governor of Nuevo Santander. Stretching from the Río Pánuco to Matagorda Bay, the new coastal province was colonized by a new model. In 1747, Escandon journeyed from Querétaro via San Luis Potosí to the Rio Grande to direct an innovative, multicolumn survey of the Texas portion of his new province. Following this investigation, Escandon initiated a massive colonial program that would add twenty-four villages, fifteen missions, some six thousand Spanish colonists, and three thousand Indians to the province during the next eight years. Escandon broke with his predecessors by focusing on commercial agricultural development and providing large financial incentives (cash bonuses) to generate settlement activity.[62]

As a result of this program, the La Bahía mission and presidio were transferred to present-day Goliad in 1749, and colonization began in the lower Rio Grande Valley. Camargo was founded in 1749, and José Vásquez Borrego, a Monclova-area rancher, established a new estate called Nuestra Señora de los Dolores some thirty leagues (79 miles) downstream from San Juan Bautista. Encouraged by Escandon, Borrego had explored the upper Nueces River for a possible settlement site but found the region too arid and too full of hostile Indians. The Dolores estate, more of a hacienda than anything yet developed in Texas, was also selected as a possible way station for travelers and soldiers en route to La Bahía.[63]

By 1750, Borrego had transferred twelve families from his Monclova ranch, had hired possibly a hundred workers, and was living in baronial splendor. Since agriculture was next to impossible, he focused on raising livestock and almost single-handedly created the cattle industry in the Rio Grande Valley. In addition, Borrego financed a series of local road projects and employed a "Flying Squadron" of field hands to defend against hostile Comanches and Carrizos. Escandon was so pleased with these developments that he expanded Borrego's land grant to include half of present-day Webb and Zapata counties.[64]

More important for our story, Borrego's estate included a ford, Paso de Jacinto or Paso de los Indios, that was used irregularly by Indians, soldiers, and travelers to cross the Rio Grande ten leagues (26 miles) upriver from Dolores.

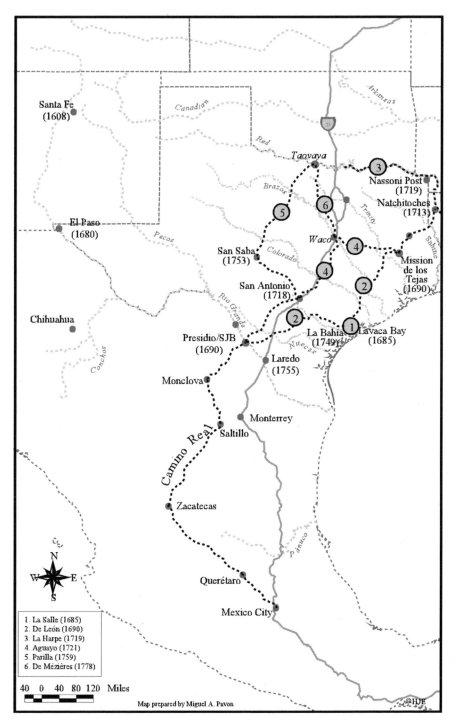

Map 4. Selected Expeditions in Texas, 1690–1778.

Santa Fe
(1608)

Canadian

Red

Arkansas

Taovaya

Brazos

③

Nassoni Post
(1719)

Natchitoches
(1713)

El Paso
(1680)

Pecos

⑤

⑥

Trinity

Sabine

San Saba
(1753)

Colorado

Waco

④

San Antonio
(1718)

④

②

Mission
de los
Tejas
(1690)

Rio Grande

Chihuahua

②

La Bahia
(1749)

Lavaca Bay
(1685)

①

Presidio/SJB
(1690)

Nueces

Laredo
(1755)

Monclova

Conchos

Camino Real

Saltillo

Monterrey

Zacatecas

Pánuco

N
W   E
S

Querétaro

Mexico City

1. La Salle (1685)
2. De León (1690)
3. La Harpe (1719)
4. Aguayo (1721)
5. Parilla (1759)
6. De Mézières (1778)

40   0   40 80 120   Miles

Map prepared by Miguel A. Pavon

@HJE

Seeing an opportunity to develop the ford and its northern bank, one of Borrego's protégés, Tomás Sánchez, established a ranch and ferry crossing there in 1750. This ferry would lead to the creation of Laredo. Escandon tried to persuade Sánchez to colonize the Nueces River but failed. Like Borrego, Sánchez saw only poor brush country lands, no water, and hostile Indians.[65]

Laredo was subsequently founded by Sánchez and two other families on May 15, 1755—without either a mission or a presidio. Named after the city of Laredo in Santander, Spain, the town would have 85 residents, nearly 1,000 head of large livestock, and 9,000 sheep and goats by 1757. Laredo would remain a tiny village for decades, however, surpassed by other river towns with much larger populations. In 1757, Reynosa had 470 inhabitants, Camargo 638, Revilla 357, and Mier 400. Matamoros would not be established until 1774. These towns traded with one another by barge and canoe.[66]

Laredo at least had the ford. As Borrego expected, a route through Laredo would cut travel time between Saltillo and San Antonio or La Bahía and would provide a closer outlet to the Gulf of Mexico than would San Juan Bautista. However, the first road between Laredo and San Antonio did not follow the future route of Interstate 35. That route would be blazed by the International and Great Northern Railroad in 1881. Laredo's first highway to San Antonio veered northeasterly, east of Cotulla, crossing the Nueces River near the future site of Fort Ewell (1852), and eventually running parallel to present-day SH 16 through Pleasanton to Bexar. According to archaeologist A. Joachim McGraw, the route and a recommended series of *parajes* (campsites) were often marked by crosses blazed into tree trunks. With limited interference from local Indian tribes, commercial traffic shifted almost immediately from the traditional Saltillo-Monclova-San Juan Bautista route (Camino Real) to the new Saltillo-Laredo-San Antonio road. By 1767, Laredo was sufficiently viable to lay out a city grid according to Law of the Indies regulations and to issue eighty-nine land grants (*porciones*) to prospective settlers. A small presidio would finally be established in 1789, raising Laredo's population to around seven hundred.[67]

If one couples the new Laredo–San Antonio road to two other routes— Aguayo's extension trail from San Antonio to Waco in 1721 and Parrilla's ill-fated path to Spanish Fort in 1759—then 1759 stands as an important date in the history of Interstate 35. In that year, a preliminary Camino del Norte, represented by a series of disjointed north-south trails, finally linked the Rio Grande with the upper Red River. While Indian tribes had used many of these same trails for centuries, no European (possibly excepting Do Campo) had been aware of a precise, if disconnected, route between the two rivers. Assuming that Parrilla visited Laredo en route to Mexico City in 1760 or during his governorship of Coahuila in 1764–65, Parrilla is the first European to have traveled between Laredo and a point very close to I-35's northern gateway in Cooke County.

The transfer of France's North American territories to England under the Treaty of Paris in 1763 provided the next wake-up call to Spanish authorities. The treaty eliminated the French threat and extended Spain's eastern boundary to the Mississippi River. This was a good news–bad news situation. The good news was the removal of the French, a probable weakening of their Indian trading partners, and a dramatic increase in Spanish territory. The bad news was that the Spanish Crown now had to contend with the emerging English threat and, possibly even worse, a collection of hostile Indian tribes that was suddenly under Spanish control.

With England, Indians, and silver in mind, the Crown responded with an inspection tour of the vast northern territories between California and Florida. The expedition party, led by the Marqués de Rubí and José de Galvez and charted by Nicholas de Lafora of the Royal Corps of Engineers, would visit every presidio in northern New Spain between 1766 and 1768 and would prompt Spain to abandon her always tenuous positions in East Texas, to shift the provincial capital from Los Adaes to the tiny (if well-managed) twenty-two-man presidio at San Antonio, and, overruling Rubí's best advice, to close San Saba for good.[68]

On his return trip to Mexico City in 1767, Rubí followed the Lower Road through La Bahía, south of San Antonio, and picked up the new Laredo Road at the El Pato junction. El Pato was located at the intersection of the San Antonio and La Bahía roads, south of the Nueces River in northeastern Webb County. From El Pato, Rubí headed south to the recently upgraded *villa* of Laredo. This southern leg of the evolving Laredo–San Antonio road included well-marked parajes that were used mainly by soldiers. Unlike most trails in colonial Texas, the Laredo Road was initially developed by Spanish military personnel—not by Indians or missionaries—to link the emerging gateway town of Laredo, with just two hundred inhabitants in 1767, to Saltillo, Monterrey, San Antonio, and La Bahía. Rubí crossed the Rio Grande at Laredo (by canoe) and observed sixty or so primitive shacks along the river.[69]

The Crown's reorganization activities in the Provincias Internas, coupled with an improved route between Saltillo and San Antonio through Laredo, boosted east-west traffic along the Camino Real. As a result, official Bexar and ad hoc Nacogdoches (founded in 1779) evolved into major trading posts. The abandonment of the San Saba and San Gabriel positions left San Antonio as the most northerly site in Spanish Texas. According to the first census in 1777, San Antonio's 1,351 inhabitants were nearly double the estimated level of 1770 and constituted an evolving melting pot of regional cultures.[70]

Fray Gaspar José de Solís had been impressed by San Antonio's fenced-in fields of corn, beans, potatoes, lentils, melons, and sugarcane and its peach orchards during his mission inspection tour of 1769. The mission ranch El Atascoso south of Bexar boasted fifty thousand acres of grazing land and thousands of head of livestock. Local farmers were able to export surplus maize to La Bahía and the Rio Grande Valley. San Antonio's local economy was indeed impressive by Texas standards, though primitive compared with Saltillo and points south. Wheat and just about everything else still had to be imported from Coahuila via expensive, escorted mule trains from Saltillo. Unlike other colonial towns in Mexico, San Antonio had no mineral riches, and the Bexar presidio had remained the local economy's principal driver. The presidio store, essentially a branch unit managed out of Mexico City, was the dominant retailer in San Antonio for decades. Since most goods were overpriced and of poor quality, smuggling and black market trade were rampant.[71]

One tangible benefit of the new organizational system was the introduction of monthly mail service in 1779, somehow running along a twelve-hundred-mile route between Arispe, Sonora, via San Juan Bautista (not Laredo) and Nacogdoches. From San Juan Bautista, mail was carried to San Antonio via the Upper Road or the Lower Road and enhanced by the start of a San Antonio River ferry service in 1786. Mail service was increased to bimonthly in 1785 and weekly in 1792, enhanced by the addition of a third route to and from Bexar, the Middle Road (Camino de la Pita), after 1807.[72]

The Roads to War, 1777–1840

*T*RAVELING along the Camino Real and the Laredo–San Antonio Road was an adventure. Traffic moved in a northeasterly direction and had to cross virtually all of Texas' north-south rivers. Wiser prehistoric peoples had utilized routes that ran parallel to rivers, not across them. Inns and hotels were nonexistent, leaving travelers to stop at the rustic parajes (campsites). Yet mail, payroll, tobacco, arms, supplies, trade goods, and missionaries were all being carried between Saltillo, Laredo, San Antonio, and Nacogdoches, typically by twenty-mule teams operated by groups of four or five drivers. Given the distance, risk, and labor required to move these mule trains, freight costs and trade goods varied considerably from point to point. From Spain, cargo was sent by ship from Cadiz or Seville via the Canary Islands to Veracruz. From there, goods were hauled to Mexico City and then north via Querétaro and Zacatecas to Saltillo. If the cargo had not already been damaged, sold or stolen, various duties, excise taxes, freight charges, interest rates, and other fees were almost certainly added to the price tag at Saltillo.[1]

From mountain-ringed Saltillo to flat Texas, variable road quality and frequent river crossings made freighting even more difficult. Roads were expected to be maintained by presidial soldiers and convicts, but many segments were neglected. Travel was slow and rising rivers caused delays, particularly during cattle drives. The trip between Saltillo and San Antonio, or between San Antonio and Nacogdoches, typically required a month. By the time merchandise was delivered to final customers, prices could be inflated beyond belief. These added costs, coupled with the problem of regular Indian attacks, provided little incentive to conduct business in Texas or to reside there.[2]

Of course, Spain could have cut travel times dramatically had seaports been established along the Gulf of Mexico. Apparently Spain feared that Texas was too far away from Mexico City, too poorly controlled by regional Spanish authorities, and too prone to the depredations of hostile coastal Indians to adopt such a strategy. In addition, Texas' north-south rivers were either too shallow or too variable to support inland shipping activity to and from the Gulf. Further, as La Salle and others had discovered, Texas' hundreds of miles of sandbars made coastal navigation a challenge. Finally, smuggling and piracy were always a problem, and the Crown was not interested in adding to her policing budget. As a result, Spain emphasized a protected overland route that may have been inefficient, inflationary, and tedious but one that was relatively secure.

Security was foremost in the mind of Commandant General Teodoro de Croix in 1777 when he concluded that the Apaches must either be stopped or be exterminated. He subsequently agreed to implement a triple-barreled plan devised by Athanase De Mézières, a remarkable Indian trader and diplomat and the lieutenant governor of Natchitoches. De Mézières's plan was simple: make an alliance with the Comanches and then encourage the Comanches (and allied Wichitas and Taovayas) to wage war against the rival Apaches, the advancing English, and the region's most dangerous enemy—the Osages.[3]

De Mézières was uniquely qualified to devise and implement this plan. Born in Paris, he had arrived in Louisiana in 1733 and, within ten years, was a wealthy Natchitoches-based trader, soldier, and planter. After marrying a daughter of St. Denis in 1746, he was commissioned to manage trade and regulate licenses along the Red River until 1763. This placed him in the middle of France's midcentury program to create a string of frontier posts between the Arkansas River and Santa Fe. The formal 1769 transfer of Louisiana to Spain provided him an opportunity to shift loyalties to the Spanish Crown.[4]

De Mézières had long-established trading relationships with Caddo tribes in northeast Texas, traded with Tawakoni and Tonkawa villages as far west as Waco, and had met the Red River–based Wichitas and Taovayas at occasional trade fairs. All of these Nations of the North had become residents of Spanish Louisiana in 1769. Aided by intelligence provided by one Antonio Treviño, by October of 1771 a series of meetings was arranged with intermediating Caddos and Norteños (excluding Comanches), encouraging De Mézières to make an overland visit to the north. He and a small military escort left Natchitoches in early 1772, heading west via Palestine to two Tawakoni villages near Waco. From Waco, he traveled up the Brazos River to Wichita villages (possibly in Young County). For whatever reason, De Mézières did not continue to the Red River villages on this trip. Instead, with seventy tribal delegates in tow, he returned to San Antonio, probably taking Parrilla's route of 1759 via San Saba. In Bexar, a treaty was concluded with the Norteños (again without the Comanches), including the ceremonial burying of a hatchet.[5]

Without the Comanches, the peace treaty eventually faltered, and De Mézières had to be recommissioned in March 1778. On this mission, he traveled northeast from San Antonio along the Camino Real to the new military post called Bucareli on the Trinity River. Joined there by a temporary forty-man military escort, De Mézières headed northwest to the Tonkawa and Tawakoni villages near Waco and then north to the Taovaya villages on the Red River, northeast of today's Ringgold. He arrived there in mid-April. While De Mézières's precise route from Waco is unclear, it must have followed or at least paralleled the future route of US 81 and much of I-35.[6]

This was De Mézières's first visit to the Taovaya villages and he was very impressed. He observed two villages—37 huts on the north bank, 123 huts on the south—and a total population of around 800. Osages had invaded the area in the early 1770s, and the villages may have been rebuilt or relocated from previous sites. Parrilla's favorite fort may have been destroyed by Osages as well. On the return trip through Bucareli (en route to Natchitoches), De Mézières managed to retrieve the two cannon that Parrilla had abandoned in 1759. Although the Comanches had declined to participate in the treaty conference, De Mézières repeated an earlier proposal that a Spanish mission and presidio be located in the Taovaya region. He believed that the proposed complex would provide a central station for four far-flung settlements—St. Louis, Natchitoches, San Antonio, and Santa Fe—as well as a defense against hostile Comanches, Osages, and English. Once again, the idea was rejected.[7]

De Mézières was one of the first Europeans to travel between San Antonio and the Red River via one continuous route. Parrilla had done it in disjointed stages. De Mézières's 1772 return route to San Antonio possibly followed the future route of US 281. His 1778 route between Waco and the Red River was similar to the future path of US 81 (if somewhat west of I-35). In 1779, in the midst of planning yet another diplomatic mission to the north, possibly including the wary Comanches, De Mézières suffered a horse-related accident en route to Waco. He returned to Bexar (via a Tonkawa trail) in ill health and died in San Antonio in November—having just been appointed a future governor of Texas.[8]

An unlikely hero, Pedro (Pierre) Vial, would continue De Mézières's legacy. Vial was enlisted to arrange a peace treaty with the Comanches and, concurrently with a retired Santa Fe presidio corporal José Mares, to find a shorter route between the provincial capitals of San Antonio and Santa Fe. Born in Lyon, France, in 1755, Vial was a practicing but unlicensed blacksmith and gunsmith by 1779. He operated along the lower Missouri River, then in Natchitoches, and most recently (and most critically) among the Taovaya villages on the Red River. It is unclear whether he met De Mézières in 1778, but his trading, language, and cultural skills became extremely valuable to Spain. Vial may have been unlicensed, but he was familiar with the French, Spanish, Caddo, and even Comanche languages.[9]

Vial and a Taovaya party had arrived unexpectedly in San Antonio in February 1785, via an unspecified route south—possibly that of De Mézières—and as the result of a chance meeting with trader Juan Baptista Bousquet (map 5). In June of that year, after volunteering to assist Croix's efforts to arrange a peace treaty with the Comanches, Vial and an associate, Francisco Xavier Chávez, followed the Camino Real eastward to Nacogdoches, then went west to Tehuacana Creek (east of Waco). A more direct route north was probably rejected for its estimated danger. From Tehuacana Creek, Vial and Chávez headed due north to the Taovaya villages, possibly along De Mézières's route of 1778, arriving there in early August. Osage attacks had forced the Taovayas and Wichitas to construct new villages on both sides of the Red River, joined by an upstream Comanche village near the mouth of the Little Wichita River. After a series of successful meetings, Vial discovered that the Comanches were willing to participate in a treaty conference—even in Bexar.[10]

Vial, Chávez, three Comanche chiefs, and a group of Comanche escorts left the Red River for San Antonio in September 1785, taking previously unknown Comanche trails south and passing near the future site of Boerne. Seizing the moment, an astonished Governor Domingo Cabello arranged the first semblance of a treaty between the Comanches and Spain. Essentially, the treaty permitted (even encouraged) Comanche attacks against the Apaches. The agreement effectively eliminated Indian attacks on Texas settlers for the next thirty years and provided Spain with its last real opportunity to colonize Texas before the Americans arrived in force. Vial and Mares would eventually formalize a series of north-south trails between San Antonio and the Taovaya villages and, in 1793, a landmark route between Santa Fe and St. Louis.[11]

These achievements made little impact on Spanish Texas. Other than California, which had only 990 Spanish residents in 1790, Texas was the least inhabited province in New Spain. Texas' non-Indian population stood at 3,103 in 1777 and would remain at 3,122 in 1809. In contrast, Coahuila had roughly 40,000 residents in 1800 and a hacienda-based economy supplying a variety of products—maize, wheat, grapes, cotton, wool, sheep, and cattle. Monterrey, to date a poor relation to Saltillo, had 6,412 inhabitants in 1803 and an emerging economy built on corn, sugar, beans, wheat, cotton, and livestock—51,532 head of cattle, 54,720 horses and mules, and 1.1 million sheep by 1804. Even New Mexico had more than 20,000 Hispanic (non-Indian) residents in 1790, and Louisiana's multinational (but non-Indian) population expanded to 50,000 in 1800. Farther south, Mexico City had an estimated Hispanic population of over 110,000 in 1793.[12]

The province of Texas had a grand total of two towns with presidios (San Antonio and La Bahía), one trading post (Nacogdoches), and two major roads. In the census of 1795, San Antonio reported 69 ranchers, 60 farmers, 30 servants, 10 merchants, 9 tailors, 6 shoemakers, 6 cart drivers, 4 fishermen, 4 carpenters, and 2 blacksmiths. The conversion of Indians to Christianity had all but stopped, and the missions had begun a gradual decline into secularization. A lack of investment capital, unresolved land titles, a presidio-centric economy, and the threat of renewed Indian attacks had prevented Bexar from developing into a more modern city.[13]

With little economic activity, the royal highway that ran between Saltillo, Monterrey, Laredo, San Antonio, and Nacogdoches deteriorated badly. In many segments, it was barely negotiable by mules. The so-called Camino Real between San Antonio and Nacogdoches was rerouted in 1795 through or near the future towns of San Marcos, Bastrop, Caldwell, Bryan, and Crockett. However, traffic would remain sparse for decades. Even with the new trails blazed by De Mézières, Vial, and Mares, few adventurers (let alone settlers) ventured north to Waco Village or via the three forks of the Trinity River to the Taovaya trading villages on the Red River. Although this northern trail would later evolve into one of North America's greatest trade routes, I-35, this was not apparent in 1800.[14]

A sharp upturn in New Spain's silver mining industry and an underdefended northeastern frontier attracted American infiltrations and raised fears of a possible Anglo invasion of Texas. American explorers, spies, and traders, including Philip Nolan, Anthony Glass, and Zebulon Pike, had filtered into Texas since the mid-1790s, and the Pinckney Treaty (1795) gave U.S. traders free access to the Mississippi River and the port of New Orleans. To the north, contraband trade between the Taovaya villages and Arkansas Post was flourishing, and a series of upper Red River survey teams had to be checked by Spanish authorities. In 1803, the Louisiana Purchase altered the landscape dramatically. An undefined ("Neutral Ground") corridor was created between the Sabine and lower Red Rivers, and Spain's claim to the Arkansas River as her northern boundary was threatened.

Checked or unchecked, American or European, the surveys and maps produced by survey teams, spies, and traders were typically less than precise. Alexander von Humboldt's excellent map of New Spain was still off target by around 170 miles. According to historian E. P. Arneson, Von Humboldt had carried state-of-the-art surveying instruments on his journey of 1803–1804—a time keeper, demi-chronometer, three-foot achromatic telescope, lunette d'épreuve, snuff-box sextant, quadrant, and variation compass—but found most of them lacking in precision. Instead, he charted his longitude bearings the old-fashioned way, by the occulation of the stars.[15]

In response to current and anticipated American incursions, new military posts were placed at Villa de Salcedo (1806) on the east bank of the Trinity River, opposite the abandoned post of Bucareli, and at San Marcos de Neve (1807), near the abandoned (relocated) San Gabriel missions in present-day San Marcos. Later, a third post was founded at Palafox, near present-day Piedras Negras on the Rio Grande. As of 1806, nearly fourteen hundred Spanish troops were stationed in Texas, mainly at Nacogdoches, and an attempt was made to expand San Marcos de Neve. In December of 1806, Felipe Roque de la Portilla led a group of twenty soldiers and sixty settlers from a coastal colony near Refugio to the new post. However, floods, renewed Comanche attacks, and neglect forced abandonment of San Marcos and Salcedo by 1813 and Palafox in 1818. The Portilla colony returned to Refugio.[16]

More successful was a plan to open new military roads. The Middle Road or Camino de la Pita, opened between Presidio de Rio Grande (Paseo de Francia) and San Antonio in 1807, was placed between the Camino Real Upper Road to Bexar and the Lower Road to La Bahía (Goliad). Since most of La Pita was in New Spain (Texas' southern boundary would be marked by the Nueces River, not the Rio Grande, until 1847), La Pita and the Laredo Road to San Antonio were intended to carry mail, cattle, and if needed, Spanish troops. The Laredo presidio remained a small but important royalist stronghold throughout the early 1800s.

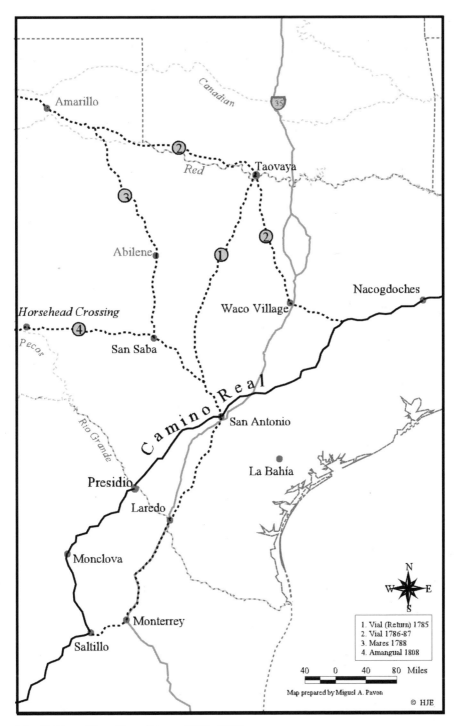

Map 5. Cross-Texas Expeditions, 1785–1808.

If New Spain was concerned with American intentions, the government's destruction of Father Miguel Hidalgo's Indian and mestizo revolt in 1811 only added to the confusion. An allied force of three hundred Mexicans, Indians, and Neutral Ground Americans responded in 1812 by capturing Nacogdoches and La Bahía and soundly and brutally defeating an undermanned royalist army at the Battle of Salado (near San Antonio) in the spring of 1813. As a larger rebel army of approximately fourteen hundred men led by José Álvarez de Toledo was being organized, an oncoming force of eighteen hundred Spanish soldiers under General Joaquín de Arrendondo was marching up the Camino Real from Saltillo.[17]

One column of the Spanish army, under Colonel Ignacio Elizondo, attacked Bexar prematurely and withdrew via the Laredo Road to royalist Laredo. Reinforced by Arrendondo's main force, mainly cavalry and including Lieutenant Antonio López de Santa Anna, the Spanish followed the Laredo–San Antonio Road back to Bexar. On August 18, 1813, the opposing forces met near the southeast corner of Bexar County, five or six miles south of the Medina River. This time, Spain's finest completely routed the rebel army. The brutal murders of Governor Salcedo and other officers after the Battle of Salado were repaid in kind—some 327 rebel prisoners were executed in San Antonio alone.[18]

The highway between Laredo and San Antonio served Spain well at the Battle of Medina. By 1800, thanks to the trailblazing efforts of Parrilla, De Mézières, Vial, and Mares, one could travel between the Rio Grande and the upper Red River over a series of defined, if extremely dangerous, north-south trails. While few of these trails would evolve into precise segments of Interstate 35, Laredo, San Antonio, and even Waco Village had become important destinations. Spain's military triumph in August 1813, was short-lived, however, and the Mexican silver industry was wracked by the internal strife.

Over 250 years after silver had been struck in Zacatecas, new discoveries, economic reforms, and capital investments had raised the value of the Mexican silver industry from around 5 million pesos in 1702 to 27 million pesos in 1804. Von Humboldt estimated in 1804 that New Spain's 500 royal mining districts and nearly 3,000 mines were producing an equivalent of 650 tons of silver—ten times the annual volume of Europe. More than half of this volume was generated from just three mining districts: Guanajuato, discovered in the 1760s; Catorce in San Luis Potosí (1778); and old reliable Zacatecas (1546). But after peaking in the early 1800s, the industry's famous cyclical quality reasserted itself. Silver production plummeted after 1810, a number of mining districts went bankrupt, loans went unpaid, and investment capital disappeared.[19]

As general business conditions in New Spain deteriorated, the tiny frontier trading centers in Texas suffered greatly. The associated political chaos made Texas desirable only to the most intrepid pioneers. Between 1800 and 1820, Texas' non-Indian population fluctuated between 3,000 and 4,000 (including slaves). The province's three largest towns in 1803—San Antonio (2,500), La Bahía (618), and Nacogdoches (770)—were nearly in ruins by 1820. Laredo's population jumped to around 1,400 in 1819, but the town was in Nuevo Santander, not Texas.[20]

Despite or possibly because of one hundred years of Spanish colonization, Texas was a mess. The subsidized mission system had collapsed, military funding for the province's two remaining presidios at San Antonio and La Bahía was cut back, and there were still a number of potentially hostile Indian tribes with which to contend. Juan Antonio Padilla observed in 1820 that the four missions of San Antonio were "in a state of decadence . . . none of them have any settlers, the principal object of their establishment." Once-friendly tribes—Caddos, Coahuiltecans, and Jumanos—had been annihilated by warfare and disease. Hard-won treaties with the Norteños were tenuous. With the threat of further civil wars in New Spain and on-again, off-again Comanche attacks, prospective traders, investors, and colonists would be scared away until after 1820.[21]

Prospects brightened with the Adams-Onis Treaty between Spain and the United States in 1819 and the creation of an independent Mexico in 1821. With Texas' boundaries fixed at the Sabine River in the east, the Red River to the hundredth meridian in the north, and the Nueces–upper Medina rivers in the south, state and municipal authorities in New Spain and then Mexico finally had confidence to issue land grants for colonization. With a population of less than 10 million in 1819 (versus around 6 million in Mexico), the United States was not exactly bursting at the seams. But America's "manifest destiny" was an unstoppable force. When the Arkansas Territory was opened to settlers in 1819, the Red River was promoted as a logical travel route west and a northern gateway into Texas.[22]

Land reform did little to reduce illegal immigration into Texas; possibly three thousand unregistered Anglos moved into the province by 1823. This total was well below the seventy-five hundred (legal) inhabitants of neighboring Natchitoches County, Louisiana, but nearly matched the entire Hispanic population of Texas. The Mexican military was in no position to remove them. Inevitably, the upper Red River Valley saw a buildup of trading post activity among Anglo-American entrepreneurs, illegal colonists, and thousands of Choctaws, Cherokees, and Chickasaws. These tribes had been evicted from their homelands in the Southeast and were being forceably relocated to the new Indian Territory (Oklahoma) via a route that came to be known as the Trail of Tears. Fort Towson, located at the confluence of the Red and Kiamichi rivers, was established in southeastern Oklahoma in May 1824, to monitor the relocation process. As if the Republic of Mexico did not have enough troubles, Anglo traders were selling guns and ammunition to the new Red River Indians, establishing French-style alliances against both Mexico and hostile Comanches.[23]

The expansion of trading activity along the upper Red River anticipated that Texas would be redeveloped by Anglos from the north. To date, Spanish attempts to colonize Texas from the south—from the Rio Grande—had failed miserably. One hundred and thirty years after De León, Spain had achieved little but ruins and chaos. Mexico had a unique opportunity to correct matters, but the new republic was in dire financial straits and was already overextended. Spain gets credit for establishing an east-west Camino Real, a military road between Laredo and San Marcos de Neve (via San Antonio), and a series of disjointed trails between Bexar and the upper Red River. However, the conversion of this rudimentary Camino del Norte into a true north-south highway, future Interstate 35, would be an Anglo affair.

Predecessor trails to Interstate 35 may be viewed as shortcut routes between St. Louis and Santa Fe (and Chihuahua). Mexico's independence immediately catalyzed American and Mexican interest in Vial's 1793 trailblazing route between St. Louis and Santa Fe. By January 1822, William Becknell had established the famous and lucrative Santa Fe Trail, a prospective trade route that had been off-limits to Americans prior to Mexican independence—Zebulon Pike had been arrested as recently as 1807. However, Mexican merchants were just as interested in trade as were Americans, and the Mexican treasury needed the additional tax revenues. St. Louis had expanded to around sixty thousand inhabitants in 1817, and pioneers were following the Missouri River westward. Missouri achieved statehood in August 1821.[24]

More than a few Anglo and Mexican merchants would devise schemes to siphon off some of the Santa Fe Trail traffic to Texas. There were also old-fashioned entrepreneurs like Moses Austin. Two recent business enterprises, a lead mining venture west of (Spanish) Ste. Genevieve, Missouri, and a speculative real estate scheme in Red River, Arkansas, may have ended badly, but the ever-entrepreneurial Austin viewed the Adams-Onis Treaty of 1819 as an intriguing business opportunity. Despite its minuscule population, Texas appeared to have excellent potential. Spain was finally free to issue valid land titles to prospective colonists in Texas, and Austin, having conducted business in Spanish-controlled territories, carried a Spanish passport. Arriving in San Antonio in late December 1820, Austin and his son Stephen would eventually convert a friendship with the self-styled Baron de Bastrop into a series of history-making empresario contracts in Spanish Texas. At least one of these contracts, the Little Colony, would straddle the future route of I-35.[25]

Energetic entrepreneurs like Moses and Stephen F. Austin, as well as the thousands of Anglo merchants and planters who streamed into Texas between 1821 and 1830, had to fend for themselves. Economically weak Mexico made no attempt to integrate Texas' emerging Anglo economy into Mexico. To avoid Mexico's added transportation costs and duties, most Anglo planters chose to transport their crops (illegally) to New Orleans, despite having to rely on snag-infested rivers to get there. More than half of the trade between the combined province of Coahuila y Texas and Mexico was illegal, conducted outside the Camino Real and official channels to avoid their inflated prices.

Some of this trade must have benefited Laredo, which expanded to around two thousand inhabitants in the mid-1820s (its peak until the 1870s). The Camino Real between Monclova and Nacogdoches via Presidio and San Antonio was still important, but Laredo had supplanted Presidio as the principal gateway into Texas. From Laredo, travelers could head north to San Antonio or, via the junction at El Pato, northeast to Texas' emerging coastal areas. Since most of the economic action was with the United States, the coastal routes had gained in importance. From La Bahía (Goliad), the La Bahía and Atascosito roads headed as far east as Louisiana.

In a hundred years of colonization, Spain had created just a handful of communities in Texas. By September 1824, Stephen F. Austin had already placed three hundred families in his first colony. One year later, Austin's colony would have eighteen hundred residents, including over four hundred slaves, and a capital (San Felipe de Austin) located at the junction of the lower Brazos River and the old Atascosito (Indian) Trail between Goliad and Nacogdoches. Austin captured four more empresario contracts between 1825 and 1831, but he was not alone. The Coahuila y Texas Colonization Law of March 1825 issued grants to four other Anglo empresarios: Robert Leftwich, Haden Edwards,

Frost Thorn, and Green C. DeWitt. Only De Witt, who settled four hundred families, would be successful.[26]

Leftwich had received authorization to settle eight hundred families over six years in the "Upper Colony" region north of the San Antonio Road. Some one hundred miles wide, two hundred miles long, and centered in Waco Village, the Upper Colony comprised twenty future counties of Texas between the Navasota River and the Cross Timbers. The massive grant was transferred to Sterling C. Robertson's Texas Association, then to Stephen F. Austin and partner Samuel May Williams, back to Robertson again, and then ultimately cancelled with Texas independence. While the Upper Colony proved controversial, this tract and Austin's adjacent Little Colony—comprising northern slices of present-day Travis and Bastrop counties—included the sites of a string of future I-35 towns between Austin and Hillsboro.[27]

The Camino Real, also known as the San Antonio or Nacogdoches Road, served as the principal mail route between Bexar, San Felipe de Austin, and Nacogdoches. However, Indian attacks and river crossing delays turned mail deliveries into irregular events. Price-gouging ferrymen did not help matters. With a second, military purpose in mind, Mexican authorities began to demand that mail routes be improved to carry stages, wagons, and carriages—and Mexican troops. Of course, no one had the money to pay for these improvements. The legislative council (*ayuntamiento*) of San Felipe de Austin endeavored to set ferry rates for the colony's river crossings and planned a series of road projects. As Santa Anna would discover in 1836, few of these plans would be converted into actual roads.

As Anglo immigration levels rose, General Manuel Mier y Terán decided to inspect Texas in 1828 as part of a so-called Mexican Boundary Survey. The Mexican Constitution of 1824 had demoted San Antonio and transferred Laredo to the new state of Tamaulipas. En route to Mexico City in March 1822, Stephen F. Austin had reported that Laredo was "as poor as sand banks" and the stretch of land between the Medina River and Laredo was "the poorest I ever saw in my life." Six years later, Mier y Terán confirmed the description. Accompanied by Jean Louis Berlandier, a French botanist and zoologist, the Terán expedition left Mexico City, now with over 150,000 residents, on November 10, 1827, and followed the "badly kept-up" Camino Real to Saltillo. The venerable Camino Real was approaching three hundred years of service. From Saltillo, Terán avoided the traditional road via Monclova to Presidio in favor of the route via Monterrey to Laredo (present-day Mexico Highway 85). The Monterey-Laredo road could hardly be categorized as a Camino Real. In many places, it was not even a road. The party lost its way several times—in ravines, at river crossings—and frequently had to hack a route through over-grown bushes that blocked the passage.[28]

When the expedition finally reached Villa de San Augustín de Laredo on February 2, Terán declared that there was "scarcely a more miserable little town than Laredo and some others located, like it, on the banks of the Río Bravo." As noted, Laredo's population had risen to approximately two thousand, ex-cluding the garrison force, but the town was more of a village than a city. Di-verting the Rio Grande waters for irrigation was believed to be cost-prohibitive, so most foodstuffs had to be imported from San Antonio or haciendas in Nuevo León and Coahuila. Few crops were grown locally, grazing lands were poor, and the town's tally of 2,150 head of livestock was underwhelming.[29]

By February 20, the party had pushed on to San Antonio. Several pack mules were added to the caravan, now comprising more than fifty people and carriages, wagons, and enough supplies for the eleven-day trip across the "immense wilderness" of South Texas. According to Berlandier, the Laredo–San Antonio Road was not much of a road either. With hostile Comanches and Lipan Apaches lurking about, the road was dominated by military traffic. Mili-tary couriers could travel the route in two to three days, but travelers were advised to have an experienced guide and a compass. Fortunately for Terán, the party saw nothing but wolves, deer, antelope, and turkeys during their journey north.[30]

Daily marches of six to eight leagues (16–21 miles) were always determined by water supplies and well-known stopping places. From Laredo, Berlandier reported a string of these parajes en route to San Antonio: Chacon, El Pato, La Parrida, Nueces River (including a military bridge constructed from tree trunks and bark), Cañada de Agua Verde, Frio River, León, San Miguel, El Guajolate, La Parrita, El Atascoso, and Medina River (map 6). Most of these parajes were located east of Interstate 35 between Laredo and San Antonio. The route passed through the eastern half of present-day La Salle County, crossing the Nueces River some twenty-five miles southeast of present-day Cotulla at the fu-ture site of Fort Ewell (1852–54). From the Nueces River, the Laredo Road veered in a northeasterly direction, eventually following segments of modern Highway 16 to Pleasanton and from there due north (parallel to US 281) to Bexar.[31]

The expedition party must have been delighted to reach San Antonio on March 1, but Berlandier's description of the town and its inhabitants was less than flattering. He compared Bexar to a large village, with no paved streets, no

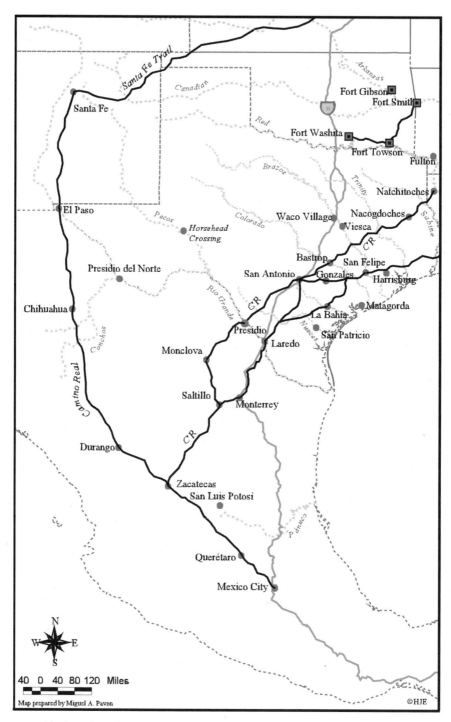

Map 6. Selected Settlements, Roads, and Trails in 1835.

public buildings, and dominated like Laredo and La Bahía by the presidio. Trading activities with Anglos may have distinguished Texas from Mexico, but Berlandier stated that the military environment ("the most pleasant life for the indolent") was holding the region back. He believed that too many residents were wasting their time in search of the next silver mine, and he recommended that Bexar be placed in "more active and harder working hands."[32]

Native Indians had also discovered that Anglos were penetrating the territory between San Antonio and Waco Village in greater numbers. Earlier territorial conflicts had pitted Norteño tribes (Tawakonis, Wacos, and even Comanches) and Anglos against entrenched Tonkawas and Apaches. Stephen F. Austin had been captured near the Nueces River by Comanches in 1822 but had been released when it was discovered that he was Anglo, not Spanish. But after 1830, all of the Texas Indian tribes were on the defensive. The powerful Comanches, a coalition of unorganized bands of guerrilla warriors, were never really defeated by the Anglos. However, they were gradually worn down by numbers and technology (six-shooters).[33]

Indian affairs would be overwhelmed by the brewing conflict between Anglo Texas and Mexico. If war was inevitable, the Mexican Army's sack of rebellious Zacatecas in May 1835, made it a near certainty. By early October of that year, a six-hundred-man Mexican army under General Martín Perfecto de Cos had seized control of Bexar, only to face an immediate revolt of armed Texans. An unruly force of four hundred rebels managed to capture Goliad on October 10 and to place San Antonio under an effective siege within weeks. After a new military commander, Edward Burleson, permitted a force of 210 Texans under Ben Milam to invade the city, Cos was forced to surrender on December 9. As Texans gained control of the strategic garrisons at Bexar (the Alamo) and Goliad (La Bahía), nearly a thousand of San Antonio's twenty-four hundred residents left town.[34]

With the possible exception of Santa Anna's final approach into Bexar and General Antonio Gaona's splinter operation through San Marcos (en route to Bastrop), the subsequent Mexican invasion of Texas avoided the future path of I-35 almost entirely. The main Mexican army followed the old Camino Real to Bexar—the somewhat circuitous route through Saltillo, Monclova, Presidio de Rio Grande (Paseo de Francia), and the Upper Presidio Road—before slogging their way due east to San Jacinto. Santa Anna had visited Laredo in 1813 under Arrendondo but ignored the mainly loyalist town in 1836. Segments of the more direct Laredo Road were in poor condition, and the preferred Upper

Road, according to General Vicente Filisola, was "solid earth and in places a mixture of sand and small stones that makes it less dusty in dry weather and prevent[s] too much mud when it is wet."[35]

Following the controversial Treaty of Velasco, the new Republic of Texas and its president Sam Houston still had to contend with hostile Indians and economics. Houston had previously lived among the Cherokees and consequently had a healthy respect for native peoples. While the Caddos and many of the Red River tribes had been decimated by disease, warfare, and forced exile into Indian Territory, the western frontier of Texas remained paralyzed by Comanche and Apache attacks for the next decade. Although Houston hoped to arrange treaties with hostile tribes, economic activities and the new republic's temporary capitals were focused on the safer southeast. San Felipe de Austin, destroyed during the Mexican conflict, gave way to the new town of Houston (1836) and its bustling population of 2,073 in 1839. By all rights, Houston or nearby Galveston (1837) could have been selected as Texas' permanent capital.[36]

Texas' second president, Mirabeau B. Lamar, had other ideas, and a few of his ideas were critical to the future path of I-35. Lamar was an expansion-minded admirer of Stephen F. Austin, a rival of Sam Houston, and a sworn enemy of Indians in general. No town named for Houston would be rewarded with the capital of Texas. Almost immediately after Lamar's inauguration in December 1838, an act of the Texas Congress charged a five-man commission with the task of selecting a new capital site. The site was to be located between the Trinity and Colorado rivers and north of the San Antonio Road. After evaluating various locations between February and April of 1839, the commissioners came up with the picturesque but nearly uninhabited site of Waterloo in Austin's Little Colony. Lamar had apparently visited the area, located on the edge of Texas' western frontier, during a buffalo hunt.[37]

San Antonio and Goliad were tainted with the past; Houston and Galveston were too far east; Bastrop and La Grange were larger settlements. But the selection of the frontier village of Waterloo was intended to send a message. Situated at a ford on the Colorado River, just north of the Onion Creek and Barton Springs stopping-off points that had served a series of Spanish expeditions and Indian tribes, Waterloo was a political statement akin to Spain's selection of Los Adaes. The statement was that Texas was going to expand to the north and to the west. Unlike Los Adaes, this expectation would actually work out. Waterloo was incorporated on January 15, 1839, within Bastrop County, and in short order, the commissioners acquired a 7,735-acre tract (for $21,000, or $2.71 per acre) from various property owners.[38]

Since most vacant lands in Texas were selling for less than fifty cents per acre, one can assume that the first group of property sellers did quite well. However, following a pattern that would repeat itself in Texas for many decades, real estate prices in Waterloo were set to explode. Construction activity began almost immediately. An act of the Texas Congress had stipulated that the new capital have a capitol, arsenal, university, schools, hospitals, churches, prison, and other buildings and infrastructure. Land and investment capital for these institutions were believed (incorrectly) to be guaranteed responsibilities of the Congress, so real estate prices could move in only one direction—up.[39]

Lamar hired Edwin Waller, a Brazoria-based planter and delegate, to manage Waterloo's startup phase and to devise what turned out to be a remarkably effective town plan. The first 217 lots (not acres) out of 306 were sold at auction in August 1839, at prices ranging from $120 to $2,700. The sellers realized a total of $182,000 from their initial $21,000 investment. Once the government records and furniture were transferred from Houston by fifty ox wagons, the Republic of Texas had a new capital. Unfortunately, Waterloo's history ended almost as soon it had begun: the instant capital was reincorporated in December as Austin—to honor Stephen F. and irritate Sam Houston—and Waller was selected as Austin's first mayor on January 1, 1840. Travis County was organized that same year.[40]

Located northwest of the San Antonio Road, Austin was planned as a future junction of probable east-west trade routes between Santa Fe and the Texas seaports and possible north-south routes between the upper Red River and northern Mexico. If these trade routes needed to be created, the Republic of Texas was ready to move—for example, in the creative but ill-fated Texas–Santa Fe Expedition of 1841. The prospective development of new trading and defense posts on the frontier would require a series of roads to link them and the organization of ranger companies to patrol the new roads.

Almost immediately, the Texas Congress established a new mail service between Austin and San Antonio, utilizing the Camino Real up to San Marcos and an old Indian trail (possibly used by Vial or Mares) north to the new capital. In addition, mail routes were opened with the United States and a General Land Office was created to address immigration issues. Most mail was carried at no cost by immigrants, soldiers, and travelers under an honor system of pickup and delivery. The pickups worked well, but the deliveries were irregular. Since mail service implied roads, a rare commodity in 1836 Texas, a Commission of Roads was authorized in 1836 to develop and regulate roads, ferries, and toll bridges. This was wishful thinking. The cash-strapped republic had no money for roads, and if any roads were built or improved, they were the result of local community activities.

On paper, the counties were ordered to lay out roads, cut down trees, clear brush, dig ditches, and organize maintenance work. All free males (except Indians) between the ages of eighteen and forty-five and all slaves between the ages of sixteen and fifty were required to work on public roads in their designated precincts (or "beats") for as much as ten days during a year. While counties could supplement these workers with convict crews, slaves were expected to shoulder most of the burden. In reality, most county road projects were ad hoc, poorly managed, and implemented by unwilling laborers. As bad as this may sound, some roads were built (or at least traced), and Texas' woeful roads were no worse than most.[41]

The delegation of road work to counties and communities in the Republic of Texas was consistent with the age-old "statute labor" or corvée system, inherited mainly from England and France and adopted widely in the United States. Between the Middle Ages and the early 1800s, English road building had relied upon a chaotic system of unpaid supervisors and forced peasant labor at the local parish level. It was not until 1555, when the Spanish were building wagon roads to and from Zacatecas, that the English Parliament enacted its first legislation governing the survey and maintenance of roads. Every English citizen was required to contribute four days of road work each year. In 1654, an *Ordinance for Better Amending and Keeping in Repair the Common Highwaies Within the Nation* added a compulsory road tax that would form the basis of English and American policy for centuries. Unfortunately, the English statute labor system accomplished next to nothing other than creating ill will among the poor souls who had to work on the roads.[42]

English roads awaited the contributions of Thomas Telford and John Loudon McAdam. Born in 1757, Telford directed a number of canal, bridge, and road engineering projects, mainly in Scotland, and was noted for his attention to road foundations. Rather than using clay or chalk as foundation materials, Telford used carefully graded, washed, and sieved stones. He also introduced a moderately cambered (three-inch) surface to promote water runoff. McAdam, born in 1756, focused on drainage. Operating out of Bristol, McAdam believed that well-drained subsoil and carefully selected surface materials six to ten inches thick could eliminate costly foundation stones entirely.

His dust surface of graded stones, reinforced with a lime-binding medium (until bituminous tar was introduced), was intended to be compacted by wheeled traffic. The surface material sandwich was eventually called macadam in his honor.[43]

OFF-RAMP: ROAD-BUILDING INNOVATIONS

These innovations benefited from ancient Roman techniques and more recent contributions from the 250-man French Corps of Roads, Bridges and Highways. Pierre Tresaguet, the director general of French roads between 1775 and 1785, is regarded as the father of modern road technology. Born in 1716, Tresaguet developed a three-layer construction process comprising a foundation of heavy stones on a cambered base, a second base layer of smaller stones, and a surface of small graded stones. In 1776, Tresaguet persuaded the minister of public works to introduce a four-class system of French roads, highlighted by *routes nationales,* which were ten inches thick and, most critically, were maintained by professional work crews.[44]

Road innovations in France, England, Spain, and elsewhere in Europe were all indebted to the Roman Empire. Roads in North America were indebted to the Indians. As indicated, most of the Caminos Reales and virtually all colonial American roads were extensions of Indian trails. Native trails like the Old Connecticut Path, the Mohawk Trail, and the Natchez Trace had crisscrossed the continent for centuries and were usually the best pathway to water supplies or hunting grounds. When the Republic of Texas was ready to plan (if not fund) interstate road projects, there would be no shortage of models.

The Old Connecticut Path was "founded" in 1636 to link the Massachusetts Bay Colony with the first English settlements on the Connecticut River. The Path was actually part of a regional loop between Boston and Hartford via Wayland, Worcester, and Springfield. The more famous Boston Post Road to New York, created in 1673 when New England's population stood at a hundred thousand, was eventually extended south to St. Augustine, Florida. Prior to 1800, other important roads with Indian roots included the Mohawk Trail (1700) between Albany and Buffalo; the Pennsylvania Road (1751) between Philadelphia and Pittsburgh; the Wilderness Road (1774) through the Cumberland Gap in southwestern Virginia; and Zane's Trace (1797) between Wheeling and Nashville via Zanesville, Ohio, and Lexington, Kentucky. With a population of seventy-three thousand in 1790, Kentucky reached statehood in 1792.[45]

The extension of Zane's Trace to Nashville prompted the reconstruction of the Natchez Trace, an old Chickasaw trail between Nashville and Natchez. An agreement with the Choctaws and Chickasaws in 1801 allowed the Trace to be converted into a U.S. military wagon road in 1803. After the War of 1812, Major General Andrew Jackson persuaded Congress to appropriate funds for a more direct (easterly) connection to New Orleans. The new route was surveyed in early 1817. By May 1820, three hundred members of the U.S. Army's First and Eighth Infantries had completed a massive 516-mile military road from Nashville via Columbus, Mississippi, to Madisonville on Lake Ponchartrain, north of New Orleans. The new road had a forty-foot right-of-way, thirty-five bridges, and nearly four miles of swampland causeways. It was destined, however, to be abandoned after Mississippi's state capital was moved to Jackson in 1822. A new shortcut route, the Robinson Road, opened between Columbus and the Natchez Trace in 1825.[46]

Another ambitious road project was initiated in 1825. In March, President James Monroe signed a bill to survey and mark the evolving Santa Fe Trail between Fort Osage, Missouri (a few miles east of Independence), and the Mexican boundary line. The Adams-Onis Treaty had set this boundary as the Arkansas River through western Kansas and Colorado. An expedition party of thirty-three men and seven wagons set off from Fort Osage in July, marking the route through Kansas as they went. Unfortunately, the Americans were unable to secure permission to survey Mexican territory. A splinter group pushed on illegally to Taos, New Mexico, but Mexico's refusal was a death knell to the official Santa Fe Trail project. Never a true highway like the Caminos Reales, the Santa Fe Trail remained an ad hoc route for decades.[47]

Despite federal funding commitments, the experiences in Mississippi and Kansas indicate that road conditions in Texas were probably no worse than anywhere else. Most U.S. roads were cleared of large stumps and stones, but that was essentially it. As in Europe, however, businessmen needed improved roads, and private enterprise was summoned to help fill the void. English-style toll-based turnpikes were introduced in the United States with the Philadelphia-Lancaster Turnpike in 1795. Like all turnpikes, it was built and owned by a private company but chartered by state government. Investors were intrigued. The Turnpike Road Company's initial public offering sold out immediately, and construction began in February 1793. The sixty-mile highway was completed by professional crews, not statute laborers, at a cost of $465,000 ($7,500 per mile) in December 1795.[48]

The Philadelphia-Lancaster Turnpike was highlighted by a striking $12,000 triple-arched stone bridge across the Brandywine Creek near Philadelphia. While most turnpikes were lightly graveled earth roads with drainage ditches, the new turnpike had a stone foundation topped with a gravel surface and a twenty-four-foot width. The turnpike operated nine tollgates (expanded later to thirteen to minimize freeloading); fares were 2.5 to 5 cents per mile and the total route fare was $2.25 per vehicle. Profits were strong from the start, leading Pennsylvania to build more than a thousand miles of turnpikes by 1808. Connecticut had 770 turnpike miles of its own, and the toll road between New York and Philadelphia was stone-surfaced by 1812. The best of these highways followed the recommendations of Pierre Tresaguet, whose work was admired by Benjamin Franklin.[49]

The public sector responded with the Cumberland Road—the last federally assisted highway project until 1916. In 1801, Secretary of the Treasury Albert Gallatin had introduced a creative plan to fund internal improvements, including canals, turnpikes, and schools, via a percentage of the sales of federally owned public lands. Starting with the Ohio Statehood Enabling Act of 1802, Congress eventually extended the land-grant concept to twenty-four states (at rates between 2 and 5 percent of public land sales) between 1820 and 1910. Texas and West Virginia had no federally owned lands and would have to fend for themselves.[50]

After preparing a complete inventory of U.S. transportation facilities in 1807, Gallatin proposed a whopping $20 million federal program to fund internal improvements, including the Cumberland Road, over the next ten years. Controversial from the start, the plan was eventually vetoed by President James Madison in 1817 as unconstitutional. In the meantime, the Cumberland Road moved forward. President Thomas Jefferson had appointed a three-man commission in March 1806, to lay out and build a free road from the farthest point of navigation on the Potomac River, at Cumberland in the Maryland Panhandle, to the farthest point of navigation on the Ohio River, at Wheeling. Cumberland had already been connected to Baltimore via the Frederick Pike.[51]

Surveyed and constructed in fits and starts, the road did not reach Wheeling until 1818, and the total project cost amounted to a jaw-dropping $1.75 million, or $14,000 per mile. However, with a sixty-six-foot right-of-way, drainage ditches, a thirty-foot roadbed, a twenty-foot paved roadway based on Tresaguet principles, a number of significant stone bridges, and a chain of hotels and taverns, the Cumberland Road was a landmark achievement. It also attracted a series of feeder roads, including the nation's first macadamized highway between Hagerstown and Boonsboro, Maryland, in 1823. With a fifteen-inch surface at the center and twelve inches at the sides, the new highway surface was five inches thicker than the prescriptions indicated in McAdam's *Remarks or Observations on the Present System of Road Making*, published in Bristol in 1816. McAdam's techniques were much cheaper (if less effective) than Tresaguet's, however, and were adopted to extend the Cumberland Road from Wheeling to Zanesville.[52]

West of Wheeling, the Cumberland Road evolved into the National Road (modern US 40) en route to St. Louis. The extension was approved in 1820 but construction was delayed until 1825. Unfortunately, the nation's only French-styled, federally financed highway project was poorly constructed west of Wheeling. McAdam roads underperformed relative to Tresaguet roads, and both the Cumberland and National highways failed to heed Tresaguet's most important recommendation: professional maintenance. Much of the surfaces of both highways were eaten away by traffic in a few short years. A bill to allow tolls for maintenance purposes was vetoed by President Monroe in 1822 as unconstitutional.[53]

Congressional appropriations and a five-year repair effort by the U.S. Army Corps of Engineers were required to continue the National Road west. By 1830, the highway project had slogged its way to Vandalia, the temporary capital of Illinois (some 60 miles east of St. Louis), when it was halted for good. In 1832 the entire National Road was transferred to the states through which it passed. The National Road was too expensive at around $13,000 per mile, twice the average cost of most turnpikes, and it would eventually be superseded by the Baltimore and Ohio Railroad. After the B&O reached Cumberland (1842) and Wheeling (1853), highway freight traffic was reduced to a trickle. In a few years, all freight traffic east of the Mississippi River shifted to railroads.[54]

Turnpikes had their run between 1800 and 1830. New York State completed four thousand miles of toll roads by 1822, and Pennsylvania reached twenty-four hundred miles in 1832. However, competition from canals, steamships, and railroads would cripple them. Canals and railroads were substantially less expensive to build and carried long-distance freight more efficiently. While turnpike construction costs averaged $5,000–$10,000 per mile, maintenance proved to be the critical factor. If maintenance was neglected, customers balked; if it was funded, profits disappeared. In addition, tollgates were costly to operate, and gatekeepers were not above lining their own pockets. Many turnpikes were simply abandoned as investment capital shifted to canals and railroads. Following the Panic of 1837, federal road funds dried up entirely, leaving highway projects to the states and counties. Of course, since most state governments were broke, road projects returned to the old county-based, statute labor system of yore.[55]

Having missed the turnpike boom and bust and Washington's brief, unsuccessful fling with national highways, the woeful road system of the Republic of Texas did not look so bad. That Texas road projects would be left primarily to the counties, despite legislation to the contrary in December of 1836, was very much in keeping with U.S. practices. The county road crews would have plenty of work to do. The condition of Texas roads, even the Camino Real, was literally as variable as the weather. Would-be entrepreneurs had observed or would discover that the road-building business was not especially enticing. For example, a group of businessmen from Houston, Galveston, La Grange, Bastrop, and Austin received a charter in January 1841 to build a new turnpike between Austin and Houston. The impressive-sounding Houston and Austin Turnpike Company even sold some stock to investors. For whatever reason, however, the road was never built.[56]

The Texas Congress at least authorized two ambitious road projects in 1839 and 1844. The first was a north-south Military Road between the Nueces River (Texas' southern border until 1847) and the upper Red River, via Austin. This was intended to monitor Indian activities along the western frontier and to enhance colonization and commercial activities. The second, a Central National Road of the Republic of Texas, was designed to connect the Military Road with an existing U.S. Military Road in southeastern Indian Territory (Oklahoma). Surveys were completed for both highways, although neither road was funded or completed as planned. As will be seen, one of the two proposals would evolve into Interstate 35.

Houston, Galveston, Austin, the coastal counties, and Red River trade were areas of priority in 1839. Goliad and Nacogdoches were fading; San Antonio was essentially ignored; and Laredo was still in Mexico. San Antonio, Texas' most famous locale, was viewed by travelers, immigrants, and President Lamar as a broken-down old Spanish town—foreign and multiethnic. Anglo Austin was marketed as the future, and transcontinental trade routes were expected to run through the capital first and Bexar second, if at all. As it turned out, these expectations would be revised by history and geography. Lamar's lofty vision for Austin would not be realized by Austin but by communities to the north that had not even been settled in 1840. And despite a slow start and occasional dips, San Antonio would surpass Austin in most economic matters until well over a hundred years later.

Austin was an Anglo professional town from the very beginning. Based on the census of 1839, Austin's population of 856 (including 145 slaves) boasted nine printers, ten lawyers, three physicians, five merchants, three architects, and twenty "professional" gamblers. By 1840, the new capital included four hundred homes, its first hotel (Bullock House), and approximately twelve hundred inhabitants. There may have been big plans for Austin, but the town was located on the edge of the frontier, and its isolation proved costly. Imported goods, at inflated prices, had to be shipped either by ox cart from the coast or by barge up the Colorado River.[57]

Austin's other challenge was Indians. Comanches refused to accept Anglo border demands, and their raids intensified. The Texas Congress was unable to provide adequate protection until local militias and ranger companies were organized. Even then, ranger posts like Little River Fort, near present-day Belton, would have to be evacuated. This, coupled with the threat of a retaliatory invasion by Mexico, gave rise to a decision to move the capital temporarily to Houston in early 1842. Armed Austinites managed to prevent the transfer of the government archives, but the city was essentially abandoned until August 1845. When the capital was restored (not permanently) after annexation in February 1846, Austin would claim just 250 residents.[58]

Texas' western frontier was in chaos, but Austin's isolation and San Antonio's economic woes would prove to be temporary. After centuries of Spanish and Mexican misrule and monopoly, Texas farmers, ranchers, and businesspeople were finally free to trade with the outside world. The ports of Houston and Galveston were bustling, export sales of cotton and sugar were expanding, and trade with New Orleans and the world was accelerating. The break in Spain's centuries-old seaport monopoly at Veracruz had already reduced transportation costs and import prices greatly. Not only had conducting business in Texas become less daunting; the elimination of the Spanish presidio system had finally allowed Texas farmers and cattle ranchers to sell their products at market prices rather than at the fixed (discounted) prices demanded by government or mission contracts.

Consequently, the development of San Antonio, Austin, and the uninhabited north—and the future of Interstate 35—hinged to a great extent on the seaports at Houston and Galveston. This required considerable effort. Coastal sandbars restricted Galveston until the late 1890s, and the cumbersome Buffalo Bayou channel southeast of Houston had to be harnessed. Typically, trading vessels docked at Galveston, then transferred their cargo to riverboats, which in turn transferred the goods to Houston-based overland carriers, and vice versa. This presented a logistical nightmare until the Port of Houston was developed in 1841 and the Buffalo Bayou Bridge was completed in 1843. Once the infrastructure was in place, however, cotton trade drove Galveston's dramatic growth in the early 1840s. By 1845, the city's population exceeded five thousand.[59]

If the ports of Galveston and Houston are important to the history of Interstate 35, so is Chihuahua. As indicated, Texas and Mexican businessmen hoped to divert some of the Santa Fe Trail traffic their way, and the traditional route between St. Louis, Santa Fe, El Paso, and Chihuahua was long, circuitous, and expensive. In response, an unlikely collection of Mexican merchants, Chihuahua-based American traders, and Texan entrepreneurs schemed to develop a new diagonal route across Texas. The new route, based possibly on Captain Francisco Amangual's expedition of 1808, passed through Comanche Springs (the future site of Fort Stockton) and headed either to San Antonio or to Fort Towson. By linking St. Louis directly with El Paso and Chihuahua, the new diagonal route saved time and also reduced a stiff five-hundred-dollar-per-wagon tariff in New Mexico. The shortcut Chihuahua Road was blazed by Henry Connelly, a Missourian who had lived in Chihuahua since 1828, in a very profitable 508-day round-trip caravan between April 1839 and August 1840.[60]

By necessity, the Chihuahua roads bypassed Laredo and Austin. As traffic volumes expanded in and around Fort Towson and Fort Washita, Presidio del Norte and Preston emerged as the two principal river crossings. Preston was downriver from the Taovaya villages and opposite Fort Washita on the upper Red River. Laredo would play a significant role in upcoming military history, but its days as a premier trade gateway would be infrequent until 1994. The Laredo–San Antonio Road continued to carry traffic between northern Mexico and Bexar, but it was not convenient to Chihuahua traffic, and the emergence of Galveston reduced the importance of Saltillo to Texas.

4

The Texas Frontier, 1840–1860

*T*HE evolving Chihuahua roads were both an opportunity and a threat to the ambitious plans of Mirabeau B. Lamar. Laredo was in Mexico and could be ignored. But Austin was the new capital of Texas and, prior to its near abandonment between 1842 and 1845, needed a push. To supplement Austin's emerging (if costly) trade with the seaports at Houston and Galveston, the push would be provided by a proposed north-south Military Road and an expedition to Santa Fe. The former would be a critical chapter in the history of I-35; the latter would be a comedy of errors.

Initiated by Lamar, the Military Road was authorized by the Texas Congress in December 1838 and reaffirmed by Secretary of War Albert Sidney Johnston in December 1839. The objective was to facilitate frontier trade and complement military defense schemes. Initially the road was intended to link Preston, the Red River crossing of the Chihuahua Road, with Austin and the village of San Patricio, west of Corpus Christi on the Nueces River. San Antonio was to be bypassed. The project was authorized because there were no wagon roads—only Indian trails—connecting the upper Red River to the populated regions of Texas in 1840. The Military Road Expedition would be commanded by Colonel William G. Cooke of the First Regiment of Infantry, a last-minute replacement for Edward Burleson and a key player in the recent "Court House Massacre" of Comanche peace delegates in San Antonio (March 19, 1840). Assisted by surveyor William H. Hunt, Cooke was commissioned to lay out a new road to connect a string of forts, way stations, and trading posts along the republic's northern and northwestern frontier.[1]

The Military Road and related forts were intended to protect prospective settlers and traders from hostile Comanches. The road was also designed to intersect with the U.S. Army's chain of forts north of the Red River—Washita, Towson, Gibson, and Smith (map 7). In 1816, a few Anglo families had settled in Jonesboro, Texas, opposite the future site of Fort Towson (1824) in Indian Territory. Trappers and Indian traders appeared more frequently after Fort Washita was founded in 1834 and Texas became independent in 1836. By then, the Anglo population of the upper Red River Valley had expanded to between six hundred and seven hundred. At Preston Bend, opposite Fort Washita, John Hart and two partners had cleared and abandoned a tract of land by 1838. The site remained vacant until another Indian trader, Holland Coffee, arrived and established Coffee's Trading Post, the predecessor to Preston. Like most Indian traders, Coffee was somewhat of a rogue. He had traded with friendly Choctaws and other tribes in the wild Red River region west of the Cross Timbers as early as 1833. He had also visited Preston Bend in 1836.[2]

Coffee almost certainly traded contraband guns and whiskey to local Indians and may have traded in cattle stolen from Anglo pioneers. His 1839 marriage to the imposing Sophia Suttenfield added to Coffee's evolving business empire. Ms. Suttenfield had somehow acquired ownership of as many as thirty slaves in a region where slavery was still rare. Coffee's claim to Hart's Preston property was somewhat murky and was clouded further by Hart's murder in 1840 at the hands of one of Coffee's partners. Still, this did not prevent Coffee from being elected to Texas' Third Congress in 1838, representing Fannin County (prior to its reorganization). In 1839, Coffee also employed one John Neely Bryan, the future founder of Dallas, and acquired nearly four thousand acres in local property.[3]

Coffee's Trading Post, situated on the south bank at the ancient Rock Bluff ford of the Red River, was located along a major east-west Indian trail and an emerging wagon road running between Missouri and southwestern Texas. By 1839, a log-raft ferry service was in operation to carry occasional bullion-laden wagons from Chihuahua en route to Forts Washita and Towson. Initially, the Chihuahua Road ran northeastward from Comanche Springs (the future Fort Stockton) via Big Spring through what would become Cooke, Grayson, Fannin, and Lamar counties, before crossing the Red River at Jonesboro. By adding a second river crossing west of the one at Jonesboro, Coffee's Trading Post facilitated a continuing westward expansion of the upper Red River Valley.[4]

A Texas congressman since 1838, Coffee must have been involved in Lamar's plans to develop a north-south Military Road between Austin and the

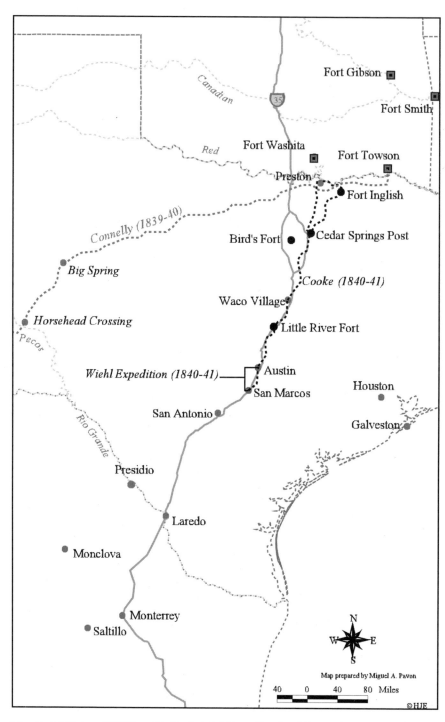

Map 7. (a) Colonel William G. Cooke's Military Road, 1840–1841.

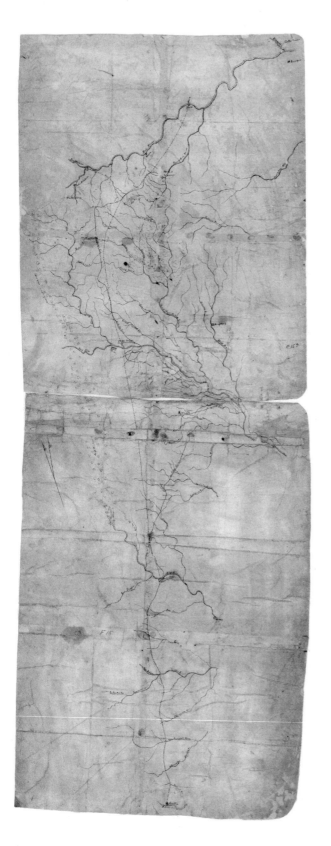

(b) Historic Sketch of the Military Road, courtesy of Texas General Land Office.

Red River. Similarly, Colonel William G. Cooke must have been aware of Coffee's Trading Post. Following the authorizations noted previously, Cooke's Military Road survey party started out in the late summer of 1840. On August 24, three companies of Texas regulars left Austin and followed a recently improved trail to Little River Fort (now Belton) en route to Fort Inglish (now Bonham) and the Red River. After Cooke arrived from San Antonio, the companies headed north to Waco and then northeast to the Red River Valley. Despite tremendous difficulties experienced en route, Cooke managed to identify and trace a suitable route for the Military Road by November 1840. Several possible terminus sites along the Red River, including Coffee's, were evaluated as well.[5]

Cooke's Military Road expedition is critical to the history of I-35. In his harrowing report from Bois d'Arc post (near Bonham) on November 14, 1840, Cooke described severe hardships: Indian attacks, escaped or stolen beef supplies, lack of water, sickness, and subsistence on dogs, mules, and horses. The expedition nevertheless managed to mark out the first north-south route between Austin and the Red River town of Preston, via Little River Post (Belton), Waco Village, and Cedar Springs Post (Dallas). Cooke noted: "I have selected a fine situation for the post on Red River, ten miles above Coffee's Station, where supplies can be easily obtained, and where it will afford most protection against the Indians. I am told by Mr. Coffee that he, with many of the settlers, were about to leave, but that our arrival has altered their determination."[6]

Cooke proceeded to establish Fort Johnston, named after Secretary of War Albert Sidney Johnston, near Denison in the winter of 1840–41. Coffee's Trading Post was renamed Preston in honor of Captain William G. Preston. Backed by Fort Washita to the north, Fort Johnston and Preston provided a convenient and less dangerous terminus point for the Military Road. With the assistance of surveyor William H. Hunt, northern segments of the new trace were then rerouted to the west and a trail to Cedar Springs (Dallas) was surveyed and marked out. A station with a few small buildings was added to Cedar Springs Post in February 1841, a few months prior to the arrival of John Neely Bryan. Bryan would subsequently found the village of Dallas.[7]

The efforts of Cooke and Hunt were tremendous, but they were only marking out these roads, identifying a suitable route of passage with markers for prospective travelers. Future persons would have to cut and then construct the Military Road. As the Spanish had discovered, cutting a road was hard work. It meant clearing a route of brush and overhanging branches, cutting down obstructing trees and stumps, removing boulders, identifying fords at river crossings (typically with Indian guides), and sometimes breaking down riverbanks for easier fording. Constructing a road involved grading work, digging drainage ditches, and adding retaining walls and bridges.

Cooke's suggested route between the frontier sites of Austin and Dallas traced a major segment of present-day Interstate 35. His trail between Dallas and the Red River gateway at Preston—the Preston Road (SH 289)—became a major highway in its own right. The Preston Road served as a branch road to Fort Washita, as a segment of the Chihuahua Road and the Texas Road, and as a feeder for the Shawnee (cattle) Trail. However, the Preston Road was sited around thirty-five miles east of future I-35. Routes between Dallas and Gainesville and between Fort Worth and Gainesville would appear much later.

While Cooke was carving out a road between Austin and the Red River, a second expedition party under Captain Joseph Wiehl had left Austin on October 8, 1840, to develop a shortcut military road between Austin and a new post at San Marcos Springs. Wiehl's Company H of the First Regiment of Infantry had been under the command of Edward Burleson, military hero, Indian fighter, and local landowner. Prior to Wiehl's expedition, travelers between Austin and San Antonio had to follow a meandering trail to the southeast of Austin, essentially following modern US 183 to a cut-off north of present-day Lockhart to the Camino Real (San Antonio Road).[8]

Wiehl's road was intended to join the San Antonio Road at a point further to the south, San Marcos. As a result, the project provided a physical link between Anglo Texas (represented by Austin), Spanish Texas (represented by the Camino Real), and Indian Texas (based on the ancient Indian trading center at San Marcos). Fortunately for Wiehl, the surrounding countryside was open and essentially free of obstacles, except for a wooded area around the Blanco River. Wiehl managed to complete the project in just ten days. Although the primitive fort constructed at San Marcos was abandoned almost as soon as it was readied, the road remained and would later be known as Stage Coach Road. Combined with Cooke's efforts up north and the existing trails between San Marcos and San Antonio, the Austin–San Marcos segment served to connect an integrated highway between the Rio Grande and the Red River.[9]

Just as Cooke and Wiehl were completing their surveys, the Republic of Texas was faced with increasingly severe financial problems. The republic was so poor that essential requirements like armies and forts, let alone highways, were cut back significantly. The unpaid Texas regular army was disbanded in March 1841. This left Cedar Springs Post, the San Marcos Post, and the entire Austin-Preston Military Road as works in progress. Yet Cooke's efforts were not in vain; a road between Austin and Preston would evolve anyway. Like most roads in nineteenth-century Texas, this road would become established through regular use.[10]

In the meantime, a segment of Cooke's Military Road project gained notoriety from President Lamar's Texas–Santa Fe Expedition in June 1841. As indicated, Chihuahua Road traffic was benefiting San Antonio at the expense of Lamar's beloved but bypassed capital. Business potential with Mexico was so attractive that a group of San Antonio merchants organized the construction of a new wooden bridge on Main (Commerce) Street during 1841. This, coupled with the abandonment or delay of the Austin-centric Military Road project, suggested that Austin's economic future had become less rosy.

Lamar responded with a double-barreled (if less than half-baked) plan to develop a trade route between Austin and Santa Fe and, in the process, to assert Texas' tenuous but not illogical territorial claims in New Mexico. Leaving a campsite north of Austin on June 19, 1841, Cooke and a motley expedition force of three hundred men followed Cooke's recently marked roadway north to Waco. Unfortunately, it was all downhill from there. The caravan meandered northwest to the upper Red River, finding and then losing a segment of Connelly's Chihuahua Trail, then wandered around West Texas and stumbled into New Mexico before being captured by Mexican authorities near Tucumcari. The expeditionary force was then marched fifteen hundred miles south to Mexico City and imprisoned. Although the survivors were eventually released in June 1842, Austin's fame and fortune would have to wait.[11]

Unlike the Spanish Caminos Reales, Cooke's Military Road (the Preston Road) would evolve from a series of small village-to-village segments, eventually stitched together by actual users. After Cooke and Hunt had identified the most suitable passages, it was up to teamsters, wagoners, merchants, immigrants, and occasional county work crews (and slaves) to do the rest. For example, Grayson County did not lay out a segment of the Preston Road through Sherman until 1847, and Travis County did not even authorize a road between Austin and Georgetown until 1848. Somehow, sections of roadway were gradually cleared of trees, fences were installed, and small-scale bridges and ferry boats were constructed along the way. Eventually, an intrepid traveler could ride from Preston via Sherman, Dallas, and Abbott (south of Hillsboro) to the more established frontier posts near Waco Village. From Waco the road south through Belton, Austin, and San Antonio was more defined, if often dangerous.[12]

However and whenever it was achieved, the Preston Road linked the upper Red River with the Rio Grande for the first time. Parrilla, De Mézières, Vial, and Mares had made the journey many decades earlier, but it was the Preston Road that formalized their trailblazing efforts. Meanwhile, the adventures of Holland Coffee and William G. Cooke were not over. Coffee's frontier homestead would serve as a magnet to future celebrities, including Robert E. Lee, Ulysses S. Grant, and future trailblazer Randolph B. Marcy. Coffee's fame did not help his longevity, however. He was killed by a nephew-in-law in self-defense in May 1846. The town of Preston currently lies beneath dammed-up Lake Texoma.[13]

The adventures depicted in Cooke's Bois d' Arc report were typical of an extraordinary career. The northernmost I-35 county in Texas is well named. Cooke was at the siege of San Antonio in 1835, participated in the Battle of San Jacinto in 1836, and served as Texas' acting secretary of war and inspector general in 1837. He even had time to open two drugstores in Houston. Returning to the military in 1840, Cooke helped to ignite the Court House Massacre in San Antonio, directed the Military Road expedition already described, established a new post at the future site of Dallas, and routed the upper half of future Interstate 35. As if that were not enough, he was captured during the Texas–Santa Fe Expedition of 1841 and endured the long march south to Mexico City. Released from prison in 1842, Cooke fought against Mexican general Adrian Woll in 1842 and the Mexican Navy in 1843, served as Texas' secretary of war in 1844, and assisted General Zachary Taylor in the Mexican War in 1846. All of this was accomplished before his death in 1847—at the age of thirty-nine.[14]

Cooke's experiences with Texas Indian tribes had confirmed what the Spanish had discovered in Zacatecas three hundred years previously: roads were necessary for wagon trains, and wagon trains needed to be protected from hostile Indians. The Republic of Texas was too poor to afford a regular army, but there were alternatives. Stephen F. Austin had employed "rangers" to patrol his colony's borderlands against Indian and Mexican attacks, and ranger companies had been organized along Texas' western frontier. With significant trade to gain or lose by the Chihuahua Road, a group of San Antonio merchants decided to hire a company of rangers under John Coffee Hays in late 1840. The objective was to protect wagon trains from robbers, unfriendly Mexicans, and Comanches. Hays had established his credentials (with Edward Burleson) against hostile Comanches at the Battle of Plum Creek, between San Marcos and Lockhart, in August 1840. In 1844, he was authorized to organize the first official group of Texas Rangers to patrol the republic's western frontier.[15]

Writing in 1858, when the tribe had been pushed back into West Texas, Butterfield Stage passenger Albert D. Richardson was especially impressed by the Comanches:

> These fierce untamed savages roam over an immense region, eating the raw flesh of the buffalo, drinking its warm blood, and plundering Mexicans, Indians and whites with judicial impartiality. Arabs and Tartars of the desert, they remove their villages . . . hundreds of miles at the shortest notice. The men are short and stout, with bright copper faces, and long hair which they ornament with glass beads and silver gew-gaws. On foot slow and awkward, but on horseback graceful, they are the most expert and daring riders in the world. In battle they sweep down upon their enemies with terrific yells, and concealing the whole body, with the exception of one foot, behind their horses, discharge bullets or arrows over and under the animals' necks rapidly and accurately.[16]

Comanche attacks, Mexican invasions, and Texan responses were not helpful to the marketing of Central Texas in the early 1840s. Comanche and Apache "plunder trails" of stolen livestock continued, some reaching as far south as San Luis Potosí and Zacatecas, and San Antonio was invaded and evacuated on two occasions. General Rafael Vásquez invaded in March 1842, and General Adrian Woll followed up in September 1842. Woll's invasion path followed a new semicircular route from Presidio, passing through Uvalde Canyon and looping north of the traditional Camino Real (Upper Road). Laredo was proclaimed the capital of a brief (283-day) Republic of the Rio Grande in 1840 and then sacked by Alexander Somervell's ragtag expeditionary force in December 1842. If the eighty-mile corridor between Bexar and Austin was nearly empty, the end points had not fared much better. San Antonio had less than a thousand inhabitants in 1845; Austin was essentially abandoned between 1842 and 1845, with possibly two hundred residents in 1844. Even by 1850, Austin's population was a modest 629, and its status as Texas' capital city would remain tenuous until the post-Reconstruction constitution of 1876.[17]

Rangers, local militias, and military posts may have deterred Indian attacks, but they were powerless to halt them entirely. Two of the new ranger posts in north-central Texas—Bird's Fort near Arlington and Fort Johnston in Denison—were involved in the nasty battle of Village Creek in May 1841. A fifty-man unit commanded by Colonel Edward H. Tarrant, and including Holland Coffee and John B. Denton, was involved in this last-recorded Indian skirmish in the Three Forks region of the Trinity valley. Denton, a minister and lawyer, was killed near the present site of Fort Worth.[18]

The incident at Village Creek led to a change in Texas' Indian policy. Assisted by Jesse Chisholm, a talented trader, guide, interpreter, and an ex-neighbor of his in Fort Gibson, President Sam Houston commissioned a series of treaty council meetings in 1843. The first, without Comanches, was held in March at Council Springs, near Torrey's Trading Post at the junction of the Brazos River and Tehuacana Creek near Waco. Houston just happened to be a shareholder in the Torrey enterprises. Although the meeting was recorded by painter John Mix Stanley, the treaty was toothless without Comanche participation.[19]

A second meeting was arranged at Bird's Fort in September. Built by Jonathan Bird in 1841, Bird's Fort was located near the future site of Birdville (nine miles east of Fort Worth) on the West Fork of the Trinity River. Chisholm was not involved in the proceedings, and the Comanches again refused to participate. However, the resulting Bird's Fort Treaty was signed by a number of tribes—the Delaware, Chickasaw, Waco, Tawakoni, Kichai, Caddo, Anadarko, Ionio, Biloxi, and Cherokee—and then ratified by the Texas Senate on January 31, 1844. The treaty divided Texas into two regions. Indian hunting grounds were restricted to territory west of a north-south treaty line running between Menard (home of the old San Saba presidio) and the future site of Fort Worth. Anglos received all lands to the east. A string of trading posts, managed by licensed merchants, was to be established along the treaty line and a "Peace Corps" of schoolteachers, blacksmiths, and mechanics would be sent to Indian villages. Anglos were prohibited from crossing the line without permission of the Texas president, and no arms or liquor were to be sold to Indians.[20]

As tenuous as it was without Comanche participation, the Bird's Fort Treaty facilitated a number of initiatives that would shape Interstate 35. The capital was restored to Austin, San Antonio's wagon train–based economy revived, and the eighty-mile stretch of land between San Antonio and Austin began to be settled by a variety of immigrant groups. One group, under the leadership of the colorful if somewhat incompetent Prince Carl of Solms-Braunfels, would establish a string of German settlements and make New Braunfels one of Texas' largest and most prosperous towns in 1850.

New Braunfels was not Prince Carl's initial area of focus. In 1843, the commissioner general for the Society for the Protection of German Immigrants in

Texas—Prince Carl—had somehow been persuaded to acquire the rights to a worthless northwestern tract of Comanche-infested land between the Llano and San Saba rivers for nine thousand dollars. The prince was not the first investor to be scammed in a Texas real estate deal, and he would not, of course, be the last. Licking his wounds but continuing to parade around Central Texas in regal dress, the prince then stumbled into an opportunity with Rafael and Maria Veramendi Garza of San Antonio.[21]

The Veramendis had obtained rights (but not clear and irrefutable ownership) to a tract of land in the future Comal County. The tract had been part of either Green De Witt's or Baron de Bastrop's original land grants. Given the prince's reputation in real estate investing, the Veramendis may have seen him as a perfect prospect. Texas was on the brink of annexation, and the unsuspecting European was probably viewed as an easy sale. The prince purchased the rights to 1,265 acres along the Comal River for eleven hundred dollars in March 1845, then added a second tract in May. The transactions were challenged immediately by Bastrop's heirs and languished in the courts until 1853. Having plunged the society into debt, Prince Carl thought it best to return to Germany in early 1845.[22]

The prince's successor, Baron Ottried ("John") Han von Meusebach, provided stronger management capabilities when they were most needed. In April of 1845, Meusebach acquired a ten-thousand-acre tract between Comal and the worthless northwestern parcel to facilitate the development of a way station along the old San Saba trail. The way station evolved into Fredericksburg. Meanwhile, the first of thousands of German immigrants had arrived in Indian Point (Indianola) on southwestern Matagorda Bay. With wagons at a premium because of the looming military confrontation with Mexico, the new arrivals were forced to struggle up the Guadalupe River to Comal Springs. Hundreds, possibly thousands, of German colonists died from disease, mainly cholera and yellow fever, at the port or en route. New Braunfels, however, would succeed. By the time that Comal County was organized in March 1846, some 7,380 German colonists were settled there.[23]

German immigration and Chihuahua Road traffic eventually generated business for San Antonio. In the early 1840s, Bexar had sunk to perhaps its lowest ebb. In addition to the Mexican invasions, traffic along the Saltillo-Laredo Road had diminished, Indian attacks were a fact of life, and except for descendants of the Canary Islanders, most of the city's upper- and middle-class Spanish families had returned to Mexico. While Galveston and Houston were in the midst of a building boom, San Antonio was in ruins and had essentially been abandoned. By 1845, the population of the most famous town in Texas had declined to seven or eight hundred persons.[24]

San Antonio's fortunes and those of Laredo recovered, thanks to Mexico. Silver trade with Chihuahua revived in 1845, and hundred-pack mule caravans began to appear on the streets of Bexar. Much of this activity was from pirate trade. Many freighters had learned to avoid high government tariffs on imported goods by bypassing the regulated Chihuahua Road. Pirate caravans simply took roundabout routes back to Chihuahua once they had exchanged Mexican silver for Texas cotton and tobacco. Chihuahua trade also flowed into San Antonio from Matamoros, near the mouth of the Rio Grande. With more than four thousand inhabitants in 1834, Matamoros had established trading relationships with upriver towns like Camargo and Laredo, the interior cities of Monterrey and Saltillo, and the seaports of Veracruz, Tampico, and New Orleans.[25]

As San Antonio's fortunes revived, the vast territory between Bexar and the Red River was being settled. Cooke's Military (Preston) Road was in varying stages of completion, whether by wagon wheels, hooves, or feet, and road projects in energetic Comal County had started almost immediately. Torrey Brothers of Houston and Tehuacana Creek had supplied wagons and provisions for the first caravan to New Braunfels. John F. Torrey liked the Comal River site so much that he established a trading post and gristmill shortly thereafter. A sawmill was added in 1848 and later a flour mill and a door, sash, and window blind business. Unfortunately, Torrey's impressive facilities and their replacements would be destroyed by fire in 1861, by tornado in 1869, and by flood in 1872.[26]

With New Braunfels as a hub, the Comal County Commissioners Court designated existing roads to San Antonio and Seguin as "first class" roads and issued a contract in January 1847 for a new road to Fredericksburg. Fredericksburg was founded in 1846 along the old trail between San Antonio and San Saba. Before construction and settlement activities could occur, the unusually capable Meusebach moved to make peace with local Comanches. This was not an easy task because the Germans were located near the very heart of the tribe's hunting grounds. Still, Germans were not Anglos, Spaniards, Mexicans, or Apaches. A meeting was arranged along the San Saba River, and the resulting treaty, for the most part, would be upheld by both sides for decades.[27]

One immigrant, Viktor Bracht, documented the Germans' progress in a book. Bracht arrived in New Braunfels via Düsseldorf and Galveston in 1846 and lived in San Antonio between 1855 and 1860. According to Bracht, who published *Texas in 1848* for prospective German colonists, "Western Texas" (including Goliad, New Braunfels, San Antonio, and the Pedernales River Valley) offered the best land in the state. Land prices ranged from thirty-seven cents to five dollars per acre. Ever the salesman, Bracht suggested that many of the "natural" (dirt) roads in the west, including the road between Fredericksburg and Austin, "compare favorably with the best highways of Europe." Bracht claimed Texas roads were excellent most of the year, though he admitted that they were prone to mud and floods during the rainy winter months. Coastal roads could become entirely submerged. Straying somewhat from reality, Bracht mentioned that "even on the Military Road and on the frontier of civilization, little thought is given to danger."[28]

Up the road from New Braunfels, the village of San Marcos began to be laid out in 1846. Like Bastrop, San Marcos had emerged from an abandoned Spanish military post along the San Antonio Road (Camino Real). The future townsite had been acquired from Green De Witt by Juan Martin de Veramendi of San Antonio in 1831. Veramendi was appointed vice governor of Coahuila and Texas in 1830 but died of cholera in 1833. One portion of Veramendi's land grant helped to establish New Braunfels; another was purchased by the remarkable Edward Burleson. Burleson had assisted Andrew Jackson at the Battle of New Orleans and gained additional fame as a ruthless Indian fighter, Texas Ranger, military commander during the Texas Revolution, and vice president of the Republic of Texas.[29]

Burleson owned around a thousand acres of local property, including the ancient San Marcos Springs, and served as San Marcos' principal investor and catalyst. When Hays County was formed by splitting off a southern section of Travis County in March 1848, the village of Stringtown was founded on the principal stage road (Hunter Road) between Austin and San Antonio. A stage-stop hotel operated by William W. Moon, who served under Burleson at the Battle of Plum Creek, began to generate coach business. Before his death in 1851, Burleson constructed a sawmill, gristmill, cotton gin, cotton press, and dam along the San Marcos River.[30]

By 1850, the northern frontier villages of Belton, Waco, Dallas, and Fort Worth had all made their debuts. Nolanville (Belton, as of 1851) was named after the adventurer Philip Nolan—although Nolan had never actually set foot in it. Bell County (1850) had been settled in the mid-1830s but was abandoned for roughly ten years because of relentless Indian attacks. In 1846, settlers returned to the Lampasas River crossing of the Preston Road (Nolanville) and established a gristmill at nearby Spicewood Spring. Until Waco was founded, one road linked Nolanville to the northwestern posts at Fort Gates (Gatesville) and Fort Graham on the Brazos. A second road, the Preston Road, connected the village with Salado, Georgetown, and Austin to the south. Unimproved land was selling for only fifty cents an acre—equivalent to about three deer hides. Whether because of hostile Indians or bad roads, Jacob Raphael De Cordova's Map of the State of Texas (1849) implied that travelers should avoid Bell County altogether. Travelers to and from Dallas were guided through Fort Milam and Bucksnort at Viesca Falls (present-day Marlin) rather than though Nolanville.[31]

Farther up the road, Waco Village had gained fame from De Mézières's visits in the 1770s and, more recently, through Torrey's Trading Post on Tehuacana Creek, eight miles to the southeast. Indian trader George Barnard apparently bought out Torrey's Trading Post in 1844 to add a northwestern extension to his existing Brazos River post at Navasota. This transaction suggests that Waco did not emerge as a way station between Austin and Dallas, as a modern Texas highway map would suggest. Rather, Waco was developed as a northwestern creation of Brazos River trade, upriver from Fort Milam at Viesca Falls. The notorious if prototypical Barnard exchanged guns, ammunition, tobacco, and whiskey for animal hides. Hides were legal tender, but most of Barnard's merchandise was contraband. Between 1844 and 1853, some seventy-five thousand hides were hauled downriver at prices ranging from fifteen cents for deer to as much as five dollars for buffalo. If freight costs to and from Houston averaged two dollars per hundred pounds, Barnard probably did very well.[32]

Had Barnard arrived in Waco twenty years earlier, he might have traded with the Waco Indians, a branch of the Wichita-oriented Tawakonis. Having displaced the Tonkawas many decades earlier, the Wacos in turn had been driven from Waco Spring by the Cherokees in the late 1820s. The Cherokees had been forced to leave their ancestral homelands in the South and had been evicted from northeast Texas as well. The relatively new Cherokee village in East Waco was visited by William M. Quesenbury in late 1845. Quesenbury had left Van Buren, Arkansas (via Fort Washita, Coffee's Trading Post, and the Preston Road) en route to Austin and San Antonio. Not only did Quesenbury meet Jesse Chisholm near the Guadalupe River; he was one of the first civilians to record a nonmilitary journey between Preston and San Antonio.[33]

Barnard's success and the concurrent development of the Preston Road attracted attention. In 1845, the frontiersman Neill McLennan founded a homestead on the east side of the Brazos River, followed by others. By 1849, George B. Erath and Jacob De Cordova, the son of a Jewish-Jamaican coffee grower, had laid out the new town of Waco. As a small Anglo-American community took root, a ferry service operated by Shapley P. Ross, one of the earliest Texas Rangers, became so popular that it would help to launch a spectacular bridge project after the Civil War. Waco was selected as the McLennan County seat in 1850 after various land contributions and real estate commissions had been extracted from interested parties. New roads, including uncompleted sections of the Preston Road, were directed south to Nolanville (Belton) and north to Waxahachie.[34]

Farther north, trading posts had been scattered around the Three Forks region of the Trinity River for nearly a decade. The most recent ventures were linked to the Chihuahua Road or anticipated future developments. Months after Cooke had established a post at Cedar Springs, John Neely Bryan arrived from Van Buren, Arkansas, in November of 1841. Bryan served as Dallas's first settler. The thirty-one-year-old pioneer had been admitted to the State Bar of Tennessee and had worked with Holland Coffee in 1839. With a keen sense of geography and business economics, Bryan had obtained a 640-acre headright claim to the bluffs below the confluence of the Trinity River forks. He then managed to encourage a few settlers at nearby Bird's Fort to relocate to his new site. Dallas would have 430 inhabitants by 1850. The town may have been named for President James K. Polk's vice president in 1844, George Mifflin Dallas; or George's brother Alexander James Dallas, a naval hero in the War of 1812; or one Joseph Dallas, a mysterious frontiersman friend of Bryan's.[35]

Dallas and twenty-five other counties in the upper Trinity River region were supposed to be settled by the Peters Land Company. The Peters Colony was initiated in February 1841, by President Lamar, via an empresario contract with W. S. Peters of Kentucky and nineteen partners. Peters had agreed to bring six hundred families into the Red River Valley and provide each with a headright to 640 acres. Like many would-be empresarios during the period of the Texas republic, the Peters Land Company was unable to fulfill its contract (despite extensions) and went bankrupt. Land claims often become confused and then reverted to the government. Even Bryan's 640-acre claim in Dallas was not confirmed until 1854.[36]

Otherwise, settlement activity was supported by the Texas Homestead Act of 1839. The act prohibited seizure of homes to settle debts, and later (1844) provided 320 acres of free land to qualifying pioneers. These parcels were distributed from the republic's vast inventory of vacant, publicly owned land. As the only state to retain her public lands, Texas was able to offer headrights virtually free to homesteaders during the republic period. But after statehood, pioneers would have to deal increasingly with real estate developers and speculators. Most of the Red River Valley settlers would be small family farmers (without slaves) from the Ohio River Valley—precisely the type of enterprising pioneers that had been missing from Spanish Texas.[37]

Dallas was an attractive site for a number of reasons. It was located at the convergence of the three forks of the Trinity River and the north-south Preston Road and provided two natural river fords. The enterprising Bryan established a ferry service at the lower crossing almost immediately and benefited from traffic generated by the Preston Road, the Chihuahua Road to Fort Towson, and two Indian trails: the Comanche Trail from Nacogdoches and the Caddo Trace from Shreveport. Bryan must have been thrilled by authorization in the Texas Congress of a "Central National Road of the Republic of Texas" in February 1844. A commission was appointed to lay out the proposed road from the Trinity River in Dallas via Rockwall and Paris to the Red River crossing at Kiomatia (opposite Fort Towson). Surveys were completed by April.[38]

Despite the lofty name, the Central National Road was planned as a modest 130-mile east-west connector road from the Preston Road to northeast Texas. The extent to which it was intended to join, upgrade, or reroute segments of the existing Chihuahua Road is unclear. According to historian J. W. Williams, the new road was planned to start in Dallas County, approximately four miles north of present-day US 80, and cross the Trinity River at Bryan's lower ferry crossing. From there, it would join the more popular Preston Road at the upper Cedar Springs crossing located three miles upstream. The Central National Road was never completed, due to an age-old problem—lack of funds. Instead, an ad hoc, stitched-together version eventually linked Dallas with Paris and Texarkana, thereby placing Dallas at the junction of an interstate highway running between St. Louis and Mexico via San Antonio. Such a crossroads location was exactly what Mirabeau B. Lamar had had in mind in 1839—for Austin.[39]

The Preston Road and the Central National Road projects had been intended to model the Spanish Crown's Camino Real strategy—build a road and colonists would follow. What happened was the exact opposite—colonists arrived and roads followed. Dallas County and the adjacent counties of Collin, Denton, Grayson, and Cooke were not organized until 1846–48. But by 1850, each was thriving. Collin County boasted nearly two thousand residents, a new general store in Plano, and a road between McKinney and Sherman. These achievements were generated by local citizens, not by state government.

Hopes to utilize the Red River for long-distance shipping were thwarted by snag-infested river conditions, however, offset partly by the emergence of Jefferson as an East Texas port and outlet.[40]

West of Dallas, a licensed trading post was established in 1845 on the South Fork of the Trinity River (near present-day Arlington), and surveyors appeared on the Clear Fork (near future Fort Worth) shortly thereafter. After annexation, ranger posts sprouted as far north as the Red River. In 1847, Fort Fitzhugh (named for William Fitzhugh) was founded on Elm Creek, three miles south of future Gainesville in Cooke County. Known also as Elm Station, the fort was located along a ranger patrol road from the Red River to Hickory Station (three miles west of where Denton now stands) and Johnson's Station (three miles south of Arlington). Fort Fitzhugh was also served by an early immigrant road that carried Illinois-based Mormons in 1845 and Captain Randolph B. Marcy and California gold rushers in 1849. The fort was abandoned in 1850, but the town of Gainesville (1850) would live on.[41]

As villages sprang up between Austin and the upper Red River, roads became necessary for trade and stagecoach connections. Unfortunately for travelers and merchants, road projects like the Preston Road depended entirely on county initiatives. The Act of March 5, 1848, authorized county courts to lay out and regulate roads whenever deemed necessary. A commission of five men would be appointed to mark out a new road to the "greatest advantage of the most inhabitants of the county." The commission would then appoint an over-seer to cut the road and make it passable. Whether a road was classified as first class (at least thirty feet wide) or second class (at least twenty feet), it had to be cleared of all trees and protruding stumps more than six inches above the ground.[42]

Prior to this act, Comal County had employed a ten-man team to lay out and mark the Fredericksburg Road from New Braunfels over a two-week pe-riod in 1847. Overseers, or "roadmasters," were appointed to supervise con-struction in five-mile segments. Germans opposed slavery, so the labor was probably contributed by local citizens and hired hands. An 1849 road project between New Braunfels and Post Hill (Fort Mason, as of 1851) was laid out by two roadmasters and a contracted team of oxen, wagon, and teamster for six days at three dollars per day.[43]

In January 1850, Texas' county courts were authorized to divide the county into precincts, designate an overseer for each precinct, and then assign able-bodied men to perform the work. All males between the ages of fifteen and fifty were required to work on public roads for as many six days per year or to provide equivalent compensation to the overseer. In many counties, equivalent compensation was often in the form of slaves. Ministers, millers, ferrymen, postmasters, and Indians were exempted from compulsory service. Workers were given two days' notice to appear (with tools) at a certain time and place.[44]

In Bell County, the first legislative act of the County Commissioners Court in October 1850 was to divide the county into four precincts, quartered by the north-south Preston (Austin-Waco) Road and the east-west Little River. After commissioners and justices were assigned to each precinct, "reviewers" were appointed to review various road projects and ferry service applications. Settlers typically had to petition the court for funds for a desired road project. If a project was approved, a "jury of view" was appointed to select the actual route, and the project was allocated to a "road precinct." Next, an overseer summoned a work crew ("hands") to open and maintain the road. For ferry services, the county court would simply license a ferry service across, say, the Leon River junction of the Preston Road and fix a schedule of rates.[45]

Of course, opening a road in Bell, Comal, or any other county was very different from building and maintaining a professionally engineered highway. It must be assumed that the Preston Road was a county-by-county affair— marked out by soldiers, compacted by wagon wheels and hooves, and maintained irregularly by county work hands under the statute labor (road tax) system. Many of these hands were local slaves or convicts.

Texas' county-based road policies were consistent with U.S. practices, but according to one expert, W. M. Gillespie, U.S. road-building policies were ineffective. In his landmark *Manual of the Principles and Practice of Road Making,* published in 1847, Gillespie offered a long list of recommendations to "harmonize the successful but empirical practice of the English engineers with the theoretical but elegant deductions of the French." He called for the replacement of the current road-tax system, borrowed from an obsolete European system of feudal vassalage, with a system that placed road repairs "under the charge of a professional road maker of science and experience." Work crews needed to be professional and paid. Gillespie favored Telford's roads over McAdam's because they were built like Roman roads, with a paved foundation. McAdam-style roads were much less expensive, relying on an unpaved roadbed with improved drainage, but they were damaged more easily by horses than by vehicles. Finding that narrow wagon wheels (less than six inches wide) did more damage than wider (twelve-inch) wheels, Gillespie opined that horses and narrow-wheeled vehicles should be penalized with higher tolls. Gillespie's recommendations would be respected by engineers but ignored by policy makers for over a century.[46]

Road improvement issues were overshadowed by the pending annexation of slave-state Texas in February 1846, and the likelihood that the annexation would trigger a full-scale war with Mexico. Fearing as much, antislavery leaders like future vice president Henry Wilson, formerly a cobbler in Natick, Massachusetts, had railed against the Polk-Dallas ticket in 1844. Even prior to annexation, Polk had sent General Zachary Taylor and nearly four thousand U.S. troops to the tiny border village of Corpus Christi in the summer of 1845 to "observe" (occupy) the disputed territory between the Nueces River and the Rio Grande. Among a series of reconnaissance expeditions, Chief Engineer Robert E. Lee surveyed Mexico's recent (1842) invasion loop into Bexar and converted the route into a segment of a new military road—a revised branch of the Chihuahua Road—stretching between San Antonio and El Paso (US 90).[47]

After war was indeed declared in May of 1846, San Antonio was established as military headquarters (Camp Bexar) and received General John E. Wool's three-thousand-man Division of the Center in August. Taylor shipped many of his troops to Fort Texas (Fort Brown), opposite Matamoros on the Rio Grande, and dispatched three supply wagons to Fort McIntosh at Laredo. The subsequent invasion of Mexico was settled essentially by the controversial Battle of Buena Vista, waged south of Saltillo, on February 23, 1847. By war's end, San Antonio's economy had been revitalized and Laredo had been incorporated into the United States. Fort McIntosh, one of a series of new posts sited along the Rio Grande, bolstered a community that had been devastated by Comanche attacks and recent floods. When a company of Texans under ex-president Lamar arrived in Laredo in November 1847, Lamar complained to Zachary Taylor that Texas' latest prize had been reduced to "very little more than a heap of ruins." Lamar remained in Laredo until the summer of 1848, overseeing the separation of Texan Laredo (with around 1,400 residents) and Mexican Nuevo Laredo (with around 600) and the organization of Webb County in January 1848.[48]

With Texas annexed, enlarged, and invigorated by military investments, Texas asked the U.S. Congress to establish a chain of forts on the state's western frontier. Mexico was defeated, but the state's fragile economy could benefit from a continuing inflow of federal funds. In addition, the Indian issue was not resolved; hostile tribes were inhibiting westward colonization and development and needed to be controlled. A proposal to build a north-south chain of forts between the Rio Grande and the Red River was approved, and the U.S. Army Corps of Engineers and the Corps of Topographical Engineers were enlisted to explore, survey, and map possible military routes for wagons, mail, and telegraph lines.

This north-south line of frontier forts would parallel the future route of I-35 (map 8). By the fall of 1848, a force of nearly fifteen hundred men under Colonel William Jenkins Worth had marched overland from Galveston Bay to Camp Maxwell in Austin. Companies were then sent to San Antonio and Fort Brown (Brownsville) to commence operations. Between 1848 and 1849, forts were established or improved at the following sites: Ringgold Barracks (Rio Grande City), Fort McIntosh (Laredo), Fort Duncan (Eagle Pass), Fort Inge (Uvalde), Fort Lincoln (on the Seco River), Fort Martin Scott (Fredericksburg), Fort Croghan (Burnet County), Fort Gates (on the Leon River), Fort Graham (west of Hillsboro), and Fort Worth.[49]

The new frontier forts were supplied mainly from San Antonio, via Port Lavaca and Indianola on Matagorda Bay. In 1849, officers of the U.S. Army's Eighth Military Department and U.S. Topographical Corps, including Lieutenant William H. C. Whiting, Lieutenant Nathaniel H. Michler, and Captain Randolph B. Marcy, conducted a series of expeditions to identify the most direct supply routes from San Antonio to El Paso and to Fort Washita. An unofficial (Austin-sponsored) expedition by Robert S. Neighbors and John S. ("Rip") Ford attempted to do the same for Austin. Whiting was also asked to survey a route for a second more westerly chain of frontier forts, while Michler completed surveys between Port Lavaca and San Antonio and between Corpus Christi and Fort Inge on the Nueces River.[50]

On July 12, 1849, Michler was ordered to evaluate the existing Military (Preston) Road between San Antonio and Fort Washita, thirty miles north of Preston, and then to survey a possible diagonal road between Fort Washita and the Pecos River. Marcy was surveying a similar diagonal route to Fort Washita from New Mexico. Leaving San Antonio with fourteen civilian workers and a wagon train of supplies, Michler evaluated Cooke's nine-year-old route that ran through the emerging towns of New Braunfels, San Marcos, Austin, Navarro, Dallas, and Preston en route to Fort Washita. After meeting up with Marcy's just-arrived expedition party from West Texas, Michler was dispatched southwest to the Pecos River.[51]

Michler's report of January 28, 1850, provided a firsthand, if uneventful, glimpse of the future route of I-35 between San Antonio and the upper Red River.

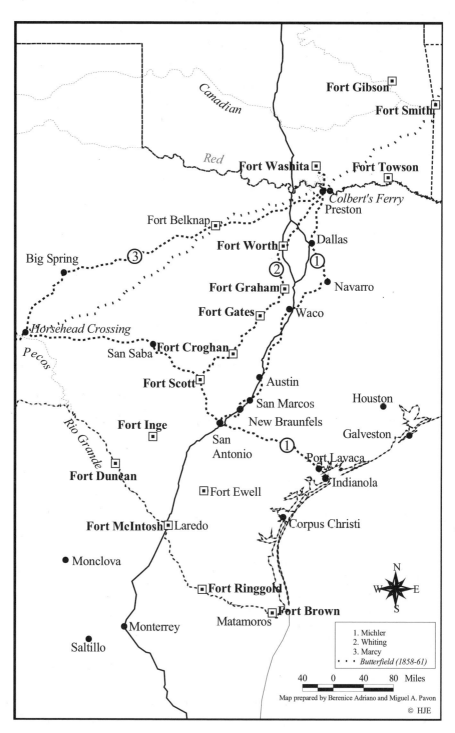

Map 8. Selected Forts and Military Routes, 1849.

Marcy's diagonal trail, which included segments of an old Kickapoo route, would be adopted by settlers, gold rushers, the Butterfied Overland Mail, and the Texas and Pacific Railroad. When Gainesville was laid out in August 1850, the city fathers designated a local section of Marcy's Trail as California Street. The U.S. Corps of Engineers revisited the trail in 1854 as a candidate route for Jefferson Davis's proposed transcontinental railroad project. Marcy was not through. He explored the Red River to its source in July of 1852 and was rewarded with the command of Fort McIntosh in Laredo in May 1856. The command gave Marcy firsthand experience with the northern (Gainesville) and southern (Laredo) gateways of I-35.[52]

The U.S. fort network needed to be supplied, and this business opportunity was critical to the continuing revival of San Antonio. In April 1849, San Antonio was designated the headquarters of the Eighth Military Department, making Bexar the center for U.S. military operations in Texas, despite occasional competition from Corpus Christi and Indianola. San Antonio was favored because of its proximity to the western forts and its ample supplies of water, timber, and locally produced (lower-priced) foodstuffs. The U.S. Army occupied the Alamo in 1850 and began to construct facilities that would become the San Antonio Arsenal by 1857.[53]

San Antonio, and a smaller depot at Austin, were initially supplied by government (not commercial) wagon trains from the port of Indianola. Indianola had been founded as Indian Point on Matagorda Bay in 1845 as a transfer station for German colonists. Austin, in turn, operated as a transfer station for the northern forts on the Colorado, Brazos, and Trinity rivers. Unfortunately, as the western line of forts moved farther west, Austin's supply depot gradually lost its significance. Forts Croghan, Graham, and Worth were closed by 1853, and the "Austin Arsenal" was out of business by 1854. A small army depot in Preston continued to support military operations in Indian Territory (Oklahoma), however, and Fort Worth would reinvent itself as a premier cattle town.[54]

In August 1850, the U.S. Army Corps of Engineers was induced to survey the Colorado River and then the Rio Grande as possible steamboat supply routes for Austin and the upriver Rio Grande forts, Fort Bliss (El Paso), Fort Duncan (Eagle Pass), and Fort McIntosh (Laredo). But as the Spanish had discovered, Texas' rivers were either too high during rainy seasons or too shallow during dry times. Traffic-blocking, river-clogging, boat-snagging "rafts"—accumulations of logs, branches, and brush—plagued inland river towns. River mouths and coastal harbors were burdened with shifting sandbars. On the Rio Grande, steamboats had played a major role in the Mexican War, and Laredo was visited by the shallow-draft steamship *Major Brown,* drawing just two feet of water, on October 24, 1847. Above Eagle Pass, however, the Rio Grande was too shallow and passage was blocked by occasional rock formations. Even between Eagle Pass and Ringgold Barracks, including Laredo, costly improvements were required to make the river navigable. Like the western frontier posts, the Rio Grande forts would have to be supplied mainly by land.[55]

Requests for surveys of the Trinity River were simply ignored. Fort Worth, located at the junction of the Clear and West forks of the Trinity River, would also have to fend for itself. Fort Worth was stranded by the fort's closing in September 1853, but a small village named for General William Jenkins Worth emerged from the tiny Fort Town community. Born in Hudson, New York, in 1794, Worth had left a hotel clerking position in Albany for a military career that included the Mexican War and a series of important survey expeditions through Texas. He died of cholera in San Antonio in May 1849 and is entombed at the intersection of Broadway and Fifth Avenue in Manhattan.[56]

Surrounding Tarrant County, named after Edward H. Tarrant of the Battle of Village Creek, had been settled since the mid-1840s. In addition to the relatively insignificant town of Fort Worth, the county included Birdville, an outgrowth of Bird's Fort; Johnson Station; and a handful of other villages. Johnson Station was founded by Colonel Middleton Tate Johnson, a lieutenant to Worth at the Battle of Monterrey and a future Civil War commander. Located around three miles south of present-day Arlington on a trail to Dallas, Johnson Station in 1849 consisted of a house with plantation, slaves, slave cabins, gristmill, sawmill, and blacksmith shop. Slaves were valuable. When Tarrant County was organized in 1850, only 32 of its 664 inhabitants were slaves, but this "property" was valued at $13,600 on the county's books. By comparison, 10,384 acres of land were valued at only $9,845, and 10,214 head of cattle at just $4,200.[57]

After the fort closing, Fort Worth's sixty-man garrison was transferred west to Fort Belknap, and a few local merchants relocated to the abandoned army barracks. By 1856, Fort Worth had its first post office, stagecoach stop, non-dirt-floored hotel (Steele's Tavern), and mercantile store (Berliner and Samuels). Tarrant County started to receive mail service from Waco in 1853 — from Fort Graham, fifty-five miles to the south, and then via Dallas by horseback rider. A new contract provided regular mail and stage service along the

Dallas–Fort Belknap line by 1856. These developments helped Fort Worth to snare the county seat from Birdville in November 1856, an action confirmed in the 1860 elections.[58]

Even with its golden location, Dallas was not much of a destination in 1850. Dallas County had grown to 2,743 residents, but the new county seat had just 163. As early as 1846, when the surrounding county had been organized, Dallas already had its first hotel (the Dallas Tavern), a post office, and general stores. Affairs improved between 1852 and 1854, when Maxime Guillot opened a wagon factory and Alexander Cockrell, a building materials supplier, acquired John Neely Bryan's real estate and Trinity River ferry business for seven thousand dollars. Bryan should have been excited by the prospects for Dallas, but ferry revenues and real estate interests were not enough to hold him. Like other adventurers, Dallas's founder left for California gold in 1849 and did not return until 1852. In that year, Bryan sold his holdings and began to focus on a railroad venture.[59]

With Bryan's properties in hand, the entrepreneurial Cockrell proceeded to construct a 520-foot-long covered toll bridge and plank approach road at Commerce Street in 1855. Both projects were needed to accommodate expanding traffic volumes and the new Sawyer stage line. Cockrell added an impressive hotel and a steam-powered sawmill shortly thereafter. This, however, would be his peak. In 1858, Cockrell was killed by a city marshal, who may have owed Cockrell money, and the bridge was washed away in a flood. Two years later, in July 1860, Dallas's best hotel was destroyed by a controversial fire. Despite these woes, Cockrell's wife Sarah would move on to bigger and better things.[60]

Sparsely populated as Dallas and Tarrant counties may have been, Cooke County, carved out of the larger Fannin District in March 1848, boasted a total population of just 220 in 1850. The county seat was located in 1850 at Gainesville, a town named for the recently (1849) deceased General Edmund P. Gaines. Gaines had been William Fitzhugh's superior during the War of 1812 and had commanded a U.S. Army post on the east bank of the Sabine River that Sam Houston may have called into action before or after San Jacinto. Gainesville remained lightly inhabited until the arrival of the Butterfield Overland Mail in 1858, but Marcy's descriptions of November 2, 1849, suggested a promising future. The Elm Creek region that bordered the "extreme frontier settlement" of Fitzhugh's Station was "one of the most beautiful locations for farmers that can be found [and] offers great inducements for others to come."[61]

By 1850, the upper Red River and upper Trinity River valleys were being settled, and the land between the Rio Grande and Nueces rivers was being folded into Texas. Still, Laredo and three cities-to-be—Dallas, Fort Worth, and Waco—were not even listed in the U.S. Census of 1850. Texas' population had soared to 212,592 (including 58,161 slaves), but no city contained as many as 5,000 inhabitants. Galveston was the state's largest town with 4,177, followed by San Antonio (3,488), Houston (2,396), New Braunfels (1,298), and Marshall (1,189). No other town had as many as 1,000 people. Austin claimed 629, Waco had just been organized, Dallas had 350 residents (in 1853), and Birdville, the seat of Tarrant County, reported 30 families.[62]

San Antonio's recovery had been impressive. Still a glorified village, unsophisticated compared with Santa Fe (let alone Chihuahua, Saltillo, and Monterrey), the town was benefiting significantly from federal largesse. The U.S. Quartermaster Department invested more than $11 million in Texas between 1849 and 1860, mainly in San Antonio, to support military and civilian payrolls, transportation, horse and mule purchases, the acquisition of animal forage, and a variety of other goods and services. Almost single-handed, the Quartermaster Department created Texas' supply depots, its modest steamboat industry, and the ports of Indianola, Port Lavaca, Corpus Christi, and Brownsville. Since traffic over the Chihuahua Road had peaked, military contracts were welcome news, producing a boom for wagon-based freighters, steamboats, and port facilities until these supply routes were eventually superseded by railroads.[63]

Somewhat like Querétaro in the 1550s, San Antonio emerged as the state's most important supply depot and transportation center. Gulf Coast seaports warehoused most of the supplies shipped from New Orleans and Mexico, and the cargo was shipped by land to San Antonio. From Bexar, the supplies were in turn distributed to forts scattered around the Texas frontier. Some 343 persons, 10 percent of San Antonio's population, were involved in the wagon or freight trade. The military supply depot, supported by a series of U.S. Topographical Corps survey expeditions, employed another 150. One U.S. Army caravan left San Antonio in May 1849, with 275 government-owned, mule-drawn wagons and 2,500 head of livestock for the grueling five-month trip to El Paso. A massive fleet of 3,000–4,000 wagons, each driven by teams of 16 to 24 mules or oxen, was operating in Texas in 1852, gradually coming to be controlled by a handful of private contractors like George H. Giddings, George T. Howard, and Charles Ogden.[64]

With the expansion of trade between the coast and the interior, calls were made to improve Texas' woeful road conditions. Counties were responsible for local roads, but longer-distance highways had been ignored. As freighters and stage companies clamored for improved highways, interior towns and their inhabitants remained unmoved. Most of the proposed turnpike and bridge schemes authorized by the state were expected to be financed by private enterprise. Few were built. When they were, the state regulated toll rates and categorized roads as either first or second class (thirty or twenty feet wide, respectively). For example, the principal road between Dallas and Waxahachie (future US 77) was widened to thirty feet and declared a first-class road in March 1851. The few bridges that were built were developed initially by private enterprises, financed by bond issues, and supported by local tax and toll revenues. A tax of two dollars might be assessed to every wagon entering a town and a tax of one dollar for every ox cart. When revenues inevitably fell below operating costs, county governments were forced to assume responsibility for bridges and their maintenance.[65]

As an incentive to build highways, free public lands were often issued to turnpike companies (Spanish-style) for rights-of-way and as a means to guide the direction of real estate and business development. Nevertheless, few turnpikes were ever built in Texas. Another idea permitted counties to assess and collect a road tax if this were approved by voters in the 1852 elections. Most voters rejected the opportunity. Still, roads and bridges occasionally got built. In Hays County, edited Commissioners Court records of November 1855, provide a glimpse of road-improvement activities in the 1850s: "All persons living near road section one, from the county line above the springs to the Black Jack Ridge near the waterhole, are by law required to work the roads and are hereby commanded to work with [the overseer]." At an April 1858, meeting, Hays County appointed overseers to reroute a segment of Stage Coach Road between San Marcos and Austin, starting at "Mitchell's Field and running on a line between [property owners] Dixon and S. B. Bales. Each named party [was] to give ground for the road."[66]

New Braunfels and San Antonio attempted to build bridges. After a ferry service had been in operation at the junction of the Comal and Guadalupe rivers since the mid-1840s, an elevated footbridge, the first in New Braunfels, was built across the Comal River to the Torrey Mill in 1851. The town's first wagon bridge, a timber affair on stone pillars, was added in 1856, replaced in 1866, and destroyed by flood in October 1870. San Antonio had at least four bridges in 1860: the West Commerce Street Bridge, built of cypress and cedar logs in 1841 on the site of the first Spanish bridge across the San Antonio River in 1736; the Navarro Street Bridge, at the site of an old Indian ford; the East

Houston Street Bridge, built to replace a ford crossing in 1853; and the St. Mary's Street Bridge in 1858.[67]

Passengers and cargo were carried in a variety of vehicles. Stagecoaches had been introduced in the 1830s and were steadily improved. In addition, there were many types of freight wagons and "prairie schooners"—most notably the Conestoga wagon. Conestogas were manufactured in Pittsburgh, introduced by the Santa Fe Trail merchants during the 1820s, and popularized by the Chihuahua traders in the 1840s. They had iron axles, five-and-one-half-foot wheels, and six-inch-wide treads and cost around two hundred dollars. The wagons were drawn by 20–30 oxen (or 10–20 mules) and could haul seven tons of cargo. As in Zacatecas, they often traveled in caravans of 100–150 wagons to improve defenses against possible Indian attacks.[68]

Old-fashioned wooden ox carts remained a common sight on Texas roads, particularly in the territory between Bexar and the Rio Grande. As described by Berlandier, the carts were drawn by teams of between two and ten oxen and were often held together by ropes and wooden pegs carved from tree limbs—virtually unchanged from the time of Cortés. Mules were preferred because of their longevity and flexibility, but oxen had their supporters. Oxen worked better in mud, carried more cargo, and were less expensive. In 1846, a team of oxen cost roughly $40–50 versus $150 or so for two draft horses. The military's brief fling with imported Arabian camels in 1856 (based northwest of San Antonio at Camp Verde) did little to threaten the livelihood of other four-legged beasts.[69]

With bridges few and far between, river crossings remained just as treacherous and potentially time-consuming as in the days of De Vaca. According to historian William Ransom Hogan, persons traveling from Galveston to Dallas in 1845 might have to journey by "raft, oxcart, horseback, canoe, and horseback again" to reach their final destination. Writing in 1856, Frederick Law Olmsted described the main road between San Antonio and Port Lavaca (and Indianola) as "a mere collection of straggling wagon ruts, extending for more than a quarter of a mile in width, from outside to outside; it being desirable in this part of the country, rather to avoid the road than follow it." Such bridges as were built were often poorly constructed and fell into disrepair. Passenger travel was an adventure. There were virtually no inns, and travelers typically had to camp out under the stars. Where there was an inn or hotel, people often had to share rooms with complete strangers. As for food service—the Coahuiltecans may have eaten better.[70]

As was the case with Spain's Caminos Reales, genuine road building in Texas was driven by military need. Roads were surveyed or built when deemed necessary to supply the continuing westward movement of U.S. military forts (and tag-along businesses) and to provide regular communications by mail and eventually telegraph. San Antonio, Austin, and Waco emerged as important mail depots for the western frontier. Military mail service was regular but slow; a civilian horseback rider required roughly ten days to travel between San Antonio and Fort Brown. An 1850 mail route between San Antonio and El Paso took either thirty days by horseback or three months by wagon.[71]

Otherwise, mail was carried by dedicated stagecoach lines. I. T. Brown and Lyman Tarbox of Houston had revived a biweekly stage line between Austin and Houston in 1845, via Washington, La Grange, and Bastrop. The twenty-dollar fare included up to thirty pounds of luggage, and the trip took around three and a half days. In August 1847, once the Military (Preston) Road was in operation, Brown and Tarbox won the first annual contract for a thousand dollars to operate a weekly, two-horse coach service between Austin and San Antonio. The coach stopped at Manchaca, San Marcos, Bonito, Guadalupe City, New Braunfels, and Cibola. In June 1849, a second weekly route was added, leaving Austin and San Antonio every Monday and Friday at 6:00 A.M. and arriving at the other terminal the following day at 6:00 P.M. In 1851, the service was improved with a four-horse coach.[72]

Between March 1847 and June 1850, Brown and Tarbox also operated the Texas U.S. Mail Line between San Antonio and Houston; the Western U.S. Mail Line between San Antonio and Port Lavaca via New Braunfels and Victoria; and a stage line between San Antonio and Corpus Christi. These and some fifty other stage companies operated in and out of San Antonio through 1881. Prior to consolidations, competition was fierce. In 1852, Brown and Tarbox lost their four-horse stage contract between San Antonio and Austin to William M. Rice of Houston. The three-thousand-dollar contract was increased to triweekly service, then increased to same-day (18-hour) service between the two terminals in 1854, for riders willing to depart either point at 3:00 A.M. In 1855, the contract was captured, in turn, by B. A. Risher of Seguin and increased to six times a week. Risher and new partner Hall also established a stage line between San Antonio and Victoria, the terminus of a new railroad line from Port Lavaca.[73]

North of Austin, the company Belton, Burney, and Blair operated a weekly mail and stage service between Austin and Waco along the Preston Road, until replaced by Sawyer and Compton in 1857. Sawyer and Compton continued to run a daily service between the two towns until the Santa Fe Railroad arrived in 1881. An alternate-day service between San Antonio and Waco began in 1861. One stop of note was the Shady Villa (the current Stagecoach) Inn in Salado, built in 1852 on a site visited by Indians for centuries, by Cooke's Military Road expedition, and later by Chisholm Trail drivers. Salado served local stages and the Western Stage Company's piece of the Great Northern Line between Memphis (via Little Rock) and San Antonio. By September 1858, Western was stopping at San Antonio, New Braunfels, San Marcos, and Austin, with connections to Waco and Dallas. When weekly mail service was extended to Laredo in 1861, Western and other stages were rolling along most of the future route of I-35.[74]

Stages, roads, and occasional bridge projects confirmed that the region between San Antonio and Austin was being filled. From a base of nearly zero in 1845, some 25,000 to 30,000 German immigrants were settled by 1860—mainly farmers, wagon makers, craftsmen, and merchants. New Braunfels had boasted a water-powered gristmill, sawmill, flour mill, and cotton gin along the Comal River since the late 1840s. They were built by William Meriwether and his slaves atop a site that had been inhabited for possibly seven thousand years. In 1859, Meriwether sold his holdings for fourteen thousand dollars to Joseph Landa, a Prussian-Jewish merchant who had arrived in San Antonio in 1844 and relocated to New Braunfels in 1847; New Braunfels's Landa Park is named in his honor. The first hotel in town, the Guadalupe, was built in 1853 and renamed after its acquisition by Jacob Schmitz in 1858. Refurbished in 1873, the Schmitz Hotel prospered from stagecoach traffic until the International and Great Northern railroad arrived in 1880.[75]

Roads between San Antonio and Georgetown were designated "public highways" (with mileposts) in 1853. The region north of New Braunfels was developing slowly. San Marcos would have only three hundred inhabitants in 1860, although cotton gins, gristmills, sawmills, and a beef factory were scattered through Hays County. A new road from San Marcos to Austin was authorized in 1852, crossing the Colorado River at Stone's Ferry in Austin. Stone's Ferry also met the stage from San Antonio and operated almost continuously between 1846 and 1886. The ferryboat was sixty feet long, and Stone charged one dollar per wagon (including oxen or horses), fifty cents per carriage, twenty-five per rider on horseback, and twelve and a half per pedestrian.[76]

Had it not been for the Civil War, railroads would have arrived meaningfully in Texas some twenty years earlier than they did. Since steamboats were limited to the Galveston–New Orleans run, the lower Brazos River, and the lower Rio Grande, this twenty-year delay—while not fatal—would have profound implications for the timing, shape, and scale of local economic and urban history. Four railroad companies had been chartered in Texas as early as 1838, and their timing should have been good: as of 1836, there were no railroads in Texas, none west of the Mississippi River, and the entire United States contained perhaps a thousand miles of track. As the cotton industry evolved, the economics of rail transportation versus ox carts, wagons, mule trains (and occasional camels) became compelling.[77]

Unfortunately, investment capital and credit were so scarce in the late 1830s and 1840s that Texas' first rail line was delayed until 1852. In that year, the Buffalo Bayou, Brazos and Colorado Railway Company (successor to the earlier Harrisburg City Company) managed to complete a modest line between the Brazos River cotton and sugar fields and the ports at Houston and Galveston. The BBB&C had received most of its investment capital from a group of Boston real estate-turned-railroad investors as well as generous grants from the state—sixteen sections of land for every mile of track laid. In return, rates for mail and freight were set by the Texas legislature. The BBB&C extended its westerly line to Richmond (on the Brazos, thirty miles from Harrisburg) by 1855 and to Alleyton, opposite Columbus on the Colorado River, by 1860. A planned northwestern extension to Austin would have to wait.[78]

By 1861, ten railroad companies were operating in Texas, together comprising less than five hundred miles of track. The principal lines ran between Marshall and Shreveport, between Indianola and Victoria, and between Houston and terminals at Galveston, Orange, Columbia, Alleyton, Brenham, and Millican. The two railheads nearest to San Antonio and Austin were Victoria (the San Antonio and Mexican Gulf line from Matagorda Bay) and Brenham (the Air Line Tap extension via Hempstead from Houston). The Air Line Tap had completed a railroad bridge across the Brazos River with slave labor, but a planned extension to Austin would also be delayed until 1871. Goods bound for interior destinations had to be transferred from the railheads to humble wagons and ox carts. Since the Civil War reduced the supply of workers and materials significantly, Texas railroad lines deteriorated badly by 1865. Stages, wagons, and carts remained in great demand.[79]

Long-distance stage lines like the Butterfield Overland Stage crisscrossed the western frontier in the pre-railroad interim. A typical journey between Tipton in Missouri (via Colbert's Red River ferry at future Denison) and San Francisco took twenty-five days. The one-way fare of $150–200 covered forty pounds of baggage. Individual segments were priced at ten cents per mile and mail was carried for ten cents per half ounce. Meals were extra. John Butterfield used state-of-the-art Concord (New Hampshire) spring coaches for the main roads, but switched to smaller Celerities (made in Albany, New York) for the rougher frontier segments. Early Concords carried four passengers, their baggage, and five to six hundred pounds of mail, followed later by six- to nine-passenger versions, priced between $900 and $1,100. Nine-passenger Celerities, made to Butterfield's own specifications, proved to be lighter and faster.[80]

Coaches averaged between six and eight miles per hour and stage drivers typically worked sixty-mile segments. Of course, travel times were dependent on river crossings, the quality of bridges (when they existed), possible robberies, Indian attacks, and general road conditions. When roads were blocked by trees, brush, or mud, passengers often had to help out with clearing and pushing chores. Relay stations were critical. Relay (or "swing") stations were designed for the pickup and delivery of mail, transfer of passengers and luggage, and changing of horses. Situated every ten to twenty miles, the stations usually included a keeper's house, stable, blacksmith shop, and dining place.[81]

Butterfield's investments and services bolstered upper Red River communities like Preston, Sherman, and Gainesville. The future I-35 gateway at Gainesville might have developed on its own, but Butterfield's investments and notoriety accelerated matters. Newspaper coverage of the Butterfield's inaugural run in September 1858, described the "fine rolling prairie" between Colbert's Ferry and the lower Cross Timbers and praised the "flourishing little town" of Gainesville. However, most readers were interested in the news dispatches from Indian territories.[82]

The line between Gainesville and San Antonio was now largely but not completely free from Indian attacks. Native tribes had been destroyed, assimilated, evicted, placed on reservations, or relocated to Indian Territory. With the Comanches finished as a serious threat, most of the upper Red River towns were left to focus on business schemes. For example, Butterfield's decision to cross the Red River at Colbert's Ferry, rather than the traditional crossing at Rock Bluff at Preston, eight miles to the northwest, was the result of a business deal. Anticipating a potential bonanza, Benjamin Franklin Colbert, a Chickasaw entrepreneur, joined with the town of Sherman to provide a free ferry service (plus a new road through Grayson County) in return for the coveted Butterfield route. Colbert's success would be repeated in later years. With Butterfield's blessing, Sherman developed as a major distribution hub, with fourteen stage lines operating through town in 1871. As indicated, Preston lies beneath Lake Texoma.[83]

Butterfield aside, some thirty-one stage lines were operating in Texas by 1860, carrying mail, passengers, and light freight. Sixteen of these lines happened to be controlled by a single (consolidated) company, Sawyer, Risher and Hall, employing over three hundred men and a thousand horses and mules. Consolidation was nothing new to the Texas transportation industry. The freight industry was already an oligopoly, and the consolidation of Texas' stage companies represented a pattern that would be repeated in railroads after the Civil War and in bus lines after 1929. In the meantime, the consolidation of smaller regional lines enhanced efficiency and promoted systemwide scheduling and management.[84]

Even without Butterfield, railroads, and steamboats, the towns of San Antonio and Austin had made considerable progress. By 1860, Bexar businesses included printers, soap and candle manufacturers, harness makers, wagon makers, iron and silver smiths, and the Menger Brewery. Austin's frontier isolation had essentially ended. In addition to the north-south Preston Road, an easterly road (through Webberville) ran to the San Antonio Road at Bastrop. Two other easterly roads connected Austin with Hempstead via Bastrop and Brenham and with Columbus via La Grange. Meanwhile, a westerly road from Austin via Fredericksburg connected to the U.S. Military Road to El Paso. Still dominated by professionals, Austin added a gristmill, sawmill, brick kiln, wagon and carriage makers, gaslights, a new capitol building (built for $150,000 in the early 1850s), and an impressive governor's mansion constructed with timber hauled by slaves from Bastrop's Lost Pines.[85]

Both towns were also starting to benefit from the emerging cattle trade, although Bexar had an edge in government beef contracts and freighting. While the legendary cattle drives would not occur until after the Civil War, cattle became an important industry in the 1840s and 1850s. New Orleans was Texas' principal cattle market until after the Civil War, but much higher prices could be received elsewhere. Entrepreneurs willing to drive thousands of herded wild and unbranded cattle north to Ohio, Kentucky, and Illinois for fattening and eventual shipment to the East Coast were usually rewarded with good profits. Some drivers even made the trek to California.

The emerging corridor between Austin and San Antonio was captured in 1856 by the keen eyes of Frederick Law Olmsted, the future designer of New York's Central Park, the "Emerald Necklace" in Boston, and a host of other famous parks. After arriving in Natchitoches, Louisiana, Olmsted and his brother John followed the Old San Antonio Road on horseback through the "Western Texas" towns of Bastrop, Austin, San Marcos, and New Braunfels en route to Bexar:

> Seven miles from San Antonio we passed the Salado, another small creek, and shortly after, rising a hill, we saw the domes and white cluster dwellings of San Antonio below us. We stopped and gazed long on the sunny scene. The city is closely-built and prominent, and lies basking on the edge of a vast plain, through which the river winds slowly off beyond where the eye can reach. To the east are gentle slopes toward it; to the north a long gradual sweep upward to the mountain country, which comes down within five or six miles; to the south and west, the open prairies, extending almost level to the coast, a hundred and fifty miles away.[86]

From Trails to Rails, 1860–1900

$\mathcal{W}$ ITH or without railroads, the combined effects of immigration, agriculture, and trade raised the population of Texas to 604,215 in 1860, including 182,566 slaves and 355 free blacks. Only 11 percent of the state's population lived in towns with more than a hundred inhabitants, and only six towns could be categorized as significant: Galveston, Houston, San Antonio, New Braunfels, Austin, and Marshall. While the state's cotton and sugar plantations spawned a large number of gristmills, sawmills, and cotton gins, most of these were scattered around the countryside—few plantation owners were likely to finance a major road or bridge project to support one or two local cotton gins. Factories were few and far between.

The 1860 census figures for communities located from south to north along the future route of I-35 are interesting. Relentless Indian attacks and the near abandonment of Fort McIntosh in Laredo kept Webb County's population at 1,397 people, none of them slaves, and well below the 2,906 residents of Nueces County, including Corpus Christi. Bexar County reported 14,454 inhabitants (including 1,395 slaves), as San Antonio reclaimed its position as Texas' largest city with 8,235 (592 slaves). Galveston was second at 7,307 (1,178 slaves), followed by Houston at 4,815 (1,069).[1]

Comal County reported 4,030 residents (including 193 slaves) and Travis County was home to 8,080 (3,136); Austin's totals were 3,494 (977). Moving north, Bell County's population in 1860 was 4,799 (1,005 slaves) and McLennan County reported 6,206 (2,395). The Brazos River plantations had raised the estimated property value of Waco's 1,938 slaves to over $1 million. While

103

Dallas County was home to 8,665 (1,080 slaves), the town of Dallas had just 775 residents, including remnants of Victor Considerant's remarkable but ill-fated La Reunion cooperative. In those days, Dallas and the northern counties were more focused on wheat, a crop that was less slave-intensive than cotton. Tarrant County reported 6,020 residents (850 slaves), including 350 in Fort Worth in 1861. Only 251 of Denton County's 5,031 residents were slaves, and Cooke County's totals were 3,760 (369).[2]

Except for the Red River crossing site, the outline for Interstate 35 was clearly in place in 1860. A wagon or stagecoach drawn by horses, mules, or oxen could follow one continuous road from Preston Station or Colbert's Ferry in Grayson County (not yet Cooke County) to Laredo. After taking the Preston Road south to Dallas, one could continue along Cooke's Military (Preston) Road through Waxahachie, Waco, Belton, and Austin. From Austin, as Olmsted described, the principal route ran through San Marcos and New Braunfels to San Antonio. From San Antonio, the old road to Laredo had deteriorated with age (and competition from the Brownsville Road), but it was still there.

The state's economic progress was gradually brought to a halt by the Civil War and would be disrupted greatly by the abolition of slavery. Slavery was a powerful economic force in Texas, though it had been introduced seriously only since the early 1820s and was concentrated in cotton and sugar-growing counties. While Governor Sam Houston and the inhabitants of eighteen counties, including Travis, Williamson, and Cooke, voted against secession in February of 1861, voting against secession was not the same as voting against slavery. If these counties and the end segments of the I-35 corridor (Webb to Bexar and Dallas/Tarrant to Cooke counties) were less slave-intensive than other counties, they and the towns and cotton plantations in between were nevertheless fully integrated with the slave-based economy. Many of the public buildings, roads, and bridges located in I-35 counties were built directly by slaves.[3]

Other than troop movements, the future route of I-35 cannot be linked to any important Civil War engagements. However, W. W. Heartsill's wartime diary provides a fascinating view of at least one soldier's trip to the front. In 1861, Heartsill traveled southwest from Marshall to Waco, there joining the Preston Road en route to Austin, San Antonio, and an eventual station at Camp Wood in Uvalde:

> April 27: . . . Fourteen miles on and we cross the Brazos River at Waco, the county-site of McLennan County. Two military companies escort us into,

and through the city-like town. April 28: A march of twenty miles and arrive at Belton (Bell County) and are pained to record the fact, that this is the only place that has not received us with some demonstrations of welcome; not that we are entitled to such demonstrations, but when the inquiry is made . . . the answer is "Belton is Union." Shame on you. A march ten miles and camp in Salado, on Salado Creek. . . . April 29: March fifteen miles and enter George-town, the county [seat] of Williamson County. Here the citizens make up for their neighbors of Belton. For each and every one of the citizens appear to use every exertion to make us feel "at home."[4]

The war period in Central Texas was highlighted by enlistments, slavery, munitions factories in San Antonio and Austin, the "Great Hanging" of at least forty suspected Union conspirators in Gainesville on October 19, 1862, La-redo's near-capture in March of 1864, and general deprivations. Union block-ades and bombardments were focused on Texas seaports, especially Galveston, and the ad hoc cotton trading centers that sprouted along the lower Rio Grande. A short-term bonanza in cotton created instant fortunes for entrepre-neurs like steamboat captains-turned-cotton traders Richard King and Mifflin Kenedy. The Battle of Glorieta Pass, an attempt by Texas Confederates to gain control of New Mexico (where Lamar had failed in 1841), was halted east of Santa Fe in March 1862. But if no significant battles or physical destruction oc-curred on Texas lands, Texans were at least successful—they defeated Union forces at Galveston (January 1, 1863) and Sabine Pass (September 6, 1863) and helped to thwart a major Red River invasion south of Mansfield, Louisiana (April 1864).[5]

At war's end, thousands of Confederate men and boys were dead, Texas' black population was free, the economy was in ruins, and the state was under military rule. In May 1865, General Philip H. Sheridan, commander of the Military Division of the Southwest, was ordered to the Rio Grande with fifty-two thousand men—less to maintain order in Texas than to monitor French military forces in Mexico. One company was sent to San Antonio, and four thousand soldiers arrived in Austin in July (joined later by George Armstrong Custer). Laredo was occupied by the 62nd U.S. Colored Infantry in October. On June 19 ("Juneteenth"), General Gordon Granger declared from Galves-ton that Texas' slave population was free by virtue of the Emancipation Proclamation.[6]

Between 1865 and 1869, a Freedmen's Bureau was established by the U.S. War Department to address the readjustment problems of emancipated slaves.

In Dallas, a Freedman's Town was settled east of downtown in 1865, and the community between Elm Street and Central Avenue evolved into the legendary Deep Ellum district. Despite many accomplishments, including the first black public school in San Antonio, the Freedmen's Bureau was abolished in 1869. Blacks were left to fend for themselves. In Austin, where blacks represented 40 percent of the population in 1870, the Antioch Colony was founded on a 490-acre tract on Onion Creek (west of Buda), and Charles Clark established Clarksville west of downtown in 1871.[7]

Amidst the confusion, the future route of I-35 would be shaped by cotton, cattle drives, and railroads. Cotton production volumes did not regain their prewar levels until 1873, but new cotton fields in north-central Texas accounted for much of the revival. The rich blackland prairies that parallel I-35 attracted thousands of settlers from East Texas and Old South states. Most were well acquainted with cotton farming and helped to accelerate the conversion of wheat-growing properties to cotton. The new settlers were part of a general expansion. The population of Texas reached 818,715 in 1870, more than 200,000 above the 1860 level. Galveston became Texas' largest city with 13,898 residents, followed by San Antonio with 12,256, Houston (9,332), Austin (4,428), and Jefferson (4,180). Austin was finally made the permanent capital of Texas in the election of 1872, defeating bids by Houston and Waco. Waco, Dallas, and Fort Worth were still small towns.[8]

In the near term, Texas' major asset was cattle, and a number of factors converged to create a unique business opportunity. These included the new railheads in Kansas, inflated live cattle prices in the Midwest, and the fact that more than 4 million wild, unbranded beeves were roaming the South Texas plains. These animals were descendants of hundreds of years of Spanish colonialism. The opportunity was simple: gather wild cattle into herds, brand them (required by law in 1866), drive the herds northward to designated (nonquarantined) railhead junctions in Kansas, and sell the beeves at market prices. Two dedicated trails, the Shawnee and the Chisholm, would be critical to the shape of I-35 (map 9).[9]

Texas entrepreneurs had driven cattle to Mexico, New Orleans, the Midwest, and western territories for decades, typically following old Indian and buffalo trails. These drives were decidedly small scale—in the hundreds and low thousands of head. Postwar drives were in the hundreds of thousands and utilized dedicated routes like the Shawnee and later the Chisholm and Western trails. Cattle-drive economics were clear: if one could herd the unbranded cattle

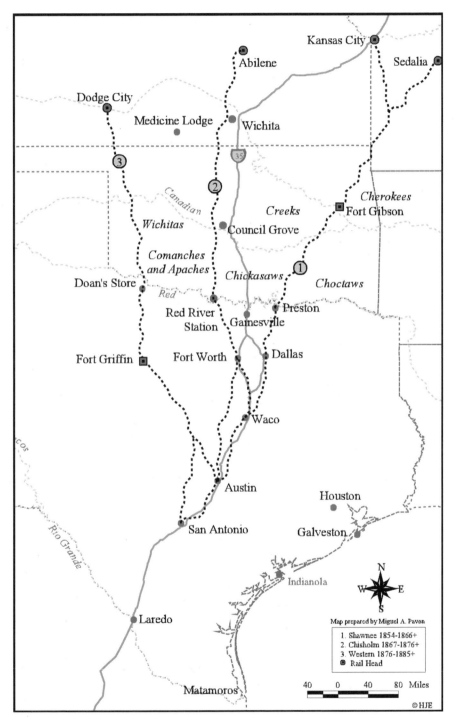

Kansas City
Sedalia
Abilene
Dodge City
Medicine Lodge
Wichita
③
35
②
Canadian
Creeks
Cherokees
Fort Gibson
Wichitas
Council Grove
Comanches
and Apaches
Chickasaws
①
Choctaws
Doan's Store
Red
Red River
Station
Gainesville
Preston
Fort Griffin
Fort Worth
Dallas
Pecos
Waco
Austin
Houston
San Antonio
Galveston
Rio Grande
Indianola
N
W E
S
Laredo
Map prepared by Miguel A. Pavon
1. Shawnee 1854-1866+
2. Chisholm 1867-1876+
3. Western 1876-1885+
⊚ Rail Head
40   0   40   80 Miles
Matamoros
©HJE

Map 9. Cattle Trails and Indian Nations, 1854–1885.

in Texas, worth only five to ten dollars locally, and sell them in the Midwest for twenty-five to a hundred dollars a head, one could realize a substantial profit after modest labor and transportation costs. According to historian Wayne Gard, "the big Texas problem was to link a four dollar steer to a forty dollar market."[10]

Tens of thousands of South Texas cattle had left the state in the 1850s (possibly fifty thousand in 1854) along the so-called Shawnee Trail to Missouri. Herds were gathered in South Texas, then driven through San Antonio, Austin, Waco, Dallas, and the Rock Bluff crossing near Preston, before moving northeast to Fort Gibson and the railheads at Sedalia (Missouri), Kansas City, or St. Louis. However, fears of "Texas Fever," a tick-borne protozoa that infected short-horn Texas cattle, reduced shipments sharply in the late 1850s, and thousands of cattle were left loose or turned loose during the Civil War. The wild cattle supply enabled the revived Shawnee Trail to carry more than two hundred thousand head in 1866. This massive scale attracted robberies and provoked renewed fears of Texas Fever. When blockades and quarantines were established in East Kansas and railheads were placed in Abilene and eventually Dodge City, the Shawnee traffic was redirected to a new, more northwesterly route, some 150 miles to the west. The new trail had better grazing lands, fewer wooded areas, less difficult river crossings, and fewer hostile Kansas farmers, Comanches, and Kiowas. The Indians were outraged about the intensified competition for water and grass supplies and the associated relocation of the buffalo herds.[11]

The new route, the Chisholm Trail, followed or paralleled a series of old Indian trails and wagon roads. Named after the Kansas-based trader, guide, interpreter, and diplomat Jesse Chisholm, it dwarfed all drive trails to date. Of Cherokee and Scots descent, Chisholm had little involvement with cattle during his long and storied career, but during and after the Civil War, he operated a string of trading posts along an old north-south Indian trading trail. One post was located at the mouth of the Little Arkansas River, at the future site of Wichita. Another was located at Council Grove on the North Canadian River (near future Oklahoma City). Chisholm was familiar with at least two other Indian trails: one between the Canadian and Red rivers, mainly following the Washita River; and the other, thanks to his diplomatic work for Sam Houston in the early 1840s, between the Red River and Tehuacana Creek (near Waco).[12]

What would be known as the Chisholm Trail was achieved simply by attaching Chisholm's trail north of the Red River, the route between Chisholm's two posts (future Oklahoma City and Wichita), to the existing Shawnee and other roads in Texas. North of the Red River, there was one and only one Chisholm Trail to the Kansas railheads. The trail crossed into Indian Territory at Red River Station, east of Ringgold and nine miles northwest of Nocona in Montague County. Red River Station had been a Texas Ranger post during the Civil War and was slightly upriver from the site of Parrilla's rout in 1759. From there, the trail headed due north, passing through present-day Duncan, Jesse Chisholm's post at Council Grove, and Enid en route to Kansas. In Kansas, the trail continued north through present-day Wichita (another Chisholm post) and across the Arkansas River to the Union Pacific railhead at Abilene. In some stretches, the "trail" was as wide as fifty miles and the cattle had left a brown wake of prairie that had once been verdant grassland.[13]

South of Red River Station there was no single cattle trail from the Rio Grande to the Red River. A number of cattle trails eventually fed into or became "the" Chisholm, Shawnee, or Western Trail. Most started in the South Texas coastal plains, the area between Matagorda Bay, Brownsville, Laredo, and San Antonio. Many but not all of the drives passed through San Antonio and the Guadalupe River crossing of the San Antonio Road in New Braunfels. Otherwise, the route through New Braunfels and other feeder trails usually converged in southeast Austin, not noted as a cattle town, at the ancient Montopolis crossing of the Colorado River. From there, the drives headed north through Round Rock (fording at Bushy Creek), Georgetown, Salado, Belton, and Waco—typically following existing stage roads and swimming across rivers and streams. From Waco, the Chisholm Trail veered to the northwest, passing through Daggett's Crossing at Fort Worth (not Dallas, which was on the Shawnee), then along present-day US 81 through Wise and Montague counties en route to Red River Station.[14]

The Chisholm Trail made Fort Worth the principal "cowtown" in Texas between 1866 and 1886. Since there were no major stores between Fort Worth and the Kansas railheads, drivers would purchase a one-month supply of provisions at Fort Worth and enjoy the local hotels and entertainment. Gainesville, finally incorporated in 1873, became a prosperous if rowdy cowtown as well. Approximately 75,000 head of cattle passed through Fort Worth in 1868, scaling up to 360,000 in 1871. Charles Daggett's ford and wagon ferry service was a major beneficiary. Fort Worth's fortunes were tied to those of Abilene, the principal railhead for the first Chisholm Trail drives, and then to Dodge. Abilene handled only 35,000 beeves in 1867 and 75,000 in 1868. But in 1869, a whopping 350,000 head were received, followed by 300,000 in 1870 and a stunning 600,000 in 1871, the greatest cattle drive—and bust—in history. The bust of 1871 was caused by a glut of cattle, deterioration in grass quality, prairie fires, and an early winter; some 250,000 wintering beeves died from starvation on the frigid plains of Kansas.[15]

When the Atchison, Topeka, and Santa Fe Railroad established a station at Dodge City, Kansas, in 1872, 175 miles southwest of Abilene, traffic from the Chisholm Trail began to shift to a new trail—the Western Trail. Like the Chisholm, the Western Trail was served by a number of branch routes in South Texas. Most passed through San Antonio, but the main trail followed a north-westerly direction, well to the west of Austin, Waco, and Fort Worth, en route to Fort Griffin and a Red River crossing at Doan's Store (east of the Texas Pan-handle). In 1880, the Western Trail handled more than half of the year's total drive (400,000 head) and prompted a fierce rivalry between Dodge City and Caldwell (on the Chisholm).[16]

The Chisholm Trail was virtually abandoned after a 300,000-head drive in 1884, and Dodge City and the Western Trail peaked in 1885. The subsequent collapse was caused by a variety of factors—severe price declines tied to the most recent cattle glut, a drought between 1885 and 1887, rising freight charges, revived fears of Texas Fever, competition from sheepmen and farmers for pasture lands, and the general inability of traditional Texas Gulf Coast breeds to adapt to the northern plains. None of this really mattered. The combination of railroads and barbed wire essentially eliminated the need for long-distance cattle drives of any kind. With railroad stations dotting the landscape, drives would rarely need to travel more than a hundred miles.[17]

While it lasted, the Chisholm Trail was critical to the history of the I-35 Corridor, spatially and economically. But if cattle drive profits helped to bolster the regional economy, revenue-poor county governments were still in no position to resume public works projects, neglected since 1861. Cattle drives made woeful road conditions even worse, and the old county system of compulsory work crews (now without slaves) was unpopular and poorly executed. A handful of bridges began to appear, but most rivers continued to be crossed the old-fashioned way, by foot or by ferry.

In 1871, Reconstruction governor Edmund J. Davis called for each adult male to sign up for work crew duty or pay a one-dollar poll tax for roads, bridges, and public schools. The first road tax in Texas was repealed in 1874 with the overturn of Radical Republicanism but was reinstated when the new Texas Constitution of 1876 authorized counties to levy taxes of as much as fifteen cents per hundred dollars of valuation for roads and bridges. Even when collected, these funds proved to be inadequate. The emergence of railroad lines and railroad towns prompted the legislature to restore the Davis program in 1879. Counties were authorized to lay out, supervise, and maintain roads and to draft work crews of males aged eighteen to forty-five for up to ten days per year. Ten days was more than twice the level of previous terms, but males were free to hire a substitute or pay a road tax of a dollar per day. The counties were already supposed to be performing these tasks, but the new legislation suggested something more formal. Unfortunately, most compulsory work crews were unmotivated, and their contributions were limited to removing stumps and large rocks and filling potholes.[18]

As increasingly large waves of settlers arrived in Texas, fresh demands were made to improve farm-to-market roads and river crossings, especially in areas devoted to cotton farming. Cotton was a cash crop that required speed to market and predictable scheduling. In cotton-rich Bell County, where the population doubled (to 18,783) between 1870 and 1880, pressure mounted to organize county road and bridge funds. In December 1868, the town of Salado had issued $2,500 in bonds to build a state-of-the-art wire and cable suspension footbridge across Salado Creek, along the Preston Road. An adjacent wagon bridge was added later. Unfortunately, both spans would be washed away by the flood of 1913, rebuilt, and washed away again by the flood of 1921. Another county project of note was the licensing of a private company in 1875 to construct and maintain a toll bridge across the Lampasas River (along future US 81).[19]

Roads began to be promoted by the media. The *Austin Daily Democratic Statesman* called for improved, macadamized (or at least straight) roads on March 26 and May 16, 1876:

[March 26]: A good many of our citizens favor the adoption of a system of macadamized roads diverging from this city to the lines of adjoining counties, or at least as far from this city as trade and circumstances seem to demand and the taxpayers can afford. That good roads, reaching out in different directions from eight to twelve miles, would greatly enhance the business of this city and tend to promote the interests and advance the price of lands throughout the entire county, no one can doubt. . . . Under proper system and management, fifty to one hundred miles of excellent road could soon be made [for] two hundred to four hundred thousand dollars, a sum that the county could very well afford.

> [May 16]: We desire to call the attention of the county court to the con-
> dition and zigzag course of many of the roads leading to the city. If we can not
> have good roads, let us at least have them reasonably straight and at least sixty
> to seventy feet wide.

Despite bad roads and cattle traffic, stagecoach lines had regained much of their prewar business. A *Scribner's Magazine* reporter described a stagecoach journey from Austin to San Antonio, via San Marcos and New Braunfels, in April 1874. Traveling in a four-horse stage with eleven other passengers (nine inside and three on top), the passengers forded the Colorado River on foot while the coach crossed on a pontoon bridge, constructed in 1869 at the foot of Austin's Brazos Street (not Congress Avenue). Later that day, after crossing the Blanco River en route to San Marcos, the party enjoyed a dinner of "but-termilk, corn bread, excellent meat and the inevitable coffee." To the north, a triweekly stage ran between Austin and Waco via Georgetown, Salado, and Belton, leaving at 6:00 A.M. but not arriving until 4:00 P.M. the following day. At Waco, connections were made to Dallas and Sherman. The typical fare was ten cents per mile.[20]

In the last few years of the stagecoach era, most of San Antonio's stage op-erators maintained offices in and around the Menger Hotel on Alamo Plaza. New services were started to the south and southwest, typically with routes laid out by contractor-owners and maintained by the counties. August Santleben and others operated lines between Bexar and Laredo and made connections with Rio Grande Valley towns. In the late 1870s, C. Bain provided service be-tween El Paso, Fredericksburg, San Antonio, and Laredo, and J. J. Ellis offered daily service between Bexar and Laredo (except Sundays), leaving each point at 6:00 A.M. Cross-border coach traffic was generated by the Sierra Mojado mines in Mexico. When the two lines merged, Bain and Ellis deployed segments of the old San Antonio–Laredo Road, passing through Pleasanton, Tilden, Sam McGill, Fort Ewell, and Callaghan Ranch.[21]

Most of the principal stage roads would be replaced by railways, bypassing a number of unlucky stage-stop communities in the process. The towns of San Marcos and Salado were affected for decades. Days were also numbered for the long-distance freighters, stage drivers, and mail lines. One of the more famous freight lines was operated by August Santleben, its fame partly attributable to Santleben's having the good sense to record his experiences in book form. Shortly after receiving a two-year contract in January 1866 to carry mail between San

Antonio and Eagle Pass, Santleben's greatest moment was his reported haul of $350,000 in silver (plus 40,000 pounds of copper) from Chihuahua to San Antonio with a Spanish-style escort of thirty men. The delivery represented the most valuable load in Bexar history. Santleben applied $1,250 of his fee to purchase a deluxe nine-seat Abbott-Downing coach, equipped with hickory woodwork, steel axles, and calfskin upholstered cushions.[22]

Santleben needed an armed escort because highways were dangerous places in Reconstruction Texas. When the railroads introduced yet another opportunity for crime, Governor Davis revived the Texas Rangers in the early 1870s. The Rangers' responsibilities were shifted from fighting Comanches and Mexican bandits to controlling postwar desperadoes. Rangers failed to halt Jesse and Frank James's three-thousand-dollar holdup of the Austin–San Antonio mail coach in May 1876, but they succeeded in capturing John Wesley Hardin in Pensacola, Florida, in August 1877; killing Sam Bass in Round Rock in July 1878; and later gunning down Clyde Barrow and Bonnie Parker near Plain Dealing, Louisiana, in May 1934.[23]

Railroads attracted attention in the 1870s because after decades of inaction and false starts, the new form of transportation was expanding greatly in Texas. More important to our story, two railroad companies eventually controlled by Jay Gould—the Missouri, Kansas and Texas (M-K-T) and the International and Great Northern (I&GN)—essentially fixed an otherwise tentative north-south trade corridor that evolved into Interstate 35. Once east-west, crossroads-forming lines like the Texas and Pacific, Southern Pacific, and Texas-Mexican railroads were completed, Gould's corridor would solidify the growth of Dallas, Fort Worth, Waco, Austin, San Antonio, and Laredo.

The railroad era in general, and Jay Gould in particular, had a profound impact on fixing routes and stimulating cities along the I-35 Corridor. Railroad expansion and Texas' explosive population growth went hand in hand. Cities boomed with new railroad stations, and these booms in turn triggered railroad needs somewhere else. If some taxpayers grumbled about the sale of massive tracts of public land to finance the new railroad projects, most transactions were quite logical. In those days, land was far cheaper than money. On the other hand, railroad construction activities accelerated the extermination of the buffalo and the remaining Indian tribes who hunted them. Millions of buffalo hides were transported by rail, briefly making Dallas and Waco major buffalo hide marketing centers. When the buffaloes were gone, Dallas and Waco moved on to cotton and other goods. The Indians were not so fortunate.

Virtually all of the pre–Civil War railroads had gone bankrupt or had been reorganized, except one—the Houston and Texas Central (H&TC), the first railroad to reach Dallas, Waco, and Austin. A series of skillful debt restructurings had provided the H&TC with sufficient capital to extend its westerly Houston-Hempstead line from Brenham to Austin in December 1871, and then add a northwest line from Millican to Waco. The H&TC then headed north. The company's charter had provided that a northern terminus be located anywhere along the Red River between Preston and Denison, an opportunity that encouraged northern communities like Dallas and Sherman to lobby the H&TC aggressively for a coveted station along the new route.[24]

Dallas had only two thousand or so inhabitants in 1870—fifteen hundred more than Fort Worth—and was not about to be bypassed by the H&TC. The town had evolved into a regional distribution center during and after the Civil War, and its proximity to the rich blackland prairies ensured a promising future. In response to the "pay to play" requirements of the era, Dallas citizens were compelled to offer the H&TC a package of five thousand dollars in cash, a three-mile right-of-way through town, and an additional 115 acres of suburban real estate to win one of the railroad's new stations.[25]

The scheme worked, and on July 16, 1872, an H&TC train from Houston pulled into Dallas's first railway station, built by local convicts one mile east of town. The arrival was celebrated by some five thousand people, including John Neely Bryan and William H. Gaston. Gaston's timely donation of the 115 acres had raised the value of his remaining real estate properties in the process and provided a future path for Central Expressway after World War II. Dallas's first telegraph service was introduced by Sarah Horton Cockrell shortly thereafter. As will be seen, the arrival of the H&TC in 1872 and the Texas and Pacific Railroad in February 1873, provided the fateful catalysts for the city's spectacular growth.[26]

By March of 1873, the H&TC operated five hundred miles of track in Texas and inaugurated an eighteen-hour express train service with Pullman cars between Houston and the Red River. Unfortunately, the H&TC's new terminus at Red River City (at the base of Colbert's Ferry) had to be abandoned almost immediately. The H&TC was beaten to the Red River by the Missouri, Kansas and Texas, and a legal battle ensued over rights and authorizations. The two companies ultimately settled their dispute by exchanging real estate interests and agreeing to co-locate at Denison. The H&TC was eventually consolidated with the Galveston, Harrisburg and San Antonio, itself controlled by Collis P. Huntington's Southern Pacific system.[27]

The M-K-T (or "Katy") had begun life as the Southern Branch of the venerable Union Pacific Railway Company. Renamed the Missouri, Kansas and Texas in 1870, the company was chartered to build the first railroad between the U.S. supply depot at Fort Leavenworth (north of Kansas City, Kansas) and Fort Gibson in Indian Territory. Once the project was completed, a lucrative land grant from the U.S. Government lay waiting. Backed by some of the nation's leading tycoons, including August Belmont, J. P. Morgan, Levi P. Morton, and John D. Rockefeller, the longer-term plan was to route the Katy from St. Louis to Mexico City. The planned route ran from Fort Gibson, opposite Muskogee in Indian Territory, to the Red River crossing at Preston, continuing through Waco, Austin, and San Antonio. From Bexar, the Katy was to cross the Rio Grande at Camargo (not Laredo) en route to Mexico City.[28]

The Katy never reached Fort Gibson, never received its land grant, and never reached Mexico. The Five Civilized Tribes of Indian Territory owned the right-of-way to Fort Gibson and were unwilling to part with it. Instead, the line was rerouted through Muskogee to a site adjacent to Benjamin F. Colbert's Red River ferry service east of Preston en route to a planned (but delayed) connection at San Antonio. Colbert had parlayed a humble raft license from the Chickasaw Nation in 1858 into a local business empire. Cash flows generated by the Butterfield Stage and its successors, military supply caravans, cattle drives, and immigrant traffic were reinvested in a sawmill, gristmill, and cotton gin on the Oklahoma side. Colbert made a fortune. Two steel-cable-guided ferryboats were in operation by 1872—just as surveyors from the Katy had selected Colbert's Ferry (future Denison) as the most appropriate site for the Red's first railroad bridge and terminus.[29]

As was the practice, land speculators, agents from the Katy and the H&TC, and the so-called Denison Town Company had already acquired much of the land surrounding the ramshackle south-bank village of Red River City and the future site of Denison—months before the actual location decisions were announced. Lots were acquired from local farmers for a generous price of twenty dollars per acre, only to be carved up into lots that would sell for as much a thousand dollars in future boom months. After the Katy and H&TC had agreed to share trackage between Red River City and a new terminus at Denison, six miles to the south, the Katy's first passenger train crossed into Texas on Christmas Day, 1872. From the south, the H&TC reached Denison via Sherman in March 1873.[30]

Everyone was happy, real estate prices soared, and the instant boom town was named after Katy vice president George Denison. By March of 1873, Denison would have three thousand inhabitants; it would also provide the birthplace for Dwight D. Eisenhower in 1890. Supply companies, banks, sawmills, a cotton compress, and stockyards appeared shortly, but every third building was a saloon. During the boom, 850 tons of goods arrived daily from St. Louis, in turn generating business for the 550 wagons, drivers, and bull-whackers required to load, unload, or distribute the building supplies, dry goods, buffalo hides, foodstuffs, cotton, and other items en route to their final destinations. An estimated nineteen thousand wagons utilized Colbert's ferry service in 1872 at roughly two dollars per vehicle, arming Colbert with ample funds with which to construct an adjacent wagon bridge in 1875.[31]

North of and along the Red River, the Katy was a builder. After Sherman turned down a pay-to-play opportunity, the Katy's next move from Denison was to loop around to Whitesboro (not Gainesville) and Denton. Denton voters had rejected a whopping $120,000 bonus demand by the Texas and Pacific (T&P) in 1872, but the town's central location apparently won a Katy station for free. Unfortunately, the Panic of 1873 intervened, and the Katy was forced into receivership through March 1876. Thereafter, much of the Katy system was stitched together from acquired branch and short lines. New construction was employed mainly to fill in gaps. From Denton, the Katy eventually forked south to both Dallas and Fort Worth, with the tracks rejoining at Hillsboro. Nearly one hundred years later, this forking pattern would be adopted by I-35. South of Hillsboro, the Katy meandered its way through Waco, Granger (not Belton), Georgetown, and Austin en route to its southern terminus at San Antonio.[32]

The Panic of 1873, prompted by the failure of Jay Cooke and Company in September, had a powerful effect on everyone, including the Texas and Pacific Railroad. Chartered by the U.S. Congress in March 1871 to build a mail and military route along the thirty-second parallel between Marshall and San Diego via El Paso, the T&P was subsequently consolidated with two other lines, stripped of $6 million in state bond financing privileges (after a public outcry), and recast as the Philadelphia-based Texas and Pacific Railway Company. The new T&P was awarded twenty sections of state land (640 acres in each section) for every mile of track laid in Texas. The land was valued at around twenty cents per acre.[33]

The Texas legislature had somehow stipulated that the T&P pass within one mile of Dallas's less-than-famous Browder Springs (south of downtown).

Otherwise, the T&P's thirty-second parallel route lay many miles south of Dallas and Fort Worth. The Browder Springs provision proved to be critical. Having already won the north-south H&TC route, Dallas was not about to let a second, history-making, crossroads-forming railroad line slip away. After the city complied (by a vote of 192–0) with the T&P's pay-to-play demand of one hundred thousand dollars, the first T&P train rolled into town on February 22, 1873. By August of that year, Chief Engineer Grenville M. Dodge (of Union Pacific fame) had steered the T&P to Eagle Ford, six miles west of Dallas, en route to a scheduled November arrival in Fort Worth.[34]

As the T&P was moving west, the Panic of 1873 halted virtually all construction activity nationwide and placed the T&P, stuck at Eagle Ford, in a precarious financial position. Fort Worth, in turn, was stranded until local residents moved to build the twenty-five-mile extension from Eagle Ford themselves, which they did in impressive fashion in July 1876. In the meantime, Fort Worth's temporary loss became Dallas's longer-term gain. With less than three thousand inhabitants in 1873, Dallas was already connected to two major railroads—the T&P and the H&TC—while Fort Worth only had the Katy. The intersections of these two great railroad lines placed Dallas at the very center of Texas' principal north-south and eventual east-west trade routes, connecting Dallas to Houston and Galveston, to a string of Red River towns between Denison and Shreveport, and eventually to California via El Paso. These junctions provided a foundation for Dallas's explosive growth in the 1900s. Thirty-three years late, William G. Cooke's Military Road and the republic's Central National Road had arrived in a somewhat different format.

The T&P's financial problems induced a change of effective (but not majority) control in 1877. The notorious Jay Gould assumed the helm. While Gould's T&P would ultimately lose a madcap construction race through West Texas to Huntington's eastward-moving and better financed Southern Pacific line, Gould would control some fourteen hundred miles of Texas trackage by the early 1880s—around 33 percent of the state's total railroad miles (map 10). This empire was assembled via a mind-boggling series of deals, beginning in 1873 with a minority investment in the Union Pacific, followed by stakes in the T&P, the Katy (while in receivership), and the I&GN. Gould's machinations were painful to his rivals and to his employees, but they somehow resulted in a logical route system. Much of this system is the predecessor to Interstate 35.[35]

Gould had refined various financial schemes developed by or with former colleagues Daniel Drew and James Fisk Jr. in their battle with Cornelius

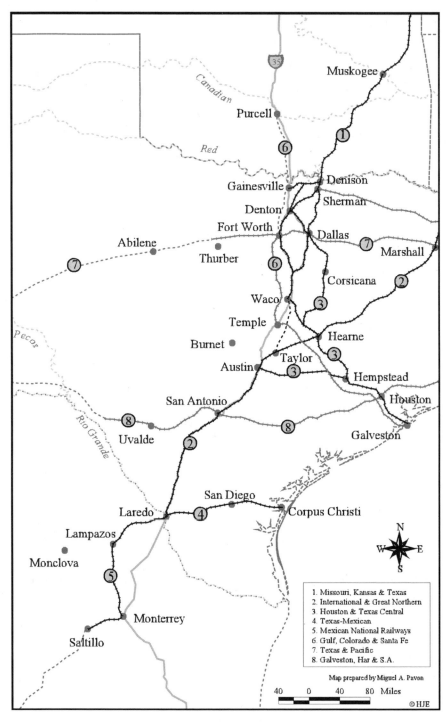

Map 10. Selected Railroads, December 31, 1881.

Vanderbilt over the Erie Railroad. Railroad holdings were typically acquired via minority interests at rock-bottom prices while a company was unprofitable or in receivership. Gould then assembled his own friendly board of directors and engineered complex cross-ownerships of companies to obfuscate matters. Next, he used his most attractive, majority-owned property to issue equity and debt; consolidated the desirable operations with other selected holdings; and milked nonstrategic operations for cash, often by underinvesting in maintenance or by applying service charges, rate discounts, and through-traffic agreements. Gould then waited for the economy and stock market to do the rest. If the plan succeeded, the values of his bargain-basement investments soared, providing fresh capital for the next round of investments.[36]

Gould was always ready to deal, provided that the deals contributed either traffic or cash flows to his core majority-owned holding company, the Missouri Pacific Railroad (Mo-Pac). As the railroad industry began to consolidate, pressured in part by the Panic of 1873, Gould emerged, almost inadvertently, as one of the few surviving empires. At that point, he was beginning to focus more on railway operations. Padded with land grants and local financial incentives, Gould's construction programs in Texas were attempts to bring order to chaos. He was no saint, but his machinations helped to create lasting north-south (Katy and I&GN) and east-west (T&P) routes in Texas that might not otherwise have been achieved. Vilified in most of the nation, Gould would be cheered in Laredo and the many fortunate towns connected to his Texas empire.

When Gould learned that the St. Louis, Iron Mountain and Southern Railroad (the "Iron Mountain") intended to merge with the recently consolidated International and Great Northern (I&GN), he moved to block the proposed merger and acquire a controlling interest in the rival Katy. The general plan was to link St. Louis traffic at Texarkana with two points along the Rio Grande: Laredo (en route to Mexico City) and El Paso (en route to California). Since the Katy intersected Gould's Mo-Pac at Sedalia, Missouri, and owned trackage between Hannibal, Missouri (via Denison) and Fort Worth, the Katy could serve as a north-south connecting route between St. Louis and the Rio Grande. Through a series of creative (if often underhanded) investments and reorganization moves, Gould gained effective control of the Katy between December 31, 1874, and January 1880.[37]

Gould eventually pushed the Katy into a merger with the I&GN (in June 1881) and shaped the future path of I-35. In the meantime, he had a number of moves to make. First, he acquired the Dallas and Wichita Railroad (D&W) in February 1880, a line cofounded by John Neely Bryan and one

hundred thousand dollars in Dallas bonds in 1872. The D&W had begun construction in 1877 but had run out of funds between Dallas and Denton (at
Lewisville) in 1879 and then forced into receivership. Gould extended the line
north to Denton by year's end. Second, he acquired the forty-two-mile Denison and Pacific Railway (D&P) in March 1880. The D&P had been surveyed
only as far as Gainesville in the summer of 1877 and had been completed with
a thousand-dollar right-of-way contribution from Gainesville in November 1879. The acquisition terms stipulated that Gainesville would remain the
Katy's western terminus until another railroad entered Gainesville. This enhanced Gainesville's position as a cattle supply and marketing center until the
Gulf, Colorado and Santa Fe arrived in January 1887.[38]

Gould then constructed a Katy line between Fort Worth and Hillsboro in
September 1881, and extended a T&P line seventy-one miles north between
Fort Worth and Whitesboro via Denton. This line paralleled the future path of
US 377. In typical Gould fashion, the Katy received trackage rights over
the T&P line via a ninety-nine-year lease. Gould now had lines running from
both Dallas and Fort Worth via Denton to the Red River. When the Katy
completed a line between Dallas and Hillsboro via Waxahachie in 1890, the
Katy would have trackage to both Dallas and Fort Worth—from Denton to
the north and Hillsboro to the south. These loops account for the present
configuration of I-35.[39]

With the loops in place, Gould merged the Katy with the I&GN in 1880. Ten
years earlier, the I&GN had been just the "I." The International Railway Company was incorporated on August 5, 1870, with ambitions to build a railroad
from Fulton's (Red River) Crossing in Arkansas through Jefferson, Palestine,
Austin, San Antonio, and Laredo. From Laredo, the line was intended to swing
west (via Durango and Mazatlán) en route to Mexico City. Much of this project was eventually completed by Jay Gould and Porfirio Díaz. Unfortunately,
plans to finance this ambitious project with Texas Permanent School Fund–related loans ($10,000, 30-year, 8 percent bonds for every mile of track laid) were
scuttled by charges of high-level corruption and bribery. The Texas legislature
eventually replaced the bond-financing package with land grants—twenty sections of land for each mile of track—and a twenty-five-year moratorium on
state taxes.[40]

In September 1873, the very month of the Panic, the International merged
with the Houston and Great Northern Railroad (H&GN). Chartered in 1866
and consolidated with the Houston Tap and Brazoria in 1870, the H&GN

operated only between Houston and Palestine. The somewhat larger International operated 177 miles of track between Hearne and Longview. As the economy recovered, the I&GN expanded westward from Texarkana and Shreveport (via Longview and Palestine) to Hearne, Round Rock, and Austin and northward from Houston (via Hearne, Waco, and Fort Worth) to Denison. Gould acquired a ten-mile branch line between Georgetown and Round Rock in 1879 in anticipation of a future merger with the I&GN—possibly influenced by the demise of train robber extraordinaire Sam Bass in July 1878. The Georgetown Railroad Company, built at a cost of $60,225, had defaulted on its debt and was acquired in foreclosure in typical Gould fashion for just $39,393. Local investors were out the difference.[41]

By 1876, the I&GN's financial position had worsened and the railroad was stalled on the north bank of the Colorado River, awaiting the construction of Austin's first railroad bridge. The I&GN had inexplicably failed to use the same rising stock market that had benefited Gould to continue the push south to San Antonio and Laredo. This delay provided Gould with an opportunity to acquire the I&GN in December 1880, then merge it with the Katy in June 1881. The merger wounded the Katy. Construction to Laredo was handed over to the I&GN and Katy trackage was leased to Mo-Pac. The merger also hurt the Iron Mountain. It surrendered to Gould's Mo-Pac system in May 1881. Gould now controlled direct routes between St. Louis and Fort Worth and was en route to San Antonio and Laredo. It was at that point that he began to manage his empire as a railroad rather than as another stock scheme.[42]

Prior to the completion of Austin's Colorado River bridge in June 1881, the I&GN had already reached Buda (then known as Du Pre), San Marcos, New Braunfels, and San Antonio between September 1880 and February 1881. San Marcos had provided a right-of-way as early as 1874 but was forced to wait out the recession, the delayed Austin bridge project, and a local real estate dispute. According to historian S. G. Reed, the I&GN had been able to obtain rights-of-way between Austin and Laredo with little difficulty except for a one-mile segment of San Marcos land owned by a loyal sister-in-law of Collis P. Huntington; the I&GN was forced to loop around the woman's property. Seven miles south of San Marcos, the tiny village of Hunter was founded in late 1880 to support the I&GN work crews. Hunter is noteworthy because it is located almost precisely at the intersection of two Camino Real routes (Hunter Road and the Old Bastrop Road), the I&GN, and Interstate 35.[43]

The I&GN and Gould hit their high-water mark in December 1881. San Antonio was reached in February 1880, and southbound construction en route to Laredo began in December that year. With land grants presold as townsite lots, future station towns like Cotulla and Webb Station sprang up along the way. Webb Station was reached on December 1, 1881, as a prelude to the I&GN's triumphant arrival in Laredo on December 15. Having concluded a face-saving West Texas peace treaty with Huntington only weeks earlier, Gould arrived shortly in Laredo as a conquering hero.[44]

The I&GN had planned to continue south to Mexico City but deferred the project to Mexican Railways. Mexican Railways had already completed a line between Laredo and Monterrey and would reach Mexico City by 1889. En route from Monterrey, Mexican Railways had the honor of constructing the first, if temporary, railroad bridge across the Rio Grande. The first work train crossed in November of 1881, followed by the first passenger train (with dignitaries) on March 8, 1882. Six weeks later, Jay Gould and his family inspected the "International works" at Nuevo Laredo and Laredo and then went sightseeing in San Antonio.[45]

The initial crossing was reported by the *Galveston Daily News* on March 9:

> The roar of cannon at about 10 o'clock this morning, at Fort McIntosh, announced the arrival of General [William T.] Sherman and party on the International Railway. . . . This evening, at 5 o'clock, the first passenger car of the International Railway crossed the Rio Grande, with General Sherman, General Poe, Colonel Morrison and Major Sumner, commanding officers of Fort McIntosh, with a large deputation of the citizens of Laredo on board. The general was received in New Laredo by the military officers of the Mexican thirteenth infantry and was saluted by a large crowd of citizens assembled on the bank of the river. After considerable hands-shaking, the train with the party returned to Laredo. . . . General Sherman expressed himself to your correspondent as highly pleased with Laredo, and believed its future commercial greatness to be already assured.

The I&GN had achieved the first unified southwesterly route between the Red River (Texarkana) and the Rio Grande (Laredo) since the trailblazing Camino Real expeditions of nearly two hundred years past. If the I&GN's Red River connection at Texarkana was some two hundred miles east of the future I-35 gateway at Gainesville, the I&GN paralleled present-day I-35 almost exactly between Georgetown and Laredo. A main line from Austin ran northeast via Corsicana to Dallas and Denison, leaving missing I-35 links between Fort Worth and Temple and between Denton and Gainesville to be filled by new

Katy construction and pieces of the rival Santa Fe. The Katy was extended from Fort Worth to Hillsboro in September 1881, and then to Waco and the new towns of Temple and Taylor (not Belton) by June 1882. These segments represented 161 miles of new trackage between Fort Worth and Taylor. There was still no connection between Temple and Austin, however, and the Katy would not reach San Antonio until 1901.[46]

The Katy had been beaten to Temple by the Gulf, Colorado and Santa Fe (GC&SF) by one year—a year of local infamy if one happened to live in Belton. Building north from Galveston since May of 1875, the GC&SF was en route via Fort Worth and Gainesville to a planned junction with the southward-building Atchison, Topeka and Santa Fe at Purcell in Indian Territory. Fort Worth citizens had already coughed up seventy-five thousand dollars and Bell County taxpayers had contributed a right-of-way and a ten-year tax moratorium based on the GC&SF's promise to establish its temporary northern terminus at Belton.[47]

In June 1880, the GC&SF had reached the Bell County line fifteen miles south of Belton when alleged cash-flow problems prompted a request for financial assistance. Having already provided the railroad with a right-of-way through town and a tax moratorium, Belton was forced to provide a new right-of-way for an alternative route, land for a relocated depot, and seventy-five thousand dollars in negotiable notes. The alternative route, circuitous and four miles longer than the original, avoided heavy costs to construct a hillside tunnel and a bridge across the Leon River. In return, the railroad promised to reach Belton by December 1 and to retain the city as the GC&SF's northern terminus for at least two years.[48]

Following a pattern typical of the 1880s, the Santa Fe and its friends had made other plans. In August 1880, the GC&SF, including the company president, quietly purchased nearly two hundred acres of prairie located eight miles northeast of Belton. The site was destined to be the new town of Temple. Railway construction was lagging, however, and the GC&SF found itself unable to meet the December 1 deadline. After a proposed extension to March 1, 1881, was invalidated by the Texas Supreme Court, Belton saved its seventy-five thousand dollars but lost its railhead. The GC&SF was focusing on Temple. The first train from Galveston arrived in Temple on February 8, 1881, and the GC&SF was in Fort Worth by December. Belton was bypassed and stranded.[49]

Real estate investors made enormous profits. Raw land in Temple acquired for around $20 per acre in 1880 was sold in 1881 for around $150 per lot.

Named after Bernard M. Temple, the GC&SF's chief construction engineer between 1878 and 1884 and a former assistant to Grenville M. Dodge, the instant if somewhat rowdy town of Temple boomed. The boom continued when the Katy reached town in March 1882, en route to Taylor and Houston. Temple would have over four thousand residents in 1890 (a thousand more than Belton), and Belton had to be satisfied with a modest tap line, built by the I&GN to recover a thirty-thousand-dollar subsidy. Bernard M. Temple went on to bigger things—he built a spectacular High Bridge across the Pecos River in 1892 on the Galveston, Harrisburg and San Antonio (GH&SA) line.[50]

As the Santa Fe moved north, Gould's railroad empire was nearing its peak. The West Texas race with Huntington was ended, via a Thanksgiving Day (1881) "peace treaty" that would link the T&P and Southern Pacific at Sierra Blanca, 110 miles east of El Paso. Yet Gould controlled 5,000 miles of U.S. railroad at December 1881, with another 475 miles under construction. Between 1879 and 1882, Gould's construction activities comprised 1,010 miles of T&P trackage, 588 miles of Katy, plus Mo-Pac (466), I&GN (257), and Iron Mountain (198). This "Southwestern" railroad empire was an extraordinary achievement for a one-time securities trader and speculator. It was not pretty but it was a genuine, logical network of routes that helped to build Dallas, Fort Worth, San Antonio, and Laredo.[51]

Unfortunately for Gould, it was all downhill from there. Unlike the higher quality Santa Fe, Gould's Southwestern system was noted for poor service, poor maintenance, and poor labor relations. In March 1886, with the T&P sliding toward its first receivership, the labor component erupted into one of the most famous (if unsuccessful) strikes in Texas history. Among many incidents of violence, an April 3 shooting match between strikers and a moving train in Fort Worth required the assistance of three hundred state militiamen from Austin. The strike collapsed on May 4, 1886, after public opinion shifted against the strikers. Within weeks, Texas Attorney General James Stephen Hogg filed a lawsuit against Gould claiming that none of Gould's railroad companies was headquartered in Texas, that he had failed to maintain the railroad adequately, and that he had diverted profits from the Texas lines to the flagship Missouri-Pacific. Hogg's accusations, of course, were old news.[52]

The Great Southwestern Strike of 1886 reminds us that railroads, bridges, and highways—whether they are initiated by entrepreneurs or civil engineers—are constructed by gangs of humble workers. Railroad building was extremely labor intensive. After a route was identified, surveyed, and approved, a roadbed was constructed, embankments were built, track was laid, wood was gathered for ties and bridges, stone was collected for piers and abutments, and bridges and trestles were erected. Bridge crews were usually sent ahead to have bridges in place by the time the track arrived. According to Grenville M. Dodge, the coordination and management of a construction corps of eight to ten thousand men, supplied by thousands of wagons and animals, had to be reduced to a logistical science. Since much of the process was transferable to highway construction, one finds that most of the first highway engineers were former railroad men.[53]

Until the Southern Pacific arrived in West Texas, approximately ten thousand railroad workers were employed in Texas in 1880. Most of the crews were filled by native white Texans, supplemented by immigrants from Ireland and Eastern Europe, relocated blacks from Old South states, and convict laborers from Texas' two state prisons. In South Texas projects, many of the workers were Mexican. The eastward-moving Southern Pacific added thousands of Chinese workers to this mix, however, and placed pressure on wage rates. White workers were paid between $2.00 and $2.50 per day—more than double the rate received by either Chinese workers or Texas cotton pickers. But rates could be halved or eliminated at a moment's notice. Railroads were routinely in and out of receivership, and labor costs were "controllable" items. When projects were completed, railroad workers were usually relieved of their duties. Even Bernard M. Temple found himself on the street in March 1884.[54]

Gould won his labor battles but eventually lost his war against Hogg. The Katy was forced to reorganize between 1888 and November 1891, and Texas' new governor—none other than James Stephen Hogg—created the long-delayed Texas Railroad Commission in April 1891. Gould had helped to defeat earlier regulatory agency proposals in 1881 and 1887, typically by delaying important construction projects—like the Katy's extension between Fort Worth and Waco in 1881—until the proposal was defeated. A personal "inspection tour" of Texas in 1887 had also contributed to the cause. But Gould's luck ran out in 1890. He charmed the otherwise hostile citizens of San Antonio, Austin, Waco, Fort Worth, and Dallas on a spring tour, predicting a great future for Dallas and informing readers of the *Austin Daily Statesman* on April 8, 1890, that the recently completed state capitol building was "the finest in the world [or] certainly the finest that I have ever seen."[55]

However, a Texas Railroad Commission was an unstoppable force in 1890, and Gould's Texas empire was forcibly reorganized. The I&GN was transferred to Mo-Pac, and a new M-K-T Railroad of Texas, with a board of directors that included John D. Rockefeller, was formed to acquire the old Katy assets. By 1890, the Katy had acquired the Dallas and Waco, a line that reached Waxahachie and Hillsboro, and was in the process of extending the Denison and Pacific from Gainesville to Wichita Falls. The arrival of the GC&SF in Gainesville in late 1886, via Fort Worth (but west of Denton), had freed the Katy to move the D&P west.[56]

Despite these expansion moves, the Katy's troubles had attracted competitors. In June 1887, the GC&SF had linked up with the AT&SF in Purcell, Oklahoma, creating a powerful Santa Fe system between Galveston and Kansas via Temple, Fort Worth, and Gainesville. In addition, the St. Louis and Southwestern ("Cotton Belt") Railway, owned partially by the irrepressible Gould, had completed a line between Sherman and Hillsboro via Fort Worth by 1888. The rival Rock Island Line connected Paris with Fort Worth between 1887 and 1893, but an eastward extension to Dallas was delayed (by the Panic of 1893) until 1903. Portions of the Rock Island's local trackage were assumed by the Cotton Belt in 1910.[57]

The Panic of 1893 was even more severe than the 1873 crisis. Triggered by a run on U.S. gold reserves prompted by the Sherman Silver Purchase Act of 1890, among other factors, the Panic plunged the nation into depression for nearly six years. When the economy finally recovered in 1900, several long-delayed projects were revived. Twenty-year-old leasing arrangements among the I&GN, the Katy, and Mo-Pac had allowed Katy trains to travel between Denison and Fort Worth and Dallas via Whitesboro (not Gainesville) and Denton. But when the I&GN, frequently in and out of receivership, refused to permit joint trackage rights between San Marcos and San Antonio, the Katy decided to build its own line in 1901. This completed, the Katy added the new Granger, Georgetown, Austin and San Antonio Railway Company in short order. The GGA&SA, chartered in 1902, reached Austin via Georgetown in June 1904, and even induced the I&GN to share trackage between Austin and San Marcos. The Katy could finally provide service between the Red River at Denison and San Antonio.[58]

The railroads revitalized San Antonio and Laredo and solidified the futures of Dallas and Fort Worth. They also bolstered the economies of relatively obscure but centrally located towns like Denison, Denton, Sherman, Temple, Taylor, and Granger. Driven by their east-west and north-south rail connections,

Dallas, Fort Worth, and San Antonio represented the future heart of the I-35 Corridor. Why it was that Sherman, Denison, or Gainesville failed to develop into a "Dallas"—each town had had its chances since Butterfield days—can be answered partly by geography. The upper Red River was not navigable, it flooded regularly, and it required costly bridge works. Unlike in most major cities in the world, proximity to a river appeared to be a liability in North Texas. The Indian Territory to the north probably did not help matters, either.

Gainesville, an old Butterfield Stage stop, appears to have peaked in 1890. The Denison and Pacific Railway had been completed through town in November 1879, two months prior to its consolidation with the Katy. With the arrival of the GC&SF from Fort Worth in 1886, Gainesville emerged as a leading cotton center. In 1888, the town boasted mule-drawn streetcars, telegraph, telephone, gas heat, electric lighting (in 1889), and a population of more than six thousand. This prominence was short-lived, however. A century later, Interstate 35's northern gateway to Texas has a population of no more than fifteen thousand people and a modest economy focused on ranching, farming, and tourism.[59]

Gainesville did not become a Dallas, and Belton did not even become a Temple. The Bell County seat was not destroyed by the Temple real estate scheme, but its future could have been very different. Belton's position on the GC&SF's western line to Lampasas, completed in 1882, was small consolation. The Belton taxpayers fumed, but Bell County at least had a railroad hub in Temple. After rebuffing overtures from Jay Gould, the GC&SF was consolidated with the Santa Fe in 1886. An electric-powered railway, the Belton-Temple Interurban, would eventually link the county rivals in 1905.

The wagon freight town of San Antonio was nearly destroyed by the railroads, only to emerge stronger than ever. Bexar had been devastated by the postwar depression in South Texas and the lack of a single railroad connection until 1877. San Antonio was the last of Texas' major cities to have one. The struggling San Antonio and Mexican Gulf Railway had been deliberately torn up by Confederate soldiers in 1863, merged (in a foreclosure) with the Indianola Railroad in 1871, and reborn as the Gulf, Western, Texas and Pacific. By 1873, its path from Matagorda Bay had reached only as far as Victoria, and it would not arrive in San Antonio until 1906. San Antonio was finally connected to the coast at Galveston by the GH&SA in February 1877, followed by the arrival of the I&GN in February 1881, and the San Antonio and Aransas Pass from Corpus Christi in 1886.[60]

Awaiting these connections, San Antonio's freighting businesses deteriorated and wagon trade with Indianola, Corpus Christi, and Galveston declined steadily. The transition from oxen and stagecoaches to the new means of transportation was a gradual one, however, lasting for decades and providing last hurrahs for era-ending characters like August Santleben. But once the necessary infrastructure was in place, the economic benefits of railroads for freight and passenger travel were clear. Ox teams could haul cargo at a rate of twenty cents per ton mile and could cover twenty miles per day. By 1909, railroads would operate at a rate of one cent per ton mile and could travel twenty miles in less than twenty minutes. Stagecoaches charged passengers ten cents a mile and operated at around six miles per hour. Railroads charged around three cents a mile and saved travelers the added expense of hotels or campsites.[61]

Railroads were the future, and fading towns like San Antonio and Laredo were ultimately revitalized by rail connections. In 1870, seven years before San Antonio received its first railroad, the entire economic output of Bexar County was just $132,000. By contrast, Galveston generated $1 million in output that year, and even McLennan County reported $345,000. While the arrival of the GH&SA (Southern Pacific) in February 1877 increased Bexar's output to $600,000 in 1880, Bexar still lagged behind Galveston ($2.4 million in value), Dallas County ($1.5 million), Harris County ($1.3 million), and Travis County ($800,000). It was the arrival of the I&GN in 1881 that was pivotal to San Antonio's economic future. The port of Galveston was not so fortunate—competition with railroads and damage wrought by hurricanes proved a devastating combination.[62]

Aside from railroads and cattle (and the supplies needed for these industries), post-1880 economic development in Texas was highlighted by cotton and to a lesser extent sugar, corn, lumber, and flour. Cotton became king as plantings replaced wheat in the prime blackland prairie belt east of present-day I-35. The emancipation of slaves, the gradual privatization of public lands, an explosion in tenant farming, and lower cost railroad transportation altered the economics of cotton and other crops. The number of Texas farms doubled. The expansion of cotton fields followed the railroad lines, taking advantage of a gradual decline in railroad freight charges to just 5 percent of traditional wagon rates. In addition, so-called postage freight rates were applied to farmers shipping cotton 187 miles or more—farms located 187 miles away from market were charged the same rate as farms 387 miles away.[63]

The railroads connected cotton and other farmers to global markets. After short-line railroads had fanned out from the major cities to the hinterlands, small towns that had escaped notice for decades suddenly appeared on major railroad itineraries. Most of the short lines provided critical farm-to-market transportation services to rural areas that were otherwise tied to challenging dirt roads. Farmers' groups prodded the Texas Railroad Commission to monitor "monopolistic" freight rates, but the commission's impact was probably minimal. Railroads gouged customers when they could, but freight rates declined mainly as a result of market forces, not regulations.

Cotton became the state's dominant cash crop and a major factor in the future route of I-35. Cotton was the most predictable crop, the highest yielding, and the least expensive to freight. From less than 60,000 bales in 1850, Texas cotton production had expanded to over 400,000 bales in 1860 and, despite the postwar devastation, recovered to around 350,000 bales in 1870. These production levels were only the beginning. A whopping 2.5 million bales were produced in 1899 on seven million acres. This was 3.5 times the 1880 acreage level but only half of that planted in 1930. Cotton acreage in Cooke County nearly tripled from 36,091 in 1890 to 108,372 acres in 1925. Waco began to host the annual Cotton Palace Exposition on a quasi-regular basis in 1894 and rivaled Dallas as the nation's foremost inland cotton center during the peak 1914–26 period. One-third of U.S. cotton production was located within a three-hundred-mile radius of Dallas by 1936. Dallas was the single leading cotton center, but Waco still managed to market two million bales in 1940.[64]

Growing, processing, and marketing cotton was more attractive than converting the product into finished goods. Factories were expensive and capital was in short supply. Just a handful of cotton (and woolen) mills had been started in places like Bastrop, New Braunfels, and Waco. In New Braunfels, John F. Torrey's cotton and wool factory was destroyed by a tornado in 1869 and a replacement mill was demolished by flood in June 1872. The new owner, Joseph Landa, added a cottonseed oil mill in 1891 after having upgraded his Landa Rock Mill (1875) with a Hungarian roller mill system. Dallas had a cottonseed oil mill in 1873, but its first cotton cloth factory was delayed until 1888. Cotton and textile-related factories were eventually developed in Waxahachie, Hillsboro, and Italy. Otherwise, humble cotton gins dotted the landscape. Hays County had fourteen gins in 1890 and neighboring Comal County had fifteen in 1904.[65]

6

Good Roads for Texas, 1870–1917

OLLOWING twenty years of feverish railway expansion in Texas, most of the right-of-way segments of future Interstate 35 had been staked out by two major rail lines and a portion of a third. The I&GN ran between Laredo, San Antonio, Austin, and Round Rock. The M-K-T (Katy) was set to operate between San Antonio and Denison via Austin, Georgetown, Granger, and Waco, splitting at Hillsboro like I-35 to Dallas and Fort Worth, and then rejoining at Denton, again like I-35. The Gulf, Colorado and Santa Fe ran slightly west of today's I-35 Corridor between Temple, Cleburne, and Fort Worth en route to Gainesville.

As one might expect, highways had received little attention during the railroad boom and continued to be managed — or more accurately, neglected — by the same old ineffective system of compulsory work crews. However, the railroad boom prompted a surge in county bridge projects, driven by railroad needs, not highways. Texas was late to bridge building because it had too many rivers to be crossed and too little money to finance the crossings. Most of the wagon bridges that were built were inclined to fail or wash away. But fortunately for Texas, by the time that its citizens were finally in a position to fund bridge projects, bridge construction technology had advanced spectacularly.

OFF-RAMP: BRIDGE-BUILDING INNOVATIONS

As early as 1825, Thomas Telford had constructed a massive 1,710-foot-long suspension bridge across the Menai Strait between the Isle of Anglesey and

Wales. Truss and cast-iron railway bridges appeared regularly after 1830, high-lighted by the U.S. Army Corps of Engineers' $39,902, 80-foot cast-iron bridge across Dunlap's Creek in Brownsville, Pennsylvania, in 1839 and Squire Whip-ple's improvements to structural stress and strain calculations in 1841. More dra-matic structures lay ahead. Benefiting from Charles Ellett's Wheeling Suspension Bridge (1849), John A. Roebling built an 820-foot double-deck railway sus-pension bridge at Niagara Falls in 1855 and the Cincinnati Suspension Bridge in 1867. In 1874, James B. Eads responded with the first steel arch bridge across the Mississippi River in St. Louis, a project that required seven years of work (and controversy) and the introduction of pneumatic caisson foundations and portland cement. Eads's innovations helped to facilitate the construction of the magnificent Brooklyn Bridge, a structure designed by John A. Roebling but completed by his remarkable son Washington in 1883.[1]

In Texas, cash-strapped county commissions must have been affected by the spectacular bridge projects that were sweeping the nation. One community even acted in astonishing fashion. On January 6, 1870, after nearly two years of construction and a jaw-dropping cost-overrun of over $100,000, Waco opened a majestic suspension bridge of its own across the Brazos River. The first major suspension bridge in Texas was built by private enterprise. The Waco Bridge Company, capitalized at $50,000 with 57 local shareholders, had re-ceived a 25-year charter in 1866 when Waco's population stood at just 1,500 and post-war city and county finances were virtually nonexistent.[2]

Designed by John A. Roebling and built by chief engineer Thomas M. Griffith and Trice Brothers of Waco, Waco's 475-foot wire and cable bridge was intended to replace Shapley P. Ross's old ferry service—still functional but plagued by occasional high waters. The new bridge, with a wooden roadway wide enough for two stagecoaches, led travelers across the Brazos to East Waco and the Preston Road to Dallas. Land on the west bank had been donated by Jacob De Cordova in 1849. Land on the east bank was acquired by the city and county for $1,720.[3]

The directors of the Waco Bridge Company could have chosen a more con-ventional iron bridge design. Instead, they opted for the relatively new suspension system after visiting Roebling's factory in Trenton, New Jersey, in August 1868. With an estimated cost of $40,000, including around $21,000 for Roebling's steel components and wire cables, the suspension bridge was supposed to be less expensive than an iron structure. Shipping costs by steamer to Galveston, by rail to Millican and, finally, by ox wagons to Waco were a manageable $8,000.

The problem was building materials. The quality of local stone was so poor that 2.7 million Waco-manufactured bricks had to be acquired for the two medieval drawbridge–like cable towers and anchor houses. If the bricks were purchased at an average cost of around $10 per 1,000, the brick costs alone were a whopping $27,000. Labor expenses were extra.[4]

Not surprisingly, the construction project was behind schedule and over budget from the start. But local investors continued their support. Two additional stock offerings (totaling $46,000) and an expensive $20,000 mortgage bond issue (at 12 percent) were required to move the project forward during 1869. After costs had reached $141,000, a shocking $101,000 over plan, the great bridge finally opened on January 6, 1870. Somehow, the investment paid off. Daily toll volumes averaged $50, despite a 50 percent discount for McLennan County residents, and the bridge generated more than $18,000 in revenues in its first year—more than its operating and interest costs. Business was enhanced by the arrival of the Houston and Texas Central's Waco Tap in East Waco in 1872 and, through the mid-1880s, by five-cent-per-head cattle drives. By September 1, 1889, after three years of legal haggling between the company and the voters, the solidly profitable bridge was transferred to the City of Waco and made toll free. The magnificent medieval motif would be "modernized" in 1914, leaving the bridge to carry vehicles until 1971 and pedestrians to this very day.[5]

Other communities attempted to follow Waco's lead. In Dallas, the flood of 1866 had destroyed the replacement to Alexander Cockrell's original Trinity River bridge and a successor structure was delayed until 1872. The new 300-foot-long Commerce Street Bridge was built by Cockrell's feisty widow, Sarah Horton Cockrell, at a cost of $65,000. The iron bridge was eventually acquired by the city for $41,600 in 1882, made free, and replaced in later years by the Commerce Street Viaduct. With the arrival of the Houston and Texas Central and the Texas and Pacific railroads, bridge traffic and local business in Dallas began to explode. To the south, Ellis County awarded thirteen bridge contracts between 1880 and 1890, including a modest $2,500 iron truss span across Waxahachie Creek. The bridge was eventually replaced in 1931 with a concrete bridge to serve US 77.[6]

In New Braunfels, which was ahead of most Texas communities in pre–Civil War bridge building, a new $15,000 iron bridge was constructed across the Comal River in 1872. The new span replaced a wooden wagon bridge that had been destroyed by flood in 1870. Unfortunately, the new bridge met the same fate in June 1872. Eventually, the Chicago Bridge and Iron Company built two new spans across the Comal in 1894. The cost was limited to $9,895 because the new structures utilized salvage iron from the recent Chicago World's Fair. The Guadalupe River was served by a temporary railroad bridge, built prior to the I&GN's arrival in December of 1880, until a $33,269 wagon bridge was added in 1887. Wagons were welcome, but livestock was prohibited.[7]

Austin's first Congress Avenue Bridge, a wooden affair across the Colorado River, was authorized by the Travis County Commissioners Court in 1875 to replace one of the two one-lane pontoon bridges that had served Austin since 1869. The new bridge was built for $100,000 by C. Baker, but construction was delayed until a right-of-way dispute was settled in 1877 with the heirs to Swisher's Ferry. As if that were not enough, the new bridge was damaged by a herd of cattle. This put Swisher back in business until a replacement span could be readied.[8]

On January 1, 1884, the second Congress Avenue Bridge opened, a more substantial six-span, iron truss bridge supported by stone piers. Tolls ranged from ten cents for a horseman to one dollar for a loaded wagon. Two years later, Travis County acquired the new bridge for $73,000 and transferred it (toll free) to the City of Austin in 1891. Unfortunately, the devastating flood of April 7, 1900, damaged much of the bridge (and all of the new city dam). Ten years later, a third structure, the present-day, 956-foot-long, reinforced concrete arch bridge, was completed at a cost of $200,000. The ill-fated second bridge, however, would not be forgotten. Six of its span sections were used to refurbish Moore's Bridge in southeast Travis County, starting in 1915.[9]

Austin's new bridge complemented other developments in town. The city's population had climbed from 4,428 in 1870 to 11,013 in 1880 thanks in part to a second railroad connection in 1876. By 1880, Austin had gristmills, flour mills, lumberyards, ice factories, a gasworks, a waterworks, a cast-iron foundry, and a mule-drawn streetcar. The University of Texas opened its doors in September 1883, and the magnificent capitol building was completed in May 1888. Austin's streets were unpaved until a section of Congress Avenue was paved with Thurber bricks in 1905, but the city had the Driskill Hotel (1886), Camp Mabry (1890), and by 1895, a new dam, a "moonlight tower" lighting system, and an electric streetcar. Austin's fling with city streetcars was a sign of progress. Streetcars roamed its downtown streets between 1875 and 1940, even if operators usually lost money with a fare of five cents per ride through 1920. The system returned briefly to mules after the devastating dam break of April 7,

1900, and was sold at auction in 1902. When the business reemerged as the Austin Electric Railway Company (AERC) in 1905, operations were interrupted by the initial paving of Congress Avenue.[10]

San Antonio remained a leading trade center for cattle, horses, mules, and wool. The transition from ox- and mule-based freighting to railroads had been painful, but once the major railroads had reached town, business began to boom. San Antonio's assessed property values nearly doubled from $8.6 million in 1881 to $16 million in 1886. The city's main plazas had been gas-lit since 1866, and a mule-drawn streetcar operated between Alamo Plaza and San Pedro Springs in 1878. Other signs of local progress included an iron works, a telephone exchange (1881), an electric streetcar (1890), and the Union Stockyards (1891). San Pedro Avenue boasted an improved roadbed, paved sidewalks, fire hydrants, and gas lamps in 1888. The pavement was supplied by the Alamo Portland and Roman Cement Works, founded in 1880 but relocated to a site nearer the railroad in 1907. The abandoned quarry (Sunken Gardens as of 1917) later became involved in a high-profile expressway dispute.[11]

By 1890, San Antonio's population had increased to 37,673, but even more dramatic growth lay ahead—the city would have 161,379 residents by 1920. Much of this growth was fostered by the city's military heritage. The predecessor to Fort Sam Houston had been established as a military post in 1876, facilitated by the city's donation of a forty-acre site in 1870, and gained notoriety for holding the Apache chief Geronimo in 1886. After an upgrade to fort status in 1890, Fort Sam Houston trained Theodore Roosevelt's Rough Riders in 1898, catalyzed the new Army Air Corps training facilities (and their successors), and provided a staging area for General John J. Pershing's "Punitive (Villa) Expedition" into Mexico (and Pershing's occasional fishing trips in New Braunfels).[12]

San Antonio's economic revival placed it neck-and-neck with Dallas in the competition to become Texas' largest city. In 1890, Dallas had temporarily emerged as the state's leading metropolis with 38,067 inhabitants, aided by the annexation of East Dallas that year. Dallas was followed by San Antonio (37,673), Galveston (29,084), Houston (27,557), and Fort Worth (23,076). Compared to other western cities, however, Dallas and Bexar were only pikers. In 1890, Omaha reported a population of 140,452, Denver had 106,713 inhabitants, and even Lincoln, Nebraska at 55,154 had nearly 20,000 more residents than Dallas.[13]

Dallas's time was yet to come. The city had already diversified from buffalo hides—it had been the nation's largest hide center in 1875—to a more lasting position as the supply and distribution capital for the emerging cotton industry. Dallas would shortly be home to a telegraph service, a gas company, the Grand Windsor Hotel (until the luxurious Oriental opened in 1893), and Belle Starr. Attracted by the city's premier railroad connections, terminal merchants Alexander and Philip Sanger and E. M. Kahn established dry goods and clothing stores on Main Street in 1872 and had full-fledged department stores in Dallas, Fort Worth, and Waco by 1898. The Neiman Marcus Company debuted in 1907.[14]

By 1890, assessed property values in Dallas had soared to $30 million, versus $4 million in 1880. Dallas boasted eight railroads; more than twenty-five miles of street railways, which became electric in 1900; more than twenty miles of (ineffective) bois d'arc block street paving; a telephone exchange (1881), the Dallas Electric Lighting Company (1882), and the Dallas State Fair and Exposition (1886). George B. Dealey's founding of the *Dallas Morning News* as a branch of the flagship *Galveston News* signaled a looming transfer in status. As regional cotton plantings expanded, the city's fortunes only brightened. The Oak Cliff community on the west bank of the Trinity River, annexed by Dallas in 1903 and now straddling Interstate 35 East, was even regarded as the "Brooklyn of Dallas."[15]

Fort Worth stayed with the cattle trade. In 1883, as refrigerated and ventilated railroad cars were being introduced, the Continental Meat Packing Company was established on the north side of town. It was reorganized as the Fort Worth Dressed Meat and Packing Company in 1890, shut down after the Panic of 1893, and revived after 1900. To utilize capacity at the adjacent Fort Worth Stockyards (established in 1890 and paved from the same Thurber brickyard that paved a section of Austin's Congress Avenue in 1905), railroad-like bonuses of fifty thousand dollars were paid to Swift and Company and to Armour and Company to establish packing plants at the yards in 1902, with a promise to add a connecting rail line shortly. The scheme worked; Fort Worth would have one of the foremost beef complexes in the United States when an estimated two million head of cattle were handled in 1910. With an additional boost provided by the I&GN's arrival in 1902, Fort Worth's population surged from 26,688 in 1900 to 73,312 in 1910.[16]

Progress was somewhat slower up north. Stimulated by the arrival of the Santa Fe, Gainesville's population reached 6,594 in 1890. But without a Red River highway bridge until 1919, travelers had to make do with old-fashioned ferries. According to A. R. Brown's permit of November 1877, ferry rates were seventy-five cents for a four-horse wagon, a quarter for a man and horse, and a nickel for a single head of livestock. Horses and mules predominated. While other towns had converted from mule-drawn streetcars to electricity, Gainesville's streetcar system operated the old way between 1884 and 1901. In July 1901, the line was abandoned entirely and a proposed electric system was rejected. Gainesville's streetcar mules moved on to greater glory, however—they were sold to the British Army and apparently served in the Anglo-Boer War.[17]

At the other end of future I-35, Laredo's population soared to 11,319 in 1890 from 3,521 in 1880, and the city emerged from a century of slumber. In 1870, Texas trade with Mexico had been concentrated at Brownsville-Matamoros. But twelve years later, Laredo had four railroad lines and new momentum. The Texas-Mexican (Tex-Mex) Railroad was completed from Corpus Christi in November 1881, and the I&GN arrived from San Antonio one month later. In 1882, the narrow-gauge Mexican National Railways (Ferrocariles Nacionales de México) line connected Laredo with Monterrey and eventually to Mexico City. That same year, a twenty-seven-mile section of the Rio Grande and Eagle Pass railroad was completed between Laredo and the Santa Tomás coal mines, the first phase of a proposed Red River Valley line between Eagle Pass and Brownsville.[18]

Pushed by Mexican president Porfirio Díaz, Mexican National Railways completed its 1,700-foot-long iron bridge across the Rio Grande in September 1888, to cap off its 837-mile line between Laredo and Mexico City. The seven iron spans of the bridge were designed to support weights equivalent to four locomotives. The journey between the two termini took thirty-six hours and was promoted as a segment of a scheduled five-day trip between New York and Mexico City. "Only two changes of sleeping cars" were required en route. According to the company's marketing brochure, the line ran from Laredo's "elegant depot" to Lampazos, a junction that served a Southern Pacific line and the mineral deposits of Nuevo León, before continuing through "the garden spots of Mexico," including Monterrey, Saltillo, and San Luis Potosí. To the north, an I&GN train left Laredo at 11:40 P.M. and arrived in San Antonio at 7:10 A.M.[19]

The new rail and cross-border linkages resulted in substantial investments in and around Laredo. Access was provided to the upriver Santo Tomás and Black Diamond coal deposits, mines that produced one hundred tons per day for the locomotive fuel market and that employed hundreds. The Guadalupe Mining Company of Philadelphia, assisted by a donation of thirty acres from the city, invested $200,000 in a massive smelting and concentrating complex in 1887. The new facilities processed 300 tons of low grade ores per day—mainly silver, lead, iron, zinc, and copper from Nuevo León.[20]

As early as 1882, one hundred new buildings were constructed in downtown Laredo, including a new county courthouse, a national bank, an opera house, and an ice factory. Mexican National Railways and the I&GN placed facilities and repair shops outside the town on donated lands; the $300,000 Mexican Railways machine shop was believed to be the largest such facility west of the Mississippi River. A waterworks, a telephone exchange, and an Edison Incandescent Lighting system soon appeared, but not without a brief clash over competing claims to the city's sudden prosperity. On April 7, 1886, at least nine people were killed and more than twenty were wounded in a riot triggered by disputed election results. After martial law was declared, the U.S. Army and Texas Rangers were sent in (via the I&GN from San Antonio) to restore order.[21]

Construction on Laredo's second Rio Grande bridge, the International (or Convent Street) Foot and Wagon Bridge, was a highlight. An act of the U.S. Congress in May 1884 had provided the International Bridge and Tramway Company with a twenty-five-year franchise to build and operate a foot, wagon, and street railway bridge between the two Laredos. The ancient ferry (*chalane*) service had operated at the foot of Flores Avenue, one block east of Convent, for over a century. After components for the new span were received from Toledo, Ohio, the 310-foot-long bridge was completed in April 1889. The cost was $150,000. The steel and wood bridge was a single-lane affair with five spans, a distinctive overhead girder structure, and toll booths placed on each side of the river. The company's rental charge was set at five thousand dollars, the same as the ferry's annual revenues. By 1890, a four-mile electric streetcar was in place to link the Mexican National Railways depot in Nuevo Laredo with the I&GN depot in Laredo.[22]

Laredo had gained access to local mineral deposits, but a few mineral-poor communities along the future route of I-35 would benefit substantially from oil. Prior to the spectacular oil strike at Spindletop on January 10, 1901, cattle, cotton, timber, and railroads had been the critical components in Texas' economic expansion, creating major cities and developing the communication lines—rail, roads, electricity, telegraph, telephone—that linked them all together. The Texas economy and the future direction of the transportation industry were both shocked by the new oil industry. Harris County became the state's leading industrial county almost overnight, highlighted by the instant

Houston Oil Company, but Dallas, Bexar, and Tarrant counties would also benefit from the boom. Some 491 oil companies were chartered in Texas in 1901.[23]

Since the later oil discoveries were located in rural areas, inland railroad centers like Fort Worth, Dallas, and San Antonio became oil towns in their own right. Two oil refineries opened in Fort Worth by 1911, and the Ranger Field discovery in 1917 added substantially to the city's business and population growth. Fort Worth had 106,482 inhabitants in 1920 and nine oil refineries in 1922. By 1940, the old frontier and cattle town was the largest inland refining center in Texas, with a massive network of pipelines and more than six hundred oil company offices. Dallas benefited greatly from the massive East Texas strike of 1930—the city would claim a total of 1,382 oil-related enterprises in 1940.[24]

Fortunately for the oil operators, the petroleum industry required its own dedicated transportation system. With its own pipelines and specially designed rail cars, the industry did not have to worry much about roads—which was all to the good since road conditions in Texas between the Civil War and the early 1900s were possibly even worse than before the Civil War. Most of the available capital, labor, and political energy had been invested in railroads and, to a lesser extent, bridges. The old system of county road crews, still managed by unpaid, nonprofessional overseers, remained ineffective and unpopular. Crews were rarely asked to report during planting and harvesting periods, and the regular use of convict workers was controversial.

When county crews were available, road building techniques followed the same old pattern. Routes were surveyed and marked; brush, trees, and stumps were removed; and the surface was "finished" (flattened) by wagon wheels, oxen, horses, cattle, and pedestrians. In 1890, the unpopular work requirement was reduced to four days per year with a dollar-a-day buy-out option. In that same year, county tax authorizations for roads and bridges were doubled to thirty cents per hundred dollars of valuation, and counties were allowed to issue bonds for bridge projects. First-class roads were to be at least forty feet wide and cleared of timber and stumps. Until 1900, counties were only encouraged, not required, to build first-class roads between the state's county seats.[25]

Old stage roads between the Red River and Austin, including the Preston Road, were in good shape during dry seasons. But few segments were even graveled as of 1900. Roadbed preparation, the application of crushed stone foundations, and drainage systems were rare. In 1875 the state legislature had approved the award of eight sections of land to finance the macadamization of

Wiehl's road between Austin and San Marcos. It did not happen. The road was eventually surfaced with caliche and gravel until a tar-surfacing road project was completed in 1919. A Dripping Springs resident complained in 1884 that "Dupree [Buda], Kyle, San Marcos and San Antonio are improving [their] roads . . . whilst Austin, or Travis County, is not only not improving the present roads, but sitting quietly by while they are lengthened and made worse [by] frequent changes."[26]

Compulsory road service was being gradually replaced with quasi-professional crews supported by tax revenues. Of course, many county voters were outraged by the new road taxes and indicated that roads were not their responsibility. Convict labor was suggested as a possible alternative when a national movement emerged to solve social problems with road-building projects. Some 588 of Texas' 3,575 state prisoners were working the railroads (not roads) in the peak year for convict projects (1892), but most of the state prison population was deployed on state farms. Conditions on these farms may have been no better than on the chain gangs, but Texas roads were never state convict projects on the scale of Georgia or the Carolinas. Still, roads in Tarrant, Dallas, and many other counties were at least partly built or maintained by local prisoners until 1933.[27]

Supported by taxes and convicts, the more populated counties in Texas increased their road and bridge activities significantly between 1890 and 1900. Fort Worth had authorized macadam or brick paving in August 1882, and had surfaced a number of downtown streets by 1890. In Dallas, Cedar Springs Road was macadamized in 1884 and the city claimed twenty miles of paved streets in 1888. Elm Street was asphalt paved by 1900. Fort Worth and Dallas were leading the emerging "Good Roads" movement, but their city roads were not linked to surrounding county roads until 1897. Outside of town, county roads consisted of flattened earth.[28]

Provisions of the Act of 1895 helped to improve matters. The act declared that any road in service for at least ten years prior to 1895 was to be declared a public road. For the first time, surveyors and engineers were employed to position one-mile markers along these roads, to construct drainage ditches, and to prepare maps. The act facilitated the layout of the Upper Georgetown Road in Travis County and its construction (by convicts) with crushed stone from Jollyville. Drainage ditches were typically dug by mule teams, convict labor, and a bit of ingenuity. A split-log drag was used in Collin County in the 1890s to grade roads and dig ditches simultaneously. A ten-foot log, two feet wide, was split down the middle and dragged along the sides of the road by a mule team. More exotic road construction technologies were on their way. The first rock crusher had been introduced in 1859, followed by the steam roller in 1869, the wheel grader in 1885, and in 1889 steam-powered crushing machines that could pulverize as much as two hundred tons of rock per day.[29]

The Act of 1895 was influenced by the farmer-oriented Good Roads movement. As early as 1880, Thomas U. Taylor had published *County Roads* to extend Gillespie's recommendations to Texas' expanding farm population. Taylor believed that good quality roads were critical to a farmer's ability to haul crops, develop more flexible trading relationships, and in turn gain higher prices. Since bad roads functioned as a large hidden tax on a farmer's profits, farmers were encouraged to pay a modest road tax to remove the larger burden. Like Gillespie, Taylor railed against the county work crew system and argued for a French-style class of professional county engineers, supported by road taxes. If the French system was the ideal, Taylor favored Telford roads over McAdam-style roads in the interim. Telfords could be twice as expensive—one with twelve inches of pavement cost between $8,000 and $10,000 per mile, versus a cost of $3,000–$8,000 for four- to six-inch McAdam roads—but lasted many years longer.[30]

By the late 1880s, the Good Roads movement had become a national phenomenon. *Harpers Weekly* complained in August 1889 that the nation's mud-plagued roads were far inferior to those in France, costly to American commerce, and burdened by a county commissioner system that "is known to be a complete failure." The League of American Wheelmen, an association of bicyclists, had already organized the National Good Roads Association in 1880 to promote the new movement. After the introduction of the English "safety" bicycle in 1885 and Irishman John B. Dunlop's pneumatic tire in 1888, a powerful lobby of four million U.S. bicyclists was demanding change. The league's publication of *Good Roads* magazine in 1892 prompted Congress to establish an Office of Road Inquiry (ORI) within the U.S. Department of Agriculture (USDA) in 1893.[31]

With the ORI, the predecessor to the Bureau of Public Roads, the federal government had finally become involved, if tentatively, in the nation's road network. The emphasis was on rural roads. Congress authorized a grand total of ten thousand dollars to the USDA to investigate road conditions, suggest building techniques, and authorize and inspect Rural Free Delivery (RFD) routes for the U.S. postal system. Since the government's last road appropriation had been in 1838, for a section of the National Road in Illinois, this tentative step was a milestone. The first RFD routes were introduced in 1896, and construction and maintenance standards were developed in 1899. By 1905, there would be some thirty-two thousand RFD routes in the United States, including, for example, five in Comal County, Texas. The league's grassroots organization and marketing strategy had been so successful that it would serve as a model for future automobile owners.[32]

The ORI also provided a clearinghouse of technical bulletins and circulars to fledgling state highway programs in New Jersey, Massachusetts, and a handful of other states. In New Jersey, the first state-aided road was a five-mile macadam highway, twelve feet wide and eight inches thick, between New Brunswick and Metuchen in 1892. In Ohio, a 220-foot section of Bellefontaine's courthouse square was paved with concrete slabs in 1891. Two years later, a four-mile stretch of brick highway was constructed along the Wooster Pike outside Cleveland. At sixteen thousand dollars per mile, however, the cost of brick roads was prohibitive. In 1898, crude oil was applied to six miles of Los Angeles roadway in an effort to control the city's dust problem.[33]

Six states had highway commissions by 1899, but fewer than five thousand automobiles were operating across the United States. In Texas, as in many other states, efforts to create a state highway agency had been repeatedly quashed. County officials were simply unwilling to relinquish their authority to the state government. In response, state officials and Good Roads advocates petitioned the federal government for help. In 1902, an ambitious proposal was made by ORI director Martin Dodge to create a U.S. Bureau of Public Roads and spend $20 million annually on U.S. highways, in cooperation with states and counties. The bill was rejected as too expensive and possibly unconstitutional. The latter concern was removed in 1907 when the U.S. Supreme Court ruled (in *Wilson v. Shaw*) that Congress had legislative power to build interstate highways.[34]

OFF-RAMP: GOOD ROADS, BETTER CARS, AND GASOLINE

The ORI's greatest success was its sponsorship of "object lesson" roads between 1897 and 1914. The concept was borrowed from Massachusetts (via France) and inaugurated with a crushed-stone section of Nichols Avenue in New Brunswick, New Jersey, in 1897. Another ninety-five object lesson roads, amounting to thirty-nine miles and supported by a road materials testing laboratory in Washington (1900) and the American Society for Testing Materials

(1899), were completed by 1905. By then, fourteen states had highway commissions and Massachusetts had a four-tiered road system borrowed from France and over 480 miles of improved state highways. These early roads were costly at twelve thousand dollars per mile and most would be destroyed by increasing vehicle weights and volumes. The ORI also worked with emerging trade groups—the American Road Builders Association (1903), National Association of Concrete Users (1905), and American Society of Civil Engineers—and helped to arrange the nation's first highway engineering course at Harvard University under Nathaniel S. Shaler. The geology professor also authored a landmark environmental work, *Man and the Earth,* in 1905.[35]

ORI-sponsored projects, in turn, catalyzed road-building activities at state, county, and local levels. Between 1907 and 1909, a one-mile segment of bituminous tar and macadam was installed in Charlestown, Rhode Island; streets were paved with concrete in Windsor, Ontario; and one mile of Woodward Avenue in Wayne County, Michigan, became the nation's first public concrete road. Constructed at a cost of $13,535, Woodward's paved section was seventeen feet wide and eight to nine inches thick, and it proved durable enough to withstand heavy military truck traffic during World War I.[36]

Led by new director Logan W. Page, the renamed Office of Public Roads (OPR) released the nation's first road census in 1907. Only 154,000 miles of an estimated two million miles of U.S. roads were improved in any way. Everyone needed good roads, but the ethos of the Progressive Era (1900–20) was to emphasize rural areas. As late as 1912, 500 of the OPR's 616 miles of object lesson roads were improved dirt roads located in rural areas. Good roads were intended to stabilize farmland values, particularly in areas bypassed by railroads. Railroad companies even supported the effort. They hoped to improve farm-to-market roads in order to build railroad freight traffic. Ironically, the railroads were unable to predict the development of commercial trucks and passenger bus lines. Their assistance to the Good Roads movement ultimately led to their decline.[37]

The Good Roads movement was started by bicyclists, influenced by Frenchmen, promoted for farmers, and popularized by automobile owners. The earliest automobiles in the United States were imported from France or Germany or reverse-engineered as American copycats or produced by former bicycle manufacturers. After decades of experimentation, the industry's breakthrough was the Panhard-Levassor Company's introduction of the world's first automobile in 1894. The innovations had begun with Etienne Lenoir's internal combustion engine patent in 1860 and had been advanced by bicycle-men-turned-engine-designers like Nicholas Otto in 1878 and Gottlieb Daimler and Carl Benz (independently) in 1885. Between 1890 and 1896, the new designs were modified by other bicycle manufacturers like Armand Peugeot, the brothers J. Frank and Charles E. Duryea, Ransom E. Olds, the brothers John and Horace Dodge, and Henry Ford. However, it was Panhard who led the pack after having acquired the French rights to Daimler's technology in 1890. Panhard's improvements were a revelation: in a Paris-Bordeaux road race in July 1895, Panhard's entry completed the round-trip course in forty-eight hours, averaging around 15 mph.[38]

In just a few years, more than a hundred auto companies came into being. Vehicle quality was poor, or at least inconsistent, and the early U.S. leader, Olds Motor Works, produced all of four thousand two-cylinder, gasoline-powered cars in 1904. The industry's first blockbuster was Henry Ford's Model T in 1908. The Model T was a dramatic improvement over Ford's first (1903) product, not to mention his "Quadricycle" of 1896. Designed and priced for middle-income Americans, particularly in rural areas, the Model T married European quality with dramatic cost savings achieved through standardization and mass production techniques pioneered by Olds in 1902. With only 1,200 pounds of weight, the 20-horsepower, four-cylinder Model T outperformed most other vehicles, particularly on bad country roads. Scale economies and sheet metalization technologies eventually lowered Model T prices to below six hundred dollars by 1911.[39]

One more breakthrough was required before gasoline would become the fuel of choice for internal combustion engines. In 1913, a new hydrocarbon-cracking process was introduced by William Burton and Robert Humphrey at Standard Oil of Indiana (Amoco), based on Louis Blaustein's earlier "Amoco" formulation of 1910 that "cracked" heavy petroleum fractions into gasolines. The new cracked gasolines had octane ratings of around 80, versus only 50–55 for traditional gasolines, as well as anti-knock characteristics. Most important to cost-conscious refiners, they now had an associated manufacturing process that nearly doubled the production yields from crude oil volumes. With higher octanes, engines could be designed with higher compression ratios and much higher power. In later years, the introduction of catalytic cracking processes (by Sun Oil in 1931) raised octane ratings to 90–92.[40]

The Model T was designed for bad roads, but the people who purchased the cars clamored for good roads. In the early 1900s, the Grange, Progressives, Populists, and railroad companies all supported the Good Roads movement. At the 1903 National Good Roads convention in St. Louis, commemorating the Louisiana Purchase Centennial, President Theodore Roosevelt and William

Jennings Bryan both cited the importance of good roads to the nation's farmers. Unfortunately, many farmers believed that good roads meant higher taxes and were less enthusiastic than the politicians. However, the growing clout of the recently formed American Automobile Association (AAA, 1902) suggested a completely new source of interest.[41]

The first Texas Good Roads Association (TGRA) was formed in 1903 by automobile enthusiasts, not farmers. It lasted only until 1907. The group's major proposal, allowing Texas counties to lease convict workers for road maintenance, was rejected by the legislature. By the time the second TGRA was organized in 1911, a series of long-distance road trips had captured the public's imagination. Between May and July 1903, Dr. H. Nelson Jackson required only sixty-three days to drive his Winton automobile from San Francisco to New York (via Idaho) over mostly unmapped routes. By June 1909, Harry Scott and James Smith had driven a 1909 Ford from New York to Seattle in just twenty-two days, beating twenty-eight other entries in the International Transcontinental road race. In October of that year, a race between Atlanta and New York was won in thirteen days and was completed by many of the thirty-eight participants. As racing began to be replaced by touring, *American Motorist Magazine* decided to chronicle a more leisurely thirty-four-day trip between Litchfield, Connecticut, and Charleston, South Carolina, in March 1911.[42]

Early road races were not limited to cars. In May 1903, the Automobile Club of America sponsored a forty-mile race within New York City to showcase another fledgling industry—commercial trucks. Among fourteen entrants, the winner was a two-cylinder, eight horsepower, gasoline-powered "Waterless" Knox driven by H. A. Knox. Knox's lightweight delivery wagon, loaded with 1,250 pounds of pig lead, covered the course in three and a half hours. In 1904, seven hundred trucks were manufactured in the United States. Most were flatbed wagons attached to an automobile. None had roofs, doors, or windshields. But truck-specific designs were beginning to appear. Early manufacturers like White (the successor to the White Sewing Machine Company), Mack Brothers (Brooklyn-based wagon makers), Reo (R. E. Olds's latest venture), Four Wheel Drive, Packard, International Harvester (the successor to McCormick Harvesting Machine Company), Rapid (Max Grabowsky's predecessor to GMC), and Ford would eventually revise the concept significantly.[43]

The AAA had published route guides since 1900, but as auto touring began to explode, the AAA prepared its landmark 1910 *Blue Book* to map the nation's emerging auto routes. With national road conditions in flux, the AAA advised its intrepid membership to carry tire chains, mud hooks, an axe, flashlight, compass, spare parts, shovel, crowbar, rope, cement, and a gun. Whether there was any room left for luggage or passengers is unclear. Otherwise, the AAA began to lobby for a national program to build long-distance, paved interstate highways based on the transcontinental railroad model. This focus on interstates set the AAA apart from the Progressives' farm road orientation.[44]

With the encouragement of the AAA and ace promoters like Carl Graham Fisher, proposals were launched to build an interstate highway between New York (or Washington) and Atlanta and a transcontinental Lincoln Highway. Fisher's Lincoln Highway concept, which raised $4 million dollars for a series of one-mile, object-lesson-like road projects, was so persuasive that some sixty interstate highway bills were presented to Congress in 1912. Proposals called for a Meridian Highway to be built between Winnipeg and Galveston (or Laredo) and a Dixie Highway between Michigan and Fisher's properties in Miami Beach. The Dixie project drew financial support from fifty counties, ten states, and hundreds of hotels, restaurants, and auto-related businesses. Other interstate highway proposals included the Robert E. Lee (New York to San Francisco), the John H. Bankhead (Washington, D.C. to San Diego), and the Jefferson Davis (Washington to San Francisco). The National Highway Association trumped them all with a plan to develop a 51,000-mile network of interstate highways, at a cost of $30,000 per mile.[45]

Back in Texas, counties had enough difficulty linking a county seat with a county line, let alone to Washington or San Francisco. Horses, mules, and wagons would last for decades, but Texas had joined the automobile age as well. The state's first recorded automobile purchase was made in 1899 by Colonel E. H. R. (Ned) Green, son of the famously wealthy and famously cheap Hetty Green and a part-time resident of Terrell and Dallas. Green raced through Terrell at an astonishing 15 mph en route to a bumpier thirty-mile jaunt to Dallas. The trip took over five hours. The second automobile sale in Texas was a "company car" issued to Texas and Pacific manager L. S. Thorne in 1902 by none other than Jay Gould. By August 25, 1903, the *Fort Worth Telegram* was reporting that Colonel R. Peterson of Paris, Texas, had won a dirt road automobile race between Fort Worth and Dallas in the "record time" of one hour and thirty-five minutes (roughly 3.5 mph). The race induced Ned Green to organize the Dallas Automobile Club in 1904 and raise the city's asphalt road mileage to three and a half by year end.[46]

Ned Green had also financed a losing political campaign of some interest. On November 9, 1903, John Nance Garner joined Congress after having defeated Green's candidate in the 15th District. Born in Red River County in 1868, Garner had relocated to Uvalde for health reasons in 1893, had entered the state legislature in 1899, and had amassed a sizable fortune from a law practice, keen business acumen, and an extraordinary talent for deal making. The "Sage of Uvalde" rarely introduced his own bills, and other than the promotion of the port of Corpus Christi, he delivered relatively few federal buildings, road projects, or bridges to his constituents. But as early as 1906, Garner did seek $10 million in federal aid for roads, railways, and waterways, with some words of advice: "Let me make a prediction. The time is coming when the federal treasury will help to build good roads."[47]

Road conditions in Texas and virtually everywhere else were so bad that early automobile owners were advised to supplement the AAA emergency list with picks and barbed wire cutters. Yet progress was being made. A 1904 amendment to the state constitution authorized Texas counties and subdivisions to issue bonds to finance the construction of gravel, macadam, or paved roads and bridges. However, approval was still required from two-thirds of the relevant taxpaying voters. By 1910, counties were also allowed to acquire land for future road projects. County bonds were subject to approval by the state attorney general and regulation by the comptroller for public accounts.[48]

The new legislation resulted in a number of county initiatives. In Bexar, a local Good Roads Association persuaded voters to approve $500,000 in county bonds in 1904 to gravel (not pave) every major road within a ten-mile radius of San Antonio. The new surfaces would be sixteen feet wide with eight-foot dirt shoulders. Most of the gravel was applied in two-inch layers—coarse on the bottom, with a finer limestone gravel on the top. Armed with modern graders and rollers, forty-horsepower Vulcan steam shovels and dump-wagon trains, the 500-men and 500-mule crews could complete one mile of roadway in twenty-two days. The total cost of the program was estimated at $3,438 per mile, including bridges, culverts, and other structures. On a per mile basis, gravel costs were the largest at $2,314, followed by earth excavation costs ($170), clearing and grubbing ($32), and rolling ($41). Crews were paid $45 per day, including $30 for ten mule teams and drivers, $12 for eight laborers, and $3 for one foreman.[49]

In Cooke County, voters in Road District No. 1 approved a $100,000 bond issue in 1909 to gravel (not pave) roads east and west of Gainesville and south to the Denton County line. Since the county's first Red River highway bridge would be delayed until 1919, travelers to and from Oklahoma had to rely on dirt roads and the twenty or so ferryboats that operated between Cooke County and Oklahoma. Subsequent road bond proposals were rejected by county voters, and Gainesville did not have a single paved street until 1919, when voters finally approved a $50,000 bond issue to pave East California Street and Courthouse Square. A promotion campaign led by the Gainesville Automobile Club, organized in January 1918, probably helped matters.[50]

Bell County got around to grading, ditching, and graveling (not paving) a new turnpike between Belton and Temple in 1912. The county had only a few hundred automobiles in 1912, and even graveled roads were considered a luxury. While most roads were of the old-fashioned dirt variety, the future direction was clear. Belton issued $150,000 in bonds to finance road graveling activities in May 1913, and other districts followed shortly. However, the traditional district-based system was determined to be inefficient for road planning and implementation. Bell's eighteen road districts were abolished in December 1917, and $1.2 million in outstanding district bonds were consolidated into a new $1.9 million bond issue for the entire county.[51]

One of Bell County's residents, Herman Brown, was in the very middle of these initiatives. Having apprenticed on local road crews since 1909, Brown began to clear, grade, and surface roads as an independent contractor in 1914. He also learned how to work with county commissioners. Brown's rough-hewn road crews, paid at a rate of $1.35 per day (after $0.75 was deducted for food and tents), labored with old-fashioned mule-drawn wagons, drags, and plows that were typically driven by black mule skinners. Brown and his brother-in-law Dan Root established a road-contracting firm in 1919 and were joined three years later by younger brother George R. Brown; their operation evolved into an extremely capable (and extremely politically influential) engineering, construction, and energy company.[52]

Texas' first macadamized (but still not fully paved) roads were completed by 1912, including a turnpike between Dallas and Fort Worth—constructed in part by convicts—and improved roads in Bexar, Harris, and a handful of other counties. Most of these improved roads were at least surfaced with bituminous tar. Dallas and Fort Worth jockeyed for position as the state's leading automobile center, encouraged by the annual State Fair road race between the two towns. Fort Worth boasted 959 registered automobiles in 1910 (among 14,286 in Texas), and Dallas County claimed 2,944 in 1912. Sam Rayburn won his first election to Congress in 1912 after campaigning through the rural Fourth District, northeast of Dallas, in a Model T.[53]

In 1911, Tarrant County approved a $1 million bond issue to pave (not gravel) county roads and another $600,000 to build bridges. Unfortunately, one of the most modern road networks in Texas helped to end Fort Worth's fledgling interurban railway system. The Northern Texas Traction Company (NTTC) had operated an electric interurban line between Fort Worth and Dallas since 1902, but the new service was fighting history. When a competing bus system, a predecessor to the Fort Worth Auto Bus Company, was added in 1917, the NTTC discovered that riders preferred buses to interurbans. The recast Fort Worth Transit Company would be entirely bus-based by 1939.[54]

Tarrant was not the only county to be burned by the brief interurban craze. Texas communities built roughly 500 miles of interurban lines by 1914, 226 miles of which were owned by the Texas Electric Railway in Dallas. Fort Worth was first, but the Dallas interurban network, which stretched between Denison and Waco with connections to Fort Worth, Cleburne, Denton, Corsicana, and Terrell, became the largest integrated system between the Mississippi River and California. "Bluebonnet" express service carried passengers at 50 mph. Farther south, a group of Pennsylvania investors had launched the Belton and Temple Traction Company and completed an interurban line between the two towns in 1905. With Temple's population approaching 11,000 in 1900 and Belton at around 4,000, the investors had hoped to extend the "twin cities" interurban north to Waco, and then south to Austin. Unfortunately, all of the interurban ventures collapsed when traffic shifted to automobiles and buses. Most were abandoned in the early 1930s.[55]

Austin still had its Austin Electric Railway Company (AERC). After a rocky start, the AERC generated a string of modest profits between 1908 and 1918 and helped to guide the city's expansion. The operation was sold to a group of hopeful New England investors in 1918. But by then, automobiles and jitneys had captured an increasingly large number of riders—enough to throw the business into federal receivership in 1921. Somehow, the business recovered, aided by a fare increase (to ten cents) and the addition of bus routes in 1928. At its peak in 1933, the route system totaled twenty-three miles. Buses became so popular, however, that the AERC's last trolley ran on February 7, 1940. The streetcar rails were torn up and sold as scrap.[56]

In the same way that railroads had succeeded stages, wagons, and steamboats, ascendant automobiles and trucks were now succeeding railroads, interurbans, and even streetcars. But, if the need for modern paved roads was becoming glaringly apparent, virtually all of the state-oriented road building proposals sent to the Texas legislature between 1905 and 1915 were rejected. There were proposals for a Texas state expert engineer in 1905, a state highway engineer in 1907, an office for a commissioner of highways in 1909, and a new state highway department in 1911 and 1913. All failed. Two measures that did pass in 1907, however, were Texas' first auto registration requirement and its first speed limit. Fees were set at fifty cents per vehicle and a speed limit of 18 mph was adopted.[57]

Counties were left to fend for themselves. In Bexar, a $400,000 three-year initiative, started in 1912, to widen six miles of Commerce Street (old US 90) to sixty-five feet, was followed by a massive $7 million road bond issue in 1914. The Bexar County Highway League, a local TGRA chapter, had somehow promoted the nation's largest horse and mule center as an emerging force of modernization. San Antonio's growth was dramatic. From a modest population of 20,550 in 1880, the city reached 53,321 in 1900, 96,614 in 1910, and via a powerful combination of railroads, oil, cotton, cattle, and military presence, a total of 161,379 in 1920. Fort Sam Houston housed 46,000 troops during World War I as the nation's the largest military post.[58]

Despite the efforts of thirty Good Roads chapters across the state, only 703 miles of Texas' 10,527 miles of improved roads were paved by 1914, mainly in Bexar, Dallas, and Tarrant counties. Since the vast majority of roads were surfaced with gravel, sand and clay, and other low-cost materials, improvement was in the eye of the beholder. States like Massachusetts and Indiana claimed that nearly 50 percent and 37 percent, respectively, of their roads were improved in 1911, but this did not necessarily mean paved. In its census of December 1914, the Office of Public Roads estimated that only 32,000 of the 257,000 miles of improved U.S. roads were paved with brick, concrete, or bituminous macadam materials.[59]

OFF-RAMP: CONCRETE HIGHWAYS AND POST ROADS

California emerged as the clear paving leader, with around nine hundred miles of concrete roads in 1914. Concrete roads were far more expensive than other surfaces, but they lasted many years longer and required less maintenance. The notion was supported by the authors of *Text-Book on Highway Engineering* in that same year. Several chapters were considered to be "somewhat of an innovation in books on roads and pavements," including one that compared the "effects of motor-car traffic" with those of "horse-drawn vehicle traffic." New York had only 244 miles of concrete roads in 1914, eleven of which were represented by William K. Vanderbilt's Long Island Motor Parkway. Having sponsored the Vanderbilt Cup Race since 1904 (won initially at 52 mph), Vanderbilt constructed a private race track between 1908 and 1914 that was twenty-four feet wide and built with five-inch-thick concrete pavement, reinforced with steel mesh.[60]

Despite the appeal of concrete highways and a surge to 1.3 million registered vehicles by 1913, federal involvement remained decidedly small scale. Most people preferred it that way. The Post Office Department Appropriation Act of 1912 provided all of $500,000 to the USDA and Postmasters General Office to improve the nation's post road system. The program carried a two-thirds matching funds requirement from participating states and local units, limited the work day to eight hours, and prohibited convict workers (in 1915). These labor restrictions were eventually declared unconstitutional. The first federal post road outlay was $27,947 ($932 per mile) for a thirty-mile dirt highway between Florence and Waterloo, Alabama, in 1913. The choice was influenced by the home state of the chairman of the Senate Committee on Post Offices and Post Roads, John H. Bankhead Jr. of Alabama. Post roads would total 450 miles in seventeen states, but the quality of the work was so uneven that the OPR eventually removed suspect county officials from the process. In the future, the OPR would work only with state highway personnel.[61]

The growing shift to centralized management was signaled by the formation of the American Association of State Highway Officials (AASHO) in 1914 and their call for a $75 million federal road improvement program. Since total federal expenditures for U.S. roads were only $550,000 in 1915, the AASHO's proposal was somewhat outrageous. Yet the surge in automobile registrations, wartime requirements (moving supplies, arms, and troops), concerns about the continuing Mexican civil war, and the last gasps of the Progressive movement had converged. AASHO would not be disappointed. A major milestone in U.S. highway history was reached in 1916 with the passage of the Federal Aid Road Bill, sponsored by Senator Bankhead and Congressman D. W. Shackleford of Missouri. The bill was signed into law by President Woodrow Wilson on July 11, 1916.[62]

The Federal Aid Road Act of 1916 provided $75 million over a five-year period (1917–21) to state programs involved with the improvement of rural post roads. The national effort was administered by the USDA's OPR division—renamed the Bureau of Public Roads (BPR) in 1918—and was eventually directed by the legendary Thomas H. MacDonald in 1919. Road projects would be managed cooperatively with approved state highway agencies (only) and were targeted exclusively to rural routes and post roads, defined as any public road that carried the U.S. mail. Cities and long-distance interstate roads were excluded completely. Federal funds would be allocated to each state based on a simple formula: one-third based on the state's share of U.S. land area; one-third based on its share of population; and one-third based on its share of rural postal road mileage. The federal cost share was set at 50 percent, but no funds would be provided to any town with a population of 2,500 or more. There was a daunting $10,000 per mile cost limitation as well.[63]

The cost-sharing formulas would be revised shortly to encourage the development of interstate highways. In the meantime, the 1916 allocation formula gave Texas the largest funding opportunity in the United States—if and when Texas was ready to create a state highway agency. As late as 1913, Texas was one of only six states (joining Florida, Indiana, Mississippi, South Carolina, and Tennessee) without some kind of state assistance program for road improvements. Texas roads continued to be managed by county commissioners, and the counties were reluctant to give up their power.[64]

However, money talks. In view of the new federal funding opportunities and wartime concerns, the Texas State Highway Act established the first state highway department in April 1917. The plans included a new three-member State Highway Commission (appointed by the governor), a state highway engineer (appointed by the commission), a new State Highway Fund, and the first authorized use of state convicts. While Governor James E. Ferguson was apparently neutral on the subject, he signed House Bill No. 2 into law on April 4, 1917 (four months before his impeachment).[65]

The State Highway Fund would be supported by automobile registration fees; gasoline taxes came later. Auto registration fees were set initially at $7.50 per vehicle or $0.35 per horsepower. Commercial vehicles (trucks) were assessed a fee based on the carrying capacity of each wheel. With 194,720 vehicle registrations in Texas in 1917, the revenues generated by these fees would be quite substantial. Half of the funds would be allocated to the State Highway Fund and half to the counties. All matching funds from the federal government were transferred to the State Highway Fund.[66]

Initially, the new Texas Highway Department (THD) focused on planning and coordination. The new agency intended to complement, not replace, the work of county commissions and attempted to work cooperatively with the counties until 1932. State financial assistance was limited to 50 percent of the cost of a planned county highway project. All road projects, including engineering surveys, plans, estimates, and financing, continued to be initiated by the counties, but all were subject to THD approval. In addition, a county road system map had to be submitted to the state highway engineer. Counties were still responsible for purchasing rights-of-way and funding road maintenance.[67]

As of June 1917, twenty-six routes were selected for the state's designated (federal funds–eligible) highway system. Routes of importance to our story included Highway 2 between Laredo and Waco via San Antonio; Highway 6 between Waco and Dallas via Hillsboro; Highway 2A and Highway 2 between Hillsboro and Fort Worth via Cleburne; Highway 16A between Dallas and Denton; and Highway 16 between Fort Worth and Gainesville via Denton. These routes would evolve (mainly) into US 81 and US 77, predecessor highways to I-35. In the meantime, most of these designated routes were old, earthen country roads and would remain unimproved until the late 1920s or even later. Roads that were not designated state roads were in even worse shape.

As it had since the 1890s, the BPR continued to provide technical advisory services in cooperation with the state highway departments. The THD had worked with laboratory test facilities at the University of Texas and Texas A&M since 1910 before launching its own Materials and Tests Division in 1919. These and other state initiatives were supplemented by the National Advisory Board on Highway Research, formed in November 1920, and recast as the Transportation Research Board in 1974. One of the major challenges was to train a new generation of highway engineers—an entirely new profession—and to reeducate the older generation of railroad men who dominated the state highway departments.[68]

Since every state had its own climate and geology, as did most subregions, standardization was difficult. So were wartime considerations. In July of 1918, James P. Nash of the University of Texas published the influential bulletin *Road Building Materials in Texas,* to help the U.S. Army identify possible sources of road materials in case of emergency. Most roads along the Texas Gulf Coast and the Rio Grande Valley were still unimproved, and World War I was very much in mind. In the tradition of Gillespie and Taylor, Nash recommended a series of alignment and grading specifications, concrete and steel drainage structures (over wood), and improved surface materials. Finding gravel roads to be unsuitable for military and other vehicles, Nash urged Texas to exploit her plentiful deposits of limestone, granite, and sandstone.[69]

Nash's recommendations were aimed at possible military actions involving Mexico (in its eighth year of civil war). San Antonio and the two Laredos had been involved in the Mexican turmoil from the start. Political exiles of all stripes relocated to San Antonio and occasionally stockpiled arms and ammunition in Laredo. Bloody battles occurred between rival forces in Nuevo Laredo on January 1, 1914, nearly spilling over to Laredo, and prompting two companies from Fort McIntosh to defend the International Bridge. Flocks of spectators used the span as an observation deck. Texas governor Ferguson met with Mexican president Venustiano Carranza in Nuevo Laredo in November 1915, to discuss refugees and the recently uncovered "Plan of San Diego." The less-than-half-baked plan had called for Mexicans somehow to retake Texas, New Mexico, Arizona, Colorado, and California, possibly with German assistance. In May 1916, Mexican terrorists attempted to destroy the I&GN railroad bridge at Webb Station, but the raid was halted by truck-borne U.S. troops from Fort Sam Houston. Some ten thousand national guardsmen were subsequently mobilized under the Defense Act of 1916, including the University of Maine band, and dispatched to Laredo in July. There they would remain, without incident, until March 1917.[70]

With one eye on Mexico and the other on the woeful state of Texas roads, the THD prepared a map showing the *Proposed System of State Highways as of June 1917.* Two of the (numbered) designated routes were proposed as Trans-Texas highways: the Texarkana–El Paso Highway (Highway 1) and the Meridian Highway (Highway 2). Highway 2, nearly the future route of Interstate 35, was honored with two branches (Laredo and Galveston) that converged at Waco. The Laredo branch followed much of the future route of I-35. The road paralleled the I&GN right-of-way through San Antonio and via Austin to Round Rock but then veered to the east to Taylor (bypassing Georgetown and Belton). From Taylor, an important railroad hub in 1917, Highway 2 headed northwest to Temple, following present day SH 95, and rejoined the present route of I-35 between Temple and Waco.

Between Waco and the Red River, comparisons with I-35 are more complex. Highway 6 (the King of Trails Highway) followed the route of I-35 north to Hillsboro, northeast to Dallas, and (as Highway 16A) north to Denton. Highway 6, Highway 2A, and Highway 2 were required between Waco and Fort Worth; Highway 2 looped between Waco and Meridian before looping

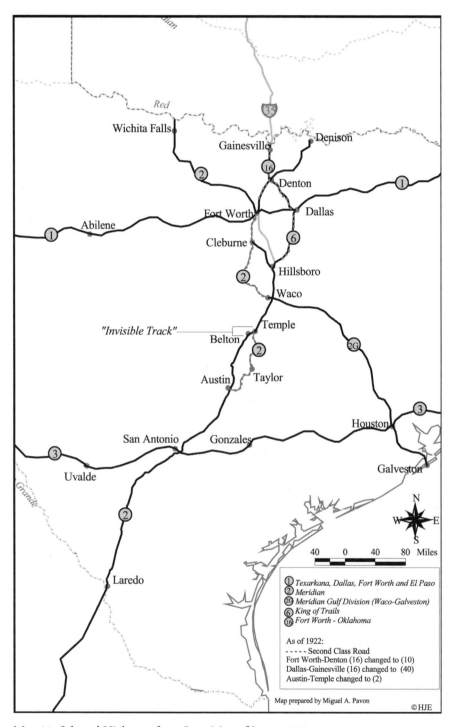

Map 11. Selected Highways from State Map of June, 1917.

back to Fort Worth, while Highway 2A ran between Hillsboro and Cleburne, another important railroad hub. From Fort Worth, the Fort Worth–Oklahoma Highway (Highway 16) was required to reach Denton (and apparently Gainesville). I-35 would eventually follow a more direct route between Round Rock and Temple, bypassing Taylor, and between Hillsboro and Fort Worth, bypassing Cleburne. Otherwise, and ignoring selected highway numbers, the 1917 map provided an outline for Texas' present-day system.

Federal Dollars for Roads, 1918–1938

*T*HE Federal Aid Road Act of 1916, the birth of the Texas Highway Department in April 1917, and the THD's state highway system map of June 1917, were all catalyzed by World War I considerations, possible actions related to the Mexican Civil War, and the explosion of U.S. automobile traffic. If the foundations for interstate highway development including future Interstate 35 were now in place, the conversion of Highway 2 and sections of other routes from a string of disjointed, mainly dirt roads into a paved interstate highway between Laredo and the Red River would take some time and a good deal of money.

The *Texas State Highway Guide* of 1918, the "official logbook" of the TGRA and the Austin Automobile Club, provides an entertaining look at road conditions in the interim. Between Laredo and Waco, drivers were directed by an unnamed route (Highway 2) to Austin and by the Meridian Road/King of Trails (Highway 2) via Taylor, Granger, and Temple to Waco. According to the guide, one could not or should not travel between Belton and Waco. From Waco to the Red River, the suggested (unnamed) route (Highway 6) ran through Hillsboro, Waxahachie, Dallas, McKinney, and Denison. One could or should travel between Hillsboro and Burkburnett via Fort Worth (Highway 2) but not between Fort Worth and Denton or between Denton and Denison. One need not bother with Gainesville—it was not even listed.

Once a desired route was identified, the guide provided detailed, if often incomprehensible, directions. The twenty-one-mile stretch of road between

Laredo and Webb Station, a future section of I-35, was described as follows:

> [Mile] (0.0): LAREDO. Jarvis Plaza and Customs House. Go west on Mata-
> moros St. 1 block. (0.1) Turn right on Santa Maria St., brick church on left.
> (0.4) Cross R.R. and straight ahead. (2.2) Turn left on end of street with road.
> (2.4) Turn right along R.R. (4.5). Turn left across two R.R.s then right along
> R.R. (5.0) Turn right across two R.R.s and then left along R.R. (5.3) Pass
> road on right. (7.0) Curve left across R.R. and then right along R.R. (10.0)
> ORVILLE. Straight ahead along R.R. (16.7) Pass road on left. (20.9) WEBB.
> Station on right. Straight ahead along R.R.

The extent to which the *Texas State Highway Guide* assisted military maneuvers during World War I is unclear. Otherwise, wartime constraints limited U.S. road-building activities to just thirteen miles of federal-aid roads by March 1919. The first federal-aid road, a 2.6-mile segment between Richmond and Albany, California, was completed in January 1918, at a cost of $53,939 — nearly $21,000 per mile. The project included grading, culverts, and a five-inch base of portland cement concrete topped with an inch and a half of bituminous concrete. Another landmark event had occurred in 1917 when the first center stripe was applied to a rural road in Marquette, Michigan.[1]

OFF-RAMP: TRUCKS

As if U.S. roads were not bad enough, wartime freighting activities had shifted a sizable portion of the nation's distribution system from railroads and horse-drawn wagons to heavy trucks. The trucks damaged existing roads significantly, and to some observers, the benefits of the new vehicles were unclear. Still, the war stimulated a revolution in truck technology. The U.S. Army owned only twelve trucks in 1911, three of them parked at Fort Sam Houston, but General Pershing's deployment of a hundred trucks to supply an unsuccessful pursuit of Pancho Villa in 1916 was a turning point. Thousands of trucks were utilized by Pershing's Motor Transport Corps in Europe, jump-starting an entire industry. To eliminate repair problems associated with over 200 different model types and some 60,000 different parts, the U.S. Army selected the White Motors light-duty truck for its Standard A vehicle and provided its own design for the heavy-duty Standard B. Other successful military trucks included the Mack AC ("Bulldog"), FWD, and Nash Quad.[2]

Galvanized by government contracts, U.S. truck production soared from 24,900 vehicles in 1914 to 300,000 in 1918. Of course, this expansion dealt a near-fatal blow to the nation's 25-million-plus horse and mule population, hurting San Antonio and other traditional suppliers. For over a decade, truck manufacturers had attempted to convince the wary owners of horse-drawn wagons that trucks were more productive than four-legged beasts. A GMC advertisement boasted that one GMC truck and driver could replace four wagons, four drivers, and sixteen horses. In *Horse, Truck and Tractor* (1913), the authors attempted to quantify a case that was still very controversial. During an eighteen-day test period, a "gasolene power-truck delivery service [made] 418 deliveries in 114 hours, covering 560 miles at a total cost of $8.76," whereas a horse-drawn vehicle made only "132 deliveries in 133 hours, covering 110 miles at a total cost of $7.49."[3]

The advantages of trucks, plus a new pneumatic, low-pressure rubber cord tire technology, was demonstrated by Goodyear Tire and Rubber Company in a series of test runs between Akron and Boston in April 1917. While muddy routes, bad roads, engine failures, and daily tire changes (twenty-eight in all) extended the first run to four weeks, three weeks over plan, the round-trip was reduced to just five days by midsummer. Goodyear's "Wingfoot Express" and Harvey Firestone's "Ship by Truck" promotion helped to create the nation's long-distance trucking industry.[4]

The emerging needs of the U.S. trucking industry and the road damage caused by trucks influenced Congress to authorize a whopping $200 million for federal road projects in February 1919. Some 1,835 construction projects, covering 15,000 miles, were under way by the end of 1920. While there were also calls for a National Highway Commission to accelerate matters, most of the nation feared intervention by another big government bureaucracy. Needy state highway departments would have to make do with federal funds and surplus army equipment—25,000 Standard A and B trucks, 1,500 tractors, and hundreds of road rollers, graders, and cement mixers.[5]

The federal government still had promotional tools at its disposal. Borrowing a page from the Goodyear test runs, a convoy of U.S. Army Motor Transport Corps vehicles—comprising seventy-five vehicles and two hundred soldiers, including Dwight D. Eisenhower—left the White House on July 7, 1919, for an epic transcontinental road trip to San Francisco. Following much of the route traced (but not built) by the Lincoln Highway project, the convoy reached its destination on September 6. West of the Mississippi River most roads and bridges were poor or nonexistent, and the average travel time of fifty miles per day was probably an achievement.[6]

The availability of federal and state funds provoked the issuance of millions of dollars in county bond financings for Texas road projects. Between 1917 and

1921, the THD built or had under construction some 682 miles of trunk (main) roads and 1,632 miles of secondary roads. Total cost for these projects was $23.5 million. Some 110 Texas counties had approved road bonds in 1919, but Texas lagged behind a number of states in road construction activities. Pennsylvania allocated $50 million for highways in 1918 and Illinois authorized $60 million.[7]

The first improved surfacing project under THD supervision was a twenty-five-mile stretch of future I-35 between the Travis and Comal county lines. Started in July 1918, a single half-inch bituminous treatment surface was applied to a fifteen-foot-wide roadway. The project was completed in March 1919, at a cost of $58,366, shared by the federal government ($22,745), the state ($14,882), and the counties ($15,938). This project and a concurrent bituminous rock asphalt surfacing project within Travis County were segments of an ambitious $3.4 million plan to build the 442 miles of Highway 2. As indicated, the so-called Meridian Highway was intended to run between Ringgold (not Gainesville), Fort Worth, Cleburne, Waco, Austin, San Antonio, and Laredo.[8]

Bypassed by Highway 2 and omitted from the *Texas State Highway Guide* of 1918, Gainesville finally woke up to the necessity of having a Red River highway bridge. The need had been discussed as early as 1903, but county voters had failed to act. Congressman Marvin Jones, a Garner protégé and future Agriculture Committee chair, spearheaded efforts to organize a Red River Toll Bridge Company in 1917. Capitalized at sixty thousand dollars, the new Company finally opened Cooke County's first bridge crossing to Oklahoma (via Highway 40) in February 1919. The bridge's history would be brief. Refurbished in 1927 after a costly fire, the bridge turned out to be too narrow for modern traffic. The span was sold to Texas and Oklahoma for thirty-five thousand dollars in 1930, dismantled for scrap, and replaced by a toll-free, state-of-the-art concrete bridge (for US 77) in 1931.[9]

While 110 counties had initiated road projects in 1919, only 15 percent of Texas' roads were improved by 1921. Few of the projects were integrated into a statewide system. A number of improved roads would simply end at the county line or be halted in midstream. Potential scale economies in planning, purchasing, construction, maintenance, and administration were neglected. Every county had its own operations and chaos reigned. Still, the worst gravel sections were usually superior to traditional dirt, sand, and clay, and so the projects continued despite the inefficiencies. In 1921, $25 million were spent on designated state highways and another $25 million were spent by Texas counties.

This $50 million investment was more than twice the total expenditures made in Texas between 1917 and 1921.[10]

In November 1921, an amendment to the Federal Aid Road Act of 1916 required states to designate certain routes as potential interstate highways, not to exceed 7 percent of the state's total road mileage. Under this "7 percent system," the Bureau of Public Roads classified roads either as paved primary/interstate highways or secondary/intercounty roads, and it gave state highway departments until 1925 to be responsible for a project's entire funding and construction process. All of the 7 percent construction contracts had to be administered by state highway departments, not by local units, to promote nationwide standards (and to cut out ineffective county commissions). The entire federal-aid route system was designated by November 1923.[11]

Despite the THD's designation of 8,865 miles of highways, or 6.9 percent of the state's 129,000 miles of roads, Texas was again ineligible for the federal funding opportunities. Texas counties simply refused to give up control of road project funds. In response, the TGRA reconfigured itself as the Texas Highway Association in 1922 and lobbied to centralize financial administration with the THD and to promote a connected system of paved highways. Some 6,532 miles of roads were surfaced in Texas in 1923, but rarely with concrete—this despite the fact that Texas was rich in gravel, rocks, limestone, and asphalt (mined in Uvalde County) and had an interested partner in Washington, Uvalde's own John Nance Garner. Most of the federal aid, including that for priority interstate highways between urban centers and county seats, had been allocated to graded earth, sand-clay, and gravel roads.[12]

Congressman Garner apparently supported plans to construct a Pan American Highway between Laredo and Mexico City (and beyond). The plans were unveiled between 1923 and 1925, after wartime tensions between the United States and Mexico had finally eased and a new highway bridge had been completed between the two Laredos in 1922. The old 1889 Convent Street Bridge had been rebuilt after a tornado in 1905 but was destroyed by a mysterious fire in April 1920. A temporary wooden structure was used until the new bridge was completed by the Laredo Bridge Company in February 1922. The new 820-foot-long span was constructed with reinforced concrete, supported by five three-hinged ribbed arches, and utilizing the existing (refurbished) stone piers and abutments from the earlier structure. The new bridge was tested almost immediately when the flood of June 1922 raised water levels to nearly forty-four feet. Approach roads on the Mexican side were destroyed, but the new bridge held firm.[13]

Mexico had focused so heavily on railroads during the Díaz regime that the nation's highway network was essentially nonexistent. In 1921, Mexico reported just 283 miles of national highways (versus an estimated 4,660 miles in 1821), and it had fewer than 45,000 registered vehicles in 1924. But when the Conference of the Pan American States met in Santiago (1924) and Buenos Aires (1925) to survey and select possible routes for a system of paved highways in Latin America, Mexican president Plutarco Elías Calles responded. He established a National Roads Commission to construct or improve over 2,600 miles of Mexican roads between 1924 and 1928, including upgrades to the ancient east-west Caminos Reales between Veracruz, Mexico City, and Acapulco. Construction on the Pan American Highway began in 1925 and the first forty-mile segment between Mexico City and Pachuca (en route to Laredo) opened in 1926. Progress was extremely slow, however, and construction funds would have to be diverted from other highway projects to maintain any kind of momentum.[14]

In Texas, the first gasoline tax was instituted (one cent per gallon) in June 1923—four years after the tax had been inaugurated in Oregon. Funds generated by the new gas tax totaled $2.9 million in 1924 and raised the probability that beleaguered road contractors would be compensated on a more timely basis. Contractors like Brown and Root had typically been paid with "paving notes," intermediate-term bonds secured only by local real estate. However, the gas tax and a proposed amendment to transfer a larger portion of the receipts to the THD were challenged by federal and state lawsuits. The gasoline tax was upheld by the U.S. Supreme Court in *Pierce Oil v. Luther Hopkins* (1924), and in *Robbins v. Limestone County* (1925) the court ruled that funds generated from auto registration fees and gas taxes could be transferred to the state.[15]

The Robbins ruling cleared the way for the Highway Act of 1925. The act gave the THD exclusive control of federally funded road projects and provided the State Highway Fund with increased control over fee and gas tax revenues. Three-fourths of these revenues were allocated to the State Highway Fund and the remainder was contributed to the Texas Available School Fund. Since a constitutional amendment of January 1, 1924, had given the THD responsibility for maintaining and evaluating 10 percent (or 18,000 miles) of Texas roads—more miles than the 7 percent road system—the new gas tax would be put to good use. Texas' state roads were subsequently categorized as first-class, second-class, or third-class. Maintenance specifications were redefined for earthen roads and surfaced roads. After four years of delay, Texas was finally eligible for the expanded BPR funding opportunities.[16]

These funding and organizational initiatives addressed a developing circular trend. As automobiles proliferated, more roads were being surfaced. As more roads were being surfaced, more automobiles and gasoline were being sold. This, is turn, added more refineries, more gasoline stations, and more wear and tear on the nation's road system. By 1925, 975,000 automobiles were registered in Texas versus only 40,000 in 1915. At the county level, for example, automobile registrations in Bell County had risen from a few hundred in 1913 to over 6,000 in 1923 in a county with a population of around 50,000.[17]

OFF-RAMP: NATIONAL TRENDS

Nationally, the surge in U.S. vehicle registrations from 7.6 million in 1919 to 19.9 million in 1925 required new schemes to coordinate exploding and increasingly chaotic traffic volumes. One major initiative was to devise a more coherent highway numbering and marking system. A Joint Board of State and Federal Highway Officials had been created by the USDA and AASHO in 1923, and states were asked to recommend 7 percent routes for a new interstate system. Selections were approved in the fall of 1925 and the new system was formally adopted in November 1926. The Joint Board designated certain routes as federal interstate highways and replaced over 250 named highways with a uniform system of numbers and markings. Some 70,000 miles of the 200,000-mile 7 percent system were now designated as numbered, interstate highways.[18]

Colorful highway names like the Bankhead, Meridian, and Dixie were replaced by simple if rather bland numbers. East-west routes were assigned even numbers—10 through 40 in northern states; 50 through 90 in the South. Thus the Dixie Overland Highway was assigned US 80 and the Old Spanish Trail between Saint Augustine and San Diego via San Antonio became US 90. North-south routes were assigned odd numbers. The Meridian Highway became US 81 and US 77 through Texas. All federal interstate highways were marked with a new black-and-white shield logo.[19]

While the nation's highways were being organized, numbered, and signed, an entirely new infrastructure of gasoline and service stations, autocamps, tourist homes, and restaurants began to proliferate. Texas was right in the middle of it. Emerging chains like Pig Stand (founded in Dallas in 1921), A&W, Dairy Queen, and countless other roadside stands and businesses were usually located on the outskirts of town. Real estate was cheaper, and they needed parking space. The first gasoline stations had evolved from horse-drawn tank wagons into curbside affairs, attached to a local general store or livery stable. As business boomed, lines formed and bypasses were constructed. This forced gas retailers to relocate to larger, free-standing filling stations on the edge of town. Gradually, national chains like Gulf Refining Company, Shell, and Standard Oil began to appear with uniform logos, standardized, often prefabricated stations, and underground storage tanks. From a single refinery in Port Arthur, the acquisitive Texas Company managed to assemble an expanding chain of four thousand Texaco gas stations by 1926.[20]

Our modern interstate highway system has been accused of destroying downtown shopping centers and blighting the roadside landscape, but this process was initiated in the early 1920s. As auto ownership soared, traffic congestion increased. This congestion, in turn, prompted county and state planners to build bypass routes around the traditional town centers. The new bypass routes, in turn, catalyzed the development of waves of service businesses on the outskirts, drawing retail sales dollars away from downtown businesses and adding new forms of advertising to the visual landscape.

Of course, every one of these "car culture" schemes, innovations, and investments depended on improved highways. As new road projects were rolled out, highway research departments experimented with new limestone, rock asphalt, and concrete formulations. Subgrade material tests and soil science tests were introduced. Various water-to-cement mixtures were tested in concrete paving projects. Efforts were made to standardize gravel gradings and road repair techniques, including the introduction of bituminous concrete patches (cold mix) and penetration patches. Not all of these innovations were successful, but road quality was clearly improving.[21]

Experimentation was everywhere. In Bell County, the home of Salado attorney-turned-governor James E. Ferguson, a nine-mile "Invisible Track Highway" had been constructed between Belton and Temple prior to 1917. The invisible tracks were bricks sandwiched between layers of concrete, crushed stones, and asphalt. The asphalt was applied with a special concave roller to produce a convex surface that, theoretically, would hold vehicles on the brick tracks and reduce skidding. Unfortunately, the new mixed surface became somewhat lumpy with use, particularly the asphalt sections. At around thirty thousand dollars per mile, the technique was also very expensive. Requests to repave the deteriorating stretch with modern materials were ignored. The THD apparently preferred to leave the Invisible Track Highway as a testament to "Pa" Ferguson's controversial legacy. Ferguson deserves credit, however, for at least one successful highway project. In 1915, he commissioned V. N. Zivley to survey the Old San Antonio Road (Camino Real) between Presidio del Rio Grande and Nacogdoches.[22]

The State Highway Act of 1925 had provided the State Highway Commission with enough financial control to meet the federal 7 percent system requirements. Auto registration fees were increased, and a portion of the fee was allocated to the THD for maintenance operations. Prior to January 1924, road maintenance had been the sole responsibility of the counties. The Act of 1925 also sought to improve management controls by requiring competitive bidding for road maintenance contracts and by specifying allocation procedures. County commissions were still involved in the decision-making process, but their authority was sharply curtailed by the act and by *Robbins vs. Limestone County*. The counties fought almost every effort to tighten state control until 1932.

Just as the THD had come into its own, it was rocked by scandal. Potential problems were foreshadowed by the resignation of State Highway Engineer Gibb Gilchrist in February 1925, immediately after Miriam A. ("Ma") Ferguson's inauguration as governor. The resignation was prompted either by a conflict between Gilchrist and the BPR's Texas district engineer (an ally of the Fergusons) or by Gilchrist's unwillingness to "play ball" with the Fergusons. According to Gilchrist: "I, along with many others, realized that we had no chance and we had no desire to serve under a Ferguson Commission." The resignation is of interest because a scandal loomed and Gilchrist, a former construction engineer with the Gulf, Colorado, and Santa Fe, returned to the THD in 1928 and became somewhat of a legend.[23]

The 1924 election campaign was a bizarre one, pitting the wife of impeached ex-governor "Pa" Ferguson against candidates backed by the powerful Ku Klux Klan lobby. A brutal period of southern lynchings (1890–1917) including the nationally publicized "Waco Horror" in May of 1916 had ended, but the Texas KKK claimed nearly a hundred thousand members in the early 1920s. Led by a thirteen-thousand-strong Dallas chapter, a KKK Day was held at the Texas State Fair in 1923. If Ma Ferguson's victory over the KKK in 1924 was a vote for decency, the Fergusons nevertheless ran an old-fashioned, Tammany

Hall–styled political patronage system that was rife with corruption. The "power behind the throne," James E. Ferguson, apparently attended every (closed-door) meeting of the State Highway Commission during his wife's administration. Between February 1925 and February 1927, there were eight different highway commissioners and four different state highway engineers.[24]

While the Fergusons may not have broken any laws personally, many of their appointee friends were found to have sold state jobs and prison pardons, received kickbacks on school supply contracts, and inflated the cost of state road projects. A number of contracts were awarded as traditional political payoffs to campaign contributors. Investigated and prosecuted by Attorney General Daniel J. Moody (a future governor), a few road maintenance contracts were found to have involved irregular bidding procedures and/or inflated bills that were three times their actual value. Suspicious contracts totaled $30 million or more—big money in the 1920s. At a fateful meeting on April 7, 1925, the commissioners had let a road-surfacing contract to the American Road Company that would (allegedly) scam over $600,000 in excess profits from the state. Twenty-two separate charges were eventually filed against the THD relating to similarly inflated prices for purchased equipment, materials, and services. Investigations continued through 1929.[25]

The credibility of the THD was hurt badly, if temporarily, and the BPR refused to fund any projects until the THD was reorganized. The BPR halted assistance to Arkansas in 1926 for similar reasons. Normalcy and BPR funding returned with Moody's victory in the gubernatorial election in 1926—"No Ma for Me, Too Much Pa" convincingly beat the "Me for Ma" forces. The THD was subsequently reorganized in 1927 and Gibb Gilchrist was invited back as state highway engineer in January 1928. Gilchrist continued in that post through September 1937—somehow including Mrs. Ferguson's second administration in 1933–34—and was eventually appointed president of Texas A&M in 1944.[26]

With order restored, THD finances were powered by the gasoline tax and license fees. Texas spent $12 million on roads in 1926, but collected $14 million from these two sources: $4 million from the gasoline tax and $10 million from auto registration fees. The gasoline tax, however, was a moving target. It was tripled to three cents per gallon in 1927, generating tax revenues of $7 million dollars, then decreased to two cents in 1928, and doubled to four cents in 1929. Despite frequent proposals for bond financings, Texas highways would continue to be funded by a "pay as you go" philosophy until the year 2000.[27]

As construction activities expanded, designated U.S. highways were always paved before state roads, and state roads were always paved before secondary roads. Federal funds were received only after BPR inspectors had given their approval to completed work. Texas would lead the nation with 3,741 miles of paved roads in 1933, followed by North Carolina with 2,427, but there was much work to do. Other than the highway between Fort Worth and Dallas, hard-surfaced in 1926, few of the other state roads in Tarrant County would be paved by 1933. Because of financial limitations, most state highway departments including the THD were left to focus on earthen, rural roads.[28]

But roads were being paved. Surfaced road milage in the U.S. nearly doubled between 1921 and 1930, from 387,000 miles to 694,000, and would double again to 1.4 million miles in 1940. During the period 1921–30, states spent nearly $8 billion on roads and received only $839 million in federal aid for their efforts. Road traffic was exploding. Registrations in the U.S. soared from 10.5 million in 1920 to 26.7 million in 1929. By 1929, over 50 percent of U.S. families owned an automobile, and every state in the nation had a gasoline tax; these ranged from two to six cents per gallon. In Texas, nearly 1.4 million vehicles were registered by 1929, versus less than 200,000 registrations when the THD was created in 1917.[29]

As competition and technological innovations broadened the market for automobiles and trucks, traffic and road conditions worsened. Higher traffic meant higher maintenance requirements, and unimproved roads were estimated to be $250–300 per mile more expensive to maintain than paved ones. Concrete paved roads were expected to last thirty to forty years but required a heavy front-end investment. Since the counties had never maintained roads very well, the THD's assumption of state road maintenance in January 1924, could only help matters. Maintenance emerged as the largest single item in the THD budget, with an allocation of $4.5 million in 1924, and the division's three thousand employees represented over half of the THD workforce. Maintenance standards would eventually have to meet BPR guidelines assigned in 1927–28.[30]

In the 1920s, the THD's labor force consisted of internal units and approved county crews. Most counties cooperated readily with the THD and were happy to share mechanized earthmovers, paving equipment, and other construction systems. The THD's maintenance fleet included 270 tractors, including Caterpillars, Holts, Monarchs, and Fordsons, 450 trucks, 500 horse-drawn "fresnos" (scrapers), and 1,000 drags. Dragging equipment was in great demand for smoothing out ruts and bumps, filling holes, and transferring ditch dirt to the main road. Magnetic nail pickers were prized as well. The THD's District Nine reported that its magnetic nail picker collected 6,062 pounds of nails, bolts, wire, and other metallic objects between 1928 and 1930. Paint-stripe machines were developed at Camp Mabry in Austin.[31]

A proposal to lease a thousand state prison convicts for THD maintenance operations was rejected, but convicts worked regularly on county and local projects. One such project even launched a career. Before joining the THD in 1927, future state highway engineer Dewitt C. Greer was employed by the new Texas State Parks Board in 1924 to build a campsite along the Guadalupe River near Boerne. The construction crew consisted of twenty-six "honor" convicts from Huntsville (all white), and by all accounts the project was a great success. It was dubbed the Pat Neff Honor Camp to honor the former governor and the work crew. All twenty-six men were eventually pardoned by the Fergusons.[32]

The THD's cost of maintenance averaged $495 per mile in 1928 but would decline with depression-era deflation to $303 in 1934. A skilled tractor operator earned fifty cents per hour in 1930, but most unskilled workers received less than twenty-five cents. The THD lobbied to raise the minimum wage to at least thirty cents per hour on state contracts in 1930. Of course, most maintenance work was labor intensive. A maintenance man in Leon County was supplied with only a pickup truck, an axe, and a lantern. Asphalt was carried to construction sites in forty- to fifty-gallon open-topped barrels and then applied manually. After spending his days applying asphalt by hand from a five-gallon jug, one Brownwood worker reported that he burned through one pair of shoes and two pairs of gloves each day.[33]

Signing was another maintenance job. Like the marking of Indian trails, the first highway markers had been stripes painted around trees or telephone and telegraph poles. The first stop sign appeared in Detroit in 1915, numbered routes were introduced in Wisconsin in 1918, and the first four-way, three-colored traffic light was placed in Michigan in 1920. By the early 1920s, signs began to indicate distance, direction to the next town, and warning and safety alerts. In Texas, some one hundred thousand markers and caution signs were installed along federal and designated state highways by 1929. Most signs were wooden affairs until metal signs were introduced in the mid-1930s, enhanced by reflectors in the 1940s.[34]

Meanwhile, an entire industry of road material contractors and their promoters had evolved to meet the state's growing needs. By 1930, the THD conducted business with forty-two sand and gravel companies, sixteen crushed stone operations, nine cement plants, three rock asphalt firms, three oil asphalt refineries, and six creosoting plants. As natural rock asphalt came to the fore, the introduction of a premixed, cold spreading and rolling process began to replace the conventional method of crushing and mixing hot asphalt (280 to 330 degrees F) in onsite drums. In addition to asphalt, contractors and material scientists continued to experiment with new road surfaces. The most unusual idea was the application of a layer of cotton fabric to a road project in Gonzales. It failed.[35]

Between 1917 and 1929, $133.5 million in road improvement projects had been completed in Texas—$57.6 million funded by counties, $43.6 million by the federal government, and $32.3 million by the state. Yet, the state role was gaining in importance. Over 2,000 miles of Texas roads received state assistance in 1929 (versus only 250 miles in 1918), and county aid would disappear entirely in 1932. In 1928, after categorizing the 16,000-mile designated system by surface type, the THD estimated that 10,000 miles were represented by dirt roads, 5,000 by gravel, stone, or shell, 1,060 by asphalt, and all of 96 miles by concrete. At around $27,000 per mile, concrete was twice as expensive as bituminous tar ($13,000 per mile) and over five times as costly as macadam and gravel ($5,100 per mile). Dirt roads continued to receive most of the attention, but the trend was toward concrete and asphalt.[36]

Some 1,037 miles of new concrete roads were built at a cost of $26 million between 1928 and 1930. Another 1,100 miles of gravel roads were upgraded with surface treatments. These totals surpassed the 1,691 miles of dirt roads that were graded and improved with drainage structures (at a cost of only $12 million). Supported by $10 million in BPR funds and a doubling of the gasoline tax to four cents in 1929, over 6,000 of Texas' 180,000 miles of roads were improved with a hard surface and/or macadam, tar, and gravel by 1929. Indiana claimed 50,000 miles of improved roads and Ohio 42,000, but definitions were key. High-type concrete and low-type gravel roads both counted as "improved."[37]

The THD introduced its first highway map in 1929, still indicating routes as straight lines—not by their actual course and mileage from town to town. Rand McNally had introduced its first road atlas in 1926 with a careful description of local surface conditions. According to Rand McNally, northeastern states, Texas, and California had the nation's best roads. Of interest to I-35 historians is the fact that the map declined to indicate any roads between San

Antonio and the Rio Grande. A more detailed depiction of Texas roads would await the introduction of the Gulf Oil Map of 1933 and the Texas Centennial Map of 1936.[38]

Old two-lane roads were becoming obsolete. In 1927, provisions of the Act of 1884 were finally revised, increasing right-of-way widths on Texas' first-class roads from 40–60 feet to a maximum of 80 feet. The federal government, however, had begun to require 100-foot rights-of-way on new highways, and the THD was encouraging 120-foot widths. All of these goals were outstripped by a 150-foot wide, four-lane highway completed between Houston and Galveston in 1929. That same year, Tarrant County approved a $5 million program to upgrade county highways to four lanes. Four lanes or two, travel times continued to be constrained by railroad grade crossings and the added expense of underpasses and overpasses. The state highway system was burdened by some 1,400 railroad crossings plus another 4,000 crossings on county roads.[39]

Counties were still authorized to initiate road-building projects and to acquire rights-of-way, thereby providing advocates of a comprehensive state highway system reasons for concern. As of 1929, the future route of I-35 still had gaps in Cooke County, north of Gainesville (US 77/SH 40), southeastern Denton County (US 77/SH 40), much of Ellis County (US 77/SH 6), and in stretches of Highway 2 between Bexar and Laredo. Congressman Garner had helped to deliver a $27,373 highway bridge across the Nueces River at Cotulla in 1925, but a gap existed in La Salle County between Dilley and Encinal. This stretch of dirt road was traveled by twenty-year-old Lyndon B. Johnson when he was a schoolteacher in Cotulla in 1928–29. While Garner was also behind a December 1928 plan to construct a Rio Grande Valley highway between Eagle Pass and Brownsville via Laredo, the *San Antonio Express* of October 29, 1929, reported that a paving project between Cotulla and Laredo was still under way.[40]

Whenever Highway 2 was actually completed, the entire route was stitched together to form US 81 (and/or US 77) between Laredo and the Red River. This was a predecessor highway to I-35 and a northern segment of the proposed Pan American Highway. Including those in Laredo, thirteen international toll bridges, with permits from the U.S. and Mexican governments, were in operation between El Paso and Brownsville by 1930. Most were narrow suspension bridges, but a few had been constructed with steel trusses and pile trestles. The most impressive span was the 1922 concrete arch bridge at Laredo. The latest Convent Street (International) Bridge was intended to link Highway 2

(US 81) with a route that would become the Pan American Highway from Monterrey. Having already survived the flood of June 1922, the new bridge remained intact through the floods of September 1932; June 1935; and June 1948. The devastating flood of 1954, however, would be another matter.[41]

If the decade of the 1920s was considered a golden era for road building, even more ambitious highway plans were afoot. In October 1929, just prior to the stock market crash, a proposal was made to build a "superhighway" between Austin and San Antonio. This segment was regarded as the most heavily traveled route in Texas after that between Dallas and Fort Worth. The new highway was intended to cut the present route (Highway 2, US 81) by eight miles and eliminate all dangerous curves and twelve grade crossings. It would also have a hundred-foot right-of-way and a forty-foot paved roadway. This superhighway would be eventually built—but not in the 1930s.[42]

Improved roads facilitated the automobile and trucking industries. There was also an explosion of bus companies. The first bus service in Texas had been started in 1907 by W. C. Chenoweth between Colorado City and Snyder in West Texas. Chenoweth served the twenty-eight-mile route with a novel six-cylinder vehicle of his own design. In Cooke County, an "auto stage" line of converted automobiles operated between Gainesville and nearby towns in 1909, eventually extended to Dallas by 1924, and then sold to Denton-based Freeman and Freeman's Red Ball service in 1929. The Freemans highlighted their smallish, customized 12- to 15-seat Reo buses before selling out to Dixie Motor Coaches that same year. Dixie owned a modern fleet of one hundred 25- to 30-passenger buses and eight terminals, but it too was soon dwarfed by larger lines.[43]

Nearly three hundred bus lines were working Texas highways in 1929, following a business pattern set by wagon freighters, stage companies, and railroads in the prior century. Together, they covered some 32,000 miles of routes and carried nearly 5 million passengers. The year also marked the opening of a $350,000, state-of-the-art bus terminal in San Antonio and the emergence of Greyhound Lines. Founded in 1913 as a seven-passenger Hupmobile service between Hibbing, Minnesota, and the Mesaba Iron Range mines, predecessors of Greyhound were reorganized as the Southland–Red Ball Motor Bus Company in Texas in 1927. By 1929, Southland–Red Ball was acquiring more regional lines and providing service between Dallas–Fort Worth and Laredo. After consolidating with three more long-distance lines—Yelloway, Pickwick, and the bus unit of the Southern Pacific Railroad—the new entity was reorganized again as Greyhound Corporation in February 1930. Greyhound's 1,800-bus national system would dominate the industry for decades.[44]

The emergence of Greyhound and other long-distance bus lines indicated that an interstate highway system was coming together, planned or not. Despite the achievements of the 1920s, the explosion of automobiles, heavy trucks, and buses had left their mark, literally and figuratively, on the nation's fledgling road network. Many recently paved roads had been so abused by expanding traffic volumes and weights that they would have to be repaved. Hundreds of new concrete and steel bridges were already obsolete. Added to these concerns was the Great Depression. Matching funds from state, county, and local sources would nearly evaporate, and an increasingly large share of U.S. road-building activities would be assumed by the federal government.

OFF-RAMP: THE GREAT DEPRESSION

The Depression years involved great hardships for most Americans, including Texans, but highway and bridge projects expanded greatly. Road projects were the beneficiaries of a number of new federal initiatives, starting with Herbert Hoover's establishment of the Reconstruction Finance Corporation (RFC) in January 1932. Franklin D. Roosevelt retained its talented director, Jesse H. Jones, and converted the RFC from a modest emergency backstop for banks, savings and loans, railroads, and farms into a $3 billion public works program. Roosevelt's own New Deal initiatives included the Federal Emergency Relief Agency between 1933 and 1935, the Civil Works Administration (CWA) between 1933 and 1934, and the Works Progress Administration (WPA) and Public Works Administration between 1935 and 1943. These public works programs were supplemented by the Agricultural Adjustment Acts (1933 and 1938), the Civilian Conservation Corps (1933), the Hayden-Cartwright Act (1934), and the National Youth Administration (1935).[45]

Thanks to the extraordinary capabilities of three prominent Texans—Vice President John Nance Garner, House Majority Leader (and future speaker) Sam Rayburn, RFC Chairman Jesse H. Jones—and seven Texan-chaired committees (Agriculture, Appropriations, Interstate and Foreign Commerce, Judiciary, Military Affairs, Public Buildings, and Rivers and Harbors), Texas received a substantial share of federal funds during the Depression years. Through June 1938, Texas received nearly $1.5 billion in New Deal funds, and it trailed only New York, Pennsylvania, and Illinois in the prime 1933–37 period. Garner was instrumental. After he became Speaker of the House on December 7,

1931, his bill to invest $1.2 billion in public works and add $1 billion to the RFC's capitalization passed both houses before being vetoed by President Hoover. The proposal would bear fruit in subsequent New Deal programs under FDR and gave Vice President Garner full reign over the flagship CWA.[46]

Still, Texas' political luminaries were focused more on national needs than on local ones. Garner, a fiscal conservative and, like Jones, a self-made millionaire, declared in the mid-1930s that "I have tried my damndest to keep out of Texas politics." The pro-Garner *Laredo Times* had even been compelled to write on July 20, 1922, that "we do not measure [Garner's] service in terms of 'pork' that has been secured." Rayburn declined to join Garner's celebrated break with FDR over the direction of the New Deal in late 1936, but the tight relationship between Texas and Washington nevertheless weakened after 1936. Local initiatives spawned from Rayburn's hideaway "Board of Education" room, a strategy (and bourbon-drinking) office started by Garner, were restricted mainly to rural electrification, farm-to-market roads, and independent oil men. After winning approval in June 1938, for his one major pet project, the Denison Dam complex, Rayburn confessed that he did not have a "favorite" contractor and that he had never introduced a bill to spend a single dollar of federal money in the district he represented.[47]

Rayburn's integrity and that of Garner may not have pleased all in Depression-wracked Texas, however—an estimated 348,000 Texans were unemployed in December 1932, and the number of Texans on relief peaked at 1.1 million in January 1935. The 40 percent of the state population living on farms (60 percent as tenants) were devastated by the plunge in cotton prices to five cents per pound in 1930. These dire economic conditions forced the THD to assume ownership of the entire state road network in 1932 and to assume all of the outstanding bond and warrant indebtedness of the devastated counties. A State Board of County and Road District Indebtedness was established to administer the county and subunit debt obligations. After October 1, 1932, one-fourth of the gas tax (one cent per gallon) was allocated to a County and Road District Highway Fund; one-half to the State Highway Fund; and one-fourth to the Available School Fund.[48]

These actions meant that after nearly a hundred years of road management, the counties' sole responsibility would be reduced to providing rights-of-way for the state's 12,800-mile and growing highway system. Based on the evidence, the reduction in county responsibilities had a positive effect. Between 1927 and 1937, some $300 million were invested in Texas roads and bridges and another

$100 million were spent on maintenance. By July 31, 1937, nearly 75 percent of the state highway system was paved. While state bridge spending totaled only $27.5 million during this ten-year period, highway engineers had discovered that an improved highway had rather limited value unless new or widened bridges were installed en route.[49]

The importance of bridges, the need for interstate coordination, and the age-old conflict between public and private sectors were all on display in the so-called Red River Bridge War of 1931. By year-end in 1931, the upper Red River was crossed by eight free interstate bridges thanks to the cooperation of the Texas and Oklahoma highway departments. Two of the eight are of special interest. The franchise for the Highway 40 (US 77) toll bridge in Gainesville, completed only in February 1919, was purchased jointly for $35,000 and replaced by a new (free) bridge on September 7, 1931. Highlighted by seven 210-foot steel truss spans, the new $334,200, 1,559-foot-long Gainesville-Marietta bridge carries traffic along US 77 (and half of I-35) to this day. In addition, the new (free) Denison-Durant bridge on Highway 6 (US 75) was opened on July 25, 1931, at a cost of $238,645. The 1,242-foot-long bridge, with four 250-foot steel truss spans and one of 80 feet, was intended to replace the 577-foot-long, 16-foot-wide toll bridge that Ben Colbert had constructed with $40,000 of his own money in 1875. Colbert's bridge had been washed away in July 1876, rebuilt by the Red River Bridge Company (RRBC) in 1892 (one year prior to Colbert's death), washed away in 1908, and rebuilt once more in 1915. This was the problem.[50]

The ensuing bridge war erupted in 1929, after the THD had sited the new (free) bridge for Highway 6 (US 75) half a mile upstream from Colbert's rebuilt bridge. Unlike the other seven Red River bridge owners, including the Gainesville enterprise, the feisty owners of the RRBC simply refused to sell out. Texas and Oklahoma responded by filing an injunction against the RRBC, halting toll collection, and sending the company into receivership. Confusion reigned when Oklahoma decided to withdraw from the joint-acquisition plan, citing a study that bridge traffic flows benefited Texas more than they did Oklahoma. In response, the THD went ahead and cut an open-ended (and ultimately illegal) deal with the RRBC in July 1930.[51]

The new Denison-Durant bridge was completed in early April 1931, three months ahead of schedule. Fearing accurately that its side deal with the THD would be declared invalid, the RRBC and its receivers managed to delay the opening of the new bridge by filing an injunction against the THD, supported by a federal court order. This in turn prompted Oklahoma governor William H. "Alfalfa Bill" Murray to action. On July 16, he issued an executive order to open both the Denison-Durant bridge and the unfinished Gainesville-Marietta bridge. Even more defiantly, Murray erected barricades to block traffic to Colbert's bridge and, citing recent interpretations of the Adams-Onis Treaty, then crossed over to the Texas side to destroy the southern approach roads.[52]

Texas governor Ross S. Sterling replied to Murray's border incursion as follows: "I feel you have exceeded your jurisdiction by all reason." On July 17, Sterling ordered four Texas Rangers to the scene and had barricades placed in front of the new bridge. The Bridge War was on. The situation, fueled by intensifying national media coverage, could be described as either tense or hilarious. Fortunately, the stalemate was broken by a creative measure. Texas Senate Bill 9, passed unanimously and signed by Sterling, permitted the RRBC to sue the THD for breach of contract, thereby allowing the RRBC to lift its injunction. The new bridge could finally open on July 25.[53]

In the meantime, Murray was determined to milk the national publicity for a few more days. He responded to the pending bridge opening by declaring martial law on July 24, dispatching thirty-three Oklahoma national guardsmen to Colbert's bridge, and then visiting the war zone himself on July 25 (armed with a pistol). The media would be disappointed. According to an Associated Press report of July 24, 1931, "hostilities apparently were limited to an incident last night on the Texas side, when Captain Tom Hickman of the rangers chased a pedestrian back across the free bridge to Oklahoma. The man was alleged to have cursed the Governor of Texas in the presence of women. . . . Lieutenant Colonel John A. McDonald, commanding the Oklahoma troops, was told . . . to hold the fort, but keep the cost down."[54]

Peace was finally restored. Whether the events of 1931 influenced the future routing of I-35 through Gainesville rather than through the traditional Red River gateway at Denison is an interesting question. But in the meantime, the ambitious Red River bridge program had at least been funded, and construction of Texas' two premier highways—Highway 1 (US 67 and US 80) between Texarkana and El Paso, and Highway 2 (US 81 and US 77) between Laredo and the Red River—began to accelerate despite daunting bridge requirements. More positively, US 80 (the Dallas–Fort Worth Road) was upgraded to an impressive four-lane highway in 1934. The road had been graveled since 1910 and paved since 1920. But when traffic volume doubled to around eight thousand vehicles per day in 1930, a major upgrade became necessary.

Over $1.5 million was spent to widen bridges and construct underpasses en route.[55]

Dallas had experimented with reinforced concrete with the Houston Street Viaduct across the Trinity River between Dallas and Oak Cliff, completed between October 1910 and February 1912, and financed by $610,000 in Dallas County bonds. The 6,562-foot-long Houston Street structure, the first of six major viaducts, had been designed with fifty-one arches to withstand the Trinity's seasonal flooding and occasional rampaging. The great flood of May 1908, had devastated downtown and left nearly four thousand people homeless. Additional viaducts and other investments (including Union Station in 1916 and Love Field in 1917) had been recommended by the George E. Kessler Plan of 1912 and the subsequent C. E. Ulrickson Plan of 1927. The 1927 plan was promoted by an officer of the Trinity Portland Cement Company. The devastating floods of 1921 and 1922 had hastened the completion of the $5 million Garza Dam on the Elm Fork of the Trinity River in 1927. Dallas followed with large bond offerings to finance additional Trinity River reclamation and viaduct projects, although construction activities were delayed until after 1929.[56]

Four new steel and concrete viaducts would be placed over the Trinity River by 1936, and several highway underpasses were constructed beneath the major rail crossings. The Houston Street Viaduct had weathered the more recent floods, but the roadway was too narrow to handle the increasing traffic volumes. Dallas's population had exploded to 260,475 in 1930, and the need for new structures was clear. The $474,000 Cadiz Street Viaduct was completed in 1932, financed by Dallas County, and a related $313,500 underpass was funded by the city and associated railroad companies. The Cadiz Street projects were followed by the $745,500 Corinth Street Viaduct (1933), the $614,800 Lamar-McKinney Viaduct (1934), and the $642,000 Commerce Street Viaduct (1934).[57]

The six-lane Commerce Street Viaduct was located on the very site of Alexander Cockrell's first covered bridge and Sarah Cockrell's replacement iron bridge of 1872. Also in 1934, a $1 million contract was let for the famous Triple Underpass at the convergence of Commerce, Main, and Elm streets. Funded jointly by the federal government, the THD, the City of Dallas, and associated railroads, the Triple Underpass provided a dramatic entrance to downtown Dallas. The project was completed in May 1936, just in time for the

Texas Centennial Exposition and President Roosevelt's speech at the Cotton Bowl in June. When plans were laid to add a park area (Dealey Plaza) to the site, *Texas Parade* could report in January 1940, that "Dallas will have one of the most beautiful city entrances in Texas when beautification work on Dealey Plaza at the Main-Commerce-Elm triple underpass is completed."[58]

Dallas's spectacular highway and viaduct projects highlighted a growing disparity between urban-oriented state roads and secondary rural roads. Most of the 521 miles of US 81 and US 77 were paved by 1930, but travelers experienced gaps when surfacing and bridge projects remained in an unfinished state. Cooke County's 57 miles of state roads on January 1, 1937, principally US 77 and US 82, comprised 17 miles of concrete, 24 miles of asphalt, 3 miles of gravel or stone, and 12 miles of graded and drained earth (dirt) roads. But these state roads represented only a tiny fraction of the county's 1,096-mile road system. Only 349 miles of Cooke County roads were surfaced with gravel or stone, 724 miles were unimproved dirt roads, and 23 miles were so-called primitive roads. Completion of a two-lane concrete highway (US 77) between the new Gainesville-Marietta bridge (1931) and the Denton County line—a future segment of I-35—was delayed until September 1933. When US 77 was improved again in 1936, traffic was slowed until a new concrete bridge was completed across Elm Creek in 1938. In the meantime, travelers had to negotiate the narrow iron bridge that had spanned Elm Creek since 1894.[59]

US 81 received a fair amount of attention. One project of note was the successor to the Invisible Track Highway between Belton and Temple. After twenty years of lumpy road, $38,480 were finally appropriated in October 1936, to reconstruct the highway and build a new bridge across the Leon River. In Waco, the famous traffic circle at the junction of US 81 and US 77 was completed in May 1935. Farther south, US 81 was finally completed between Dilley and Encinal, but travelers were delayed by a new bridge project across the Frio River (between Dilley and Derby). The new 2,000-foot-long, $200,000 steel and concrete bridge was intended to replace an existing low-water structure.[60]

After a slow start, the THD managed to build over four thousand new bridges by 1937 and to refurbish hundreds of old ones. Thirty-five older bridges along the highway between San Antonio and Austin (US 81) were replaced, widened, or refurbished. Narrow, low-load bridges with timber trestles and old iron trusses, like the timber–steel truss bridge across the Blanco River at San Marcos, were replaced by larger metal truss and concrete structures. Austin's new $279,000 Montopolis Bridge, sited at the ancient ford of the Colorado River, included five 200-foot steel truss spans. In New Braunfels, a state-of-the-art concrete arch bridge was completed across the Guadalupe River in 1934, replacing an 1887 structure that had in its day been the state of the art. A new underpass was added below the I&GN in 1936. Even more imposing was the new Lancaster Avenue Bridge across the Clear Fork of the Trinity River in Fort Worth. When completed in early 1938, the $600,000, 2,976-foot structure carried rerouted US 80 traffic along a forty-foot-wide roadway.[61]

Improvements to US 81 focused on straightening curves (to one degree or less) and removing railroad crossings. The improved segment between Austin and San Antonio, designed to be expanded to two to three times its traffic load in 1936, was regarded as the flagship highway within the THD's so-called cardinal route system. South of Austin, grade crossings were removed by relocating the highway outside the town centers. Three railroad crossings between Kyle and Buda were eliminated, via a new bypass route, and two more crossings were bypassed in San Marcos. In San Antonio, the $266,500 Nogalitos Street underpass was built to carry US 81 traffic beneath the Katy and Texas and New Orleans railway crossings.[62]

San Antonio benefited from federal public works, military largesse, and the efforts of a firebrand New Dealer—Congressman and future Mayor Maury Maverick. After his defeat in 1938, Maverick declared "that the surprising thing was not that he had been defeated for re-election, but that he had ever been elected in the first place." Thanks to Maverick and local preservationists, funds (and jobs) were received to restore the Riverwalk, the La Villita district, the Espada aqueduct, the otherwise unrecognizable Spanish Governor's Palace, and the badly decayed Spanish missions. San Antonio had actually been promoting its Spanish colonial heritage since the state had acquired the Alamo in 1883, and "mission-style" railroad stations were built by the Southern Pacific (1902) and the I&GN (1907). Commerce Street served as an urban section of the Old Spanish Trail, completed in 1929 between St. Augustine, Florida, and San Diego.[63]

Farther south, plans were made to upgrade US 81 and the International Bridge at Laredo. Laredo's population had more than doubled between 1910 and 1930, from 14,855 to 32,618, and the number of registered vehicles in Webb County had tripled to 6,395 since 1922. Congestion was becoming a problem, and the Pan American Highway from Mexico City was on its way. Thanks to the efforts of President Lázaro Cárdenas and five thousand workers, the epic 762-mile road project was completed to Laredo by year's end in 1935 (map 12). State Highway Engineer Gilchrist and BPR Chief MacDonald confirmed the achievement in June 1936. A few mountainous sections remained to be paved, but the two-lane highway remained Laredo's principal route to Monterrey (and Mexico City) for decades. From Monterrey, the Pan American Highway bypassed the ancient Camino Real towns of Saltillo, Zacatecas, and Querétaro in favor of Linares, Victoria, Valles, Tamazunchale, and Jacala. From Jacala, the road zigzagged the remaining 175 miles (via Pachuca) to Mexico City. Officials boasted that no grade was steeper than six degrees and no curve was sharper than twenty-eight degrees. Of course, these levels were somewhat frightening by U.S. standards—US 81 in Texas had no curve sharper than one degree.[64]

To promote the Texas Centennial, the state's first color highway map was released in 1936 and thirteen tourist information stations were placed at major highway junctions. The Centennial Exposition itself was held in Dallas and attracted over six million visitors between June and November. The new highway map presented the future course of I-35 as three routes—US 81, US 377, and US 77. US 81 marked the route between Laredo and Waco and shared the Waco-Hillsboro stretch with US 77. From Hillsboro, the route split into two branches, just as it does today. One branch, US 81, continued to Fort Worth (en route to Ringgold), where it picked up US 377 to US 77 at Denton. The other branch, originating from Corpus Christi via Waco, left Hillsboro en route to Waxahachie, Dallas, and Denton. From Denton, US 77 headed north to Gainesville and Oklahoma.[65]

Since 1 percent of a state's federal highway funds could be used for landscaping, a landscape architect (Jac L. Gubbels) was hired in 1933 to manage the THD's 800,000 acres of rights-of-way. By 1939, over one million trees and shrubs were planted, many cultivated in a greenhouse built by a National Youth Administration (NYA) project team, and an estimated eighty tons of wildflower seeds were sown. The Civilian Conservation Corps (CCC) employed 102,760 Texans through January 1, 1938, in projects that included state parks in Bastrop, Goliad, San Saba, and other historic locations, roadside parks (390), and scenic turnouts (316). Nearly two hundred of these projects employed NYA students and school-age youths. The THD provided land, construction materials, supervision, and transportation to the sites, leaving the youths to do the rest. The land contributions took some doing. The THD was not authorized to purchase land, so the two- to three-acre park sites had to be donated by

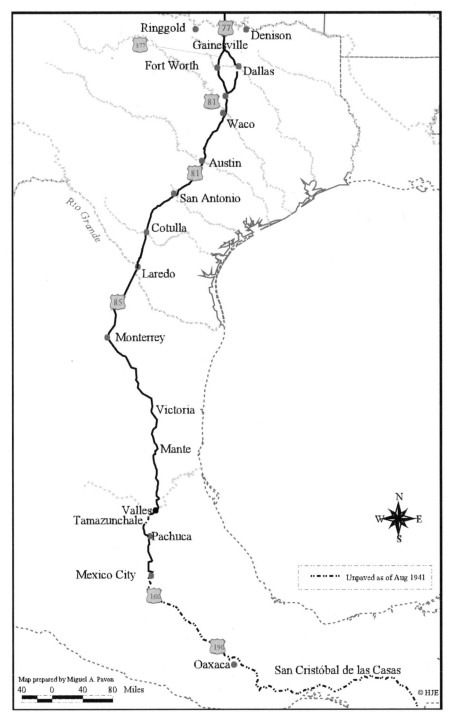

Map 12. Pan American Highway, 1936.

counties or property owners. For example, Dallas County allocated five thousand dollars to purchase and donate eight park sites in 1936.[66]

The NYA, initiated in June 1935, with a $50 million annual budget, eventually employed 500,000 youths between the ages of sixteen and twenty-five. The NYA was one of the few decentralized federal programs managed by individual state directors. The Texas directorship, thanks to the support of Governor James V. Allred and the intervention of Sam Rayburn, was somehow handed to twenty-six-year-old Lyndon B. Johnson. Having served on a Johnson City road crew in his early years, Johnson was receptive to roadside park projects and apparently did an excellent job as Texas' NYA director between 1935 and 1936. More than twenty thousand Texans received NYA assistance in 1936, and nearly $2 million in NYA funds were invested in the state. Daily wages were between a quarter and a dollar, enough money in those days to keep most high school and college students in school. One project close to Johnson's heart recruited a hundred farm youths and students to build three new dormitories at Southwest Texas State Teachers College in San Marcos.[67]

Parks and beautification programs made a significant contribution to Texas' roadside landscape. The NYA and a special relationship with Rayburn even served as a springboard for Johnson's spectacular rise in national affairs. Otherwise, beautification programs did little to offset the continuing proliferation of urban sprawl. Roadside stands and gas stations had responded to the exploding automobile sales of the 1920s, the paving of highways, and the creation of bypass routes. Commercial advertisements were banned from Texas highways in 1927 but were always permitted along adjacent properties. In the 1930s, the evolving car culture was taken to the next level. Drive-in window service was introduced, and the first standardized highway coffee shops, restaurants, and motor courts (some even with air conditioning) made their appearance.[68]

Business successes ranging from E. Lee Torrance's chain of Alamo Plaza Hotel Courts (started in Waco in 1929) to Howard D. Johnson's restaurant franchising concept (launched on Cape Cod in 1935) were achieved through private enterprise. Most Americans were not that skillful or fortunate. Government programs were required to provide massive amounts of funds for new construction projects and thereby create jobs for thousands of unemployed workers. During the depression years, between 35 percent and 45 percent of all U.S. workers on federal relief were involved with roads. About half a million were working on the nation's roads in 1932, funded in part by the first federal fuel tax (one cent per gallon) in that same year. As of September 1938, 47 percent of WPA employees were assigned to road projects.[69]

By 1938, 5,131 miles of the 19,218-mile Texas state highway system had been paved with "high type" surfaces, another 10,494 miles had been "improved," and only 3,593 miles of state roads remained in an "earthen" condition. These, of course, were state roads. Most of Texas' 151,099 miles of county roads remained in their natural state—127,039 miles were dirt, 23,288 miles were improved, and only 772 miles were paved. Depressed wage rates had at least helped to control the THD's maintenance budget. After tripling between 1924 ($142) and 1930 ($428), maintenance costs per mile declined to $355 in 1940. During the depression, the THD could usually hire a truck and driver for around $8 per day and employ local workers for less than $3.50. Foremen made no more than $125 per month. To spread employment opportunities, no one was permitted to work more than thirty hours per week.[70]

Working the roads was no vacation. In a December 1937 letter to Secretary of Labor Frances Perkins from Ogden, Utah, the wife of a federal road camp employee complained about leaky tents, gasoline lanterns that did not light, bare cots, poor food, perpetually dirty clothes, often frozen water supplies, and other matters. Workers started their day at 4:00 A.M., typically without breakfast, for their daily shift in the cold. Men regularly blamed their superiors for mismanagement and wasteful practices. An Indian worker exclaimed to the writer's husband that "my ancestors lived like princes compared with this."[71]

As one would expect, many other groups were less than enthusiastic about the federal programs. Private contractors were often outraged that they had to compete with, or were replaced by, subsidized government projects. Public Works Administration grants enabled state highway departments to hire workers directly, a form of competition that nearly sent firms like Brown and Root into bankruptcy by 1936. There was also corruption. In February 1934, the Texas Rehabilitation and Relief Commission had to be converted from a county-based patronage system for the Fergusons to a more evenhanded state agency. Meanwhile, black workers were often excluded entirely from New Deal programs. An ardent New Dealer like Governor James V. Allred vetoed a proposal to add even segregated CCC camps for Texas blacks. Texas' black population would have to put up with segregation and Jim Crow policies until the 1960s.[72]

State officials had their own concerns. As the federal share of U.S. road expenditures skyrocketed from less than 10 percent in 1930 to 53 percent in

1939, traditional state and local matching requirements were largely abandoned. The WPA field organizations began to bypass the traditional state apparatus, in much the same way that states had usurped county powers, creating bad feeling in the process. There was also a brewing conflict between rural and urban interests. The Hayden-Cartwright Act of 1934 had permitted the use of federal highway funds for primary farm-to-market type roads that were unconnected to the designated national system. But when city roads were finally made eligible for federal assistance (in 1933), farming areas were forced to compete more aggressively.[73]

To accelerate national rural road-building activities, 1.4 million miles of rural roads were designated as RFD routes in 1938, and secondary farm-to-market roads became eligible for federal assistance. The transition from horse-drawn wagons and railroads to trucks had been gradual, but by 1940 it was nearly complete. Improved roadways to market centers had become critical to farmers and the cattle business. For example, nearly 86 percent of the 166,025 cattle received at San Antonio's Union Stockyards in 1940 were delivered by trucks; only 14 percent by rail. But if rural roads needed to be paved, they were typically last in line for funds. Even the BPR had de-emphasized rural roads in favor of urban projects and new expressways. County engineers and work crews were disparaged, but the votes were in the cities.[74]

No chronology of I-35 would be complete without a few words about Texas music. Music has always been an important component of highway and road-trip folklore, and an estimated 20 percent of U.S. automobiles were equipped with car radios by the late 1930s—inventor William Lear sold the rights to the technology in 1924 to Paul V. Galvin, who in turn commercialized the concept as "Motorolas." As it happens, places along the future route of I-35 can lay claim to having spawned some of the nation's greatest musical innovators. In Dallas, blues and folk masters Blind Lemon Jefferson and Huddie ("Leadbelly") Ledbetter performed regularly in Deep Ellum before 1918; Oak Cliff's Aaron Thibeaux ("T-Bone") Walker recorded his first sides in 1929, followed by Mississippian Robert Johnson's two existent recording sessions in San Antonio (1936) and Dallas (1937).[75]

Meanwhile, James Robert (Bob) Wills arrived in the emerging western swing capital of Fort Worth in 1929 to organize Wills' Fiddle Band, then the Fort Worth Doughboys, the Light Crust Doughboys, and finally the Texas Playboys (in Waco) in 1933. Also in 1933, Ellis County's Ernest Tubb began his first radio shows in San Antonio following the death of his idol, Jimmie Rodgers, and Willie Nelson was born in Abbott. Rodgers, Mississippi-born but Texas-styled, had spent his last years in and around Bexar. He, Tubb, and the later Hank Williams would influence William Orville (Lefty) Frizzell's first recordings in Dallas in 1950 and those of Dallas's Ray Price shortly thereafter. Back in San Antonio, "Tex-Mex" (conjunto) pioneer Santiago Jimenez recorded his first sides in 1936, shortly before the birth of his musical heirs—sons Flaco and Santiago and the late Doug Sahm.[76]

Texas' touring musicians, like most highway travelers, discovered that city routes had become clogged and congested. As indicated, one solution was the development of bypass roads around the central business district, but these routes became clogged as well. Another possible solution, city streetcar systems and interurban railways, had been unable to compete with automobiles and buses and had died out. In the same way that railroads had received the bulk of investment capital between 1870 and 1900, automobiles and highways had returned the favor since the 1920s. Local railway systems, and many national ones, were through.

OFF-RAMP: PARKWAYS

Another idea, parkways, was promoted to relieve urban and suburban congestion and promote beautification. Borrowed from England and extended by the BPR, the concept was popularized by New York City's network of limited access (autos-only) commuter parkways. The fifteen-mile Bronx River Parkway in Westchester County, proposed in 1907 and finally completed in 1924, was the first highway to eliminate traffic signals and grade crossings. The cost was a whopping $1 million per mile, but the route became so popular that the Saw Mill and Hutchinson River parkways were started shortly thereafter. These roads, in turn, were followed by the Southern State Parkway on Long Island and the Henry Hudson (River) Parkway into Manhattan. In the early 1930s, the BPR countered with the Mount Vernon Memorial Parkway, Skyline Drive in Virginia, the Blue Ridge Parkway, and the Natchez Trace Parkway. These early experiments in limited-access highways were predecessors to future expressways.[77]

Most parkways followed the contour of the land and, as a result, soon became obsolete. They worked well in a 45 mph world, but with higher speed limits, the narrow eighteen-foot (curbed) roadways, with regular twists and turns, had become too dangerous. Newer highways were engineered to cut *through* hills in order to remove the dangerous curves. As eight-degree curves were reduced to one to two degrees, parkways became straighter and, inevitably, less parklike. Parkways evolved into less attractive expressways, typified by Chicago's eight-lane Lake Shore Drive in 1933, which included one of the nation's first cloverleaf junctions; the Meadowbrook Parkway to Jones Beach, Long Island, in 1934; and a ten-lane stretch of superhighway in St. Louis.[78]

Parkways, freeways, and expressways would soon become controversial issues. In the meantime, WPA programs built 572,000 miles of U.S. highways by 1940, 67,000 miles of city streets, and 78,000 bridges. The CWA resurfaced another 255,000 miles of road. Despite these massive achievements, most of the new roads were improved, not necessarily paved, and the quality of recently paved roads was inconsistent. Nearly two-thirds of the U.S. highway system was paved with asphalt in 1940, but much of this network had not been designed for speeds higher than 50 mph. Like the experience during World War I, many roads were unable to withstand the demands of heavy trucks and buses. Higher strength pavements were required for larger load capacities, particularly those associated with military convoys. The 1938 load limit of seven thousand pounds per axle was insufficient, and many new roads were obsolete by the time they were completed.[79]

Road failures emphasized the need for improved research, especially regarding the impact of trucks. The BPR and the Highway Research Board of the National Research Council continued to work in conjunction with state highway departments, universities, and experimental stations to develop new construction techniques and materials. Progress could be painfully slow. Continuously reinforced concrete, introduced in 1921, was finally tested in 1937 at a site at Stilesville, Indiana. The BPR had released standard specifications for road materials and bridge designs as early as 1924, but standards were difficult to achieve. The road-construction industry was extremely fragmented, and local conditions, skill sets, and materials varied greatly. Unlike for railroads and gasoline retailers, no national chains emerged to develop standards by force of their oligopoly power. Yet trade associations like the American Society for Testing Materials somehow managed to introduce standards for pavements, asphalts, alignments, grades, intersections, grade separations, paint, concrete and metal culverts, passing zones, bridges, and even accounting procedures.[80]

Like most state highway departments, the THD attempted to procure newly standardized materials and equipment from Texas manufacturers. The goal was to reduce costs and create local jobs. Of course, the manufacturers and their lobbyists had their own ideas on the subject, and these were not always consistent with THD objectives. No less an authority than Gibb Gilchrist reported in 1936 that highway engineering in Texas had had to overcome two great obstacles since 1916—"an almost universal opposition to proper location" and the "keen propaganda that surrounded the sales organization and promotion force of highway materials."[81]

A National System, 1938–1960

$\mathcal{M}$OST states, including Texas, viewed parkways and freeways as luxuries during the depression years. The predecessors to Interstate 35—US 81 and US 77—operated as well-defined (if undivided) interstate highways which, to the delight of local merchants, passed through Texas cities in a zigzag, time-consuming (and oft-confusing) fashion. As early as 1938, the THD was involved in three divided highway projects: an upgraded roadway between Dallas and Fort Worth; a four-mile stretch of US 81 north of Austin, including "service" (frontage) roads; and a freeway between Houston and Galveston—but when the first Texas Highway Planning Survey was released in 1940, the focus was on rural roads, traffic levels, finances, and road life (not parkways or expressways). But things change.

OFF-RAMP: AUTOBAHNS AND TOLL ROADS

If the first controlled-access parkways were constrained by sharp curves, narrow lanes, and dangerous curbs, they would soon be superseded by expressways and a new generation of toll roads. All were influenced to some extent by the German autobahns. The first autobahn segment had opened in May 1935, and some 800 miles (of a planned 4,300-mile system) were completed by 1938. The autobahns received tremendous publicity and were inspected carefully by Thomas Mac-Donald. While impressed, the BPR chief viewed the new concept as a luxury, a propaganda tool, and even unsuitable. Autobahns had been designed to bypass German cities just as U.S. cities had emerged as a focus area for BPR highway planners. During 1937, congressional hearings were held to evaluate the possible development of autobahnlike superhighways in the United States. No decisions were made.[1]

A few states began to circumvent the venerable but somewhat stodgy BPR. In 1937, the highly regarded Merritt Parkway was completed in southwestern Connecticut without BPR assistance. The following year, the Pennsylvania Turnpike Commission managed to secure a $26 million grant from the PWA, plus a $32 million loan guarantee from the RFC, to build a new 162-mile four-lane toll road between Harrisburg and Pittsburgh. The Pennsylvania Turnpike would utilize a right-of-way owned by the unfinished Southern Pennsylvania Railroad. In direct defiance of the state's own highway department and the BPR, the Pennsylvania Turnpike opened in 1940 and eventually connected Pittsburgh with Philadelphia. It collects tolls to this day.[2]

The Federal Aid Highway Act of 1938 had authorized the BPR to assess the feasibility of building six transcontinental toll highways. The results, presented in *Toll Roads and Free Roads* in 1939, were negative—the BPR's quantitative analyses indicated that there was not enough traffic to justify any of the proposed routes. Only 172 miles of the proposed highways (in the Northeast, California, and Florida) were expected to cover their projected costs. Another 666 miles were likely to cover only 80 percent of their costs. For the vast remainder of proposed miles, projected revenue would be insufficient. Many of these traffic projections would be proven wrong, but the BPR controlled the purse strings. Proposals to build long-distance superhighways—like a PWA-assisted toll road between Washington, D.C., and Jersey City and a freeway between Minnesota and the Gulf of Mexico—were rejected. The BPR also dismissed "visionary" designers like Norman Bel Geddes as crackpots. In 1939, Bel Geddes had wowed millions of New York World's Fair attendees with his twelve-lane, 100 mph-based superhighway concept at the General Motors Futurama pavilion.[3]

The BPR preferred to stick with its guiding philosophy of free highways and incremental development. Stodgy or not, this approach favored a free network of "interregional" highways, utilizing existing rights-of-way wherever possible, designed in conjunction with "master plans" and state highway departments, and funded by gasoline taxes. BPR expressways were designed to accommodate higher speeds than twisty parkways and would be depressed (or elevated) through central business districts in urban areas. Highways would be upgraded to more than two lanes only when traffic exceeded two thousand vehicles per day. The BPR had argued that even two-lane interstates like nearly completed Route 66 between Chicago and Los Angeles were of questionable value. When the BPR finally agreed to support a superhighway for the dense Washington-Boston corridor, the new expressway (present day I-95) paralleled US 1 and involved eight state highway departments.[4]

Texas was not a priority area for BPR (or any other) expressway schemes, but congestion problems were looming. Although the undivided US 81 and US 77 functioned reasonably well over long distances, urban centers could be a challenge. Between Laredo and Waco, US 81 ran as Convent and Bernardo in Laredo; as Nogalitos, Alamo, Broadway, and the Old San Antonio Road in San Antonio; as Congress, Lavaca, Guadalupe, and 45th in Austin; and as Robinson (joining US 77), South 18th, Washington, and Elm in Waco. US 81 and US 77 were one and the same route between Waco and the fork at Hillsboro. From Hillsboro, US 81 entered Fort Worth as Hemphill and continued as Jennings and North Main before veering northeast (as US 377) to Denton. From Hillsboro, US 77 passed through Waxahachie, entered Dallas as Houston, and continued through town as McKinney, Orange, Cedar Springs, and Maple before heading northwest to the fork at Denton. From Denton, US 77 ran due north through Gainesville before crossing the Red River into Oklahoma.[5]

By 1940, these zigzag urban routes were part of a 19,000-mile network of paved highways (within an expanded 22,600-mile state system). Texas' population had increased to 6.4 million, including 2.9 million in urban areas, and the petroleum-rich state had become industrialized. The value of Texas manufactured goods in 1940 reached $1.5 billion, eleventh in the United States (between Wisconsin at $1.6 billion and North Carolina at $1.4). Unfortunately for Dewitt C. Greer, the new state highway engineer in July 1940, Texas' economic development opportunities were checked by World War II. Non-military highway construction projects ground to a complete halt until after 1945. In the course of his twenty-seven-year stewardship at THD, however, Greer would have the good fortune to preside over the greatest period of highway building since the Roman Empire.[6]

Like all wartime highway departments, the THD focused on the improvement of access roads to military facilities. This focus provided a fateful catalyst to the development of additional divided highways. Plans to upgrade US 77 through Dallas County had been hatched as early as 1939, but the war accelerated the timetable. By 1941, a four-lane divided highway (Hines Boulevard) was completed between downtown Dallas and Love Field, which had been established northwest of town in 1917. Since the highway was routed through a so-called blighted area, right-of-way properties were purchased for only $300–500 per acre. By 1949, real estate along Hines Boulevard (US 77) commanded prices of $10,000–20,000 per acre.[7]

Military considerations influenced the construction of a new traffic circle in northwest Dallas, west of Love Field where US 77 joined SH 114, US 183, and Storey Road. The project was intended to remove existing railroad crossings. Supported by the WPA, Public Roads Administration (successor to the BPR), THD, Dallas County, City of Dallas, and two railroad companies, the new circle opened on October 14, 1941. Plans were also made to upgrade US 77 between Dallas and Waxahachie and between Dallas and Lewisville. Access roads were built to new production facilities like the North American Aviation plant in Grand Prairie west of Dallas and the Consolidated Aircraft bomber facility northwest of Fort Worth.[8]

Farther north, US 77 was upgraded to a four-lane highway to the Red River bridge when a new army training camp, Camp Howze, was established six miles north of Gainesville in 1942. Traffic concerns had already prompted Gainesville to install its first three hundred parking meters in April. In addition to soldiers, US 77 continued to carry the Gainesville Community Circus, a regional troup that had performed throughout Texas and Oklahoma since 1930. A more serious regional project, initiated by the Flood Control Act of 1938 and the efforts of Sam Rayburn, had authorized the Army Corps of Engineers to build an $80 million hydroelectric dam and lake complex at the mouth of the Washita River, five miles northwest of Denison. After its completion in 1944, Lake Texoma inevitably submerged remnants of Preston, Holland Coffee's Trading Post, and Ben Colbert's bridge.[9]

Similarly, some seventy-three miles of Bexar County highways were upgraded to enhance access to San Antonio's military facilities. This objective spawned a THD project to reroute US 81 around San Marcos in 1941. The new bypass was opposed by local officials and merchants, who feared a loss of downtown business activity. But with San Antonio's military bases to be considered, the new four-lane divided highway was pushed through. It provided a more direct route between Austin and San Antonio, saving at least ten minutes and eliminating three railroad grade crossings. Sixteen different trains had traveled daily along the Katy crossing alone.[10]

Two new traffic circles were also installed in San Marcos, one en route to Luling (SH 80), and the other on the road to Seguin (SH 123). The total cost of the projects ($237,000) compared favorably with a THD estimate that the cost of new railroad overpasses or underpasses would have totaled $350,000. Military projects were everywhere. A thirty-mile stretch of SH 21 between San Marcos and Bastrop—a segment of the Old San Antonio Road (Camino Real)—was reconstructed with state and federal funds as a military access road. In Austin, the concrete-arched Lamar Street Bridge was completed in 1942 to provide an alternative route for military traffic along US 81. Between Austin, Bastrop, and Paige, between 15,000 and 25,000 men, 9,000 tons of stone, and 600 tons of asphalt were deployed to improve and widen segments of US 290, SH 71, and SH 95. An upgraded highway (US 190) was also built to South Camp Hood in Killeen (west of Belton) in 1942. With the addition of North Camp Hood, located seventeen miles to the north and near the site of old Fort Gates, the two camps were consolidated as the 217,337-acre Fort Hood in 1951.[11]

Supplies of asphalt, tar, and gasoline were directed to military needs or rationed between 1941 and 1945. To conserve fuel, the highway speed limit was temporarily reduced to 35 mph. There were shortages of just about everything—except the THD's cash position. With nonmilitary construction activity at a standstill, Greer was able to invest $30 million in surplus construction funds in short-term government securities. Annual gas tax revenues ran 35 percent below their prewar levels, but Texas would have more highway investment funds available in 1945 than it had in 1940.[12]

The BPR, transferred from the USDA to the Federal Works Administration (FWA) in July of 1939 and renamed the Public Roads Administration (PRA), focused on military needs as well. The nation's showcase highway projects were military affairs. The threat of a possible Japanese invasion path through Alaska or Central America prompted the immediate development of a highway to link the northern frontier with the Lower 48 states and a stepped-up effort to complete the Pan American Highway. Under the leadership of Francis C. (Frank) Turner, a Texas A&M graduate and future "father of the interstate highway system," 10,000 work troops managed to complete an unbelievable 1,480-mile gravel road—the Alaska-Canada (AlCan) Highway—between Edmonton and Fairbanks in October 1943. The challenging stretch of Pan American Highway between Mexico City and Panama City was declared complete on October 12, 1942, to commemorate the 450th anniversary of the arrival of Columbus, but at least 243 miles were still unimproved in 1945.[13]

OFF-RAMP: PLANNING THE NATION'S NETWORK

In Washington, highway building took a backseat to highway planning. The Defense Highway Act of 1941 and the Federal Highway Amendment of 1943 made funds available to states for master planning and, for the first time, for purchase of rights-of-way. The introduction of master planning principles was a response to the contention that New Deal projects had favored job creation in rural areas over quality road engineering in urban contexts. Some 1.4 million miles of U.S. roads had been paved by 1941 (versus only 387,000 miles by 1921), but this was still not enough to relieve rising congestion levels. Many feared that the nation's metropolitan transportation systems were sliding into chaos. A National Interregional Highway Committee was assembled in April 1941, to plan the next generation of defense-oriented ("strategic") U.S. highways; the committee was chaired by PRA chief Thomas MacDonald and included Rexford G. Tugwell, a somewhat utopian advocate of "greenbelt" towns modeled on England's "garden cities" movement. In 1943, Congress authorized MacDonald to reevaluate the need for a system of U.S. expressways as well.[14]

The Interregional Highway Committee's recommendations were released in January 1944, as *Interregional Highways,* a landmark work that outlined the modern interstate highway system. The committee recommended a twenty-year program, at $750 million per year, to build a 39,000-mile system of interregional highways across the nation. The massive scale was a compromise between the 26,700-mile system recommended in *Toll Roads and Free Roads* and a larger 48,400-mile proposal. The highways would mainly follow existing routes, but their actual location would be determined by the state highway departments and regional metropolitan authorities. Around 9,500 miles would be assumed by urban expressways, including 5,000 miles of so-called circumferential roads (loops) and bypass routes. The remaining miles would be located in rural areas. The plan was to connect every U.S. city with a population greater than 300,000, plus fifty-nine of sixty-two cities in the 100,000–300,000 range. Three Ohio cities (Akron, Canton, and Youngstown) were somehow left out.[15]

Bypass routes and loops were major features of the report. The committee had been influenced by a study in Newport News, Virginia, indicating that a new seven- to ten-mile bypass had reduced drive times by nearly 50 percent in off-peak periods and by substantially more during rush hours. Since bypasses were appropriate for through traffic but not for traffic intending to stop and park within downtown areas, connector roads were needed to link bypasses to city centers. Parking garages, preferably multistory or underground, were necessary as well. In large cities, loops and urban expressways (elevated and/or depressed) were recommended to manage traffic flows. San Antonio, for one, had proposed a loop system for years. According to the January 1940, issue of *Texas Parade:* "Completion of a loop highway around San Antonio and improvements and modernization of other roads radiating to neighboring communities have been made a primary objective of the San Antonio Chamber of Commerce."[16]

In 1944, only seventeen states (including Texas) had laws permitting the development of limited-access highways. The construction of new routes had been found to be much cheaper than widening existing ones, especially when the legal rights of abutters had to be addressed. In Westchester County, New York, land acquisition costs for the new Saw Mill Parkway were $139,000 per mile, while acquisition costs to widen the existing Albany Post Road averaged $792,000. New highways were also favored because few of the nation's existing parkways and freeways could meet the requirements (speed, volume, weight) for next-generation expressways. The Pennsylvania Turnpike, the New York and Merritt parkways, and a handful of other freeways were approved, but scenic highways like New York's Taconic Parkway were not. Bridges were another problem. Only 347 (4.1 percent) of 8,435 highway bridges met the recommended widths—nearly 96 percent would have to be widened or replaced.[17]

Finally, the committee estimated construction costs for a range of traffic volumes and pavement types. A two-lane, 24-foot-wide stretch of "intermediate" quality pavement serving less than 1,000 vehicles per day was estimated at $40,000–60,000 per mile. For volumes between 3,000 and 10,000 vehicles per day, a divided four-lane, "high type" highway would run $100,000–150,000 per mile. In some urban areas, where expressways would have to be depressed or elevated, costs could exceed $1 million per mile. In New York, East River (now FDR) Drive required a $2 million investment per mile, and the elevated Gowanus Parkway came in at $3 million per mile. Elevated urban expressways were discouraged for reasons other than costs: "Even [if] attractively designed, elevated roadways are aesthetically undesirable in the midst of some parts of cities, such as residential areas. They also tend to divide a community and to act as barriers, at least psychologically, between the divided sections."[18]

Following intense debates among the vested constituencies—urban, rural, and the proponents of freeways and toll roads—many of the committee's recommendations were included in the landmark Federal Highway Act of 1944. Signed by President Roosevelt on December 20, 1944, the act authorized a forty-thousand-mile interstate system, instituted a generous 50–50 federal-state matching requirement, and provided ample funding opportunities for urban expressways. The act was intended to replace and significantly expand the Defense Highway Act of 1941, which had funded strategic military highways used to carry convoys and troop mobilizations. While there was no special funding status for interstates, the 1944 act authorized the development of a

"National System of Interstate Highways" to "connect by routes, as direct as practicable, the principal metropolitan areas, cities and industrial centers, to serve the national defense, and to connect at suitable border points with routes of continental importance in the Dominion of Canada and the Republic of Mexico."[19]

The Act of 1944 designated four federal road networks—primary, interstate, farm-to-market, and urban—and required state highway departments to submit interstate route candidates to the PRA by July 1945. After an inevitable two-year delay, 37,700 miles (2,900 miles in urban areas) were finally designated in 1947. The selected routes were presented in the PRA's celebrated map of August 2, 1947 (map 13): *National System of Interstate Highways Selected by Joint Action of the Several State Highway Departments as Modified and Approved by the Administrator, Federal Works Agency, Public Roads Administration.* While 6,375 miles of Texas roads, 27 percent of the state system, had already been designated as strategic military highways, less than one-third of this total was approved for new interstates. However, the expanded federal funding opportunities for urban projects were welcome—THD assistance to Texas cities had just begun in October 1943—and the PRA map foreshadowed the famous I-35 forks at Hillsboro and Denton.[20]

The PRA's lofty intentions aside, no federal funds were targeted specifically for interstates until 1954. As a result, the actual construction of the mapped road system stalled until the mid-1950s. One of the very few postwar expressway projects that were started in Texas—surprisingly (and reluctantly)—was a modest stretch of US 77 in Cooke County. It was not easy. US 77 (future I-35) had emerged as an interstate highway candidate in 1944, and Jac Gubbels, the THD's landscape architect-turned-planner, recommended that "US Interregional (Superhighway) 77" be rerouted to the western edge of downtown Gainesville. The existing route, along California Street, crossed two railroad lines and required passage through congested Courthouse Square. Gubbels's scheme had been rejected by local businesses for over a decade, and wartime traffic generated by Camp Howze had not altered many opinions. The town that had delayed construction of a Red River highway bridge until 1919 rejected the rerouting plan for US 77 in June 1944.[21]

Money talks, however. When it became clear that the THD and the PRA were fully prepared to reroute US 77 to another town, or to designate US 75 (at Denison) or US 377 (at Whitesboro) as Texas' principal northern gateway, Gainesville citizens had a change of heart. The rerouting plan and the four-lane

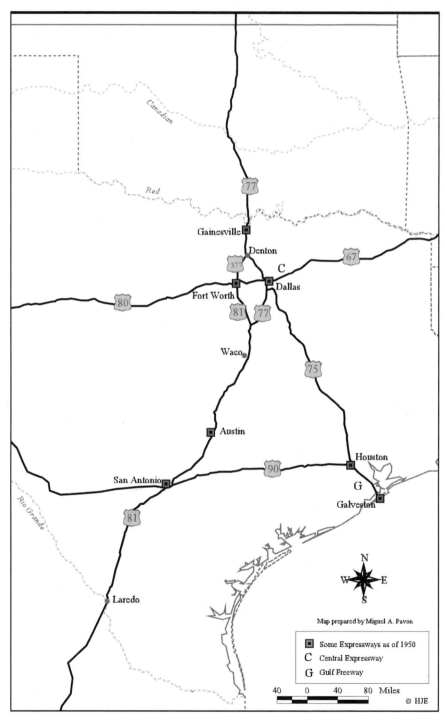

Map 13. PRA Approved Interstate Routes as of August 2, 1947.

superhighway project were subsequently approved in December 1944, and surveys were completed in January 1945. By a vote of 719–530 in November 1945, Gainesville voters approved $98,000 in bonds to purchase rights-of-way through town. Cooke County voters added another $85,000 in February 1946, by a vote of 1,856–626, for countywide rights-of-way. In return for these timely actions, the THD agreed to build thirty-five miles of farm-to-market roads in Cooke County over the next three years. Typical of most agricultural regions, the number of farms in Cooke County had declined from 3,507 in 1900 to 2,130 in 1945, but a majority of the survivors were family-owned.[22]

Construction on the first segment of US Superhighway 77 (I-35) started in July 1947. Nearly $2 million in contracts were let for grading, drainage, and concrete paving work. These and other projects were completed in Gainesville during 1948, including a new $165,251 Elm Creek bridge south of town, a $200,000 underpass to eliminate the Katy rail crossing, and overpasses for the Santa Fe rail crossing and east-west US 82. By 1950, Cooke County had one of the first controlled-access highways in Texas. The first segments of the more ambitious Houston Expressway–Gulf Freeway between Houston and Galveston had opened in 1948, but the entire Gulf Freeway was not completed until 1951.[23]

The Texas highway system had risen to 30,146 miles in 1948 and represented around 20 percent of total state expenditures. This compared with 15,681 miles of railroads and 196,230 miles of rural roads. While 27,733 miles of the expanding state system were paved with asphalt and 4,835 miles with cement (or brick) in 1950, Texas' rural routes remained largely unimproved. Federal funding for designated farm-to-market (FM) roads had been delayed until Sam Rayburn inserted a provision into the Highway Bill of 1944. Rayburn recalled that he had "hauled cotton down [one of his district's roads] when mud was so deep it came to the wagon hubs." Postwar inflation raised construction costs (land, wages, and materials) significantly, and most road projects, including FMs, would have to wait. In addition, because the 1944 act had prioritized interregional routes, urban expressways, and existing primary roads, political battles intensified among the various constituencies. New transcontinental superhighways, which would come later, were an easier sell—they satisfied nearly everyone.[24]

After a slow start, some 1,518 miles of controlled-access expressways were under construction in Dallas, Fort Worth, Houston, and San Antonio by 1950. These projects took advantage of federal funding opportunities for urban highways and the THD's formation of an Urban Projects division in 1945. The first 3.5-mile section of the $21 million Gulf Freeway opened in October 1948, after less than two years of work. In San Antonio, the first 0.7-mile stretch of US 87 expressway (future I-10) was completed for $1.5 million northwest of downtown in July 1949. This modest start was enhanced by a $3.9 million bond issue to fund additional right-of-way purchases. The issue was approved by San Antonio voters in October 1949—two years after they had rejected a larger $5 million package.[25]

The new urban initiatives were designed to address rising traffic volumes and to reverse the apparent decline of many U.S. cities. Urban expressways were viewed by the BPR—the name was revived from 1949 until 1967 and the agency was transferred to the Department of Commerce—as a double-barreled solution. They could improve access to downtown areas and clear so-called blighted areas in the process. Of course, the catch was that suburbanization and associated urban decline were themselves the results of improved highway systems. Not only did the new urban expressways enhance this decline, but the elimination of "blighted" areas destroyed traditional urban neighborhoods and habitats.

To facilitate the BPR's schemes, a profession of city and regional planners was invented to devise and implement the new master plans. "Hub-and-spoke" systems were preferred in metropolitan areas. The hub was the central city, and the spokes were the new urban expressways, radiating out to a new circumferential loop road. As will be seen, the loop roads may have made sense, but many of the hub-and-spoke systems tore up neighborhoods, parklands, and historic areas, often displacing religious sites, businesses, and thousands of people in their path. Once the damage was done, the new expressway systems might be credited with enhancing access throughout most metropolitan areas. Yet if the goal was to revive central business districts, promote diversity, and increase pedestrian activity, the plans failed miserably. Downtowns are credible today because of office towers and occasional large-scale entertainment venues; most of the old department stores, movie theaters, and independent businesses are long gone.

Controversial as the BPR's postwar planning philosophy may have been, many important constituencies opposed it from the start. Highway engineers, chambers of commerce, trucking companies, and business people wanted urban expressways to move vehicles faster and to reduce congestion, period. In response, many regions dispensed with the planning and focused on the building.

Texas' first urban expressway, the Houston Expressway (US 75), was opened in 1948 from the city's northwest border through downtown to an eventual southeast connection with the more ambitious Gulf Freeway (US 75) project. The new six-lane highway had three-hundred-foot rights-of-way, carved through blighted areas acquired by the city, and two-way frontage roads on each side. When the completed Gulf Freeway between Houston and Galveston opened in 1951, it averaged 69,000 vehicles per day in its first full year of operation — 40,000 more than the 1948 level.[26]

Close behind was the first two-mile section of the Central Boulevard Expressway (US 75) in Dallas, opened in December 1948, along the old right-of-way of the Houston and Texas Central. The project had been delayed by the city's inability to obtain necessary rights-of-way and a need to construct an 11,400-foot-long storm sewer to control possible flooding. A creative solution was found when the city purchased rights-of-way from both the H&TC and Texas and New Orleans railroads between 1944 and 1946. This solution also happened to destroy a number of traditional black neighborhoods on the east side of Dallas, a syndrome reconfirmed in a grisly manner when the Freedman's Town Cemetery was discovered (and relocated) during a highway construction project in 1986.[27]

The nondesignated Central Expressway project accelerated the timetable through which the recently completed (designated) US 77 expressway at Gainesville was extended south to Dallas. In Fort Worth, two four- to six-lane expressways (including two-lane frontage roads) were under construction as of October 1948. These new expressways, US 81 and US 80, were also routed through blighted or undeveloped areas to minimize right-of-way costs. Similarly, thirty miles of US 81 and US 90/87 in San Antonio were being upgraded to four- to eight-lane divided highways, once again routed through blighted or sparsely populated areas of Bexar. The estimated cost of the project was $38 million, or $1.4 million per mile, but highway engineers confidently predicted a thirty-year life for the new roads. Plans to upgrade US 81 between Temple and Belton were delayed indefinitely, pending Bell County's provision of necessary rights-of-way.[28]

Bell County at least had plans, whether it would implement them or not. Laredo had been dormant for nearly two decades. The city had been honored as the southern terminus of the Blue Star Memorial Highway, a north-south transcontinental route selected in 1947 (dedicated in 1950) to honor the armed forces who had served in World War II. However, a series of proposals to upgrade US 81

and to add a second highway bridge had either been rejected by Laredo's political powers or been shelved. The Blue Star's fame was brief, but the highway
followed the future route of I-35 in Texas (I-35W rather than I-35E) almost
precisely. From Laredo, the Blue Star was routed along US 81 to Fort Worth,
then via US 377 and US 77 to Denton, Gainesville, and Oklahoma City.[29]

If the Blue Star Highway was a nonevent, Laredo still had the Pan American
Highway. One could even argue that the Blue Star and the Pan American were
one in the same road. Over 700,000 vehicles had crossed the Rio Grande via the
Convent Street (International) Bridge en route to or from segments of the Pan
American Highway in 1946. In addition to tourist trade, the one bridge and
the Mexican Railways single-track railroad span handled some 60 percent of
the cross-border freight between the United States and Mexico in 1950. This
expansion, in turn, prompted an International Traffic Committee to reaffirm
Laredo's gateway status in 1953. US 81 would be upgraded and linked more
closely with the Pan American Highway (Mexico 85). A second highway
bridge, like the rejected $665,000, 1,362-foot-long structure proposed by the
THD and the Mexican Ministry of Communications and Public Works in
February 1940, would eventually be built as well—in 1976.[30]

The new expressway projects were intended to relieve traffic congestion, but
they were not enough. After a decade of sluggish growth, auto registrations
exploded to nearly 45 million in 1949, versus 31 million in 1945, and the
$8.4 billion invested in U.S. highways between 1946 and 1950 represented
the greatest road construction effort in U.S. history. A coterie of Texas power
brokers—highlighted by Senator Lyndon B. Johnson, Speaker Sam Rayburn,
oil and gas magnates like Herman and George Brown (having launched Texas
Eastern with the purchase of two underpriced military pipelines), Sid W.
Richardson, and talented lieutenants like John B. Connally—were right in the
middle of it. The fortunes of Johnson and the Browns had bonded with the
Marshall Ford Dam project (Mansfield Dam, 1937) and Corpus Christi Naval
Air Station (1940). The political foundation laid by John Nance Garner and
Sam Rayburn was now extended to an oil, gas, and highway lobby of epic
proportions.[31]

Texas highways continued to receive their share of funding from Washington, but postwar investments were being eroded by postwar inflation and
dramatic increases in traffic volume. In response to the political gridlock in
Washington, a number of "end-run" turnpike projects were introduced based
on the successful Pennsylvania model. These projects were in direct defiance of

the BPR and the state highway departments. A brief but powerful turnpike craze resulted. By 1950, Colorado, Maine, Maryland, New Hampshire, New Jersey, New York, Ohio, Oklahoma, and West Virginia had either completed or authorized toll roads. Some 1,461 miles of toll roads were open by January 1955, with another 1,398 miles under construction. At the peak of this activity eight years later, over 3,500 miles of toll roads were open across the nation. Not all of these roads were profitable, however, affirming at least some of the BPR's prewar warnings on the subject. Only high-volume urban routes could be described as successful.[32]

THD officials must have paid some attention to toll road developments north of the Red River. In July 1953, the hundred-mile, state-of-the-art Turner Turnpike opened between Oklahoma City and Tulsa. Named for ex-governor Roy Turner, the four-lane divided highway was designed for daily traffic of 15,000 vehicles and speeds of up to 70 mph. Fares were $1.40 for cars, $3 for buses, and $4 for trucks. The turnpike included four cloverleaf interchanges, a 15-foot-wide median strip, 12-foot wide shoulders, no grade crossings, and six licensed service plazas. The roadbed comprised twelve inches of compacted "selected soil," topped with seven inches of crushed stone and surfaced with two inches of asphaltic concrete. Like the toll bridge companies of years gone by, the turnpike itself was expected to retire its bonds in thirty to forty years and then become a freeway.[33]

The Turner Turnpike project had to be on people's minds when the Texas Poll was conducted in November 1952. Poll results indicated that Texas residents were lukewarm about their current highway system but were positive about the need for new (free or toll) expressways. Since all politics are local, the state legislature responded by approving a Texas Turnpike Authority (TTA) in August 1953. Initially, the TTA intended to build a turnpike between Dallas and Fort Worth, parallel to US 80, and to provide a Dallas junction for future expressways planned for US 77 and US 80. The Dallas–Fort Worth corridor was generating traffic of thirty thousand vehicles per day and drivers had to will their way through forty-five separate traffic signals.[34]

Even more ambitious toll road proposals were in the works. Plans to build a $150 million turnpike between Gainesville and Houston via Dallas and a $125 million road between Irving and San Antonio had been scrapped, but three other projects were soon added to the Dallas–Fort Worth Toll Road effort. Toll roads were authorized between Gainesville and San Antonio; between Waco and Houston; and between Houston and Corpus Christi. A TTA plan to add a toll road between Dallas–Fort Worth and Houston was also on the drawing board. Versions of these four projects would eventually be built as freeways.[35]

Like other turnpike commissions, the new TTA defied the THD's traditional pay-as-you-go philosophy in favor of the so-called Maine model. In Maine, turnpike bonds were issued and secured only by the future revenues of the highway. The state of Texas had refused to issue state bonds for highway projects, but the Texas Supreme Court permitted the quasi-public TTA to do so. Capitalized by a successful $58.5 million bond offering to fund construction, purchase rights-of-way, and relocate a section of the Trinity River, the TTA eventually opened the Dallas–Fort Worth Toll Road in August 1957. By June 1958, toll revenues exceeded operating costs and fixed interest charges. The turnpike became so successful that the bonds were paid off in December 1977, some seventeen years ahead of schedule, and the highway was transferred (as a freeway) to the THD. In October 2001, now a segment of I-30 between I-35E and I-35W, the freeway was renamed the Tom Landry Highway to honor the legendary Dallas Cowboys coach.[36]

The innovative highway-only service plazas on the Turner, Dallas–Fort Worth, and other U.S. turnpikes helped to promote a concept that has become nearly synonymous with interstate and other highways—fast food chains. As indicated, A&W, Pig Stand, Howard Johnson, and others had already introduced chains of highway-oriented restaurants to the nation's roadscape. By the late 1940s, drive-in stands were everywhere, and standardization and franchising concepts had been demonstrated successfully. But as highway lanes increased and travel times fell, the established chains were unable to provide service that was fast enough, or convenient enough, for a nation increasingly consumed with speed.

New chains like Jack-in-the-Box in San Diego (1950), Whataburger in Corpus Christi (1950), McDonalds in San Bernadino (taken national by Ray A. Kroc in Des Plaines, Illinois, in 1955), Church's Fried Chicken in San Antonio (1952), Kentucky Fried Chicken in Corbin, Kentucky (1955), and Pizza Hut in Wichita (1958) became as much a part of the new expressway and turnpike systems as the roads themselves. Luby's in San Antonio (1947) was not really "fast food," but it was faster than old-fashioned restaurants. Meanwhile, enterprises like Best Western in Long Beach (1946), Holiday Inns in Memphis (1953), Ramada Inns in Flagstaff (1954), and Marriott in Washington, D.C. (1955) introduced motel chains that were modern, predictable, and easily accessible.[37]

Of course, in the early 1950s, the founders of these chains could have no idea that the best was yet to come—the interstate highway system. Having been jarred by the turnpike boom, the BPR and the American Association of State Highway Officials (AASHO) struck back with the Federal Aid Highway Acts of 1952, 1954, and 1956. These acts even made federal funds available to state turnpike authorities, allowing them to redeem their outstanding revenue bonds and become freeways. After a sluggish start, 5,620 miles of interstate highways were completed by 1953. In that same year, long-time BPR chief Thomas MacDonald retired (to Texas A&M) after thirty-four years of service.

The funds earmarked for interstate construction, all of $25 million in 1952, were matched on a 50–50 basis with participating states. These funds represented the first time that interstate highways had been targeted specifically. Again, the Act of 1944 had lumped in interstates with funding allocations for primary roads. In the Federal Highway Act of 1954, the concept was expanded significantly. The act authorized $875 million for the nation's roads: $315 million for primary; $210 million for secondary; $175 million for urban; and $175 million for interstates. Since primary, interstate, and urban highways were becoming interdependent, the act could be viewed more simply as providing $665 million for interstates and $210 million for secondary roads. The 1954 act also raised the federal cost share to 60 percent. Unfortunately, the early interstate highways were obsolete by the time they were completed. Most would have to be upgraded in future years.[38]

As of January 1954, the Texas state highway system had expanded to 50,581 miles, including 24,295 miles of THD-maintained FM roads. Vehicle registrations stood at 3.5 million. Every road in the state was either paved or programmed (and funded) to be paved. However, very few miles of Texas highways were divided four-lane affairs with frontage roads (a Texas specialty to control acquisition costs). Other than the Gulf Freeway between Houston and Galveston, no two cities were yet connected by an expressway. Most of Texas' divided highways were relatively small segments within city limits. Ambitious plans were unveiled, but implementation was difficult.[39]

In Dallas, the Central Expressway (US 75) had been completed north to Richardson but south only to a point north of Loop 12. Two 2,723-foot bridges, one old and one new, would be utilized by US 75 across the Trinity River. One had been built by Dallas County in 1910 and widened to twenty-four feet by the state in 1938 at a cost of $225,326. The second bridge, twenty-eight feet wide, was constructed in 1950 at a cost of $669,073. On the drawing board were plans to upgrade US 77 and US 80 to expressway status. As of early 1954, however, Dallas County had approved bonds only for the US 80 portion. Meanwhile, the Sam Houston Toll Road Corporation was authorized in February 1954, to build a toll road between Dallas and San Antonio—provided that construction began no later than January 1, 1955. The deadline was missed.[40]

In 1955, six federally approved interregional highways in Dallas and two other routes were designated as freeways by House Bill 451 of the 52nd Texas Legislature. The federal designations were tied to the BPR's *General Location of the National System of Interstate Highways,* published in September 1955. The so-called Yellow Book contained a map of interstate routes approved for designation in August 1947, as well as one hundred urban area maps depicting the intended routes of designated urban interstates. To date, 44.5 miles of expressways had been completed through Dallas County and another 125.6 miles were programmed. Dallas County's Metropolitan Highway Needs Plan of 1952 had recommended that all expressways have three-hundred-foot rights-of-way, with new interchanges planned for US 67, US 77, and US 80.[41]

Sections of the new US 77 expressway had been completed through Gainesville, but further progress was stalled in Cooke and Denton counties, en route to Dallas. Rights-of-way still needed to be acquired in Cooke County, and a $1.7 million bridge project across the Garza–Little Elm Reservoir was still under construction in 1955. The new 1,022-foot-long span would have 26-foot-wide roadways. The reservoir itself and a related dam for the Elm Fork of the Trinity River were intended to control Trinity River flooding and provide an additional water supply for Dallas. Plans had been approved to widen US 77 north to the Red River, but construction funds were limited and the THD was leaning toward a still wider expressway solution for US 77. This would require additional right-of-way purchases and additional funds.[42]

For many years, the "I" in I-35 stood for "Interregional" in Travis County. As early as 1945, a four-lane, twenty-three-mile Interregional Highway had been planned to upgrade US 81 between Round Rock and Kyle, en route to a junction with the so-called San Antonio Highway (US 81). Planners had also sought to reroute US 81 away from downtown Austin, preferably via Austin's two-hundred-foot-wide East Avenue. After several possible routes through and around Austin were evaluated, the East Avenue route was selected. Right-of-way purchases followed, and construction began in 1952. In addition to its width, East Avenue provided a location east of the vast and growing domain of the University of Texas and formalized an existing dividing line of sorts.

In 1928, a consulting firm had recommended that Austin's black community— then roughly 17 percent of the city's population—be guided to an existing "Negro District" east of East Avenue and south of the city cemetery. The proposal was rejected, but the intention became the reality. Austin's black community has been centered in East Austin for decades, and East Avenue (US 81/I-35) was and still is viewed as a significant dividing line.[43]

The first 1.5-mile section of Austin's Interregional Highway (US 81) was completed in July 1952. The project would be highlighted by a new six-lane East Avenue Bridge over the Colorado River a few blocks east of Congress Avenue. When completed in July 1954, the $771,206, 1,052-foot span boasted a welded (rather than riveted) steel girder–type structure with a concrete deck and two thirty-eight-foot roadways. Unfortunately, the new bridge remained closed until the entire Interregional Highway project was completed. The objective of 1957 proved wishful thinking. Construction costs were averaging $500,000 per mile and rising, including around $50,000 per mile for a new "whiteway" lighting system, and progress was slow. By February 1960, a two-mile, six-lane segment in downtown Austin (with frontage roads and eight underpasses) was still incomplete, and the target date was extended to year-end, 1962. By then, the expressway was obsolete. The Interregional would eventually have to be expanded to six lanes with a double deck in downtown Austin in 1975.[44]

San Antonio fared better. US 81 had been completed through Bexar by late 1954 and a six-mile segment of the San Antonio Expressway (I-10) between Nogalitos Street (US 81) and the Fredericksburg Road (US 87) was nearing completion. Bexar's expressway system, comprising US 81 (I-35), US 90 (I-10), US 87, and inner Loop 13 had been planned in 1945. Roughly $20 million in right-of-way purchases had been completed, shared by the City of San Antonio (67 percent) and Bexar County (33 percent). Only part of Loop 13 was ever built, however. It would be superseded by the more ambitious Loop I-410 project, located two miles farther out.[45]

As highway construction projects stalled and costs escalated, the Texas gas tax was raised to five cents per gallon in 1955. Since 1951, one-fourth of these tax revenues had been devoted to county farm-to-market roads and to servicing old county debt obligations. A second fourth went to the Available School Fund. The State Highway Fund received the balance. As for registration fees, which had benefited from a near doubling of Texas vehicle registrations between 1945 and 1950 (to 3.1 million), the State Highway Fund and the counties continued to share these revenues on a 75–25 basis.[46]

While Texas was moving somewhat tentatively into expressways, its north-ern neighbor was building one of the largest independent highway systems in the nation. By 1955, the Turner Turnpike linked Oklahoma City via Tulsa with Joplin, Missouri, and plans were readied to extend the network south to the Red River. I-35 was still in the planning stages in 1955, and if Gainesville (US 77) and Denison (US 75) were logical junction candidates for the Turner's southern extension, it is of some interest that the honor eventually fell to Burk-burnett, north of Wichita Falls. Burkburnett boasted a new $1 million bridge and a seventeen-mile Red River Expressway (I-44) by December 1964, even if the new expressway was dead-ended six miles southeast of Wichita Falls.[47]

The location of I-35 eventually followed the PRA Map–Blue Star Highway route of 1947. But it could have been different. If a northwestern route through Burkburnett was unlikely, I-35 could have been routed along US 81 north through Ringgold to another junction with the Turner Turnpike. Or I-35 could have been directed northeast from Dallas (via US 75) through Denison—Deni-son lay in Democrat Sam Rayburn's home district but had been the birthplace of Republican President Eisenhower. Yet I-35 was routed due north. Gainesville sat in Republican-leaning Cooke County and may have been rewarded for (reluctantly) approving the relocation of US 77 in 1945. Bypassed communities like Sherman (US 75) and Decatur (US 81) must have felt slighted.

By 1955, the expressway version of the Blue Star Highway had been com-pleted only in segments. Four- to eight-lane "superhighways" US 81 and US 77 were scheduled to be completed in 1961, but contracts had been let in stages: $1.2 million for 14.5 miles in Bell County; $1.5 million for a four-mile section in Austin; and $2.3 million for 6.7 miles in Bexar County. Each of these con-tracts included grading, surfacing, and structures work. The THD had already invested $275 million in the new expressways, and most of the necessary rights-of-way had been acquired. But gaps remained. Williamson County had asked the state to purchase its remaining rights-of-way, something the state was pro-hibited from doing until after 1956. In Hays County, a dispute arose over compensation due to property owners as US 81 was widened through San Mar-cos. The city had approved $300,000 for right-of-way purchases, but it had not been enough.[48]

With US 81 moving forward, some 743 miles of multilane highways were either completed or under contract in Texas by November 1955. A three-mile segment of the Central Expressway in Dallas was already carrying fifty-two thousand vehicles daily, and a $1 million contract was let for a new highway bridge across the Trinity River at the junction of US 77 and US 67. New three-level interchanges were under way at the junction of US 81 and US 84 in north Waco and in northwest Fort Worth. Texas' first three-level interchange had been constructed at the western end of the Baytown Tunnel in Houston.[49]

OFF-RAMP: LANDMARK LEGISLATION

Nationally, the Federal Highway Act of 1954 and the Cold War prompted more ambitious proposals. In July of that year, on behalf of an incapacitated President Eisenhower, Vice President Richard M. Nixon delivered a speech that was anything but mundane at a state governors' conference in Lake George, New York. Nixon suggested that a massive ten-year interstate highway initiative was needed to accelerate the expanded program laid out by the 1954 act. The price tag was a shocking $50 billion.[50]

As a follow-up to Nixon's speech, President Eisenhower appointed retired general Lucius D. Clay, then chair of Continental Can Company, to chair an advisory committee on a National Highway Program. Eisenhower's interest in transportation issues was predictable. Born in the one-time transportation hub of Denison, Texas, in 1890 and the son of a Katy railroad employee, Eisenhower had been reared in the former cattle drive capital of Abilene, Kansas, had served at Fort Sam Houston in 1916, and had participated in the U.S. Army's first transcontinental truck convoy in 1919. His substantial logistics planning and management skills had been critical to the Allies' successful D-Day invasion and subsequent victory in World War II. Having been impressed by the German autobahn system as well, Eisenhower must have seen the potential benefits of transcontinental interstate highways as clearly as anyone.[51]

The Clay Committee, assisted by Francis du Pont (who had replaced Mac-Donald as BPR chief in 1953), Senator Prescott S. Bush of Connecticut, and Frank Turner, issued its report in January 1955, estimating the total U.S. highway needs at around $101 billion and recommending a $27 billion, ten-year program to build the designated interstate system. The report called for a new Federal Highway Corporation, empowered to issue $25 billion in bonds, like state turnpike authorities, and supported by dedicated gasoline taxes—not tolls. In addition, the sponsors hoped to raise the federal cost share from 60 percent to 95 percent. These new ideas were not widely accepted. The Clay Committee plan was rejected in the U.S. Senate by a vote of 60–31 in May 1955, prompting House Speaker Rayburn to note the heavy influence of powerful interests (trucking, oil, tires) who favored a bond financing program over pure user taxes. These same interests (and the AAA) would ultimately agree to gasoline and other user taxes as preferable to tolls.[52]

The need for an interstate system was an unstoppable force, however, and cooler heads prevailed. Some of the Clay Committee's recommendations even found their way into the Federal Highway Act of 1956, signed by President Eisenhower while he was recuperating at Walter Reed Medical Center on June 29. The Act of 1956 expanded the federal role dramatically and categorized the interstate system as one single gigantic highway project. The renamed National System of Interstate and Defense Highways was increased to 41,000 miles (the Senate wanted 42,500 and would eventually get it) with a scheduled completion date in 1969. All of the added mileage was in urban areas. The act created the Federal Highway Trust Fund and raised the federal share of interstate construction costs to a whopping 90 percent—slightly below the Clay Committee's target. As recently as 1930, the federal share had been below 10 percent. The act also converted the venerable BPR into the Federal Highway Administration (FHA).[53]

The projected cost of the 41,000-mile system was pegged at $27.6 billion, lower than Nixon's figure but shocking nevertheless. The Highway Trust Fund would receive contributions from a series of taxes, including a one cent per gallon increase in the federal gasoline tax to three cents (four cents in 1959), taxes on tires, excise taxes on vehicles, and a higher usage fee for heavy trucks. All of these taxes were scheduled to be phased out in 1972. The act provided federal funds for advance right-of-way land acquisitions but prohibited tolls and phased out the old population and geography allocation formulas. After 1959, interstate funding allocations would be determined by "system needs." Last, interstate highway contractors were required to pay no less than prevailing local wage rates, a law already covered by the Davis-Bacon Act (and so controversial that Senator Lyndon B. Johnson scheduled a medical exam on the day of the vote).[54]

Most of the new interstates would have four twelve-foot-wide lanes with ten-foot shoulders. Two-lane highways were permitted only until 1966, when all interstates were required to be four-lane divided expressways with no at-grade intersections. Access would be controlled via restricted entrances and exits, with interchanges at all freeway intersections. Speed limits were set at 70 mph in flat terrain, 60 mph in rolling terrain, and 50 mph in mountains and designated urban areas. The new interstate highways were routed near but not through small communities. Existing principal highways were retained as business routes. In large cities, interstates would pass through developed areas and near enough to the central business district to carry some of the heaviest traffic loads. Eventually, but not in 1956, public hearings were required in any community affected by a proposed route.[55]

The new interstates would provide travel that was faster, safer, and more productive for interstate commerce. While massive swaths of real estate were required to implement these improvements, service stations, restaurants, and other commercial businesses were banned entirely from interstate highways. New overhead highway signs were introduced with a warning that "since the letters and numerals must be large to be readable [from at least 700 feet], most town names will be too long to be included." The AASHO also introduced a numbering and marking plan based on the now familiar red, white, and blue interstate shield logo. Unveiled in August 1957, the new logo was based on designs submitted by the THD and the Missouri Highway Department. It made its Texas I-35 debut in 1961, on a stretch south of Hillsboro.[56]

Texas was allocated 2,905 miles of the 41,000-mile interstate highway system, representing 7 percent of the U.S. total and 6 percent of the state highway system. Texas' new interstates would make up four east-west routes (I-10, I-20, I-30, and I-40), four circumferential loops around Dallas, Fort Worth, Houston, and San Antonio, and one and only one north-south route, Laredo-Gainesville (I-35), splitting at Hillsboro and Denton. Four other north-south routes—I-37 between Corpus Christi and San Antonio, I-45 between Dallas and Galveston, I-27 between Amarillo and Lubbock, and I-44 between Wichita Falls and the Red River—would eventually be added to the list, but these routes are intrastate expressways that were built to interstate standards.

As of October 1956, the Texas road system included 37 U.S. highways, 210 state highways, and 2,358 FM roads. Expressways were rare. Other than the Gulf Freeway and the Central Expressway, the only expressways depicted in the 1956 *Texas Highway Map* were US 77 between Lewisville and Denton and five sections of US 81—between the Randolph Air Force Base exit in San Antonio and south of New Braunfels; north of Austin to the Pflugerville exit; between Belton and Temple; the portion coinciding with US 77 north of Waco to Abbott; and between Burleson and south of Fort Worth. Somehow, "Superhighway" US 77 in Gainesville was not represented as an expressway.[57]

The new interstate highway system was administered in traditional fashion by the THD, with one exception. The Act of 1956 had created a revolving fund through which states could purchase rights-of-way in advance, based on a successful 1947 California model. The THD, previously dependent on counties and towns to obtain rights-of-way for all highway projects, could now acquire rights-of-way for interstates for the first time in its history. In December 1956, the THD purchased its first right-of-way under the new guidelines, spending $5,890 to widen US 87 five miles east of its junction with US 80 in Dallas County.[58]

While the process of upgrading US highways like US 81 and US 77 into interstate-quality expressways would be slow, some progress was being made. The northern and southern segments of US 81 in Austin, totaling 13.7 miles, were completed by year's end in 1956. Construction continued along the middle (East Avenue) segment, however, between 1st and 15th streets. The downtown project necessitated the demolition and relocation of Samuel Huston College, recently merged with Tillotson in 1952, between 11th and 12th streets. Farther north, a ten-mile section of US 81 in Bell County was under construction during 1957, including a depressed rigid frame underpass/bridge structure in Troy (five miles north of Temple). The new structure was built with timber columns and reinforced steel at a cost of $41,706.[59]

The year 1957 was marked by a number of events. A massive loop road (future I-635) was proposed for Dallas County, and the Dallas–Fort Worth Toll Road opened in August, after twenty-three months of construction. The six-lane divided highway included ten entrances and exits, six fare stations, and a lighting system comprising a thousand mercury vapor lamps. A licensed mid-point plaza with two service stations and two restaurants opened on both sides of the highway. The toll for passenger cars was fifty cents. Despite lower than projected traffic volume of around 14,000 vehicles per day in 1957, versus an estimate of 20,000 and a capacity of 65,000, the turnpike somehow managed to break even (after operating costs and interest charges) by June 1958.[60]

Two other highlights of 1957 involved the completion of gateway bridge projects at both ends of future I-35. US 77 between Gainesville and the Red River was upgraded in time to serve a new deck-plate, girder-type bridge between Gainesville and Ardmore, Oklahoma. Planned in 1953 by a Joint Conference of the Texas and Oklahoma Highway Departments—a more peaceful mechanism than those in the 1930s—the new Red River bridge was opened on August 26, 1957, to supplement the older 1931 truss span. Since old truss-type bridges were difficult to widen, Cooke County's upgraded expressway (future I-35) was accommodated by using the 1931 structure for one direction of US 77 and the new bridge for the other. This same concept had been applied to a US 75 bridge project in Dallas in 1950.[61]

At the other end of I-35, the $1.5 million Friendship (International) Bridge opened in Laredo in February 1957. The new four-lane, 860-foot-long span was not the second highway bridge that had been proposed in 1940, however. Rather, the new structure replaced a temporary pontoon bridge that had been constructed by the U.S. Army Corps of Engineers following the massive flood of June 1954. Floodwaters had crested to a near record of sixty-one feet, but the sturdy 1922 structure had not been washed away. The old bridge was demolished only when sections of a collapsed bridge in Eagle Pass had smashed into Laredo's Mexican Railways bridge and stormed downriver. The 1957 version, built jointly by the City of Laredo and the Mexican Government on a 60 percent–40 percent cost share basis, featured a unique prestressed concrete, continuous-beam design to defend against future floodwaters (until the Amistad Dam was constructed upriver in 1969).[62]

As the new International Bridge was being built, plans were made to upgrade US 81 in Laredo to an expressway. As early as 1929, the THD had encouraged the city to develop north-south and east-west bypass routes. The city had declined. Like San Marcos and Gainesville merchants in the 1940s, many Laredoans viewed downtown traffic congestion as a boon to local businesses — not something with which to tamper. But Laredo's colonial streets, despite ample widths of 55.6 feet (twenty varas), were becoming increasingly overburdened after two hundred years of service. Meanwhile, the old, single-track railroad bridge, dedicated by William T. Sherman in 1882, had to be reconstructed after the floods of 1932 and 1954.

Encouraged by the International Traffic Committee's recommendations, the new International Bridge, and Mexican plans to upgrade 150 miles of the Pan American Highway to a divided highway between Nuevo Laredo and Monterrey, Laredo finally approved the US 81 expressway initiative in 1955. An estimated 1.5 million automobiles crossed the International Bridge in 1958, representing 80 percent of the tourist traffic with Mexico, and construction along US 81 (I-35) between North Laredo and Cotulla began in 1959. Proposals to add a second highway bridge and an eastern expressway to Corpus Christi were again rejected.[63]

According to the 1958 State Highway Map, expressways were completed between northwest Dallas and Denton, between North Waco and Hillsboro, between Buda and South Austin, and between Lytle and southwest San Antonio. Entering 1959, Texas had completed 444 miles of interstates, including 402 interstate bridges, with another 436 miles under construction. By year end, a $20 million, 7.9-mile section of Stemmons Freeway (I-35E) opened as part of the planned 95-mile route of I-35E between Hillsboro and Denton. The Stemmons would be a massive ten-lane affair with three lanes of frontage roads on each side. Completions, however, were becoming expensive. Costs per mile were ranging between $500,000 and $2 million, with some sections reaching as high as $6 million.[64]

One costly (and questionable) project was a four-level, roadway-stacking interchange in Fort Worth, completed in 1958 at the junction of I-35W and I-30. Nicknamed the "pretzel" (or the "mixmaster") by local denizens, the interchange utilized a "haunched slab-span design" of continuously reinforced concrete slab (due to a shortage of structural steel). The concrete paving was ten inches thick with a reinforcing steel mat. The interchange had been planned in 1945–47 as a cloverleaf but was revised in 1952. The final stacking design was determined by railroad tracks to the south and west, a housing project on the northwest side, and a plan to add a Lancaster Avenue overpass in the near future. A completely different junction for the I-35W interchange was apparently not considered.[65]

Pretzel-like interchanges and increasingly expensive urban expressway projects contributed to an escalation in construction costs. As progress slowed and costs mounted, the estimated price tag for the entire interstate highway program, projected at $27 billion in 1956, was revised upward to $40 billion in 1960. Even this revised figure excluded about another $6.5 billion in funds required to purchase selected toll roads and to reroute various railroad and utility lines. In partial response, the federal gasoline tax was raised to four cents in 1959.[66]

OFF-RAMP: THE CRITICS SOUND OFF

Criticism began to appear. Lewis Mumford, the noted urbanist and co-chair of the June 1955 symposium "Man's Role in Changing the Face of the Earth," railed against the environmental damage caused by interstates. The new highways were "covering over and removing from cultivation the very [agricultural] land—often, indeed, the richest alluvial soils—whose existence at the beginning made the [city's] growth possible." In a September 1957 speech, Mumford recommended that the entire interstate highway program be halted until comprehensive metropolitan land use plans could be developed and evaluated. The prophetic, somewhat elitist, and overly pessimistic Mumford stated that the nation's cities and countryside were being destroyed by people "who hadn't the faintest notion of what they were doing" and the "religion of the motor car."[67]

Even less than rabble-rousing publications like *Readers Digest* were becoming concerned. In the July 1960 article "Our Great Big Highway Bungle," the magazine suggested that the "dream" of an interstate highway system had become a "nightmare: of recklessness, extravagance, special privilege, bureaucratic stupidity and sometimes outright thievery." *Readers Digest* was most concerned that the BPR's supervisory role had all but disappeared. Highways were being built willy-nilly, particularly in urban areas, with little regard to cost or location.[68]

Corruption and waste were rampant. Many contractors, right-of-way property owners, and service providers were being overcompensated without effective supervision. In Wilmington, Delaware, a new ten-mile stretch of interstate highway had a cost of $5 million per mile, cut the city in half, and forced over six hundred tax-paying homes and businesses to relocate. In Reno, Nevada, four bridges across the Truckee River were constructed at a cost of $41 million to route I-80 through town, when a northern bypass route would have required no bridges and would have saved $23 million. The process was repeated across the nation. The implication was that the interstate system was being driven by a massive "highway lobby" of automobile, trucking, oil and gas, engineering, and construction companies and powerful trade associations.[69]

If that were not enough, the magazine discovered that more than two thousand interstate-ready bridges and underpasses were too low, at fourteen feet of clearance, to accommodate various military weapon systems (missiles and radar) and their vehicles. Since the interstate system had been sold to the American public in part as a military defense, mobilization, and evacuation network, this discovery was curious. Input from the Department of Defense had somehow not been solicited. In 1967, when the THD learned that some 254 bridges in Texas would have to be upgraded or replaced to meet the new DOD overhead clearance standard of sixteen feet, a THD official stated that the announcement "fell like a bombshell [with] lots of screaming and squirming."[70]

Routings were also being questioned. A major thrust of the 1956 act had been to build urban expressways to relieve traffic congestion and to facilitate interstate commerce. Inevitably, many of the new expressways were being routed through neighborhoods, parklands, and districts of historical importance. Texas towns would not escape this process, but cities like Baltimore, Boston, New Orleans, New York, Philadelphia, San Francisco, and Washington would be impacted greatly. The route selections were almost always driven by economics and politics. Not illogically, cost-conscious highway departments almost always sought to acquire rights-of-way through a city's least expensive real estate markets. If many of these markets happened to include low-income, often minority neighborhoods—too bad.

In fact, many planners turned the issue on its head. Routing an expressway through a city's "blighted" area, they claimed, meant the bulldozed path was then ripe for "urban renewal." The concept was pioneered by Robert Moses, a master planner who was building 899 miles of urban expressways through greater New York City by 1964—nearly double the 459 miles built in all of Los Angeles. The fortunes of the residents and businesses displaced by this renewal process were left unspoken. Politics prevailed; rarely was an urban expressway routed through a city's middle- and upper-income areas. Viewing the federal role in these endeavors as a "subsidization of chaos," Mumford informed readers in 1959 that the majestic Verrazano Narrows Bridge between Brooklyn and Staten Island had displaced some eight thousand residents of Bay Ridge, leaving the remaining citizens with a noisy elevated highway to contemplate.[71]

The nation's largest interstate highway builder, Texas, was relatively unscathed by and immune to these criticisms. Most Texans recognized that if interstates like I-35 did not exist, the cost of doing business in Texas would be higher than in states having such highways. But based on a series of "before and after" economic impact studies commissioned by the THD and BPR and conducted by the Texas Transportation Institute (TTI) at Texas A&M, important issues were raised and quantified. Impact studies were prepared for Dallas and San Antonio in the 1950s and nine other towns in the 1960s, including future I-35 sections of San Antonio, Austin, Temple, and Waxahachie. The objectives were to measure the impact of expressways on urban property values and to determine whether bypassing the old through-routes had had any effect on local business activities, land use, property values, and travel patterns. Of course, when the numbers began to sour, future studies were halted.

In Dallas, a 3.6-mile section of the 30-mile-long Central Expressway (US 75) was selected as the TTI study area. The Central Expressway, completed between 1947 in early 1953, was routed through a number of so-called blighted neighborhoods and industrial areas, as would-be future sections of I-35. The value of land that abutted the frontage roads ("A-Bands") was compared before construction (1941–45) and after (1951–55). As one might expect, the A-Band values increased by 405 percent over the ten-year period versus a control group increase of only 134 percent. However, and somewhat surprisingly, the values of "B-Band" properties, located a few blocks away from the frontage roads, increased by only 110 percent, versus 132 percent for the control group. If one did not own the abutting property, one actually underperformed the overall real estate market.[72]

In San Antonio, a 3.7-mile section of the combined US 81/US 87 express-way, completed between 1947 and 1954, was selected as the study area. The study area section had witnessed the removal of a blighted neighborhood, two manufacturing areas, several shopping districts, and a rare middle-class neighborhood. In this study, A and B Bands were combined, probably to improve the reported results, and the enlarged abutting land values were again compared before construction (1941–45) and after (1952–56). Over the ten-year period, abutting land values rose by 318 percent versus only 87 percent for the control group, and unimproved land values increased by even more—by 393 percent versus only 83 percent for the control. While the San Antonio results were consistent with those in Dallas, it would have been useful to have had data from pure B-Band properties as well. Otherwise, both studies confirmed that abutting frontage road properties were the places to be—preferably before routes became official.[73]

Waxahachie, Temple, and Austin were analyzed in three of the TTI's nine bypass studies. The 11.5-mile bypass study section in Waxahachie, purchased by Ellis County between July 1955, and July 1956, ran parallel to the MKT railroad line. Completed between August 1956, and September 1959, the section had entailed construction costs of $4.5 million or $391,000 per mile. Surprisingly, the new bypass was found to have no apparent impact on the seventy-two retail businesses operating in the Waxahachie study area between 1958 and 1962—their gross revenues totaled $6.7 million in 1958 and $7 million in 1962. This modest expansion (3.5 percent) was well below the retail sales growth in all of Waxahachie (up 13.1 percent during the period), below that of nearby Corsicana (up 19.7 percent), and below that for the state of Texas (up 17.8 percent) during the five-year period. While some study area businesses may have benefited from I-35, most were either hurt by the new bypass or underperformed their peers.[74]

Results in Temple were even cloudier. Again, the prospect of converting traditional agricultural lands into commercial and industrial properties caused an explosion in local land values. Between 1945 and 1964, Temple land values within the three-mile study section of the US 81 expressway (I-35) soared by 2,562 percent. But a comparison of business activity between I-35, opened in 1954, and old US 81 during the 1954–61 period indicated no significant change in Temple's total revenue growth. Traffic-oriented businesses on old US 81—gas stations, motels, and restaurants—were hurt severely by I-35. Despite a strong general economy, the old US 81 businesses suffered a 1 percent decline in revenues between 1954 and 1961.[75]

In Austin, the TTI study area was an eight-mile stretch of US 81 (future I-35) some four miles north of downtown, north of the US 290 interchange and one mile east of old US 81 (North Lamar Boulevard). The study area had consisted mainly of unimproved agricultural or pasture land when the three-hundred-foot rights-of-way were acquired in 1948 by the City of Austin and Travis County. The relatively expensive ($100,000 per mile) purchase price, years before construction would even start, reflected the market's anticipation of increased valuations. Unimproved land prices had averaged $525 per acre in the study area between 1941 and 1948 but only $130 per acre in four "control group" tracts scattered around Austin.[76]

The Austin study section was completed in June 1954, as an interregional highway with four lanes, divided by a median strip, with two additional frontage lanes on each side. With several at-grade crossovers, the new highway would not be upgraded to interstate status until later. Austin's population in 1961 (192,500) was more than double the 1940 level (87,930), and the study area had become urbanized and residential. Between 1958 and 1961, average unimproved land prices in the study area soared to $3,114 per acre, versus control group prices of only $707. Again, the new expressway reduced business activity at traffic-oriented businesses along old US 81—gas stations, restaurants, and motels—without impacting total business activity. If much of the lost revenue was offset by residential-related businesses and new commercial enterprises, total revenue growth in Austin was minimal.[77]

The TTI studies appeared to confirm the investment appeal of raw, future (abutting) frontage road property—a process set to be repeated along Texas 130 intersections—and the damage done to businesses located along the old highway (e.g., US 81). Still, it must also be assumed that an entire metropolitan region benefits from an interstate highway or suffers without one. Consider the case of Taylor. Like Temple, Taylor was established as a railroad town (in 1876) and served as a junction for the I&GN and Katy railroads in their heyday. Driven by railroad traffic, Taylor emerged as one of Texas' leading cotton centers by 1900 and, as late as 1920, held a coveted position on Highway 2 and future US 79 to Shreveport. But Taylor was bypassed when a more direct route was chosen for Highway 2 in 1922 and for future US 81 (I-35). Taylor has underperformed the I-35 towns of Temple, Georgetown, and Round Rock ever since, and a 1974 decision to reroute US 79 away from downtown may not have helped matters.[78]

9

Interstate 35 Comes to Pass, 1960–2000

*T*N much the same manner that the Federal Aid Road Act of 1916 had shifted management responsibilities from counties to state highway departments, the Federal Highway Act of 1956 solidified the New Deal era trend in which the state role, in turn, was subservient to that of the federal government. State highway departments remained powerful entities, but decision making was increasingly centralized, bureaucratized, and politicized out of Washington. The construction of Interstate 35 in Texas and most other U.S. interstate projects became less a function of local initiative and more a function of accessing federal purse strings in a timely manner. Old-fashioned economic cycles remained a fact of life, however, and stops, starts, and delays would be the norm for decades.

According to the *Texas Highway Map* of 1960, the following expressway sections of Interstate 35 had been completed: from north Laredo to south Cotulla; Lytle to San Antonio; northeast San Antonio to south San Marcos; north Buda to Austin; Austin to north Round Rock; north Jarrell to south Waco; Elm Mott to Hillsboro; Burleson to south Fort Worth; south Waxahachie to north Waxahachie; northwest Dallas to north Sanger; and between Gainesville and the Red River. In metropolitan areas, San Antonio had completed thirteen miles of I-35, a downtown expressway (US 81) between Division and Broadway, plus a southwestern section of Loop I-410. Austin's East Avenue Expressway (US 81) was nearing completion between the south and north city limits. In Fort Worth, a segment of the North-South Freeway had reached Lancaster and the east-west Toll Road was in operation to Dallas. The Stemmons Freeway (US 77) had been completed to Dallas's northwest corner, the Central Expressway (US 75) was nearing completion, and an elevated freeway was planned to connect the two.

Some 884 miles of interstate highways were completed in Texas by June 1961, with another 1,425 miles under construction. The next highlight was the completion of the final 1.7-mile ($2.4 million) segment of I-35 in Austin in March 1962. Designed to handle volumes of 30,000 vehicles per day, the Austin project included a new 900-foot overpass at Sixth, Seventh, and Eighth streets, built with prestressed concrete (at $4.34 per square foot) rather than steel ($5.14). A new Montopolis Bridge and interchange were under construction at US 183 in anticipation of a possible loop road around the Texas capital. But unlike I-410 in San Antonio, Austin's disjointed loop-road candidates—US 183 (north and east), US 71 (south), Mo-Pac and Loop 360 (west), and the new Texas 130 (east)—would never be tied into a true loop system.[1]

Loop or no loop, the hundred-mile stretch of I-35 between Round Rock and San Antonio was nearing completion. The "US 81 Freeway" between Kyle and Buda opened in October 1962, and forty-three miles of I-35 were completed through both ends of Bexar County. The Bexar project, fourteen years and $50 million in the making, gave San Antonio more expressway miles than any U.S. city other than greater New York and Los Angeles. Remaining gaps included an upgrade of a 7-mile section of expressway in north Austin (to interstate standards); a 3.2-mile segment in San Marcos, including a new interchange to replace the twenty-year-old traffic circle; and the remaining 21 miles of (55-mile) I-410 in Bexar.[2]

Farther north, I-35E was completed across the western portion of the Garza–Little Elm Reservoir in Denton County, followed by the opening of segments north and south of Farmers Branch in August 1963. The last 3.8-mile segment of Stemmons Freeway opened in October. Other downtown Dallas sections were still in progress, and the first 15-mile (northside) segment of the $23 million LBJ Freeway (Loop I-635), a massive undertaking with 350-foot rights-of-way, commenced in 1964. The Stemmons Freeway (I-35E) would boost the fortunes of Farmers Branch and Carrollton in the same way that the Central Expressway (US 75) had fostered Richardson and Plano. These and other suburban boom towns were eventually linked by I-635. In Fort Worth, a $14 million segment of I-35W between the Tarrant County line and Denton was still in the pipeline but a 10.6-mile segment of Loop I-820 was dedicated in September 1963. The total cost was $12 million, or $1.1 million per mile.[3]

These projects pushed Texas' interstate highway mileage to nearly 1,300, at least 400 miles more than the June 1961, total and nearly 500 miles more than in California. Another 1,163 miles were under construction. Few of Texas' interstate segments were longer than 60 miles, however, and the remaining portion of the state's 3,032-mile system was still on the drawing board. Construction budgets continued to be eroded by reality. The target completion date for the entire U.S. system was extended from 1969 to 1972, and the estimated total cost rose from more than $40 billion to $50 billion. The principal cost culprits were bridges and interchanges. Some 13,000 bridges and 12,000 interchanges had been constructed to date, but right-of-way expenditures and construction costs in urban areas had gotten out of hand. The revised $50 billion projection would be revised again and again.[4]

New structural materials like prestressed concrete, "slip form" pavement sections, asphalt binders, and grooved pavements were introduced, as was new equipment. By embedding pretensioned cables into a structure to produce a desired stress condition, prestressed concrete bridges allowed legal load limits to be raised from 16,000 pounds (in a timber-steel world) to over 72,000 pounds. Petroleum-based asphalts still had their problems. Some 15 million tons of paving asphalt had been installed on U.S. roads through 1959—roughly 50 percent as asphaltic cement, 40 percent as a solvent-thinned "cutback" material, and 10 percent as an asphalt emulsion—but according to one expert, Dr. R. N. Traxler of the TTI, the wrong binder formulation had often been applied. New equipment offerings would include diamond-bladed rotary saws, portable rock-crushing machines ("rockbusters"), and the L-360, a massive 175-foot-long earth mover with a 360-ton capacity. The THD had replaced the venerable short-handled No. 2 Scoop, which required six men and thirty minutes to fill a dump truck, with a modern front-end loader that did the same job in just five minutes.[5]

Another new piece of equipment, the computer, was contributing to the planning, engineering, management, and monitoring of highway and bridge projects. A THD Bridge Division employee boasted in 1960 that "the computing machine" in Austin had reduced bridge-design paperwork from nearly five hundred pages to fifty, small enough to fit in just two manila folders. Within five years, a computer systems employee predicted that the THD's new Control Data 1604-A would lead to a series of innovations that would affect everyone in the department. Assuming that data could be transmitted to and from the computer via telephone or telegraph, the employee suggested that computers would make it "possible and economical to communicate with the districts" on a daily basis.[6]

Improved equipment, surface materials, and signage were intended to boost highway safety. While interstate highway accidents were more common, and often more spectacular, than those occurring on the roads they replaced, the older highways had more frequent intersections and a higher probability for crashes. The elimination of dangerous intersections, curves, and crossovers and the improvement of road surfaces and signage have almost certainly saved thousands of lives. The bypassing or elimination of colorful World War II–era traffic circles in San Marcos, Waco, and Dallas reduced intersections that had become dangerous with rising speeds. Interstate signs, conforming to the catchy *Interstate Manual for Signing and Pavement Marking of the National System of Interstate and Defense Highways,* debuted in Texas on a stretch of I-35 ten miles south of Hillsboro, near Abbott, in August 1961.[7]

Highway safety improvements in Dallas were of little value on November 22, 1963. En route to a scheduled luncheon at the Dallas Trade Mart following a morning speech in Fort Worth, President John F. Kennedy and Governor John B. Connally were shot at 12:30 P.M. from a sixth-floor window of the Texas School Book Depository on Houston Street—near Elm Street, facing Dealey Plaza, and one block north of John Neely Bryan's cabin. The dying president was rushed in six minutes to Parkland Memorial Hospital, via Elm, the Triple Underpass, the recently completed Stemmons Freeway (I-35E), and Hines Boulevard (US 77). The president, vice president, and governor had hoped to shore up support in a state that was leaning increasingly to the rival Republican Party.[8]

The Kennedy and Johnson administrations, starting with the Federal Aid Highway Act of 1962, encouraged regional transportation planning. In Waco, with 132,352 residents in 1964, "Origin and Destination Surveys" considered the adequacy of 11,591 parking spaces located in a 99-block area of the city's central business district. This parking capacity would prove to be more than adequate as I-35 began to transfer more and more businesses from downtown Waco to frontage roads and suburbs. However, the city that had led Texas into the modern era with a majestic suspension bridge in 1870 was lagging on I-35. Other than the planned bypass for Waco Circle, still functioning today south of downtown at the intersection of US 81 and US 77 and two local roads (La Salle and Valley Mills), I-35 was unfinished between Waco's Fourth Street (south of the Brazos River) and Elm Mott to the north as of January 1966. Rights-of-way were the principal problem. In response to this and another gap south of Cotulla, the THD was empowered in late 1963 to purchase all remaining rights-of-ways along I-35.[9]

Laredo's I-35 activities were moving along. The 3,142-mile Pan American Highway to Panama City was finally "completed" in April 1963, excluding various jungle-covered sections of Panama, and the combined population of the two Laredos was nearing 150,000. The city fathers had approved the future route of I-35 to San Antonio in 1955, but the segment between Cotulla and Laredo was not finished until 1965. More important, the path of I-35 to Laredo's one highway bridge would remain stalled at Victoria Street, just north of the ancient San Augustin district. The halt helped to preserve the city's colonial heritage, but the old downtown route (US 81) between I-35 and the International Bridge was becoming increasingly congested. Between Cotulla and San Antonio, I-35 was finished only between Lytle and a section of I-410. Old US 81 remained in use between Cotulla and Lytle.[10]

Work proceeded between San Antonio and Georgetown. By December 1965, Bexar County had constructed 147 miles of designated interstate highways, 79 miles of which were either I-35 or I-410 (map 14). On January 19, 1966, the 55-mile Loop I-410 was finally opened after ten years of effort and a capital cost of $32 million ($582,000 per mile). The cost excluded $7 million for right-of-way purchases and future outlays for a planned interchange at I-410 and I-35. Mayor Walter W. McAllister participated in the ribbon-cutting ceremony. In Austin, a $20 million contract (at nearly $2.9 million per mile) was let to upgrade a seven-mile section of I-35 north of US 290 to interstate standards. A ten-mile segment of I-35 between Round Rock and Georgetown was moving to completion in early 1966.[11]

By February 1966, 176 miles of I-35 remained to be finished. I-35E between Hillsboro and Waxahachie opened in May 1966, and the entire stretch of I-35E between Hillsboro and Dallas in early 1967. The completion of one segment, however, had upset a few residents. An enterprising youth group had borrowed a section of the surfaced (but unfinished) roadway north of Hillsboro for Thursday night drag races. In Dallas County, I-35E was completed except for a small gap south of downtown. The first (3.2-mile) segment of the LBJ Freeway (Loop I-635) between Stemmons Freeway and Farmers Branch opened in March 1967, in anticipation of completion of the entire loop in 1971. In Fort Worth, the final section of I-35W between Hillsboro and Fort Worth was dedicated in March 1967, as the northeast section of Loop I-820 neared completion. The next task would be the former US 377 segment between Fort Worth and Denton.[12]

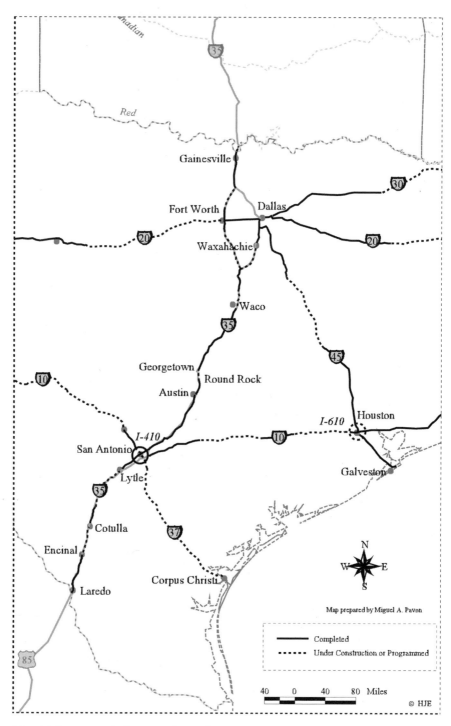

Map 14. Interstates in Progress, December 31, 1965.

The THD was managing 68,000 miles of highways in 1967, supported by a $500 million budget and 17,000 employees. The corresponding figures for 1927 were 18,000 miles, $29 million, and 6,900 employees. Over 80 percent of Texas' 3,033-mile interstate system was now built, under construction, or programmed. I-35 was the furthest along. According to the *State Highway Map* of 1968, gaps in I-35 were limited to the following segments: between Encinal and Devine; between Waco and Elm Mott, including an uncompleted bridge across the Brazos River; and between Highway 114 north of Fort Worth and Denton. In addition, I-35 was stalled in downtown Laredo and awaited an interchange (the Fratt) to link I-35 with Loop I-410 in northeast San Antonio. Sections of Loop I-635 in Dallas County were also under construction.[13]

OFF-RAMP: NEIGHBORHOOD REVOLTS

Despite this progress, public opinion in urban areas had turned skeptical, at best, toward interstate highways. Not only had delays and cost overruns become routine, but even the highway routings were being challenged. In addition, the Federal Highway Beautification Act of 1965, promoted by Lady Bird Johnson and influenced by the president's earlier experience with the NYA, had established regulations for landscaping, billboards, and junkyards. The act was somewhat toothless but did call attention to an increasingly questionable visual landscape. The federal aid highway acts had permitted input from local citizens but only gradually. In 1950, state highway departments were required to hold public hearings only for projects that bypassed cities and towns. This requirement was extended to projects (other than interstates) routed through cities and towns in 1956 and to all interstate highway projects in 1958. By 1969, hearings were required at the route selection stage and again at the route design stage (combinable in 1974).[14]

Ten years after Mumford's diatribes, community groups had woken up to a new reality. More than a few city dwellers discovered that they were quite happy in their present neighborhood, blighted or not, and began to challenge the highway planners. Since the costs of construction and right-of-way purchases in urban areas were exorbitant, averaging over $2 million per mile in 1969, a number of neighborhood groups concluded that society had more pressing needs (schools, hospitals, crime fighting, etc.) than urban expressways. According to a *Business Week* article of July 19, 1967, more than twenty U.S. cities were fighting the construction of planned highways. In March 1969, the FHA followed up with a list of sixteen cities, including Boston, Memphis, and New Orleans, where historical, community, neighborhood, and or environmental impact studies were under way in response to proposed interstate projects.

Community groups were not always successful. Residents of Boston's Back Bay failed to halt the extension of I-90 through their neighborhoods, but local groups in Cambridge managed to stop a proposed Inner Belt expressway in its tracks. In Memphis, a planned route of I-40 through Overton Park was also forced to a halt. Local opposition was so strong in New Orleans that the Vieux Carré project, a proposed six-lane, 108-foot-wide, 40-foot-high elevated expressway along the city's French Quarter riverfront, was canceled by Secretary of Transportation John A. Volpe in July 1969.[15]

No Texas cities appeared on any "revolt list," but location battles involving the proposed ten-mile North Expressway (US 281) in San Antonio, and later the I-35 extension through downtown Laredo, were as good as anyone's. As indicated, Dallas, Fort Worth, Austin, and San Antonio had accommodated— even encouraged—highways, cattle trails, and railroads for many decades. Texas cities have always contained poverty-stricken areas but never dense urban neighborhoods of the eastern variety. When communities such as Laredo, San Marcos, Temple, and Gainesville attempted to fight off expressway plans, it was local merchants, not neighborhood groups, that had led the battles.

With the possible exception of Austin, Texas' major cities were only too happy to build modern interstates. Houston has its "spaghetti bowl" interchanges at I-45, Fort Worth has its "pretzel," and Dallas will have its "high five" when a $261 million five-level interchange at I-635 and US 75 is eventually completed. Most I-35 and other highway projects in Dallas, Fort Worth, and San Antonio have been started and completed with little difficulty other than old-fashioned delays and cost revisions. Black residents of East Dallas and East Austin were simply powerless to save their neighborhoods, which were segregated, relocated, or simply destroyed. If homes and businesses had to be bulldozed, efforts were made to be (or at least look) fair. When FHA Administrator Frank Turner learned that the Turner home in Fort Worth would have to be razed to make way for I-35W, he apparently warned his own mother: "You'll just have to move."[16]

San Antonio, where I-35, I-10, and Loop I-410 had been approved in the mid-1950s with little opposition, represented the very model of modern highway planning. The urban expressway spokes were intended to carry traffic rapidly through town, controlled by the first circumferential loop in Texas, which opened in January 1966. To avoid the affluent northeastern neighborhoods of Alamo Heights, I-35 was routed east of US 81 (the Old San Antonio Road) and then looped around Fort Sam Houston into the city's ancient downtown. From downtown, I-35 was directed through a number of less well-heeled neighborhoods before rejoining US 81 (the Old Laredo Road) at the city's southwest corner. Interchange projects included the elevated structure at I-35 and I-10 in 1965, the I-35/US 90 interchange adjacent to El Mercado on the northwest edge of downtown in 1967, and the four-level I-10/I-37 interchange in 1968. The $9.7 million interchange at I-10/I-37, comprising twenty-seven major structures within a sixteen-block area, was intended to be finished in time for the HemisFair (World's Fair) in April 1968.[17]

All had been well in San Antonio until 1959. In that year, the THD and the city determined that an expressway should be constructed to link San Antonio International Airport (on the north side of future I-410) to a downtown junction with I-35. After considering thirteen possible routes, planners settled on a scheme to relocate congested US 281 to a new route (I-37) west of San Pedro Avenue. Fatefully, the new six-mile expressway was routed through corners of Los Olmos and Brackenridge parks, including the old portland cement quarry at Sunken Gardens. Local resistance was immediate. The City of Los Olmos refused to approve the plan and forced the so-called North Expressway to be rerouted entirely within San Antonio.[18]

The rerouting prompted opposition from the formidable San Antonio Conservation Society. Not in any way to be confused with a low-income neighborhood association, the society had led efforts to restore and preserve San Antonio's rich network of missions, historical structures, and riverways. Having recently stopped an underground parking garage planned for Travis Park, the battle-tested society helped to defeat (barely) the first North Expressway bond financing proposal in June 1960. But a powerful marketing blitz organized by the City of San Antonio, the THD, and the highway industry won convincing approval for a subsequent $3.5 million bond issue in January 1961. As right-of-way purchases and relocation activities were set to begin, the society returned the favor with a series of lawsuits and injunctions and some serious lobbying. They delayed the project indefinitely. At a testy public hearing with Mayor McAllister and THD officials, one conservationist even threatened to "throw [herself] under the bulldozers."[19]

San Antonio's capture of the 1968 World's Fair, a pet project of Governor John B. Connally, provided a tremendous (if money-losing) showcase for the city. While millions of urban renewal dollars became available as a result of the process, HemisFair forced some sixteen hundred people, businesses, and religious institutions to move, and the large-scale projects that replaced them were debatable. Hopes of ending the North Expressway dispute in time for Hemis-Fair's April 1968, opening were also disappointed. The society had persuaded Secretary of Transportation Alan S. Boyd to order an "environmental impact study" of the proposed expressway route in November 1967, based on paragraph 4(f) of a recent amendment to the Department of Transportation Act of 1966. Drafted by Senator Ralph W. Yarborough of Texas at the urging of well-connected society members, the amendment required impact studies and possible route revisions when federally funded projects passed through wildlife areas, historic districts, or parklands.[20]

As the legal battle continued, new US DOT Secretary John A. Volpe, a former Massachusetts contractor, public works commissioner, and governor, shocked most observers by halting the Vieux Carré expressway project in New Orleans in July 1969. The North Expressway did not involve a historic district issue as in New Orleans, however, and Volpe was willing to approve the San Antonio project in December 1969, providing that the controversial middle (parkland) section be evaluated by an independent consultant. Otherwise, Texas stood to lose all past and future federal funding for the North Expressway. Since money talks, the THD reluctantly agreed in August 1970, and freed up $8.6 million in construction funds for the expressway's upper and lower sections in November 1970.[21]

The eagerly awaited consulting report, released in June 1971, reaffirmed the middle parkland route section and should have ended the dispute then and there. It did not. Continuing legal actions stalled the release of federal construction funds once more and prompted the city and state, in exasperation, to proceed on their own, without federal funding. Supported by a U.S. District Court ruling in December 1973, a $22.6 million construction contract—the largest single contract in THD history—was finally issued for the middle section in November 1974. Nineteen years after it was planned, ten years after HemisFair, and at a cost of $40.4 million—nearly four times the initial estimate—the North Expressway finally opened as an upgraded section of US 281 (not I-37) in February 1978. The renamed McAllister Freeway, dedicated by the city's feisty, eighty-eight-year-old former mayor, has been cited as one of the best-designed urban expressways in the United States, with embankments, retaining walls, and noise-abatement walls sourced from stone quarries in Kerrville and Austin.[22]

Opponents of the North Expressway could be consoled by the fact that the battle had contributed to the passage of a series of environmental and preservation laws that stand to this day—the National Historic Preservation Act of 1966, Section 4(f) of the DOT Act of 1966, and the National Environmental Policy Act (NEPA) of 1969. The new federal laws worked to enhance, halt, or delay a number of questionable interstate highway projects elsewhere in the nation, including an I-35 extension project in downtown Laredo. NEPA's requirement that environmental impact statements be conducted on all federally funded project proposals became especially controversial. Another important milestone, the Federal Highway Act of 1973, allowed disputed interstate projects to be replaced with urban mass transportation programs (or, as amended in 1976, with less divisive highway initiatives).[23]

As the battle over the North Expressway was raging, preservationists had created the first two historical districts in Texas—the King William District (1968) and an expanded La Villita site (1969)—with urban renewal funds catalyzed by HemisFair. These sites would be joined by the Alamo Plaza Historical District (1978), improvements to the San Antonio Missions National Historic Park, and Cattleman Square (1988). In addition, I-35, Loop I-410, and I-10 were all completed through San Antonio by May 1970, and a 1.4-mile elevated section of I-37 en route to Corpus Christi was under construction.[24]

The Federal Highway Act of 1956 had pegged the completion date for the entire U.S. interstate highway system at 1969. Despite many impressive achievements, the expanded 42,500-mile system was only 70 percent complete at the beginning of 1970, and the projected cost had escalated to $60 billion and rising. Even worse, the revised projection excluded the potential cost of replacing more than 300,000 bridges that had been built before 1930. At an average cost of $200,000, the cost of replacing 300,000 bridges would itself total $60 billion. Given the cost pressures, efforts were made to refurbish rather than replace as many bridges as possible. If crown-width roadways of forty-four feet (including shoulders) was the goal, sixteen-foot shoulderless affairs were the norm for most of Texas' 18,351 bridges. Old pre-1930 truss bridges usually could not be widened, but a number of old two-way bridges, like the Trinity River bridge in Dallas, the Red River bridge in Gainesville, and the Montopolis Bridge in Austin, could be redeployed as half of a two-bridge system once a second bridge was added.[25]

By May of 1970, 2,284 miles of Texas interstates were open (2.8 miles more than in resurgent California). Some 497 miles of I-35 were completed, with another 93 miles either under construction (15) or programmed (78). The final sections included seven miles of I-35W, the segment between Waco and Elm Mott, various gaps between Encinal and Dilley, and a controversial mile in downtown Laredo. Texas' I-35 record compared favorably with that in other states. By January 1971, 1,179 of the 1,567 miles planned for I-35 between Duluth and Laredo were open to traffic. Minnesota had completed 171 of 258 planned miles, Iowa had 132 of 218, Missouri had 75 of 115, and Kansas had 186 of 236. The I-35 completion leader, however, was Oklahoma, with 233 of 243 miles. Oklahoma's remaining ten miles were a hilly stretch of old US 77 between Wynnewood and Davis, constructed in the 1920s by convict labor.[26]

In Austin, the already obsolete Interregional Highway began to be upgraded with a new elevated roadway in 1971. Consisting of two forty-foot-wide decks supported by massive single column piers, I-35's new upper level was scheduled to open in 1974, as part of a 1.5-mile downtown development project, but was delayed until late 1975. I-35 was and is a work in progress in Austin. Construction of a multilevel interchange at US 290, access roads, and an additional bridge across the Colorado River were expected to continue at least through 1980. This would be wishful thinking. The $30 million interchange at US 290 was finally completed in 2002, and a $90 million interchange project at SH 71 in south Austin is targeted for early 2005.[27]

Temple also opted for an elevated roadway. A $3.6-million, 2.7-mile elevated section of I-35 was opened between SH 36 and Loop 363 in February 1970, after three years of work. The elevated highway structure was designed to eliminate dangerous crossovers and was preferred over a possible bypass route. It has also split the city in two. Efforts were made to improve the structure's questionable aesthetic qualities, including landscaping and the application of a decorative finish to the undersection retaining walls. One landscaper ventured that "a beautification plan [would] make the underpart of the structure more appealing." Based on the dark, Bronx-like structure depicted in the April 1970, issue of *Texas Highways,* the landscaper had his work cut out for him.[28]

Dallas had 165 miles of freeways after the Stemmons, Carpenter, Hawn, Central, and Thornton expressways were completed and connected in 1975 and the Dallas–Fort Worth Toll Road was converted to a freeway in 1977. Dallas' Loop I-635 and Fort Worth's I-820 projects were nearing completion, although cutbacks in federal funding delayed a $40 million, nine-mile, ten-lane extension of I-635 to the new DFW Airport until November 1973. This was not the only project to be delayed or stretched out. Distributions from the federal Highway Trust Fund had become irregular during the Vietnam War.

Coupled with inflation and delays caused by public participation under the new federal guidelines, remaining interstate projects in Texas and the nation would be completed in fits and starts.[29]

Progress continued, but progress reports became even more suspect than usual. Few officials were willing to acknowledge the delays, the mounting costs, and the gap between available funds and planned highway projects. In March 1974, one official claimed that the interstate system was 98 percent complete, with remaining segments expected to be finished by 1979. But six years later, in March 1980, other officials reported that just 94 percent of the system was actually open. The whereabouts of the missing 4 percent was unclear. To add to the confusion, the FHA deemed that only 8,234 miles (19 percent) of the 42,500-mile system was "officially complete" with specified lighting systems, rest areas, landscaping, and fencing—this after some $76 billion had been invested in U.S. interstates since 1956.[30]

By 1977, the last unfinished segments of I-35 were located in downtown Laredo, between Encinal and Artesia Wells, and at the $70 million-plus Fratt interchange project linking I-35 with I-410 in northeast San Antonio. Traffic volumes at Fratt had nearly doubled from 40,000 vehicles per day in 1970, necessitating an increase to eight lanes, new frontage roads and bridges, realignments, the installation of 13½-inch reinforced concrete pavement (three times the normal design load), and a new 3,000-foot bridge above the MKT railroad tracks. Between project start (1980) and completion (1983), the contractors somehow managed to implement all of these reconstruction activities without having to detour local highway and rail traffic. At one point, more than twenty cranes were deployed onsite.[31]

The Fratt interchange project, delayed for years, would be completed ahead of its revised schedule. Otherwise, delays and budgetary concerns affected everyone in the 1970s and early 1980s. Proposals to build a new THD headquarters were rejected or vetoed, and the THD head count was cut from a peak of 20,000 in 1972 to 14,000 in 1980. In 1975, following the first oil shock and a growing interest in mass transportation, the name of the venerable State Highway Department was changed to the State Department of Highways and Public Transportation. It would be changed again in 1991 to the Texas Department of Transportation (TXDOT).[32]

In Laredo, plans to extend I-35 south from Victoria Street to a second highway bridge were finally approved in 1974. Over 25 million people were crossing the city's single international bridge—nearly five times the annual traffic volume of 1954—and Laredo's downtown traffic snarl and air quality had only worsened with time. Since the U.S. General Services Administration (GSA) had hoped to build a new inspection station to monitor cross-border drug trafficking, a combined I-35 extension, bridge, and inspection complex became increasingly attractive to city officials. They hoped the new complex would provide a boost to a regional economy that had been devastated by the recent closing of Laredo Air Force Base.[33]

Feasibility studies for the one-mile extension of I-35, the second highway bridge, and a new border inspection station had actually started in 1966. However, an agreement between the City of Laredo and the Mexican Public Works, Toll Roads, and Bridges departments was not finalized until May 1970. By December, Laredo was cleared to make a formal request to the THD to extend I-35 south to meet the new bridge complex and to request a bridge construction permit from the U.S. Coast Guard. Estimated costs were $23.4 million: $6.2 million for the I-35 extension, from the THD and FHA; $3.3 million for the bridge, rights-of-way, and approach roads, split 70–30 percent between Laredo and Mexico; and $13.9 million for the border station, from GSA.[34]

Unlike the North Expressway project in San Antonio, which was routed through parklands, the I-35 extension route passed directly through neighborhoods. These neighborhoods included a so-called blighted section of Laredo's original San Augustin and Old Mercado districts, platted in 1767. Rights-of-way for the new construction projects were expected to claim eighteen city blocks, including one of the city's five original plazas, Central Plaza. As in San Antonio, local opposition would manage only to delay the I-35 project, not defeat or even reroute it. Compliance features of the National Historic Preservation Act, Section 4(f) of the DOT Act, and NEPA postponed the project only until the target area could be surveyed by the Texas State Historical Survey Committee and environmental impact statements could be prepared by the U.S. Coast Guard, on behalf of the GSA.[35]

As the impact statements were being prepared, the Texas State Historical Survey Committee managed to have the San Augustin de Laredo district listed in the National Register of Historic Places in September 1973, and formally designated as a Historical District in February 1974. In that same month, the U.S. Coast Guard completed its surveys and impact analyses. The results indicated that the integrated highway, bridge, and border station project would have an "adverse impact" on the newly declared historic district, but alternative bridge sites and highway routes were determined to be impractical. I-35 had already been completed to Victoria Street, and a possible relocation to the east was blocked by a large Southwestern Bell Telephone complex. Southwestern Bell was happy where it was.[36]

Less fortunate were the 390 residents, 148 homes, 26 small businesses and the elementary school that had to be evicted. Fourteen structures of "significant architectural value" were targeted for the wrecking ball. To reduce tensions, the City of Laredo agreed to establish a Laredo Historical Commission to prepare land use regulations for the preserved San Augustin District. Otherwise, and as in all highway-related evictions, the displaced persons and businesses were compensated for their moving costs, legal expenses, and possible rent or mortgage increases. Property owners were reimbursed at fair market values. Of course, since most highway projects tended to inflate property values in abutting areas, evicted property owners lost possible future gains.[37]

The formal designation of the San Augustin de Laredo Historic District enabled the U.S. Coast Guard to issue a bridge construction permit in March 1974. Construction began almost immediately at a site located one-fourth of a mile downstream from the venerable Convent Street (International) Bridge. The new 1,007-foot-long reinforced concrete Lincoln-Juarez Bridge, with seven lanes, eleven spans, and eighteen northbound traffic lanes converging from Nuevo Laredo, opened in November 1976. Mexican engineers made the structure resistant to floodwaters and added a seventh lane to accommodate a possible rail line. Unfortunately, travelers had to wait another five years for the I-35 extension to be completed one mile south, above the Tex-Mex right-of-way, to meet the new bridge. When the extension finally opened in March 1981, "after what truly has seemed like an eternity to many Laredoans," as the *Laredo Times* put it, another seven months of work were required to complete the five-lane approach road and the toll plaza. By then, of course, rising traffic volumes had indicated a need for additional bridges and traffic lanes.[38]

The siting of the Lincoln-Juarez Bridge is debatable. The two Laredos needed a new transportation and international border complex but not one that was outdated by the time it was implemented and that destroyed ancient neighborhoods in its path. While community groups had been unable to reroute the project, timely actions had preserved most of the San Augustin district, including the capitol building of the short-lived Republic of the Rio Grande. The Old Mercado District north of San Augustin was eventually designated as a historic district in 1985. I-35 was essentially completed between the Red River and the Rio Grande, but the last mile of this great achievement was bittersweet.

The opening of Laredo's one-mile extension in October 1981, following the completion of other remaining gaps and interchanges, should have marked the finish of I-35 in Texas. It did not. Various sections of I-35 still needed to comply with FHA interstate standards, and the highway would and will continue to be improved, widened, and refined into the new century. Thus it is difficult to state precisely the year in which I-35 was finally completed. The entire 1,593-mile length of I-35 between Laredo and Duluth was not declared officially complete until the Leif Erikson Tunnel, named for the Viking explorer, opened in Duluth on October 28, 1992—tweaking the five hundredth anniversary of Columbus's "discovery" of North America in the process. The U.S. interstate highway system was deemed to be 99.7 percent complete that year.[39]

Completed on paper but a perpetual work in progress in reality, the more than five hundred miles of I-35 between the Rio Grande and Red River represent a towering engineering achievement, if only a fraction of the Texas highway system. As of September 2000, the annual TXDOT budget stood at around $4.4 billion (en route to $5.2 billion in 2003) and the state system comprised 78,856 miles of roads—3,233 miles of interstates, 6,421 miles of interstate frontage roads, 12,110 miles of U.S. highways, 16,129 miles of state highways, and 40,963 miles of farm-to-market roads. This road system serves a population that continues to expand. Texas' population surged to 20.9 million in 2000, nearly 23 percent above the 1990 level. After Harris County (3.4 million, up 21 percent since 1990), each of the next four largest counties in Texas happens to lie along I-35: Dallas County (2.2 million, up 20 percent); Tarrant County (1.4 million, up 24 percent); Bexar County (1.4 million, up 18 percent); and Travis County (0.8 million, up 41 percent).[40]

The combined population of the eighteen counties through which I-35 passes reached 7.74 million in 2000, nearly 27 percent above the 1990 level. With population growth like this, the great achievement of I-35 has been slighted by the age-old problem of expanding highway traffic. In this most recent boom, the impulses have been immigration from other states, the expanding Texas economy, the rise of "technopoli" in Dallas and Austin, and most critically, the North American Free Trade Agreement (NAFTA). Enacted in December of 1993 by the governments of the United States, Canada, and Mexico, NAFTA was intended to gradually eliminate tariffs on all goods traded among the three nations and to remove barriers to overland transportation services. It has produced an explosion of highway traffic in Texas.[41]

In an irony of history, Laredo, somewhat of a poor relation since 1755, has been at the very center of NAFTA-related highway, bridge, and economic activity. Laredo captured nearly 40 percent of total cross-border trade between the U.S. and Mexico in 2000 (totaling $247 billion) and around 55 percent of all trade between Texas and Mexico. The city's 2000 population of 176,576, 44 percent above the 1990 level, has created a metropolitan area of around 500,000, if one includes Nuevo Laredo's 300,000-plus residents. The boom, in turn, has placed great pressure on the city's infrastructure, especially I-35 and the regional bridge system. When trucking companies in the three nations gain full access to one another's market—Mexican trucks are presently restricted to a twenty-mile area north of the U.S. border until environmental, safety, and wage-rate concerns are resolved—the burden on I-35 will become even heavier.[42]

I-35 between Laredo and Dallas has emerged as the single largest trade corridor in the United States, with an estimated 17 million vehicles, including three million trucks and 330,000 railcars, passing through Laredo in 2000. Some 50 percent of this volume occurs between Laredo and San Antonio; volume tapers off to around 20 percent en route to Austin and points north. Laredo has developed a growing portfolio of distribution, freight forwarding, customs brokerage, and intermodal services and has created more warehouse space (60 million square feet) than in San Antonio and Austin combined. A string of new retail shopping centers along I-35 has even introduced urban sprawl to the Rio Grande. In anticipation of this remarkable growth, Laredo was designated a TXDOT district in 1993—the first new district in over sixty years.[43]

It took Laredo decades to add a second highway bridge in 1976 but less than ten years to add two more. The speculative 1,216-foot-long, eight-lane Colombia–Solidarity Bridge complex was completed twenty miles west of town in July 1991, for $47 million, financed by Laredo via a bond issue and by the state of Nuevo León. Laredo's second new bridge, the eight-lane, 1,000-foot World Trade Bridge, opened for commercial traffic (only) northwest of downtown in April, 2000. Including a new border inspection station, a 1.5-mile connection to I-35, a major new interchange, and approach roads, the entire complex was completed for around $211 million, funded by the two Laredos, TXDOT, and bonds secured by dedicated toll revenues. In addition, the extension road to the (autos-only) Lincoln-Juarez Bridge was widened to six lanes in 1998, and two frontage roads were added in 2000 at a total cost of around $33.5 million. While the widening projects inevitably required additional slices of the adjacent neighborhood, most of the damage had already occurred in the mid-1970s.[44]

The hazards of private enterprise were displayed by the recent bankruptcy (and near closure) of the $90 million, 22-mile Camino-Colombia toll road between the Colombia-Solidarity Bridge and I-35. Opened in October, 2000, the highway was undone by traffic volumes that ran 87 percent below plan and by a prohibitive toll structure ($3 for autos and $16 for trucks). A proposed toll road between Colombia-Solidarity and La Gloria, Mexico, on Highway 85, plus a semicircular eastern loop road to a possible fifth bridge sited southeast of downtown, may be delayed or even reconsidered. Meanwhile, plans to provide water and wastewater connections to the nearly 400,000 Texans who inhabit scores of third-world-style colonias like Pueblo Nuevo in Webb County have also been scaled back; the latest proposal calls for the provision of just 10,000 connections at seven Rio Grande Valley colonias in 2006.[45]

The failure of Camino-Colombia has had no adverse impact on a slew of toll road projects planned for Central Texas. Tolls are still prohibited on U.S. interstate highways, but Congress agreed in 1987 to provide 35 percent of construction costs to nine demonstration states (including Texas) willing to build new toll roads. The program was extended to all fifty states when the Intermodal Surface Transportation Efficiency Act (ISTEA) was passed in 1991. A proposed toll road between Austin and San Antonio was scuttled by neighborhood and environmental groups in February 1984, but a new project has emerged to take its place: on October 3, 2003, ground was broken on Texas 130, a ninety-one-mile semicircular toll road planned to connect north Georgetown (on I-35) with Seguin on I-10.[46]

Texas 130 was jump-started when a $1.5 billion contract was let on June 14, 2002, to complete a forty-nine-mile segment between I-35 in Georgetown and US 183 in southeast Austin by December, 2007. The four-lane, expandable highway will include a train-enabled median strip, fifteen toll plazas, thirty intersections, and a connecting east-west toll road (Texas 45 North) to I-35 at Round Rock. Another east-west connector, Texas 45 Southeast (between US 183 and I-35 in South Austin), is targeted for 2010. The entire $3.6 billion Central Texas Turnpike project will be financed with bonds secured by projected toll revenues and with contributions from the state, the City of Austin, and Travis and Williamson counties. The Texas Transportation Commission's sale of $2.2 billion in bonds ended TXDOT's pay-as-you-go philosophy in grand fashion but has charted a new financial course from predictable gasoline taxes to uncertain turnpike revenues. The cash flow projections assume that average weekday toll transactions between Georgetown and US 183 increase from 42,161 in 2008 to 119,173 in 2015, 196,867 in 2025, and 267,857 in 2042.[47]

Texas 130 is intended to relieve some of the pressure on I-35 in Central Texas. The effects of NAFTA and dramatic increases in population, vehicle registrations, technology business formation, and suburbanization have all combined to raise traffic congestion ratios and to place an added burden on I-35's pavement and bridge structures. Trucks, the greatest culprit, account for an estimated 9 percent of all I-35 traffic in the stretch between Georgetown and San Antonio. If the region grows from around 2.6 million residents presently to an estimated 4.1 million people in 2020, daily traffic volumes along I-35 are expected to soar by 2020: from 210,000 to 330,000 vehicles in downtown Austin; and from 162,000 to 235,000 at the junction with I-410 in San Antonio. Even if Texas 130 manages to remove 30,000 vehicles per day from I-35 by 2025, the total will represent only 12 percent of I-35's projected volume for that year. The five-county region already faces a possible compliance problem with federal ozone air quality standards, and fast-growing communities like Kyle and Buda (among others) are concerned about available water supplies.[48]

A recent I-35 Trade Corridor Study (1999) estimated that "urban core" sections of I-35 in Dallas, Fort Worth, Austin, and San Antonio would need a whopping sixteen lanes or more by 2025 (versus six to eight lanes in operation in 1996) to handle the projected traffic volumes. Where the rights-of-way would be found and how they would be funded to accommodate these new urban lanes were matters left unspoken. The authors preferred to consider relief routes like Texas 130, double-decking schemes as in downtown Austin, a possible dedicated "NAFTA Truckway" between Laredo and Dallas, various mass transit and demand-management schemes, electronic payment and traffic monitoring systems, and longer-lived pavement. Pavement was specified as a six-inch lime-treated subgrade, topped with a six-inch cement-stabilized base, a one-inch asphalt binder, and a thirteen-inch section of continuously reinforced concrete. Since engineering and administration represent a fixed cost of around 25 percent of interstate highway construction expenses, the economic incentive was, as usual, tilted toward larger scale projects of almost any kind.[49]

A number of "I-35 relief" proposals are afoot. Plans have been readied to extend Texas 130 north to Dallas with a privately owned and operated turnpike system; I-35 could be "deforked" via a straight line between Hillsboro and Denton; and the proposed I-69 NAFTA Superhighway between the lower Rio Grande Valley and Houston (and points north) could divert truck traffic to the east. A proposed 423-mile freight tunnel between Laredo and Dallas could conceivably redeploy fourteen miles of Superconducting Super Collider tunnel abandoned around Waxahachie in 1993. In the meantime, TXDOT has unveiled a $2 billion plan to widen a forty-five-mile stretch of I-35 between Georgetown and Buda, outraging a number of East Austin neighborhood groups in the process, and Hays County voters recently approved a semicircular eastern loop (FM 110) around San Marcos after the original design was rerouted away from the Camino Real.

Some of these ideas may be integrated into an evolving (but highly controversial) $180 billion proposal to integrate six-lane toll roads, rail, and utility lines into a 4,000-mile network of privatized "Trans-Texas" transportation corridors. Privately owned and operated Trans-Texas turnpikes are preferred by influential policy makers. Few legislators are willing to raise the twenty-cents-per-gallon gasoline tax substantially—a five-cent hike would add only $500 million to the state's annual transportation coffers—and private projects are likely to face minimal regulation and public scrutiny.[50]

The Trans-Texas Corridor plan was triggered by House Bill 3588, signed into law on June 10, 2003, and passage of Proposition 14 on September 13, 2003. The new legislation established a revolving state bond fund called the Texas Mobility Fund and associated Regional Mobility Authorities to issue bonds secured by toll road revenues. In addition, the new laws authorize the State Highway Fund to spend as much as 20 percent of Texas' annual federal highway obligation authority on Trans-Texas corridors and enables TXDOT to engage in rail projects for the first time. Travis and Williamson counties responded with the Central Texas Regional Mobility Authority, the state's first, but one of its powers—an ability to convert eligible free state highways like US 183 into toll roads—has already met with resistance. Most voters recall that state highways were already built with taxpayers' funds. Passage of Proposition 14 also allowed TXDOT to supplement its traditional pay-as-you-go financing method with short-term notes (to bridge occasional cash flow deficits) and/or with up to $3 billion in long-term bonds secured by the State Highway Fund. Still, some observers wondered recently in *Time* magazine whether the Trans-Texas Corridor concept is an "innovative solution to the U.S.'s overcrowded highway system or a Texas-size boondoggle." We will see.[51]

Of course, new highway corridors and bypasses contribute to the controversial issue of urban sprawl. Conceding as much in an August 2001 policy shift, an increasingly privatized TXDOT intends to exclude frontage roads and excessive on-and-off ramping on future projects. Controlled or not, sprawl is difficult to define. In *The Costs of Sprawl Revisited* (1998), the Transportation Research Board of the National Research Council defined sprawl as a type of suburban peripheral growth that "expands in an unlimited and noncontiguous (leapfrog) way outward from the solidly built-up core of a metropolitan area." Others have defined sprawl as a "discontinuous development pattern," where undeveloped tracts remain interspersed among developed areas and are filled in later. The costs associated with sprawl reflect the "type, density and/or location of development," or the "physical, monetary, temporal [and] social/psychological resources [and] costs to individuals, communities and society."[52]

OFF-RAMP: SPRAWL

These definitions are somewhat confusing, and so is the subject matter. The landmark predecessor report, *The Costs of Sprawl* (1974), had sought to quantify the cost impact of urban sprawl on a region's infrastructure, housing, transportation, energy, environment, and quality of life. While most of the report's controversial recommendations have been ignored, the emergence of the "smart growth" movement is one of its legacies. Smart growth programs are designed to control growth, to facilitate compact (pedestrian and mass transit–oriented) development, and to retain local retailers. Oregon's Land Conservation and Development Act of 1973 created one of the nation's first such programs, highlighted by a new metropolitan government and a controversial Urban Growth Boundary (UGB) initiative to regulate growth within and around Portland. By controlling land usage within the UGB line, and outside of it, sprawl has been contained, densities have increased, and Portland's downtown has become more vibrant.[53]

However, many people in Portland (and in other "smart" towns like Boulder, Colorado) have discovered that higher densities lead to a surge in housing and rental prices. Like sprawl, smart growth is debatable. In the 2000 elections, smart growth initiatives were rejected in Colorado and Arizona, and light rail systems were defeated in Austin and San Antonio. Smart programs are intended to preserve the environment and retain local tax dollars, which they do; but many voters perceive that the primary beneficiaries of these programs are owners and developers of urban real estate. For example, real estate values adjacent to Dallas Area Rapid Transit stations are roughly 25 percent above those at comparable properties in Dallas County. Meanwhile, lower-income people are hurt by rising rents and regressive sales taxes required to pay for new transit systems and other smart growth investments. So-called affordable housing programs are helpful, but typically serve as insufficient "band-aids."[54]

If poor people are hurt by rising real estate prices, the implication is that poor people should relocate from smart central cities. Unfortunately, the least expensive real estate is found in the suburban fringe, and controlled growth programs are designed to reduce the availability of such alternatives. Otherwise, the suburbanization of jobs has brought suburbanites closer to their place of work—in miles, if not necessarily in commuting time. Technopoli like Dallas and Austin have fueled the movement of fledgling technology businesses and their employees to inexpensive real estate in suburban fringe areas. New satellite towns like Plano and Richardson on US 75, Round Rock on I-35, and the master-planned communities of Las Colinas west of Dallas and the Woodlands north of Houston have become cities in their own right. In theory, commuting travel times should have been reduced by these developments, but congestion is often as intense in the satellites as in the central cities.[55]

In many cases, congestion along I-35 is so severe that real estate developers have been forced to pay large sums to TXDOT to relocate on and off ramps to sites of commercial interest. Round Rock's new 328-acre La Frontera mixed-use development site has raised local commuting times significantly and awaits expensive remedies like Texas 45 that, in turn, will generate additional sprawl and traffic congestion. Texas 130 is likely to unleash a brand new wave of sprawl in the region east of I-35. When public hearings are held, they are often too late (or powerless) to affect large, momentum-building projects. Real estate interests have always been intertwined with transportation planning and always will be, but eyebrows are raised when a state representative allows a Texas homebuilding association official to vote as his proxy in regional planning meetings. One ambitious developer has already proposed an instant city of twenty thousand at the future junction of Texas 45 South and I-35 in Buda. On the other hand, when a proposed "Very Big Box" retail project in South Austin was challenged by a neighborhood group, the retailer's attorney replied, quite fairly, that "if you can't do it on I-35, where can you do it?"[56]

Interurbans, light rail systems, and subways might have been appropriate solutions for these emerging growth corridors had they been in place in 1950 and been allowed to guide future development. But fifty years later, they have a lot of expensive catching up to do. The cost of light rail systems run between $20 and $50 million per mile, excluding tunnels, and the economic rationale is somewhat cloudy—the General Accounting Office has estimated that express buses in Dallas cost only $1.74 per revenue mile versus a $12.54 per mile price tag for light rail. Undaunted, light rail is moving ahead in Houston, where the first 7.5 miles of a planned 80-mile system opened on January 1, 2004, and in Dallas. In 2000, Dallas voters approved a $2.9 billion, 75-mile extension of DART to complement the evolving Trinity Railway Express (TRE) commuter line. TRE opened along former Rock Island trackage in Dallas' Union Station in December 1997, and has been extended via DFW Airport to the old T&P station in Fort Worth. Projected weekday daily ridership is 8,200—impressive, but still a tiny fragment of the DFW marketplace.[57]

Farther south, Austin voters barely rejected a $1.9 billion, 52-mile light rail system in the 2000 elections but in 2004 approved a more modest $60 million, 32-mile commuter rail between Leander and downtown. A more ambitious $1 billion commuter rail network between Georgetown and San Antonio is inching its way forward. Encouraged by 1997 legislation authorizing a commuter rail district between Williamson and Bexar counties, the proposed rail network appears to be contingent on relocating the Union Pacific's twenty-seven daily freight trains to new (unfunded) trackage along Texas 130. One study projected that the commuter rail line would attract a modest weekday ridership of 8,000 passengers in 2000, ramping up to 11,000 in 2020. These estimates are probably low, but passenger rail systems rarely if ever make money; fares would probably cover only 55 percent of the line's operating and maintenance expenses, requiring regional taxes (35 percent) and federal funds (10 percent) to make up the difference. More positively, the front-end capital costs of commuter rail are far lower per mile than those of competing light rail systems, especially when existing trackage can be utilized, as in the case of the Leander-Austin project.[58]

If a conventional commuter rail system sounds appealing, would it not be fun to take a French-style *train à grande vitesse* (TGV) between Dallas and San Antonio (map 15)? Interest in high speed trains started with the U.S. High Speed Ground Transportation (HSGT) Act of 1965 and the establishment of an Office of HSGT within the Federal Railroad Administration in 1969. By 1986, six states had formed consortii to build private HSGT systems, including Texas, California, and Florida. No system was built. In each case, the promoters were unable to convince prospective investors that estimated traffic volumes could cover capital and operating costs. Despite the addition of ISTEA funds (1991), loan guarantees, and funds to remove highway and rail grade crossings (1994), no HSGT projects have been built. Amtrak's new but slower Acela Express between Boston and Washington typically averages less than half of its 150 mph clock speed in the real world. If rising energy prices revive interest in HSGT to lessen the nation's exposure to foreign oil, proposed systems in Florida and California—where a $20 billion-plus, 680-mile TGV system is planned to link San Diego with San Francisco via Bakersfield—appear to be first in line.[59]

HSGT systems have been constrained by front-end costs of around $30 million per mile and unpredictable traffic volumes. However, the cost of an eight-lane urban expressway, excluding its associated sprawl and air pollution effects, is running in excess of $30 million per mile; even rural-oriented, four-lane Texas 130 is at $30 million. Since the target market for HSGT is pegged at trips of between 150 miles (competing well with cars) and 500 miles (competing well with airplanes), a Texas system would appear to be ideal. A triangular, 125–200 mph rail system linking Dallas–Fort Worth, Houston, and San Antonio, with stops in Austin, Waco, and College Station, was even sponsored by the newly created Texas High Speed Rail Authority in 1989. The 245-mile Dallas-Houston segment was projected to have equivalent demographics in 2015 to the 11.0 million inhabitants (and 5.2 million TGV riders) of the 264-mile Paris-Lyon line in 1988. Unfortunately for the sponsor, it failed to recognize that France has a long tradition in public transportation, much higher gasoline prices, and fewer competing airline flights and airline lobbyists.[60]

Forecasting Texas HSGT ridership levels is a challenge, especially with competing airlines and the chronically unprofitable Washington–New York Metroliner to be considered. A 750-mile franchise was actually awarded to the Texas TGV consortium in May 1991, but the project died when financing milestones were unmet. If the recent surges in energy prices have altered the cost/benefit dynamics of HSGT, front-end capital costs, passenger demand, and other issues are still daunting. Existing systems like the French TGV, the Japanese "bullet train" (Tokaido Shinkansen), and the German Intercity Express require exclusive rights-of-way, straight alignments, and dedicated bridges and tunnels. These are expensive. And because 186 mph French TGVs must slow down to make station stops and then reaccelerate to regain their peak speed, the average effective speed of TGVs is a less than compelling 130 mph.

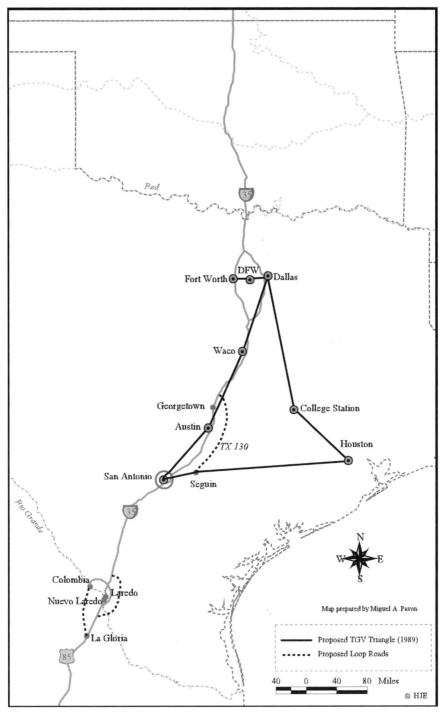

Map 15. Proposed Texas TGV (1989) and Proposed Loop Roads.

While test TGV has reached 322 mph, and experimental Magnetic Levitation (Maglev) trains have also exceeded 300 mph, these systems are more energy intensive and require new propulsion systems and controls and even more capital. Proposed Berlin-Hamburg, Shanghai-Beijing, and Osaka-Tokyo Maglev lines have been either scrapped or reconsidered.[61]

Even if a TGV system were built parallel to I-35, within a Trans-Texas corridor scheme or not, one is left wondering how an inbound passenger at San Antonio's shiny new TGV station would be transported to a meeting at the UT Medical Center, located outside Loop I-410, or to a job at the new (taxpayer-assisted) Toyota truck plant located south of I-410 in southern Bexar. The expensive answer is that connecting rail and subway systems would have to be built (or extended in the case of Dallas) to link TGV passengers to and from suburban sites of interest. Not only would these integrated systems cost a large pile of money, probably funded via sales taxes, gasoline taxes, excise taxes, and tolls, but it is unclear who the principal beneficiaries of these investments might be. In short, automobiles are not going away.

Conclusion

ALK of TGV systems, light rail, and commuter rail lines would have warmed the heart of Lewis Mumford. Mumford's advocacy of planned, integrated mass transit systems and pedestrian-centric environments remains timely, even if the execution would be challenging and extremely expensive. Some of his highway solutions, such as depressed urban expressways and scenic, autos-only parkways like the Taconic, are challenging as well. The costs of depressing an urban expressway are daunting, as was recently confirmed by Boston's off-the-charts Fitzgerald Expressway ("Big Dig") project. The parkways concept may work well in the Catskills, but most drivers are unwilling to drive at reduced speeds of 50 mph to negotiate twists and turns. In addition, parkways are not applicable in urban areas or in monotonous terrain. Sections of US 281 north of San Antonio and SH 71 west of Austin are attractive because of the hills and dales, not because of the highway. In other words, I-35 was not, and Texas 130 is not, a candidate for a Taconic-like parkway.

Mumford would be pleasantly surprised by the revitalization of many U.S. cities after decades of decline. If much of this revival has been based on relatively narrow finance, legal, accounting, and sports venues, it is better than the alternative. Mumford would certainly be outraged by urban sprawl, but beauty is in the eye of the beholder. In 1940, only 15 percent of the U.S. population lived in suburbs. Sixty years later, this figure has soared to 60 percent and is still climbing. Most people live within suburban sprawl and probably even enjoy it. A stretch of sprawl between San Marcos and New Braunfels would represent pasture-eating, chain-store sameness to Mumford but a modern, convenient, and enjoyable place to live, work, and shop to many others. Even if the suburbanization of America is nearing its peak, spacious I-35 hubs like Dallas, Fort Worth, Austin, San Antonio, and Laredo would appear to be less likely, or less equipped, to benefit from a possible return to density.

Texas' major cities are relatively new, were laid out by wagon roads, and typically lack the type of dense urban neighborhoods that have made interstates controversial in many cities. While I-35 ripped out sections of Dallas, Fort Worth, Austin, San Antonio, and Laredo, the damage was limited by the fact that the ripped-out sections were not particularly dense. There have been occasional tiffs. In Laredo, I-35 was halted north of historic San Augustin Plaza for nearly fifteen years before it was extended south to the Rio Grande. San Antonio's North Expressway battle was waged over parklands but not people. In Austin, the construction of a second (elevated) highway above I-35 isolated East Austin from downtown in the 1970s and marshaled local resistance to subsequent widening plans. Otherwise, most Texas interstate highway projects, including Interstate 35, have proceeded rather smoothly.

As for the impact of I-35 on smaller towns along old US 81 or US 77, the record is mixed. On the positive side, a number of historic town centers along the path of I-35 were bypassed by the interstate, including New Braunfels, San Marcos, Georgetown, Belton, Waxahachie, and Gainesville. This may not have helped their local economies, but it at least preserved their historic courthouse squares. On the negative side, interstates like I-35 must be criticized for damaging local communities. They have required massive swaths of right-of-way, particularly to accommodate cloverleaf and multilevel stacked interchanges, and have often bulldozed their way through long-established businesses, local institutions, and neighborhoods that lay in their path. In addition, the frontage roads have generated thousands of convenient chain-store establishments but in the process have destroyed thousands of independent small businesses, often located on downtown main streets.

Of course, these criticisms are national in nature, not specific to Texas or to I-35. The largest interstate highway builder in the United States has been relatively unscathed by and immune to the general controversies. Most Texans have concluded that if interstates like I-35 did not exist, the competitive position of the Texas economy would suffer. The larger question—what if no urban interstates had ever been built in the United States and long-distance interstates had been routed away from urban areas, like German autobahns?—is moot. They have been built, they are a fact of life, and regional economies have adjusted to their reality. The tradeoff of speed, safety, and efficiency versus visual pollution, sprawl, and sameness is well documented. Fortunately, the rights-of-way for the interstate system including I-35 have already been assembled and the related environmental damage has been confined. If well-intended bypass schemes like Texas 130 are likely to repeat many of the problems associated with the interstate experience, the alternatives are not especially clear.

Mass transportation systems might once have played a significant role in moving I-35 corridor inhabitants to where jobs, stores, or homes are located; but not now. Cities like Boston and New York extended their subway systems to the suburbs to guide future development. They did not attempt to string suburbs together after such growth had occurred in helter-skelter fashion. If Texas' interrurban railway and electric streetcar systems had somehow managed to survive, our present-day congestion and air pollution problems would be less onerous. But now that metropolitan areas have become so sprawled, rail connection opportunities have limited potential and limited investment appeal. Critics of proposed fixed rail systems are correctly concerned about their "spatial inflexibility" and their inevitable orientation to downtowns that are no longer downtowns in the traditional sense. In other words, no rail system is capable of handling regional shopping areas like the one-mile "big box" strip of I-35 that sprouted between Parmer and Howard in North Austin—the strip's 1.3 million (and rising) square feet of retail space was designed solely for the automobile.[1]

Good or bad, I-35 and its frontage roads, interchanges, feeder roads, traffic congestion, and sprawl are facts of daily life. They are also part of a long-running continuum driven by migration, trade, warfare, technology, entrepreneurship, and ample doses of government funding. The roots of I-35 were introduced thousands of years ago with the earliest stone age peoples of Central Texas, including the first rockshelters, waterside settlements, and trails. The roots advanced with occasional linkages between North American Indian tribes and the great civilizations of Mexico. As hunting and gathering gave way to agricultural villages, tributary relationships, and interregional trade, the trails began to be formalized. When villages became cities, trails became roads.

European exploration, plunder, and colonialism introduced modernity to preexisting civilizations, destroying these civilizations in the process but building a foundation of cities and the roads necessary to connect them. Conquistadors, silver magnates, and missionaries prompted the construction of Caminos Reales between Veracruz and Saltillo by 1578, but it took a military threat from

France to extend these routes into mineral-poor Texas in 1689. By 1759, a series of military-oriented Spanish expeditions had established a rudimentary north-south route between Saltillo and Taovaya villages of the upper Red River, via San Antonio.

Military funding from Spain extended the Caminos Reales to Laredo, San Antonio, and San Marcos, and military funding from the Republic of Texas and the U.S. Congress catalyzed the development of a rough north-south Military Road between San Marcos and Preston via Austin and Dallas. After waves of adventurers, Indian traders, real estate speculators, ferry operators, homesteaders, slaveholders and trail drivers had filled in this north-south corridor with commerce, it was up to profit-minded stage operators, freighters, and railroad tycoons to create order out of chaos, armed, of course, with sizable government contracts and land grants.

Cotton farmers, civil engineers, automobile owners, truckers, bus companies, retailers, purveyors of items from hamburgers to high technology, and new generations of real estate speculators, among many others, contributed to the advances of the last century. However, the final shape of I-35 has been influenced mainly by government policies associated with two world wars, the New Deal, the Cold War, incentives to suburbanization, and NAFTA. Traffic congestion along I-35 has prompted a flurry of new transportation ideas in the same way that wagon and stage traffic spawned turnpikes and railroads; railroads spawned trucks, buses, and two-lane highways; and two-lane highways spawned interstates. One hopes that the state's recent policy shift to privatized, debt-financed toll roads will follow the success of the Dallas–Fort Worth Toll Road and not the record of Camino-Colombia.

If Interstate 35 remains a work in progress, the past refuses to go away. In July 1980, as the new I-35 border complex in Laredo was being readied, a team of archaeologists from the University of Texas at San Antonio was commissioned to investigate the leveled site known as Block 12, between Grant and Zaragosa streets, prior to construction. Hundreds of artifacts from the Spanish colonial period were unearthed and catalogued for posterity. More important, the archaeological investigation confirmed earlier studies suggesting that the site was indeed ancient. Starting with the Middle Archaic period, hunters, gatherers, and their successors had probably occupied Block 12 since 1800 B.C. If this is true, the site has provided a Rio Grande crossing point for some 3,800 years—3,760 years before I-35 appeared on any map. With history as our guide, the next 3,800 years should be just as interesting.[2]

$\mathcal{N}otes$

1. A. Joachim McGraw and Fred Valdez Jr., *Investigation of Prehistoric Rockshelters and Terrace Sites along Portions of the Salado Creek Drainage, Northern Bexar County, Texas,* Center for Archeological Research, University of Texas at San Antonio (hereafter cited as CAR, UTSA), Report no. 55 (1978), 2, 3; Daniel R. Potter et al., *Archeological Salvage Research at 41BX 901: A Prehistoric Quarry in Bexar County, Texas,* CAR, UTSA, Report no. 211 (1992), 5; Thomas R. Hester et al., *Archeological Survey of Area Proposed for Modification in the Salado Creek Watershed, Bexar County, Texas,* CAR, UTSA, Report no. 3 (1974), 3.

2. *Texas Highways,* August 1963, 12–15, and September 1970, 3.

3. *Texas Highways,* May 1966, 15, and September 1970, 3; Parker Nunley, *A Field Guide to Archeological Sites of Texas* (Austin: Texas Monthly Press, 1989), 150; *Austin American-Statesman,* May 3, 1997, and August 12, 2002.

4. Wilson W. Crook Jr. and R. K. Harris, "Trinity Aspect of the Archaic Horizon," *Bulletin of the Texas Archeological and Paleontological Society* 23 (1952): 7, 28; W. W. Newcomb Jr., *The Indians of Texas* (Austin: University of Texas Press, 1961), 9; Dessamae Lorraine, *Archeological Excavations in the Fish Creek Reservoir* (Dallas: Southern Methodist University, 1969), 1, 2, 17; Michael Collins, *Cooke County, Texas* (Gainesville: Cooke County Heritage Society, 1981), 3.

5. Nunley, *Field Guide,* 150.

6. Daniel E. Fox, *Traces of Texas History* (San Antonio: Corona Publishing Company, 1983), 9; Newcomb, *Indians of Texas,* 16.

7. Nunley, *Field Guide,* 38.

8. Don Worcester, "Indian and Buffalo Trails," in *Pioneer Trails West,* ed. Donald E. Worcester, Western Writers of America (Caldwell, Idaho: Caxton Printers, 1985), 1–3.

9. Jeremiah F. Epstein et al. (eds.), *Papers on the Prehistory of Northeastern Mexico and Adjacent Texas,* CAR, UTSA (1980), 85, 88; C. Roger Nance, *The Archeology of La Calsada* (Austin: University of Texas Press, 1992), 139.

10. Nunley, *Field Guide,* 150.

11. Nance, *Archeology of La Calsada,* 1, and "La Calsada and the Prehistoric Sequence in Northeast Mexico," in Epstein et al., *Papers,* 41; J. M. Adovasio, "The Evolution of Basketry Manufacture in Northeastern Mexico, Lower and Trans-Pecos Texas," in Epstein et al., *Papers,* 96.

12. *Cambridge Encyclopedia of Latin America* (Cambridge: Cambridge University Press, 1992), 168; George E. Stuart, *National Geographic Archeological Map of Middle America* (Washington, D.C.: National Geographic Society, 1968); Samuel Salinas Alvarez, *Historia de*

los Caminos de Mexico (Mexico: Banco Nacional de Obras y Servicios Publicos, 1994), 28; Robert J. Sharer and David C. Grove (eds.), *Regional Perspectives on the Olmec* (Cambridge: Cambridge University Press, 1989), 275.

13. Richard E. W. Adams, *Ancient Civilizations of the New World* (Boulder: Westview Press, 1997), 71; Stuart, *National Geographic Map.*

14. Salinas Alvarez, *Historia,* 52, 54, 60.

15. Charles C. Kolb, "Commercial Aspects of the Classic Teotihuacan Period," in *Research in Economic Anthropology,* ed. Barry L. Isaac (Greenwich, Conn.: JAI Press, 1986), 155; Salinas Alvarez, *Historia,* 34; Stuart, *National Geographic Map;* Michael D. Coe, *Mexico: From the Olmecs to the Aztecs* (New York: Thames and Hudson, 1994), 144; *Austin American-Statesman,* November 27, 2003.

16. Salinas Alvarez, *Historia,* 88, 92; Ross Hassig, *Trade, Tribute and Transportation* (Norman: University of Oklahoma Press, 1985), 31, 67; Geoffrey Hindley, *A History of Roads* (Secaucus, N. J.: Citadel Press, 1972), 22, 23; *Cambridge Encyclopedia of Latin America,* 183, 187.

17. Hassig, *Trade, Tribute,* 157

18. Newcomb, *Indians of Texas,* 29.

19. Newcomb, *Indians of Texas,* 20.

CHAPTER 2

1. [Cabeza de Vaca], *Adventures in the Unknown Interior of America,* anotated translation by Cyclone Covey (Albuquerque: University of New Mexico Press, 1961; reprint 1998), 12–15; [Cabeza de Vaca], *The Account: Alvar Nuñez Cabeza de Vaca's Relacion,* anotated translation by Martin A. Favata and Jose B. Fernandez (Houston: Arte Publico Press, 1993), 11–14.

2. Frederick W. Hodge (ed.), "The Narrative of Alvar Nuñez Cabeza de Vaca," in *Spanish Explorers in the Southern United States 1528–1543* (New York: Scribner, 1907), 71, 72.

3. Bernal Díaz del Castillo, *The Discovery and Conquest of Mexico,* ed. Irving A. Leonard (New York: Farrar, Straus and Cudahy, 1956), Introduction, p. xxx; Samuel Salinas Alvarez, *Historia de los Caminos de Mexico* (Mexico: Banco Nacional de Obras y Servicios Publicos, 1994), 156–216.

4. John W. Reps, *Cities of the American West* (Princeton: Princeton University Press, 1979), 25, 35, 37; Luis Weckmann, *The Medieval Heritage of Mexico* (New York: Fordham University Press, 1992), 378, 427; Hugh Thomas, *The Conquest of Mexico* (London: Hutchinson, 1993), 560; *Cambridge Encyclopedia of Latin America* (Cambridge: Cambridge University Press, 1992), 413; Ross Hassig, *Trade, Tribute and Transportation* (Norman: University of Oklahoma Press, 1985), 221.

5. Peter W. Rees, "Origins of Colonial Transportation in Mexico," *Geographical Review* 65 (1975): 329, 330; Salinas Alvarez, *Historia,* 218.

6. Paul Johnson, *The Renaissance* (London: Weidenfeld and Nicolson, 2000), 10; Geoffrey Hindley, *A History of Roads* (Secaucus: Citadel Press, 1972), 25, 26, 30, 35, 37, 51, 52, 55.

7. D. A. Brading and Harry E. Cross, "Colonial Silver Mining: Mexico and Peru," *Hispanic American Historical Review* 52, no. 4 (November 1972): 571, 573, 576.

8. Herbert E. Bolton, *Coronado* (Albuquerque: University of New Mexico Press, 1949), 358; Fr. Angelico Chavez, *Coronado's Friars* (Washington, D.C.: Academy of American Franciscan History, 1968), 58, 59; Salinas Alvarez, *Historia,* 188; Hodge, *Spanish Explorers,* 285.

9. Bolton, *Coronado,* 358; Chavez, *Coronado's Friars,* 62.

10. Bolton, *Coronado,* 360; Chavez, *Coronado's Friars,* 67.

11. Samuel Eliot Morison, *The European Discovery of America: The Southern Voyages* (New York: Oxford University Press, 1974), 525–27; James E. Bruseth and Nancy E. Kenmotsu, "From Naguatex to the River Daycao: The Route of the Hernando de Soto Expedition through Texas," *North American Archeologist* 14 (1993): 200, 217; [Cabeza de Vaca], *Adventures,* 14; Timothy K. Perttula, *The Caddo Nation* (Austin: University of Texas Press, 1992), 19.

12. *Handbook of Texas Online,* www.tsha.utexas.edu/handbook/online.

13. Peter J. Bakewell, *Silver Mining and Society in Colonial Mexico* (Cambridge: Cambridge University Press, 1971), 1; Salinas Alvarez, *Historia,* 220; Philip Wayne Powell, *Soldiers, Indians and Silver* (Berkeley: University of California Press, 1952), 14.

14. Richard L. Garner, "Long Term Silver Mining Trends in Spanish America," *American Historical Review* 93, no. 4 (October 1988): 913, 914; Richard L. Garner, *Economic Growth and Change in Bourbon Mexico* (Gainesville: University Press of Florida, 1993), 109.

15. Bakewell, *Silver Mining,* 20; Hassig, *Trade, Tribute,* 175.

16. Salinas Alvarez, *Historia,* 218, 222; Powell, *Soldiers, Indians,* 18, 22; Hassig, *Trade, Tribute,* 175, 176.

17. Hassig, *Trade, Tribute,* 161, 164–66; Robert C. West, "The Mining Community in Northern New Spain," *Ibero-Americana* 30 (1949): 77.

18. Bakewell, *Silver Mining,* 22; Hassig, *Trade, Tribute,* 196; David G. Ringrose, "Carting in the Hispanic World," *Hispanic American Historical Review* 50 (1970): 37, 38; West, "Mining Community," 87.

19. Hassig, *Trade, Tribute,* 193; Max L. Moorhead, "Spanish Transportation in the Southwest," *New Mexico Historical Review* 32 (1957): 109–11.

20. Bakewell, *Silver Mining,* 20; Powell, *Soldiers, Indians,* 22.

21. John C. Super, "Miguel Hernandez: Master of Mule Trains," in *Struggle and Survival in Colonial America,* ed. David G. Sweet and Gary B. Nash (Berkeley: University of California Press, 1980), 300; Bakewell, *Silver Mining,* 20; Powell, *Soldiers, Indians,* 22, 25, 26.

22. John W. Clark Jr., "The Legal Basis of the Roads," in *A Texas Legacy: The Old San Antonio Road and the Caminos Reales,* ed. A. Joachim McGraw, John W. Clark Jr., and Elizabeth Robbins (Austin: Texas Department of Transportation, 1991), 399.

23. Powell, *Soldiers, Indians,* 27.

24. Bakewell, *Silver Mining,* 28, 29; Donald E. Chipman, *Spanish Texas* (Austin: University of Texas Press, 1992), 51; Powell, *Soldiers, Indians,* 155.

25. Chipman, *Spanish Texas,* 52, 53.

26. Nicolas Sanchez-Albornoz, "The Population of Colonial Spanish America," in *Cambridge History of Latin America,* vol. 2, ed. Leslie Bethell (Cambridge: Cambridge University Press, 1984), 4; *Cambridge Encyclopedia of Latin America,* 131, 132; Woodrow W. Borah, "New Spain's Century of Depression," *Ibero-Americana* 35 (1951): 3.

27. Chipman, *Spanish Texas,* 54.

28. José Carlos Mariátegui, *Seven Interpretative Essays on Peruvian Reality,* trans. Marjory Urquidi (Austin: University of Texas Press, 1971), 39.

29. Marc Simmons, *The Last Conquistador* (Norman: University of Oklahoma Press, 1991), 12; Chipman, *Spanish Texas,* 56–59; Max L. Moorhead, *New Mexico's Royal Road* (Norman: University of Oklahoma Press, 1958), 5, 8.

30. William C. Foster (ed.), "Texas and Northeastern Mexico," Introduction to Juan Bautista Chapa's *Historia de Nuevo Leon* (Austin: University of Texas Press, 1997), 3; Garner, "Long Term Silver Mining Trends," 913.

31. Carl Newton Tyson, *The Red River in Southwestern History* (Norman: University of Oklahoma Press, 1981), 15, 16; Chipman, *Spanish Texas*, 72, 76; Albert C. Rose, *Historic American Highways* (Washington, D.C.: American Association of State Highway Officials, 1953), 26; A. Joachim McGraw, "Spanish Eyes Turn to the Northern Frontier," in *A Texas Legacy*, 49–50.

32. Foster (Chapa), "Texas and Northeastern Mexico," 3, 21.

33. Chipman, *Spanish Texas*, 80; William C. Foster, *Spanish Expeditions into Texas 1689–1768* (Austin: University of Texas Press, 1995), 18, 33; *El Camino Real*, TXDOT Travel and Information Division brochure; Foster (Chapa), "Texas and Northeastern Mexico," 122.

34. Chipman, *Spanish Texas*, 82; Foster, *Spanish Expeditions*, 17, 20.

35. Foster, *Spanish Expeditions*, 22.

36. Chipman, *Spanish Texas*, 87; Foster, *Spanish Expeditions*, 33; Elizabeth A. Robbins, "The First Routes into Texas," in *A Texas Legacy*, 61, 62; Foster (Chapa), "Texas and Northeastern Mexico," 2, 215 (note); Perttula, *Caddo Nation*, 85.

37. Foster, *Spanish Expeditions*, 7, 30.

38. Chipman, *Spanish Texas*, 94, 96; Foster, *Spanish Expeditions*, 51, 60.

39. Foster, *Spanish Expeditions*, 77, 87; *El Camino Real* (TXDOT brochure); *Texas Highways*, December 1974, 6.

40. Harry W. Crosby, *Antigua California* (Albuquerque: University of New Mexico Press, 1994), 196.

41. Chipman, *Spanish Texas*, 106; Richard G. Santos, *Aguayo Expedition into Texas* (Austin: Jenkins, 1981), 115; Foster, *Spanish Expeditions*, 101.

42. Tyson, *Red River*, 18, 23; Garner, "Long Term Silver Mining Trends," 913.

43. Tyson, *Red River*, 18; Herbert E. Bolton, *Athanase de Mezieres* (Cleveland: Arthur H. Clark Company, 1914), 36, 37; Noel M. Loomis and Abraham P. Nasatir, *Pedro Vial and the Roads to Santa Fe* (Norman: University of Oklahoma Press, 1967), 36.

44. Tyson, *Red River*, 20–25; Chipman, *Spanish Texas*, 112, 113; Foster, *Spanish Expeditions*, 109, 112.

45. Chipman, *Spanish Texas*, 117; Foster, *Spanish Expeditions*, 127, 130, 132; Janet R. Fireman, *The Spanish Royal Corps of Engineers in the Western Borderlands* (Glendale: A. H. Clark and Company, 1977), 53.

46. Tyson, *Red River*, 19, 20; Bolton, *Athanase*, 44, 45; Loomis and Nasatir, *Pedro Vial*, 38; Chipman, *Spanish Texas*, 119; Tyson, *Red River*, 26–30, 33.

47. Tyson, *Red River*, 34; Santos, *Aguayo Expedition*, 18, 19.

48. Chipman, *Spanish Texas*, 120, 121; Foster, *Spanish Expeditions*, 145, 148; Santos, *Aguayo Expedition*, 17–20.

49. Santos, *Aguayo Expedition*, 17–20, 107, 108; Foster, *Spanish Expeditions*, 150–52.

50. Santos, *Aguayo Expedition*, 150–95.

51. Santos, *Aguayo Expedition*, 107, 108; Chipman, *Spanish Texas*, 124; Tyson, *Red River*, 23.

52. Chipman, *Spanish Texas*, 131.

53. Jesus F. de la Teja, *San Antonio de Bexar* (Albuquerque: University of New Mexico Press, 1995), 7, 105; Reps, *Cities*, 64, 65, 71.

54. Chipman, *Spanish Texas,* 135, 140; Jack Jackson, *Los Mestenos* (College Station: Texas A&M University Press, 1986), 35; De la Teja, *San Antonio,* 46.

55. De la Teja, *San Antonio,* 97, 98, 105.

56. Loomis and Nasatir, *Pedro Vial,* 52; Chipman, *Spanish Texas,* 147, 151.

57. Frances Stovall, *Clear Springs and Limestone Ledges* (San Marcos: Hays County Historical Commission, 1986), 15; Chipman, *Spanish Texas,* 157, 158, 161; Loomis and Nasatir, *Pedro Vial,* 60; Elizabeth Ann Harper, "The Taovaya Indians in Frontier Trade and Diplomacy," *Chronicles of Oklahoma* 31, no. 3 (1953–54): 280; *Handbook of Texas Online,* 1171–74.

58. Elizabeth Ann Harper John, *Storms Brewed in Other Men's Worlds* (College Station: Texas A&M University Press, 1975), 385; Harper, "Taovaya Indians," 268–76; Bolton, *Athanase,* 58; David Dary, *The Santa Fe Trail* (New York: Knopf, 2000), 33–35; Lathel F. Duffield, "The Taovayas Village of 1759: In Texas or Oklahoma?" *Great Plains Journal,* Spring (April 2, 1965): 45.

59. Harper, "Taovaya Indians," 268–76; John, *Storms Brewed,* 301, 350; Duffield, "Taovayas Village," 39, 40; Weddle, *New Handbook,* 1171–74.

60. John, *Storms Brewed,* 351, 352.

61. Weddle, *New Handbook,* 1171–74.

62. Chipman, *Spanish Texas,* 166, 168, 169; Jerry D. Thompson, *Sabers on the Rio Grande* (Austin: Presidial Press, 1974), 9, 10.

63. Chipman, *Spanish Texas,* 168; Thompson, *Sabers,* 13, 14.

64. Thompson, *Sabers,* 14–16.

65. Thompson, *Sabers,* 20, 21; Gilberto Miguel Hinojosa, *A Borderlands Town in Transition* (College Station: Texas A&M University Press, 1983), 5; Kathleen da Camara, *Laredo on the Rio Grande* (San Antonio: Naylor, 1949), 11.

66. Thompson, *Sabers,* 23; Hinojosa, *Borderlands Town,* 6, 7; Da Camara, *Laredo,* 12, 13.

67. Hinojosa, *Borderlands Town,* 9, 13, 16; A. Joachim McGraw and Kay Hindes, "The Development of the Regional Road Network," in *A Texas Legacy,* 161; Da Camara, *Laredo,* 14.

68. Lawrence Kinnaird, *The Frontiers of New Spain* (Berkeley: Quivira Society, 1958), 7, 28–34; Chipman, *Spanish Texas,* 172–79, 191; Foster, *Spanish Expeditions,* 182.

69. Foster, *Spanish Expeditions,* 192; Kinnaird, *Frontiers,* 34; Chipman, *Spanish Texas,* 180.

70. Chipman, *Spanish Texas,* 187–89, 193.

71. Foster, *Spanish Expeditions,* 200, 204, 224; De la Teja, *San Antonio,* 114

72. De la Teja, "The Camino Real," in *A Texas Legacy,* 48; Robert S. Weddle and Robert H. Thonoff, *Drama and Conflict* (Austin: Madrona Press, 1976), 69.

CHAPTER 3

1. A. Joachim McGraw, "Early Roads across the South Texas Landscape," in *A Texas Legacy: The Old San Antonio Road and the Caminos Reales* (Austin: Texas Department of Transportation, 1991), 131; De la Teja, "The Camino Real," in *A Texas Legacy,* 43–48.

2. De la Teja, "Camino Real," 43–45.

3. Donald E. Chipman, *Spanish Texas* (Austin: University of Texas Press, 1992), 190, 191; Noel M. Loomis and Abraham P. Nasatir, *Pedro Vial and the Roads to Santa Fe* (Norman: University of Oklahoma Press, 1967), 79.

4. Loomis and Nasatir, *Pedro Vial,* 66; Herbert E. Bolton, *Texas in the Middle Eighteenth Century* (Austin: University of Texas Press, 1970), 79–83.

5. Bolton, *Texas in the Middle Eighteenth Century,* 95, 122; Elizabeth Ann Harper, "The Taovaya Indians in Frontier Trade and Diplomacy, 1769–1779," *Southwestern Historical Quarterly* (hereafter cited as SWHQ), October 1953, 186.

6. Bolton, *Texas in the Middle Eighteenth Century,* 113, 114; Carl Newton Tyson, *The Red River in Southwestern History* (Norman: University of Oklahoma Press, 1981), 53.

7. Elizabeth Ann Harper John, *Storms Brewed in Other Men's Worlds* (College Station: Texas A&M University Press, 1975), 515.

8. John, *Storms Brewed,* 544, 553.

9. Elizabeth Ann Harper John (ed.), "Inside the Comanchera 1785," SWHQ 98 (1994–95): 28; Loomis and Nasatir, xv.

10. John, "Inside the Comanchera," 27, 29, 31, 33, 41; John *Storms Brewed,* 649, 650.

11. John, *Storms Brewed,* 663; John "Inside the Comanchera," 48, 52; Chipman, *Spanish Texas,* 199.

12. Chipman, *Spanish Texas,* 206; David J. Weber, *The Spanish Frontier in North America* (New Haven: Yale University Press, 1992), 195, 265, 274; Robert S. Weddle and Robert H. Thonoff, *Drama and Conflict* (Austin: Madrona Press, 1976), 66; Jesus F. de la Teja, *San Antonio de Bexar* (Albuquerque: University of New Mexico Press, 1995), 5, 100, 101; Angela Tucker Goldston, "Monterrey: Development of an Urban Area," thesis, Austin, 1978, 15, 25.

13. Chipman, *Spanish Texas,* 205; Jack Jackson, *Los Mestenos* (College Station: Texas A&M University Press, 1986), 592.

14. *El Camino Real,* TXDOT brochure.

15. Texas Section, American Society of Civil Engineers, *The Texas Engineer,* Centennial Edition, December 1936, 12.

16. Frances Stovall, *Clear Springs and Limestone Ledges* (San Marcos: Hays County Historical Commission, 1986), 9; Chipman, *Spanish Texas,* 224; John W. Reps, *Cities of the American West* (Princeton: Princeton University Press, 1979), 79.

17. Chipman, *Spanish Texas,* 218, 235–37; Ted Schwarz, *The Forgotten Battlefield* (Austin: Eakin Press, 1985), 45.

18. Chipman, *Spanish Texas,* 222; A. Joachim McGraw, "The Development of the Regional Road Network," in *A Texas Legacy,* 161.

19. John H. Coatsworth, "The Mexican Mining Industry in the Eighteenth Century," in *The Economies of Mexico and Peru During the Late Colonial Period,* ed. Nils Jacobsen and Hans-Jurgen Puhle (Berlin: Colloqium Verlag, 1986), 42; Alexander Von Humboldt, *Political Essay on the Kingdom of New Spain* (New York: Knopf, 1972), 147, 148, 152; Garner, *Economic Growth,* 113.

20. Reps, *Cities,* 79; Juan Antonio Padilla, "Texas in 1820," SWHQ 23 (1919–20): 60, 61.

21. Padilla, "Texas in 1820," 60, 61.

22. Tyson, *Red River,* 83, 85.

23. David J. Weber, *The Mexican Frontier 1821–1846* (Albuquerque: University of New Mexico Press, 1982), 162; Tyson, *Red River,* 88, 90.

24. David Dary, *The Santa Fe Trail* (New York: Knopf, 2000), 63, 69.

25. Charles A. Bacarisse, "Baron de Bastrop," SWHQ 58 (1954–55): 319–24; Gregg Cantrell, *Stephen F. Austin* (New Haven: Yale University Press, 1999), 54–85.

26. Cantrell, *Stephen F. Austin,* 172, 183, 184.

27. Cantrell, *Stephen F. Austin,* 183, 184, 205, 232–35, 261; *Handbook of Texas Online.*

28. Kathleen da Camara, *Laredo on the Rio Grande* (San Antonio: Naylor, 1949), 15; Jack Jackson (ed.), *Texas by Teran* (Austin: University of Texas Press, 2000), 35; Jean Louis Berlandier, *Journey to Mexico,* trans. Sheila M. Ohlendorf (Austin: Texas State Historical Association, 1980), 139, 180; Jackson, *Texas by Teran,* 3, 13.

29. Berlandier, *Journey,* 262, 263; Jackson, *Texas by Teran,* 35.

30. Berlandier, *Journey,* 271–75; Jose Maria Sanchez, "A Trip to Texas in 1829," SWHQ 29 (1925–26): 251.

31. Sanchez, "Trip to Texas," 251; Berlandier, *Journey,* 272–75; La Salle County Historical Commission, www.historicdistrict.com.

32. Jackson, *Texas by Teran,* 17, 18.

33. W. W. Newcomb Jr., *The Indians of Texas* (Austin: University of Texas Press, 1961), 343, 336.

34. Randy Roberts and James S. Olson, *A Line in the Sand* (New York: Free Press, 2001), 42–46, 56–59.

35. Jerry D. Thompson, *Sabers on the Rio Grande* (Austin: Presidial Press, 1974), 71, 72; Weber, *Mexican Frontier,* 142; Jose Enrique de la Pena, *With Santa Anna in Texas,* trans. Carmen Perry (College Station: Texas A&M University Press, 1975), 20; Stephen L. Hardin, "The Old San Antonio Road in the Texas Revolution," in *A Texas Legacy,* 225.

36. Reps, *Cities,* 129, 134.

37. Reps, *Cities,* 135.

38. Mary Starr Barkley, *History of Travis County and Austin* (Waco: Texian Press, 1963), 7; Reps, *Cities,* 135.

39. Reps, *Cities,* 135, 136.

40. Barkley, *History of Travis County,* 40; Reps, *Cities,* 137, *Handbook of Texas Online.*

41. Stephen L. Hardin, "People and Events along the Caminos Reales," in *A Texas Legacy,* 237, 238.

42. Geoffrey Hindley, *A History of Roads* (Secaucus, N. J.: Citadel Press, 1972), 59, 60; Charles L. Dearing, *American Highway Policy* (Washington, D.C.: Brookings Institution, 1941), 12, 13.

43. U.S. Department of Transportation (USDOT), *American Highways 1776–1976* (Washington, D.C.: Federal Highway Administration, 1976), 13; Hindley, *History of Roads,* 63, 65.

44. Hindley, *History of Roads,* 74, 75.

45. Albert C. Rose, *Historic American Highways* (Washington, D.C.: American Association of State Highway Officials, 1953), 23–26, 35–38; Robert H. Scotland, "Old Connecticut Path," Wayland Historical Society, April 3, 1968.

46. Rose, *Historic American Highways,* 44, 50, 51; USDOT, *American Highways,* 24.

47. Dary, *Santa Fe Trail,* 92–96, 104.

48. Rose, *Historic American Highways,* 37, 38.

49. USDOT, *American Highways,* 9, 10, 12; Rose, *Historic American Highways,* 37, 38.

50. Dearing, *American Highway Policy,* 32; USDOT, *American Highways,* 17, 19.

51. USDOT, *American Highways,* 17–20.

52. USDOT, *American Highways,* 19, 20, Rose, *Historic American Highways,* 52, 53.

53. Rose, *Historic American Highways,* 53; USDOT, *American Highways,* 20.

54. USDOT, *American Highways,* 21, 22.

55. George R. Taylor, *The Transportation Revolution* (New York: Harper Torchbooks, 1951), 23; Dearing, *American Highway Policy,* 37.

56. S. G. Reed, *A History of the Texas Railroads* (New York: Arno Press, 1941), 25.

57. Kenneth W. Wheeler, *To Wear a City's Crown* (Cambridge: Harvard University Press, 1968), 30–32.

58. John Edward Weems, *Austin 1839–1989* (Austin: Austin American-Statesman, 1989), 8.

59. Wheeler, *To Wear a City's Crown,* 54, 69, 71, 78

60. Max L. Moorhead, "Spanish Transportation in the Southwest," *New Mexico Historical Review* 32 (1957): 120; Roy L. Swift and Leavitt Corning Jr., *Three Roads to Chihuahua* (Austin: Eakin Press, 1988), 35, 38, 41; A. Morton Smith, *The First 100 Years in Cooke County* (San Antonio: Naylor, 1955), 4.

CHAPTER 4

1. J. W. Williams, "The National Road of the Republic of Texas," SWHQ 47 (1943–44): 218.

2. Mattie Davis Lucas and Mita Holsapple Hall, *A History of Grayson County, Texas* (Sherman: Scruggs, 1936), 18, 24, 35; Graham Landrum and Allan Smith, *An Illustrated History of Grayson County* (Fort Worth: Historical Publishers, 1967), 1.

3. Landrum and Smith, *Illustrated History,* 1–3; Michael V. Hazel, *Dallas: A History of Big D* (Austin: Texas State Historical Association, 1997), 2.

4. Landrum and Smith, *Illustrated History,* 4.

5. Gerald S. Pierce, "The Military Road Expedition of 1840–41, *Texas Military History* 6 (1967): 115.

6. Adjutant General Records, Army Correspondence, William G. Cooke to Branch T. Archer, November 14, 1840, Archives and Information Services Division, Texas State Library and Archives Commission.

7. Lucas and Hall, *History of Grayson County,* 47; Pierce, "Military Road," 123, 126.

8. Pierce, "Military Road," 132, 133; Frances Stovall, *Clear Springs and Limestone Ledges* (San Marcos: Hays County Historical Commission, 1986), 70.

9. Pierce, "Military Road," 133, 134; Stovall, *Clear Springs,* 70.

10. Pierce, "Military Road," 127.

11. Harry Warren, "Col. William G. Cooke," SWHQ 9 (1905–1906): 217; Roy L. Swift and Leavitt Corning Jr., *Three Roads to Chihuahua* (Austin: Eakin Press, 1988), 49; Jerry D. Thompson *Sabers on the Rio Grande* (Austin: Presidial Press, 1974), 102.

12. Pierce, "Military Road," 119, 127.

13. Landrum and Smith, *Illustrated History,* 4.

14. *Handbook of Texas Online.*

15. Walter Prescott Webb, *The Texas Rangers* (Austin: University of Texas Press, 1965), 33, 60, 61.

16. Albert D. Richardson, *Beyond the Mississippi* (Hartford: American Publishing Company, 1867), 224–30.

17. A. Joachim McGraw and Stephen L. Hardin, "The Evolution of the Old San Antonio Road and the Camino Reales," in *A Texas Legacy: The Old San Antonio Road and the Caminos Reales* (Austin: Texas Department of Transportation, 1991), 229; Thompson, *Sabers,* 111–16; John W. Reps, *Cities of the American West* (Princeton University Press, 1979), 138, 139; Kenneth W. Wheeler, *To Wear a City's Crown* (Cambridge: Harvard University Press, 1968), 39; W. W. Newcomb Jr., *The Indians of Texas* (Austin: University of Texas Press, 1961), 349.

18. Edmond F. Bates, *History and Reminiscences of Denton County* (Denton: McNitzky, 1918), 8.

19. Stan Hoig, *Jesse Chisholm* (Niwot, Colo: University of Colorado Press, 1991), xi, xii, 8, 12, 16, 26, 52, 57; Julia Kathryn Garrett, *Fort Worth: A Frontier Triumph* (Austin: Encino Press, 1972), 43–46.

20. Garrett, *Fort Worth,* 43–46; Hoig, *Jesse Chisholm,* 57.

21. *Texas Highways,* October 1973, 20–22; Oscar Haas, *History of New Braunfels and Comal County, Texas* (Austin: Steck Company, 1968), 17; Writers Program of the Texas WPA, *Texas: A Guide to the Lone Star State* (New York: Hastings House, 1940), 445, 446.

22. Haas, *History of New Braunfels,* 22; WPA, *Texas Guide,* 445, 446.

23. *Texas Highways,* October 1973, 23, 24; WPA, *Texas Guide,* 445, 446.

24. Wheeler, *To Wear a City's Crown,* 39.

25. Wheeler, *To Wear a City's Crown,* 43.

26. Haas, *History of New Braunfels,* 140.

27. Haas, *History of New Braunfels,* 74.

28. Viktor Bracht, *Texas in 1848* (San Antonio: Naylor, 1931), ix, 82, 84, 142, 143.

29. Stovall, *Clear Springs,* 20.

30. Stovall, *Clear Springs,* 71, 80, 83, 93, 96, 172.

31. George W. Tyler, *The History of Bell County* (San Antonio: Naylor, 1936), 42, 82, 88, 113.

32. Roger N. Conger, *A Pictorial History of Waco* (Waco: Texian Press, 1964), 5, 6.

33. Lee David Benton, "An Odyssey into Texas: William M. Quesenbury With the Cherokees," *Chronicles of Oklahoma* 60 (1982–83): 116–31.

34. Conger, *Pictorial History,* 6, 8; Reps, *Cities,* 151; *Handbook of Texas Online.*

35. A. C. Greene, *Dallas: The Deciding Years* (Austin: Encino Press, 1973), 4, 7; Patricia E. Hill, *Dallas: The Making of a Modern City* (Austin: University of Texas Press, 1996), xviii; Hazel, *Dallas,* 2.

36. Garrett, *Fort Worth,* 51, 54; Hill, *Dallas: The Making,* xix.

37. Robert H. Thonoff, *San Antonio Stage Lines, 1847–81* (El Paso: Texas Western Press, 1971), 4, 5, 7–9; Thomas T. Smith, *The U.S. Army and the Texas Frontier Economy* (College Station: Texas A&M University Press), 155; Stovall, *Clear Springs,* 128; Garrett, *Fort Worth,* 51, 52; Hill, *Dallas: The Making,* xix; Greene, *Dallas: The Deciding Years,* 6.

38. Williams, "National Road," 207, 208.

39. Williams, "National Road," 208; J. W. Williams, *Dallas Morning News,* April 1, 1945.

40. J. Lee and Lillian J. Stambaugh, *A History of Collin County* (Austin: Texas State Historical Association, 1958), 44, 57.

41. A. Morton Smith, *The First 100 Years in Cooke County* (San Antonio: Naylor, 1955), 4, 7; Bates, *Reminiscences of Denton,* 153.

42. Agnes S. Calvin, "A History of Roadside Development in Texas," thesis, Southwest Texas University, San Marcos, May 1941, 8, 9.

43. Haas, *History of New Braunfels,* 74.

44. Calvin, "History of Roadside Development," 9, 10; Earl F. Woodward, "Internal Improvements in Texas in the Early 1850s," SWHQ 76 (1972–73): 171.

45. Tyler, *History of Bell County,* 123, 126, 149, 150.

46. W. M. Gillespie, *A Manual of the Principles and Practice of Road Making* (New York: Barnes, 1852), 3, 191, 193, 194, 200, 218, 341, 342, 346.

47. Henry Wilson, *History of the Rise and Fall of the Slave Power in America* (Boston: Houghton Mifflin, 1872–77), 604, 606; Thomas T. Smith, *The U.S. Army and the Texas Frontier Economy* (College Station: Texas A&M University Press, 1999), 17, 138.

48. T. T. Smith, *U.S. Army,* 19–26, 49, 138; William H. Goetzmann, *Army Expeditions in the American West, 1803–1863* (Lincoln: University of Nebraska Press, 1979), 149; Thompson, *Sabers,* 141–61; Kathleen da Camara, *Laredo on the Rio Grande* (San Antonio: Naylor, 1949), 18; Swift and Corning, *Three Roads,* 56.

49. T. T. Smith, *U.S. Army,* 28; Rupert N. Richardson, Introduction to Roger N. Conger et al., *Frontier Forts of Texas* (Waco: Texian Press, 1966), viii–xiii.

50. Goetzmann, *Army Expeditions,* 211; T. T. Smith, *U.S. Army,* 139.

51. Goetzmann, *Army Expeditions,* 234; W. Turrentine Jackson, *Wagon Roads West* (Berkeley: University of California Press, 1952), 43.

52. Nathaniel H. Michler, *Bureau of Topographical Engineers Report to U.S. War Department,* July 23, 1850, 30, 31; *Gainesville Daily Register,* August 30, 1948 (*hereafter cited as Gainesville DR*).

53. T. T. Smith, *U.S. Army,* 30, 32.

54. Averam B. Bender, "Military Transportation in the Southwest, 1848–1860," *New Mexico Historical Review* 32 (1957): 124–29; T. T. Smith, *U.S. Army,* 31, 33.

55. Bender, "Military Transportation," 142; T. T. Smith, *U.S. Army,* 148; Goetzmann, *Army Expeditions,* 237.

56. Garrett, *Fort Worth,* 65, 66.

57. Garrett, *Fort Worth,* 58, 60.

58. Reps, *Cities,* 151; Garrett, *Fort Worth,* 82–83, 128, 137–38, 157, 173.

59. Hill, *Dallas: The Making,* xviii; Greene, *Dallas: The Deciding Years,* 7.

60. Greene, *Dallas: The Deciding Years,* 9, 12; Hazel, *Dallas,* 6, 8, 9.

61. Collins, *Cooke County,* 7, 8; A. M. Smith, *First 100 Years,* 16; Randolph B. Marcy, *Report to U.S. War Department,* July 23, 1850 (Washington, D.C.: U.S. War Department, 1850), 220, 221.

62. *US Census 1850;* Garrett, *Fort Worth,* 83, 108.

63. T. T. Smith, *U.S. Army,* 11, 13.

64. T. T. Smith, *U.S. Army,* 50, 135.

65. Wheeler, *To Wear a City's Crown,* 45.

66. Haas, *History of New Braunfels,* 75; Stovall, *Clear Springs,* 131, B26.

67. Haas, *History of New Braunfels,* 80, 83; San Antonio Public Library, *A Chronology of the Historic San Antonio River.*

68. Wheeler, *To Wear a City's Crown,* 82.

69. Wheeler, *To Wear a City's Crown,* 82.

70. Marilyn McAdams Sibley, *Travelers in Texas* (Austin: University of Texas Press, 1967), 38, 41; Wheeler, *To Wear a City's Crown,* 81; William Ranson Hogan, *The Texas Republic* (Norman: University of Oklahoma Press, 1946), 54.

71. T. T. Smith, *U.S. Army,* 162.

72. Thonoff, *San Antonio Stage Lines,* 3, 9, 10, 12.

73. Thonoff, *San Antonio Stage Lines,* 3–12; T. T. Smith, *U.S. Army,* 155; Stovall, *Clear Springs,* 128.

74. Kathryn Turner Carter, *Stagecoach Inns of Texas* (Waco: Texian Press, 1972), 176, 189; Thonoff, *San Antonio Stage Lines,* 14–18; Tyler, *History of Bell County,* 137.

75. John S. Spratt, *The Road to Spindletop* (Dallas: Southern Methodist University Press, 1955), 246; Haas, *History of New Braunfels,* 95, 149, 150; Harry Landa, *As I Remember* (San Antonio: Carleston, 1955), 13, 14; T. Lindsay Baker, *Building the Lone Star* (College Station: Texas A&M University Press, 1986), 144–45.

76. B. P. Gallaway (ed.), *Texas: The Dark Corner of the Confederacy* (Lincoln: University of Nebraska Press, 1994), 68; Mary Starr Barkley, *History of Travis County and Austin* (Waco: Texian Press, 1963), 266–71.

77. Charles S. Potts, *Railroad Transportation in Texas* (Austin: University of Texas, 1909), 15, 32; Wheeler, *To Wear a City's Crown,* 90, 103.

78. Potts, *Railroad Transportation,* 26–28, 35; Woodward, "Internal Improvements," 173, 174; Wheeler, *To Wear a City's Crown,* 97, 98; Andrew F. Muir, "Railroads Come to Houston, 1857–61," SWHQ 64 (1960–61): 47.

79. S. G. Reed, *A History of the Texas Railroads* (New York: Arno Press, 1941), 124.

80. Waterman L. Ormsby, *The Butterfield Overland Mail* (San Marino: Huntington Library, 1942), 42–45; Emmett M. Essin, "The Ox-Bow Route," in *Pioneer Trails West,* ed. Donald E. Worcester, Western Writers of America (Caldwell, Idaho: Caxton Printers, 1985), 206; Carter, *Stagecoach Inns,* 7.

81. Lucas and Hall, *History of Grayson County,* 79–82; Carter, *Stagecoach Inns,* 7–10.

82. Ormsby, *Butterfield Overland,* 42–45.

83. Essin, "Ox-Bow Route," 205; Wayne Gard, *The Chisholm Trail* (Norman: University of Oklahoma Press, 1954), 27.

84. Essin, "Ox-Bow Route," 205; Gard, *Chisholm Trail,* 27. Wheeler, *To Wear a City's Crown,* 83; Potts, *Railroad Transportation,* 15.

85. Wheeler, *To Wear a City's Crown,* 119; Larry Jay Gage, "The City of Austin on the Eve of the Civil War," SWHQ 63 (1959–60): 430; Weems, *Austin,* 9.

86. Frederick Law Olmsted, *A Journey through Texas* (New York: Dix, Edwards, 1857), 109–53.

CHAPTER 5

1. *US Census 1860.*

2. *US Census 1860;* A. C. Greene, *Dallas: The Deciding Years* (Austin: Encino Press, 1973), 15; Roger N. Conger, "Waco: Cotton and Culture on the Brazos," SWHQ 75 (1971–72): 56; Michael V. Hazel, *Dallas: A History of Big D* (Austin: Texas State Historical Association, 1997), 11, 12.

3. B. P. Gallaway (ed.), *Texas: The Dark Corner of the Confederacy* (Lincoln: University of Nebraska Press, 1994), 5; Stephen B. Oates, "Texas under the Secessionists," SWHQ 67 (1963–64): 171; Allan C. Ashcroft, *Texas in the Civil War* (Austin: Texas Civil War Centennial Commission, 1962), 8, 9; Oscar Haas, *History of New Braunfels and Comal County, Texas* (Austin: Steck Company, 1968), 153; John Edward Weems, *Austin 1839–1989* (Austin: Austin American-Statesman, 1989), 10.

4. W. W. Heartsill, *Fourteen Hundred and Ninety One Days in the Confederate Army* (Marshall: Heartsill, 1876), 9–11.

5. Ashcroft, *Texas in the Civil War*, (Austin: Texas Civil War Centenial Commision, 1962), 7, 14, 21; Texas Historical Commission (THC), *Texas in the Civil War*, brochure (Austin: Texas Historical Commission, 1962).

6. Julia Kathryn Garrett, *Fort Worth: A Frontier Triumph* (Austin: Encino Press, 1972), 230; Ashcroft, *Texas in the Civil War*, 29; Jerry D. Thompson, *Sabers on the Rio Grande* (Austin: Presidial Press, 1974), 216; Weems, *Austin*, 11; THC, *Texas in the Civil War*, brochure.

7. Garrett, *Fort Worth*, 241; Michael Collins, *Cooke County, Texas* (Gainesville: Cooke County Heritage Society, 1981), 17; Weems, *Austin*, 12; San Antonio Public Library, *Chronology*; Writers Program of the Dallas WPA (1936–1942), *The WPA Dallas Guide and History* (Dallas: Dallas Public Library, 1992), 292, 296; Texas Historical Commission, *African Americans in Texas*, brochure, p. 13, and *Texas Independence Trail*, brochure.

8. W. C. Nunn, *Texas under the Carpetbaggers* (Austin: University of Texas Press, 1962), 137, 145, 237.

9. Wayne Gard, *The Chisholm Trail* (Norman: University of Oklahoma Press, 1954), 4.

10. Gard, *Chisholm Trail*, 26, 28; Ron Tyler, "The Cowboy Trails," in *Pioneer Trails West*, ed. Donald E. Worcester, Western Writers of America (Caldwell, Idaho: Caxton Printers, 1985), 186, 187.

11. Gard, *Chisholm Trail*, 28, 54; James E. Sherow, "Water, Sun and Cattle: The Chisholm Trail as an Ephemeral Ecosystem," in *Fluid Arguments: Five Centuries of Western Water Conflict*, ed. Charles Miller (Tucson: Unversity of Arizona Press, 2001), 146, 149, 150.

12. Gard, *Chisholm Trail*, 72, 73; Stan Hoig, *Jesse Chisholm* (Niwot, Colo: University of Colorado Press, 1991), 162, 165.

13. Hoig, *Jesse Chisholm*, 133; Sherow, "Water, Sun," 142.

14. Haas, *History of New Braunfels*, 201; *Texas Highways*, August 1967, 20, 21; Gard, *Chisholm Trail*, 76–79; Tyler, "Cowboy Trails," 293.

15. Garrett, *Fort Worth*, 258, 266–68, 282–84, 288, 315; Nunn, *Texas under the Carpetbaggers*, 136, 137; Donald E. Worcester, *The Chisholm Trail* (Lincoln: University of Nebraska Press, 1980), 13–16; John W. Reps, *Cities of the American West* (Princeton: Princeton University Press, 1979), 556; Albert C. Rose, *Historic American Highways* (Washington, D.C.: American Association of State Highway Officials, 1953), 88; Sherow, "Water, Sun," 147, 148.

16. Reps, *Cities*, 556; Rose, *Historic American Highways*, 88.

17. Gard, *Chisholm Trail*, 253, 257, 259, 263; Terry G. Jordan, *North American Cattle Ranching Frontiers* (Albuquerque: University of New Mexico Press, 1993), 231, 236–39.

18. Nunn, *Texas under the Carpetbaggers*, 168, 169; Agnes S. Calvin, "A History of Roadside Development in Texas," thesis, Southwest Texas University, San Marcos, May 1941, 10; John S. Spratt, *The Road to Spindletop* (Dallas: Southern Methodist University Press,

1955), 25; John D. Huddleston, "Good Roads for Texas," thesis, Texas A&M University, 1981, 24.

19. George W. Tyler, *The History of Bell County* (San Antonio: Naylor, 1936), 268, 270, 282, 286, 306.

20. Nunn, *Texas under the Carpetbaggers,* 155–57; Robert H. Thonoff, *San Antonio Stage Lines, 1847–81* (El Paso: Texas Western Press, 1971), 4, 5, 7–9, 25; Edward King, *Texas 1874* (Houston: Cordovan Press, 1874), 75–80; Weems, *Austin,* 14.

21. Thonoff, *San Antonio Stage Lines,* 26, 29, 31, 32.

22. Thonoff, *San Antonio Stage Lines,* 22; Boyce House, *City of Flaming Adventure* (San Antonio: Naylor, 1949), 166.

23. John D. Huddleston, "Austin, Texas in 1876," thesis, University of Texas, 1976, 28; Webb, *Texas Rangers,* 297–303, 371–88, 540–44.

24. Charles S. Potts, *Railroad Transportation in Texas* (Austin: University of Texas, 1909), 39, 40, 49; Nunn, *Texas under the Carpetbaggers,* 159.

25. Garrett, *Fort Worth,* 324; S. G. Reed, *A History of the Texas Railroads* (New York: Arno Press, 1941), 209; Hazel, *Dallas,* 16.

26. Hazel, *Dallas,* 19; Patricia E. Hill, *Dallas: The Making of a Modern City* (Austin: University of Texas Press, 1996), 3.

27. Reed, *History of Texas Railroads,* 211, 213; Nunn, *Texas under the Carpetbaggers,* 160.

28. Stewart H. Holbrook, *The Story of American Railroads* (New York: Crown Publishers, 1947), 216; Reed, *History of Texas Railroads,* 375, 376.

29. Holbrook, *Story of American Railroads,* 217; Reps, *Cities,* 576; Vincent V. Masterson, *The Katy Railroad* (Norman: University of Oklahoma Press, 1953), 165; Ruth Ann Overbeck Perez, "The Red River Bridges," thesis, University of Texas, 1969, 8, 9.

30. Masterson, *Katy Railroad,* 176–79, 184, 191; Reed, *History of Texas Railroads,* 210.

31. Masterson, *Katy Railroad,* 180, 181; Perez, "Red River Bridges," 22; Holbrook, *Story of American Railroads,* 217.

32. Reed, *History of Texas Railroads,* 378; Collins, *Cooke County,* 21; Edmond F. Bates, *History and Reminiscences of Denton County* (Denton: McNitzky, 1918), 170.

33. Reed, *History of Texas Railroads,* 150, 151; Potts, *Railroad Transportation,* 53; Garrett, *Fort Worth,* 320, 322.

34. Hill, *Dallas: The Making,* 3, 4.

35. Masterson, *Katy Railroad,* 206, 220.

36. Holbrook, *Story of American Railroads,* 68; Julius Grodinsky, *Jay Gould* (Philadelphia: University of Pennsylvania Press, 1957), 401.

37. Grodinsky, *Jay Gould,* 253.

38. Masterson, *Katy Railroad,* 222; *Gainesville DR,* August 30, 1948.

39. Masterson, *Katy Railroad,* 219, 223, 226; Reed, *History of Texas Railroads,* 378–80; A. Morton Smith, *The First 100 Years in Cooke County* (San Antonio: Naylor, 1955), 79.

40. Garrett, *Fort Worth,* 319, 323; Nunn, *Texas under the Carpetbaggers,* 160; Reed, *History of Texas Railroads,* 150–52.

41. Potts, *Railroad Transportation,* 54, 55; Reed, *History of Texas Railroads,* 322, 323.

42. Grodinsky, *Jay Gould,* 261, 265.

43. Reed, *History of Texas Railroads,* 320; David C. Humphrey, *Austin: An Illustrated History* (Northridge: Windsor, 1985), 77; Al Lowman, *A Windshield Tour of the Historic El Camino Real* (San Marcos: Convention and Visitors Bureau, 2000).

44. J. B. Wilkinson, *Laredo and the Rio Grande Frontier* (Austin: Jenkins Publishing Company, 1975), 366, 370.

45. Pressler and Langermann, *Map of the State of Texas* (1879); *Galveston Daily News,* April 27, 1882.

46. Masterson, *Katy Railroad,* 223, 234; Reed, *History of Texas Railroads,* 380.

47. *Gainesville DR,* August 30, 1948; Tyler, *History of Bell County,* 313.

48. Weldon Green Cannon, "Bernard Moore Temple," thesis, Texas Christian University, 1987, 45–50.

49. Cannon, "Bernard Moore Temple," 50, 52, 56, 57.

50. Tyler, *History of Bell County,* 318; Masterson, *Katy Railroad,* 228.

51. Grodinsky, *Jay Gould,* 267, 608.

52. Ruth A. Allen, *The Great Southwest Strike* (Austin: University of Texas, 1942), 14; Masterson, *Katy Railroad,* 239.

53. Grenville M. Dodge, *How We Built the Union Pacific Railway,* U.S. 61st Congress, 2nd Session, 1909–1910, Sen. Doc. No. 447, Washington (1910), 13, 14.

54. Allen, *Great Southwest Strike,* 22; Alton K. Briggs, "The Archeology of 1882 Labor Camps on the Southern Pacific Railroad," thesis, Austin, 1974, 34; William H. Harris, *The Harder We Run* (Oxford University Press: New York, 1982), 34.

55. Robert L. Peterson, "Jay Gould and the Railroad Commission of Texas," SWHQ 58 (1954–55): 423, 427.

56. Masterson, *Katy Railroad,* 240–42; *Gainesville DR,* August 30, 1948.

57. Masterson, *Katy Railroad,* 240–42; Potts, *Railroad Transportation,* 62, 67, 68; *Gainesville DR,* August 30, 1948; WPA, *Dallas Guide,* 138.

58. Masterson, *Katy Railroad,* 250, 268; Potts, *Railroad Transportation,* 56, 64; Reed, *History of Texas Railroads,* 380, 385.

59. Collins, *Cooke County,* 27, 29.

60. Nunn, *Texas under the Carpetbaggers,* 163; Potts, *Railroad Transportation,* 32; Thonoff, *San Antonio Stage Lines,* 34.

61. Potts, *Railroad Transportation,* 16; Reed, *History of Texas Railroads,* 182.

62. Vera Lea Dugan, "Texas Industry 1860–1880," SWHQ 59 (1955–56): 154.

63. Spratt, *Road to Spindletop,* 56, 63.

64. Spratt, *Road to Spindletop,* 66; WPA, *Dallas Guide,* 7, 13; *Texas Parade,* October 1936, p. 5; *Gainesville DR,* August 30, 1948.

65. Haas, *History of New Braunfels,* 85, 150; Landa, *As I Remember,* 61; T. Lindsay Baker, *Building the Lone Star* (College Station: Texas A&M University Press, 1986), 145, 146; WPA, *Dallas Guide,* 13.

CHAPTER 6

1. Albert C. Rose, *Historic American Highways* (Washington, D.C.: American Association of State Highway Officials, 1953), 65, 71; Richard M. Barker and Jay A. Puckett, *Design of*

Highway Bridges (New York: John Wiley, 1997), 4, 8, 11, 14; M. S. Troitsky, *Planning and Design of Bridges* (New York: John Wiley, 1994), 18, 23–25.

2. Roger N. Conger, "The Waco Suspension Bridge," *Texana* 1, no. 3 (1962–63): 181–85, 194.

3. Conger, "Waco Suspension Bridge," 181, 188, 189.

4. Conger, "Waco Suspension Bridge," 187, 190, 193.

5. Conger, "Waco Suspension Bridge," 192–97, 214–23; T. Lindsay Baker, *Building the Lone Star* (College Station: Texas A&M University Press, 1986), 262.

6. Michael V. Hazel, *Dallas: A History of Big D* (Austin: Texas State Historical Association, 1997), 19; Baker, *Building,* 262; Writers Program of the Dallas WPA (1936–1942), *The WPA Dallas Guide and History* (Dallas: Dallas Public Library, 1992), 154.

7. Oscar Haas, *History of New Braunfels and Comal County, Texas* (Austin: Steck Company, 1968), 85, 87, 204, 208, 210; Harry Landa, *As I Remember* (San Antonio: Carleston, 1955), 75, 76.

8. John Edward Weems, *Austin 1839–1989* (Austin: Austin American-Statesman, 1989), 16; Baker, *Building,* 162, 163.

9. Weems, *Austin,* 17, 18; Baker, *Building,* 39, 162–65.

10. Huddleston, "Austin, Texas," 12; Weems, *Austin,* 14, 22, 24, 25; Baker, *Building,* 15, 16; A. T. Jackson, "Austin's Street Car Era," SWHQ 53 (1949–50): 236, 238, 241, 243.

11. Boyce House, *City of Flaming Adventure* (San Antonio: Naylor, 1949): 162, 169, 170; Baker, *Building,* 3; Barker and Puckett, *Design,* 17; *Texas Highways,* June 1978, 16.

12. House, *City,* 192; Green Peyton, *San Antonio* (New York: McGraw-Hill, 1946), 104, 107; Landa, *As I Remember,* 94; Lewis F. Fisher, *Saving San Antonio* (Lubbock: Texas Tech University Press, 1996), 404.

13. John W. Reps, *Cities of the American West* (Princeton: Princeton University Press, 1979), 669.

14. WPA, *Dallas Guide,* 64–67, 78, 125; *Handbook of Texas Online.*

15. Hazel, *Dallas,* 24, 31; Ted Dealey, *Diaper Days of Dallas* (Nashville: Abingdon Press, 1966), 79; Patricia E. Hill, *Dallas: The Making of a Modern City* (Austin: University of Texas Press, 1996), 5, 6, 29; WPA, *Dallas Guide,* 74, 80.

16. Vera Lea Dugan, "Texas Industry 1860–1880," SWHQ 59 (1955–56): 160; Oliver Knight, *Fort Worth* (Fort Worth: Texas Christian University Press, 1990), 137, 177; Baker, *Building,* 87–89; *Texas Highways,* June 1978, 20.

17. *Gainesville DR,* August 30, 1948.

18. *Laredo Directory of 1889,* p. 8; J. B. Wilkinson, *Laredo and the Rio Grande Frontier* (Austin: Jenkins Publishing Company, 1975), 363.

19. E. R. Tarver, *Laredo: The Gateway between the United States and Mexico* (Laredo: Daily Times, 1889), 1, 10, 18, 20; *Laredo Directory of 1889,* 38.

20. Jerry D. Thompson, *Warm Weather and Bad Whiskey* (El Paso: Texas Western Press, 1991), 48; Tarver, *Laredo: Gateway,* 2, 9; *Laredo Directory of 1889,* 11.

21. Thompson, *Warm Weather,* 50, 51; Tarver, *Laredo: Gateway,* 39; Wilkinson, *Laredo and the Rio Grande Frontier,* 371–73; Thompson, *Warm Weather,* iii, 93, 145.

22. *Laredo Directory of 1889,* 16, 38; Wilkinson, *Laredo and the Rio Grande Frontier,* 395; Tarver, *Laredo: Gateway,* 2; City of Laredo Web site, www.cityoflaredo.com; Jerry D. Thompson, *Laredo: A Pictoral History* (Norfolk: Donning Company, 1986), 259.

23. John S. Spratt, *The Road to Spindletop* (Dallas: Southern Methodist University Press, 1955), 282, 283.

24. Knight, *Fort Worth,* 199; WPA, *Dallas Guide,* 7.

25. *Texas Highways: Golden Anniversary 1917–1967,* vol. 14, no. 9 (September 1967): 6; Reverdy T. Gliddon, "Texas Highway Administration," thesis, Austin, 1951, 12; J. R. Canion, "Historical Background of Road Building in Texas," thesis, Austin, 1936, 85.

26. Frances Stovall, *Clear Springs and Limestone Ledges* (San Marcos: Hays County Historical Commission, 1986), 416; *Austin Daily Statesman,* February 19, 1884.

27. Knight, *Fort Worth,* 158; Donald R. Walker, *Penology for Profit* (College Station: Texas A&M University Press, 1988), 57.

28. Stovall, *Clear Springs,* 416; Dealey, *Diaper Days,* 23; WPA, *Dallas Guide,* 74, 76.

29. Canion, "Historical Background," 86, 87; *Texas Highways,* November 1964, 18, 19.

30. T. U. Taylor, *County Roads* (Austin: University of Texas, 1890), 2, 4, 6, 8, 9.

31. *Harpers Weekly,* August 3, 1889, 633–36; Rose, *Historic American Highways,* 89–93; Peter J. Hugill, "Good Roads and the Automobile in the United States 1880–1929," *Geographical Review* 72, no. 3 (1982): 327; Bruce E. Seely, *Building the American Highway System* (Philadelphia: Temple University Press, 1987), 12.

32. Hugill, "Good Roads," 330.

33. Rose, *Historic American Highways,* 94–99; Frederic L. Paxson, "The Highway Movement 1916–1935," *American Historical Review,* January 1946, 240.

34. Richard F. Weingroff, *Public Roads Online,* vol. 60, no. 1 (1996; hereafter cited as PRO), www.tfhre.gov/pubrds; Hugill, "Good Roads," 332.

35. Seely, *American Highway System,* 13, 16, 20–22, 30; William L. Thomas Jr., ed., *Man's Role in Changing the Face of the Earth,* vol. 1 (Chicago: University of Chicago Press, 1956), xxxi; Paxson, "Highway Movement," 239; Hugill, "Good Roads," 332.

36. Rose, *Historic American Highways,* 105, 106.

37. Seely, *American Highway System,* 9, 27.

38. James J. Flink, *America Adopts the Automobile, 1895–1910* (Cambridge: MIT Press, 1970), 12, 13, 19.

39. Rose, *Historic American Highways,* 102; Gerorge H. Dammann, *Illustrated History of Ford, 1903–1970* (Glen Ellyn, Ill.: Crestline, 1970), 7, 9, 19, 26; Flink, *America Adopts,* 275; Hugill, "Good Roads," 337; John A. Jakle and Keith A. Sculle, *The Gas Station in America* (Baltimore: Johns Hopkins University Press, 1994), 49.

40. Jakle and Sculle, *Gas Station,* 59, 91–93; *Texas Parade,* December 1950, 5, 6.

41. Seely, *American Highway System,* 19.

42. *Texas Highways: Golden,* 10, 14; Rose, *Historic American Highways,* 102; Howard Lawrence Preston, *Dirt Roads to Dixie* (Knoxville: University of Tennessee Press, 1991), 98, 103, 106; *Texas Highways* 12, no. 1, 1965.

43. Robert F. Karolevitz, *This Was Trucking* (Seattle: Superior, 1966), 16–19, 33–37; James H. Thomas, "Trucking: History and Legend," thesis, Oklahoma State University, 1976, 5, 16; Robert M. Roll, *American Trucking* (Osceola, Wis.: Motorbooks International, 1979), 18, 72, 98, 124, 160.

44. Preston, *Dirt Roads,* 99, 104, 114.

45. Preston, *Dirt Roads,* 36, 45, 52–54, 60, 61; Paxson, "Highway Movement," 242; Seely, *American Highway System,* 38.

46. *Texas Highways,* February 1962, 14, and May 1962, 6; Knight, *Fort Worth,* 171; Dealey, *Diaper Days,* 96, 105, 106; Richard Morehead, *Dewitt C. Greer* (Austin: Eakin, 1984), 32.

47. Bascom N. Timmons, *Garner of Texas* (New York: Harper and Brothers Publishers, 1948), 3, 14, 19, 25, 30, 32, 48; Lionel V. Patenaude, *Texans, Politics and the New Deal* (New York: Garland Publishing, 1983), 30.

48. Gliddon, "Texas Highway Administration," 12, 16; Knight, *Fort Worth,* 173; Canion, "Historical Background," 95

49. *Texas Highways,* August 1931, 5, 6.

50. *Gainesville DR,* August 30, 1948.

51. George W. Tyler, *The History of Bell County* (San Antonio: Naylor, 1936), 346, 347.

52. Joseph A. Pratt and Christopher J. Castaneda, *Builders* (College Station: Texas A&M University Press, 1999), xii, 21–24; Robert A. Caro, *The Years of Lyndon Johnson: The Path to Power* (New York: Knopf, 1982), 370, 371.

53. Knight, *Fort Worth,* 172; *Texas Highways: Golden,* 14; *Texas Highways,* February 1962, 14; WPA, *Dallas Guide,* 87, 155, C. Dwight Dorough, *Mr. Sam* (New York: Random House, 1962), 112.

54. Knight, *Fort Worth,* 177.

55. George W. Hilton and John F. Due, *The Electric Interurban Railways in America* (Palo Alto, Calif.: Stanford University Press, 1960), 376–79; Tyler, *History of Bell County,* 340.

56. A. T. Jackson, "Austin's Street Car Era," 244–47; *Austin American-Statesman,* November 3, 2000.

57. State Highway Commission, *History of the Texas Highway Department* (Austin: State Highway Commission, 1939), 3.

58. *San Antonio Express,* July 19, 1936; Fisher, *Saving San Antonio,* 69, 70; Kirk Kite, "History of the Texas State Department of Highways and Public Transportation," thesis, 1981, 5; WPA, *Texas Guide,* 343.

59. Preston, *Dirt Roads,* 30, 37; American Association for Highway Improvement, *Good Roads Yearbook, 1917* (Washington, D.C.: American Association for Highway Improvement, 1917), 28, 475.

60. Hugill, "Good Roads," 342, 343; Rose, *Historic American Highways,* 106; *Texas Parade,* September 1940; Arthur H. Blanchard and Henry B. Drowne, *Text-Book on Highway Engineering* (New York: John Wiley and Sons, 1914), viii, ix.

61. Weingroff, PRO; Rose, *Historic American Highways,* 108.

62. Weingroff, PRO.

63. Seely, *American Highway System,* 49.

64. Gliddon, "Texas Highway Administration," 21.

65. Gliddon, "Texas Highway Administration," 29; *Texas Highways: Golden,* 17; John D. Huddleston, "Good Roads for Texas," thesis, Texas A&M University, 1981, 38.

66. *Texas Highways: Golden,* 17.

67. Gliddon, "Texas Highway Administration," 34.

68. Weingroff, PRO; *Texas Highways: Golden,* 21.

69. James P. Nash, *Road Building Materials in Texas* (Austin: University of Texas, 1918), 5, 7–15.

70. *Cambridge Encyclopedia of Latin America* (Cambridge: Cambridge University Press, 1992), 234, 235; Gilberto Miguel Hinojosa, *A Borderlands Town in Transition* (College Station: Texas A&M University Press, 1983), 118, 119; Don M. Coever and Linda B. Hall, *Texas and the Mexican Revolution* (San Antonio: Trinity University Press, 1984), 76, 79; J. B. Wilkinson, *Laredo and the Rio Grande Frontier* (Austin: Jenkins Publishing Company, 1975), 394, 396; John H. Coatsworth, *Growth against Development: The Economic Impact of Railroads in Porfirian Mexico* (Dekalb: Northern Illinois University Press, 1981), 1, 2.

CHAPTER 7

1. Bruce E. Seely, *Building the American Highway System* (Philadelphia: Temple University Press, 1987), 51; Albert C. Rose, *Historic American Highways* (Washington, D.C.: American Association of State Highway Officials, 1953), 112.

2. Seely, *American Highway System,* 51; Rose, *Historic American Highways,* 112.

3. Herbert N. Casson, Rollin W. Hutchinson Jr., and L. W. Ellis, *Horse, Truck and Tractor* (Chicago: F. G. Browne, 1913), 1–3, 34, 35.

4. Philip L. Cantelon and Kenneth D. Durr, *The Roadway Stor,* (Rockville, Md.: Montrose Press, 1996), 6.

5. John D. Huddleston, "Good Roads for Texas," thesis, Texas A&M University, 1981, 44; Peter J. Hugill, "Good Roads and the Automobile in the United States 1880–1929," *Geographical Review* 72, no. 3 (1982): 343.

6. Frederic L. Paxson, "The Highway Movement 1916–1935," *American Historical Review,* January 1946, 244.

7. J. R. Canion, "Historical Background of Road Building in Texas," thesis, Austin, 1936, 103, 104.

8. *Texas Highways,* February 1956, 34; Canion, "Historical Background," 106.

9. *Gainesville DR,* August 30, 1948; Irvin M. May Jr., *Marvin Jones* (College Station: Texas A&M University Press, 1980), 38.

10. Canion, "Historical Background," 108.

11. Reverdy T. Gliddon, "*Texas Highway Administration,*" thesis, Austin, 1951, 37, 38; Seely, *American Highway System,* 62.

12. P. J. R. MacIntosh, "The Biggest Highway Job in History," *Texas Monthly,* December 1929, 598; Paxson, "Highway Movement," 249.

13. Jerry D. Thompson, *Laredo: A Pictoral History* (Norfolk: Donning Company, 1986), 264, 265; *Laredo News,* May 29, 1983; W. E. Simpson, Consulting Engineers, *Plan for a Reinforced Concrete Bridge across the Rio Grande for the Laredo Bridge Company* (1920).

14. Samuel Salinas Alvarez, *Historia de los Caminos de Mexico* (Mexico: Banco Nacional de Obras y Servicios Publicos, 1994), 62, 64, 102, 111; Highway Education Board, *Highway of Friendship* (Washington, D.C.: Highway Education Board, 1924), 1; Catherine Cate Coblentz, *Pan American Highway* (Washington, D.C.: Pan American Union, 1942), 4, 5.

15. Canion, "Historical Background," 117, 118; Gliddon, "Texas Highway Administration," 40; Paxson, "Highway Movement," 249; Robert A. Caro, *The Years of Lyndon Johnson: The Path to Power* (New York: Knopf, 1982), 371.

16. *Texas Highways: Golden,* 22.

17. George W. Tyler, *The History of Bell County* (San Antonio: Naylor, 1936), 340, 347.

18. Rose, *Historic American Highways,* 119; Howard Lawrence Preston, *Dirt Roads to Dixie* (Knoxville: University of Tennessee Press, 1991), 130.

19. Preston, *Dirt Roads,* 130.

20. John A. Jakle and Keith A. Sculle, *Fast Food* (Baltimore: Johns Hopkins University Press, 1999), 43, 165, 172, 186; *Texas Highways,* October 1964, 14; John A. Jakle and Keith A. Sculle, *The Gas Station in America* (Baltimore: Johns Hopkins University Press, 1994), 55, 100, 114, 131, 132; Preston, *Dirt Roads,* 141.

21. Canion, "Historical Background," 115.

22. Canion, "Historical Background," 134; *Texas Highways: Golden,* 107; Huddleston, "Good Roads," 71.

23. *Texas Parade,* June 1936, 28; Gibb Gilchrist, *An Autobiography (Preliminary)* (Austin: Texas Department of Transportation, 1991), 47; Richard Morehead, *Dewitt C. Greer* (Austin: Eakin, 1984), 15.

24. Michael V. Hazel, *Dallas: A History of Big D* (Austin: Texas State Historical Association, 1997), 37, 38; Patricia E. Hill, *Dallas: The Making of a Modern City* (Austin: University of Texas Press, 1996), 100, 101; Gilchrist, *Autobiography,* 48; Leon F. Litwack, *Trouble in Mind* (New York: Knopf, 1998), 115, 136; Philip Dray, *At the Hands of Persons Unknown* (New York: Random House, 2002), 216–19.

25. Kirk Kite, "History of the Texas State Department of Highways and Public Transportation," thesis, 1981, 23, 27, 31, 33; Ken Anderson, "Konvicted," *Texas Alcade,* July–August, 2000, p. 31; Huddleston, "Good Roads," 75.

26. Gilchrist, *Autobiography,* 51, 52; Seely, *American Highway System,* 83.

27. Canion, "Historical Background," 140, 141; *Texas Highways: Golden,* 23.

28. Robert H. Talbert, *Cow Town Metropolis* (Fort Worth: Texas Christian University, 1956), 131; Preston, *Dirt Roads,* 159.

29. Seely, *American Highway System,* 72.

30. MacIntosh, "Biggest Highway Job," 580; *Texas Highways: Golden,* 120, 121.

31. *Texas Highways: Golden,* 120–26; State Highway Department of Texas, *Seventh Biennial Report,* December 8, 1930, 88.

32. *Texas Highways: Golden,* 36, 121; Morehead, *Dewitt C. Greer,* 16, 17.

33. *Texas Highways: Golden,* 120, 140–42.

34. *Seventh Biennial,* 82, 83; Hugill, "Good Roads," 344; *Texas Highways: Golden,* 129, 147–51.

35. *Seventh Biennial,* 40, 41, 71, 75; *Texas Parade,* August 1937, 17; *San Antonio Express,* October 17, 1931.

36. MacIntosh, "Biggest Highway Job," 610; *Texas Highways: Golden,* 122; *Seventh Biennial,* 41, 97.

37. Bryan C. Utecht, "Facing the Highway Problem," *Texas Monthly,* January 1929, 9.

38. *Texas Highways: Golden,* 130; Hugill, "Good Roads," 334.

39. Canion, "Historical Background," 145, 146.

40. *State Highway System of Texas,* January 1, 1929 (map); Canion, "Historical Background," 133; *San Antonio Express,* October 29, 1929; Robert A. Caro, *Years of Lyndon,* 166, 172.

41. *Seventh Biennial*, 52; Thompson, *Laredo: Pictorial*, 266, 267.

42. *San Antonio Express*, October 29, 1929.

43. *Texas Highways*, April 1975, 25; *Gainesville DR*, August 30, 1948.

44. Utecht, "Facing," 23; Jack Rhodes, *Intercity Bus Lines of the Southwest* (College Station: Texas A&M University Press, 1988), 33, 47–50, 62; Carlton Jackson, *Hounds of the Road* (Bowling Green, Ohio: Bowling Green University Popular Press, 1984), 8–13; Osgar Schisgall, *The Greyhound Story* (Chicago: J. G. Ferguson, 1985), 9; *Gainesville DR*, August 30, 1948.

45. Rose, *Historic American Highways*, 122–24.

46. Lionel V. Patenaude, "The New Deal and Texas," thesis, University of Texas, Austin, 1953, 76–78, 334; Patenaude, *Texans, Politics*, 165, Timmons, *Garner*, 134, 151.

47. Robert A. Caro, *Master of the Senate* (New York: Alfred A. Knopf, 2002), 124, 401; Caro, *Path to Power*, 467, 617; Anthony Champagne, *Congressman Sam Rayburn* (New Brunswick, N.J.: Rutgers University Press, 1984), 48; C. Dwight Dorough, *Mr. Sam* (New York: Random House, 1962), 128, 255, 265, 272, 414, 485; Patenaude, "New Deal," 70; Patenaude, *Texans, Politics*, 33, 42, 102.

48. *Texas Highways: Golden*, 23; Kite, "History of Highways," 65; Patenaude, "New Deal," 255, 341; Patenaude, *Texans, Politics*, 3.

49. Gibb Gilchrist, *Texas Highway Department 1927–1937* (1938), 31.

50. Gilchrist, *Texas Highway Department*, 84; *Seventh Biennial*, 50; Ruth Ann Overbeck Perez, "The Red River Bridges," thesis, University of Texas, 1969, 22–26.

51. Perez, "Red River Bridges," 51, 55, 57, 98, 110.

52. *New York Times*, July 18, 1931; Perez, "Red River Bridges," 117, 120–124.

53. *New York Times*, July 18, 1931; Perez, "Red River Bridges," 134, 138, 139.

54. *New York Times*, July 25, 1931.

55. Gilchrist, *Texas Highway Department*, 137; *Texas Parade*, April 1937, 20.

56. Baker, *Building*, 59, 60; Hill, *Dallas: The Making*, 106; Writers Program of the Dallas WPA (1936–1942), *The WPA Dallas Guide and History* (Dallas: Dallas Public Library, 1992), 85, 87, 94, 155; Hazel, *Dallas*, 34.

57. WPA, *Dallas Guide*, 155.

58. WPA, *Dallas Guide*, 97, 109, 155; Hill, *Dallas: The Making*, 118.

59. *Gainesville DR*, August 30, 1948; A. Morton Smith, *The First 100 Years in Cooke County* (San Antonio: Naylor, 1955), 193–94, 198–200; *Gainesville DR*, August 30, 1948.

60. *Texas Parade*, September 1936, 23; October 1936, 21; December 1936, 27; June 1937, 25.

61. Gilchrist, *Texas Highway Department*, 93, 97, 99; *Texas Parade*, May 1938, 7.

62. *Texas Parade*, December 1936, 24, and Nov 1937, 23; Gilchrist, *Texas Highway Department*, 116.

63. Lock's Good Road Maps of Local and Transcontinental Auto Routes, *Old Spanish Trail* (map); Lorrie K. Owen et al., *Dictionary of Texas Historic Places* (New York: Somerset, 1996), 128; Lewis F. Fisher, *Saving San Antonio* (Lubbock: Texas Tech University Press, 1996), 119, 122, 127, 147, 164, 168, 182–85, 194, 199; Patenaude, "New Deal," 99.

64. *Texas Parade*, May 1937, 221; Coblentz, *Pan American Highway*, 5; Rose, *Historic American Highways*, 121; Gilchrist, *Texas Highway Department*, 62; Salinas Alvarez, *Historia*, 118, 124, 134. *Texas Parade*, August 1936, 10, 28, 29; September 1937; February 1938, 20.

U.S. Department of Transportation (USDOT), *American Highways 1776–1976* (Washington, D.C.: Federal Highway Administration, 1976), 140.

65. *Texas Highways: Golden,* 28, 48; WPA, *Dallas Guide,* 98.

66. *Texas Highways: Golden,* 24; Gilchrist, *Texas Highway Department,* 130; Caro, *Path to Power,* 347; *Dallas News,* May 20, 1936; State Highway Commission, *History of the Texas Highway Department,* 14; Patenaude, *Texans, Politics,* 107.

67. *Texas Parade,* September 1936, 5; *Texas Highways: Golden,* 165; Caro, *Path to Power,* 340–44, 360–68; Patenaude, *Texans, Politics,* 99.

68. Jakle and Sculle, *Fast Food,* 50; Caro, *Master,* 403.

69. John A. Jakle, Keith A. Sculle, and Jefferson S. Rogers *The Motel in America* (Baltimore: Johns Hopkins University Press, 1996), 18, 91–100, 107; Charles L. Dearing, *American Highway Policy* (Washington, D.C.: Brookings Institution, 1941), 93; Seely, *American Highway System,* 89.

70. Dearing, *American Highway Policy,* 270, 271; *Texas Highways: Golden,* 27.

71. Gerald Markowitz and David Rosner, eds., *Slaves of the Depression* (Ithaca, N.Y.: Cornell University Press, 1987), 53–55.

72. William H. Harris, *The Harder We Run* (New York: Oxford University Press, 1982), 106; Caro, *Path to Power,* 372; Patenaude, *Texans, Politics,* 88, 92, 107.

73. Dearing, *American Highway Policy,* 97.

74. *Texas Highways: Golden,* 28; Tom W. Nichols, "The Trucking of Livestock in the San Antonio Area," thesis, University of Texas, 1941, 12.

75. *Handbook of Texas Online;* www. Amazon.com.

76. Bill C. Malone, *Country Music U.S.A. (*Austin: University of Texas Press, 1985), 82, 83, 155, 160, 231, 288; www. Amazon.com.

77. Seely, *American Highway System,* 84, 152; Robert A. Caro, *The Power Broker* (New York: Vintage Books, 1975), 162.

78. *Texas Highways: Golden,* 106; Seely, *American Highway System,* 152–54.

79. *Texas Highways: Golden,* 100; Seely, *American Highway System,* 91.

80. Seely, *American Highway System,* 102, 108, 121, 126; USDOT, *American Highways,* 329.

81. Texas Section, American Society of Civil Engineers, *The Texas Engineer,* Centennial Edition, December 1936, 108.

CHAPTER 8

1. Richard F. Weingroff, *Public Roads Online,* vol. 60, no. 1 (1996; hereafter cited as PRO); Bruce E. Seely, *Building the American Highway System* (Philadelphia: Temple University Press, 1987), 147.

2. Seely, *American Highway System,* 163; Thomas J. Schlereth, *US 40* (Indianapolis: Indiana Historical Society, 1985), 18.

3. Weingroff, PRO; Jose A. Gomez-Ibanez and John R. Meyer, *Going Private* (Washington, D.C.: Brookings Institution, 1993), 167; *Texas Parade,* September 1938, 31; Seely, *American Highway System,* 170.

4. Seely, *American Highway System,* 170.

5. WPA, *Texas Guide,* 173, 235, 264, 311, 336, 359.

6. *Texas Highways: Golden,* 34.

7. *Texas Parade,* October 1948, 19.

8. *Texas Parade,* December 1941, 3, 21, and May 1942, 6, 7; Hill, *Dallas: The Making,* 164.

9. Michael Collins, *Cooke County, Texas* (Gainesville: Cooke County Heritage Society, 1981), 58, 60, 62; *Texas Parade,* June 1942, 7; *Gainesville DR,* August 30, 1948; Carl Newton Tyson, *The Red River in Southwestern History* (Norman: University of Oklahoma Press, 1981), 179.

10. *Texas Parade,* March 1942, 26.

11. *Texas Parade,* August 1940, 17, 18, and March 1942, 26; *Texas Highways,* May 1960, 7; *Handbook of Texas Online.*

12. Seely, *American Highway System,* 177, 178; *Texas Parade,* April 1943, 12.

13. Albert C. Rose, *Historic American Highways* (Washington, D.C.: American Association of State Highway Officials, 1953), 129–30. *Texas Parade,* August 1941, p. 26; November 1941, p. 14; February 1942, 30, 31, May 1943; Rose, *Historic American Highways,* 121, 122, 129, 130; U.S. Department of Transportation (USDOT), *American Highways, 1776–1976* (Washington, D.C.: Federal Highway Administration, 1976), 150.

14. Mark H. Rose, *Interstate* (Lawrence: Regents Press of Kansas, 1979), 19; Weingroff, PRO; *Interregional Highways: Report of the National Interregional Highway Committee,* January 12, 1944, vii.

15. *Interregional Highways,* 4–12; Seely, *American Highway System,* 56, 57.

16. *Interregional Highways,* 56, 57.

17. *Interregional Highways,* 81–84, 89, 93–105.

18. *Interregional Highways,* 114, 115.

19. Texas Highway Department, *Texas and the Interstate Highway System* (Austin: Texas Highway Department, 1957), 5; introduction to the act, quoted in Kirk Kite, "History of the Texas State Department of Highways and Public Transportation," thesis, 1981, 120.

20. USDOT, *American Highways,* 469; Kite, "History of Highways," 120.

21. A. Morton Smith, *The First 100 Years in Cooke County* (San Antonio: Naylor, 1955), 216, 221; *Gainesville DR,* August 30, 1948.

22. *Gainesville DR,* August 30, 1948.

23. A. M. Smith, *First 100 Years,* 218, 221; *Texas Highways: Golden,* 101; *Gainesville DR,* August 30, 1948.

24. Reverdy T. Gliddon, "Texas Highway Administration," thesis, Austin, 1951, 99; *The Leadership of Speaker Sam Rayburn,* (Washington, D.C.: U.S. Government Printing Office, 1961), 35; Dorough, *Mr. Sam,* 305.

25. *Texas Highways: Golden,* 29.

26. *Texas Parade,* October 1948, 20, 21; *Texas Highways: Golden,* 29.

27. *Texas Parade,* October 1948, 22, 23; Michael V. Hazel, *Dallas: A History of Big D* (Austin: Texas State Historical Association, 1997), 51; Texas Historical Commission, *African Americans in Texas,* brochure, 20.

28. *Texas Parade,* October 1948, 24, 26, 28.

29. *Austin American,* September 11, 1947; *Texas Highways,* December 1954, 26.

30. *Austin Statesman,* May 7, 1946; WPA, *Texas Guide,* 306; *Texas Parade,* April 1958, 14, 18.

31. Seely, *American Highway System,* 192; Robert A. Caro, *Master of the Senate* (New York: Alfred A. Knopf, 2002), 247, 248; Caro, *Path to Power,* 469, 598.

32. Seely, *American Highway System,* 192, 205; *Texas Highways,* October 1955.

33. *Dallas News,* July 19, 1953.

34. *Austin Statesman,* November 30, 1952; Kite, "History of Highways," 131, 133.

35. *Dallas News,* October 30, 1953.

36. Kite, "History of Highways," 131–33; *Austin American-Statesman,* October 28, 2001.

37. John A. Jakle and Keith A. Sculle, *Fast Food* (Baltimore: Johns Hopkins University Press, 1999), 132–258; John A. Jakle, Keith A. Sculle, and Jefferson S. Rogers, *The Motel in America* (Baltimore: Johns Hopkins University Press, 1996), 142–273; Seely, *American Highway System,* 207.

38. USDOT, *American Highways,* 470; Weingroff, PRO; Seely, *American Highway System,* 213.

39. *Texas Highways,* January 1954, 2.

40. *Austin American,* February 18, 1954.

41. *Texas Highways,* August 1955, p. 11; Weingroff, PRO.

42. *Dallas News,* January 14, 1954; *Texas Highways,* June 1955, 16.

43. *Austin Statesman,* May 7, 1946; *Texas Highways,* January 1976, 37; Jill Kruse and Chris Hall, *IH-35: History and Future Alternatives,* Issue Paper (Austin: Downtown Austin Alliance, 1996), 4, 5.

44. *Construction and Maintenance,* March 1953, 11; *Austin American,* Aug 4, 1953, May 11, 1954 and May 17, 1956; *Texas Highways,* January 1958, 17.

45. *Texas Highways,* November 1954, 179, 180.

46. Kite, "History of Highways," 69, 129.

47. *Dallas Morning News,* June 10, 1955.

48. *Austin Statesman,* November 7, 1955; *Texas Highways,* November 1955, 9.

49. *Texas Highways,* July 1955, 36, and November 1955, 9.

50. Weingroff, PRO.

51. Weingroff, PRO; *Texas Highways,* January 1957.

52. USDOT, *American Highways,* 172, 173; Seely, *American Highway System,* 214, 215; Weingroff, PRO; Tom Lewis, *Divided Highways* (New York: Viking, 1997), 109; Seely, *American Highway System,* 215–17; M. H. Rose, *Interstate,* 88, 89; Dorough, *Mr. Sam,* 488.

53. Weingroff, PRO.

54. Weingroff, PRO; Caro, *Master,* 678.

55. Texas Highway Department, *Texas and the Interstate,* 9, 25.

56. *Texas Highways,* August 1961, 2.

57. *Texas Highways,* October 1956, 2.

58. *Texas Highways,* February 1957, 7.

59. *Texas Highways,* January 1957, 1, and September 1957, 18.

60. *Dallas News,* August 25, 1957, and Feb 10, 1958; *Texas Highways,* December 1957, 7; *Fort Worth,* September 1958.

61. *Texas Highways,* November 1957, 7, and January 1958, 18.

62. Jerry D. Thompson, *Laredo: A Pictoral History* (Norfolk: Donning Company, 1986), 269, 271. *Texas Parade,* May 1955, 19; April 1958, 17; April 1959, 16–18.

63. *Texas Parade,* May 1949, 13; February 1951, 17; April 1958, 14, 18.

64. *Texas Highways,* January 1958.

65. *Texas Highways,* March 1958, 2, 7.

66. Karl Detzer, "Our Great Big Highway Bungle," *Readers Digest,* July 1960, 46.

67. William L. Thomas Jr., ed., *Man's Role in Changing the Face of the Earth,* vol. 1 (Chicago: University of Chicago Press, 1956), 383, 384; Lewis Mumford, *The Highway and the City* (New York: Harcourt, Brace and World, 1963), 234.

68. Detzer, "Our Great Big," 45–47.

69. Detzer, "Our Great Big," 48–50.

70. *Texas Highways,* April 1960, 16; Detzer, "Our Great Big," 48–50.

71. Mumford, *The Highway,* 219; Caro, *Power Broker,* 940.

72. William G. Adkins, "Economic Impacts of Expressways in Dallas and San Antonio, *Traffic Quarterly,* July 1959, 335–40.

73. Adkins, "Economic Impacts," 340–44.

74. Jesse L. Buffington, *Economic Impact of Interstate Highway 35E on Waxahachie, Texas,* Texas Transportation Institute Bulletin no. 35, Research Report no. 4–6 (1966), 9, 43; *Texas Highways,* July 1967, 20.

75. *Texas Highways,* April 1966, 40.

76. Jesse L. Buffington, *Economic Impact Restudy: Austin, Texas,* Texas Transportation Institute Bulletin no. 26, Research Report no. 4–4 (1964), 6, 15, 26.

77. Buffington, *Economic Impact Restudy,* 6, 15.

78. Reijo Helaakoski, "Economic Effects of Highway By-passes on Business Activities in Small Cities," thesis, University of Texas, 1991, 45, 47.

CHAPTER 9

1. *Dallas News,* June 29, 1961, *Texas Highways,* June 1962, 6, 7, and April 1964, 38.

2. *Texas Highways,* October 1961, 21; May 1962, 16; June 1962, 6, 7.

3. *Texas Highways,* August 1963, 3; October 1963, 12, 22; April 1964, 11.

4. *Texas Highways,* February 1964, 12, 13.

5. *Texas Highways,* April 1958, 6; July 1960, 12–15. *Texas Highways: Golden,* 132, 133. *Texas Highways,* April 1954, 24; January 1963, 9; February 1964, 13; January 1966, 11.

6. *Texas Highways,* February 1960, 3; April 1964, 33.

7. *Texas Highways: Golden,* 132, 133; *Texas Highways,* January 1963, 9; February 1964, 13; January 1966, 11.

8. William R. Manchester, *The Death of a President* (New York: Harper and Row, 1967), 164.

9. *Waco Urban Transportation Plan,* vol. 3 (1966), xii, xiv, xvii, 5, 31; *Texas Highways,* May 1963, 21.

10. *Laredo Urban Transportation Plan,* vol. 2 (1964), 3, 35, 69, 155; *Texas Highways,* June 1962, 19, and April 1963, 18.

11. *San Antonio Express,* Supplement, January 16, 1966; *Texas Highways,* March 1965, 23; December 1965, 19; February 1966, 33; March 1966, 8.

12. *Texas Highways,* March 1965, 21, 22; November 1965, 27; May 1966, 13; July 1966, 3; March 1967, 1; May 1967, 7.

13. *Houston Post,* January 6, 1965, and July 17, 1966.

14. *Texas Highways: Golden,* 43; U.S. Department of Transportation (USDOT), *American Highways 1776–1976* (Washington, D.C.: Federal Highway Administration, 1976), 371.

15. Helen Leavitt, *Superhighway-Superhoax* (New York: Ballantine Books, 1971); Richard O. Baumbach Jr. and William E. Borah (Afterword by Diane L. Donley), *The Second Battle of New Orleans* (Tuscaloosa: University of Alabama Press, 1981), xv, xvi.

16. *Austin American-Statesman,* April 15, 2001; Tom Lewis, *Divided Highways* (New York: Viking, 1997), 240.

17. *Texas Highways,* January 1967, 27, and November 1967, 29.

18. Gruen Associates for USDOT, FHA, *San Antonio North Expressway Study,* June 1971, 4; Lewis F. Fisher, *Saving San Antonio* (Lubbock: Texas Tech University Press, 1996), 286.

19. *San Antonio Express,* January 11, 1961; *San Antonio Express,* October 17, 1963; Fisher, *Saving San Antonio,* 266, 290; Gruen, *San Antonio North,* 5.

20. Gruen, *San Antonio North,* 4, 5; Fisher, *Saving San Antonio,* 297, 304.

21. Fisher, *Saving San Antonio,* 321–25, 329; Gruen, *San Antonio North,* 5, 6; *San Antonio Express,* December 9, 1970.

22. *San Antonio Express,* January 29, 1978; Fisher, *Saving San Antonio,* 330–33.

23. USDOT, *American Highways,* 374; Baumbach and Borah, *Second Battle,* 244, 245, 256; Richard F. Weingroff, *Public Roads Online,* vol. 60, no. 1 (1996).

24. Fisher, *Saving San Antonio,* 371, 375, 384, 387, 496; *Texas Highways,* May 1970, 2.

25. *Texas Highways,* February 1964, 15; May 1964, 8; September 1970, 28; March 1974, 27.

26. *Texas Highways,* September 1970, 28, and March 1974, 27; *Austin American-Statesman,* January 10, 1971.

27. *Texas Highways,* September 1973, 1; *Daily Texan,* February 14, 1975; *Texas Highways,* January 1976, 37; Hilton Hagan, *An Informal History of the Texas Department of Transportation* (Austin: Texas Department of Transportation, 1991), 49; *Austin American-Statesman,* January 3, 2005.

28. *Texas Highways,* March 1967, 17, and April 1970, 21.

29. *Texas Highways,* September 1970, 25, and November 1973, 25.

30. *Texas Highways,* March 1974, 27; Kirk Kite, "History of the Texas State Department of Highways and Public Transportation," thesis, 1981, 137.

31. Amado Felipe Cavazos, *Zachry* (San Antonio: Metro Press, 1993), 130–33.

32. Hagan, *Informal History,* 40, 46, 64; Cavazos, *Zachry,* 130–33.

33. USDOT, U.S. Coast Guard, *Final Environmental Impact/4(f) Statement for Proposed International Bridge Project at Laredo, Texas* (1974), 10, 11, 13.

34. Coast Guard, *Final,* 2, 3, 13.

35. Coast Guard, *Final,* 11, 17.

36. Coast Guard, *Final,* iv, 19, 39, B-60a, B-60b.

37. Coast Guard, *Final,* ii, 14, 15, 20.

38. Coast Guard, *Final,* 1, 4–7, B-60a; *Laredo Times,* March 5, 1981.

39. Hagan, *Informal History,* 52, 54; *Austin American-Statesman,* November 26, 2000.

40. *TXDOT Pocket Facts,* September 30, 2000; *2000 U.S. Census; Austin American-Statesman,* December 31, 2003.

41. *2000 U.S. Census.*

42. *Corpus Christi Caller-Times,* November 18, 2000; *Austin American-Statesman,* March 25, 2001.

43. *Wall Street Journal,* September 13, 2000; *Corpus Christi Caller-Times,* November 18, 2000.

44. *San Antonio Express,* June 2, 1999; TXDOT; *Austin American-Statesman,* March 24, 2001; *San Antonio Express,* April 9, 2000, and April 15, 2000.

45. *San Antonio Express,* June 2, 1999, and April 9, 2000; *Houston Chronicle,* August 1, 1999; *Austin American-Statesman,* December 10, 2002, and January 7, 2004.

46. Jose A. Gomez-Ibanez and John R. Meyer, *Going Private* (Washington, D.C.: Brookings Institution, 1993), 171; *Austin American-Statesman,* October 4, 2003.

47. *Austin American-Statesman,* August 30, 2002; August 31, 2002; September 28, 2003; October 4, 2003. *Official Statement,* Texas Transportation Commission, August 7, 2002.

48. TXDOT SH130 Traffic Forecast, Executive Summary, November 1, 2000, 13; Carter and Burgess, Inc., *Austin-San Antonio Commute Rail Study* (1999), 1, 2; CAMPO *Newsletter* 8, n0.1 (April, 2000): 3; *Austin American-Statesman,* November 29, 2002.

49. I-35 Steering Committee, pp. S-7, S-8, III-6; III-17, III-19, VII-50, V-1.I-35, VII-20.

50. TXDOT SH130 Traffic Forecast, 13. *Austin American-Statesman,* April 1, 1998; November 15, 2000; March 12, 2001; April 5, 2001; April 10, 2001; July 9, 2001; March 1, 2002; April 6, 2002; September 26, 2003; November 5, 2003. *Wall Street Journal,* August 8, 2001; *Christian Science Monitor,* October 21, 1999; *Austin Chronicle,* September 6, 2002, and September 20, 2002.

51. *Austin American-Statesman,* June 20, 2003, and August 22, 2003; House Research Organization, *Analysis of HB 3588,* May 9, 2003; "A Big, Fat Texas Boondoggle?" *Time,* December 6, 2004.

52. *Austin American-Statesman,* August 2, 2001; Transportation Research Board, *The Costs of Sprawl Revisited* (Washington, D.C.: National Academy Press, 1998), 68; Richard B. Peiser, "Density and Urban Sprawl," *Land Economics* 65, no. 3 (1990): 193.

53. Transportation Research Board, *Costs of Sprawl,* 35, 37; Gerrit J. Knapp, "The Pure Effects of Urban Growth Boundaries on Metropolitan Portland, Oregon," *Land Economics* 61, no. 1 (1985): 26; Alex Marshall, *How Cities Work* (Austin: University of Texas Press, 2000), 162, 163, 166.

54. *Wall Street Journal,* March 27, 2002.

55. Joel Garreau, *Edge City* (New York: Anchor Books, 1992), 209, 229.

56. *Austin American-Statesman,* October 14, 2002; January 14, 2003; August 26, 2003.

57. *Austin American-Statesman,* March 12, 2001; December 24, 2001; October 16, 2003; January 2, 2004. *Fort Worth Star Telegram,* October 17, 2000; Dallas Area Rapid Transit (DART) Web site, www.dart.org.

58. Carter and Burgess, Inc., *Austin-San Antonio Commuter Rail Study* (1999), 1, 2; CAMPO *Newsletter* 8, no. 1 (April, 2000): 3; *Austin American-Statesman,* March 9, 2002; October 9, 2002; October 24, 2003; December 29, 2003.

59. US DOT Web site, *HSGT Report; Wall Street Journal,* February 2, 2000; California High Speed Rail Authority Web site, www.cahighspeedrail.ca.gov.

60. Transportation Research Board, *In Pursuit of Speed,* Special Report 233 (Washington, D.C.: Transportation Research Board, 1991), vi, 5, 6; California High Speed Rail Authority

Web site, www.cahighspeedrail.ca.gov; Marc H. Burns, *High Speed Rail in the Rear View Mirror* (Austin: M. H. Burns, 1995), 22; Texas Transportation Institute, *Ridership and Related Issues,* Texas A&M University (1991), 1.

61. Burns, *High Speed Rail,* 10, 18; Transportation Research Board, *In Pursuit,* 4, 5; *Austin American-Statesman,* February 9, 2004.

CONCLUSION

1. *Austin American-Statesman,* September 21, 2003.

2. William J. Folan et al., *Laredo, Texas: Gateway Community on the Texas Borderlands,* (San Antonio: Center for Archeological Research, University of Texas at San Antonio, 1986), 36, 37.

MAPS

Map 1. Pre-Columbian Civilizations. Sources: *Cambridge Encyclopedia of Latin America* (Cambridge: Cambridge University Press, 1992); W. W. Newcomb Jr., *The Indians of Texas* (Austin: University of Texas Press, 1961); Parker Nunley, *A Field Guide to Archeological Sites of Texas* (Austin: Texas Monthly Press, 1989); George E. Stuart, *National Geographic Archeological Map of Middle America* (Washington, D.C.: National Geographic Society, 1968); William R. Swagerty, "Protohistoric Trade in Western North America," in *Columbian Consequences,* vol. 3, ed. David H. Thomas (Washington, D.C.: Smithsonian Instutution Press, 1991).

Map 2. The First Europeans: Selected Routes, 1519–1564. Sources: Stanley A. Arbingast, *Atlas of Mexico* (Austin: Bureau of Business Research, University of Texas at Austin, 1975); Herbert E. Bolton, *Coronado* (Albuquerque: University of New Mexico Press, 1949); James E. Bruseth and Nancy E. Kenmotsu, "From Naguatex to the River Daycao: The Route of the Hernando de Soto Expedition through Texas," *North American Archeologist* 14 (1993); Donald E. Chipman, *Spanish Texas* (Austin: University of Texas Press, 1992); Frederick W. Hodge (ed.), *Spanish Explorers in the Southern United States 1528–1543* (New York: Scribner, 1907); Albert C. Rose, *Historic American Highways* (Washington, D.C.: American Association of State Highway Officials, 1953).

Map 3. Silver Mining and Caminos Reales, 1519–1608. Sources: Samuel Salinas Alvarez, *Historia de los Caminos de Mexico* (Mexico: Banco Nacional de Obras y Servicios Publicos, 1994); Peter J. Bakewell, *Silver Mining and Society in Colonial Mexico* (Cambridge: Cambridge University Press, 1971); *Cambridge Encyclopedia of Latin America* (Cambridge: Cambridge University Press, 1992); Philip Wayne Powell, *Soldiers, Indians and Silver* (Berkeley: University of California Press, 1952); Robert C. West, "The Mining Community in Northern New Spain," *Ibero-Americana* 30 (1949).

Map 4. Selected Expeditions in Texas, 1690–1778. Sources: Herbert E. Bolton, *Texas in the Middle Eighteenth Century* (Austin: University of Texas Press, 1970); William C. Foster (ed.), "Texas and Northeastern Mexico," Introduction to Juan Bautista Chapa's *Historia de Nuevo Leon* (Austin: University of Texas Press, 1997); William C. Foster, *Spanish Expeditions into Texas 1689–1768* (Austin: University of Texas Press, 1995); A. Joachim McGraw, John W. Clark Jr., and Elizabeth Robbins (eds.), *A Texas Legacy: The Old San Antonio Road and the Caminos Reales* (Austin: Texas Department of Transportation, 1991); Richard G. Santos, *Aguayo Expedition into Texas* (Austin: Jenkins, 1981); J. W. Williams, *Old Texas Trails* (Burnet: Eakin Press, 1979).

Map 5. Cross-Texas Expeditions, 1785–1808. Sources: Elizabeth Ann Harper John, *Storms Brewed in Other Men's Worlds* (College Station: Texas A&M University Press, 1975); Elizabeth Ann Harper, "The Taovaya Indians in Frontier Trade and Diplomacy," *Chronicles of Oklahoma* 31, no. 3 (1953–54); Elizabeth Ann Harper, "The Taovaya Indians in Frontier Trade and Diplomacy, 1769–1779," *Southwestern Historical Quarterly,* October 1953; Noel M. Loomis and Abraham P. Nasatir, *Pedro Vial and the Roads to Santa Fe* (Norman: University of Oklahoma Press, 1967); Roy L. Swift and Leavitt Corning Jr., *Three Roads to Chihuahua* (Austin: Eakin Press, 1988).

Map 6. Selected Settlements, Roads, and Trails in 1835. Sources: William Ranson Hogan, *The Texas Republic* (Norman: University of Oklahoma Press, 1946); U.S. War Department Map of 1844; J. H. Young, *New Map of Texas* (Philadelphia: S. Augustus Mitchell, 1837).

Map 7. (a) Colonel William G. Cooke's Military Road, 1840–1841. Sources: Joseph Milton Nance, *After San Jacinto* (Austin: University of Texas Press, 1963); Gerald S. Pierce, "The Military Road Expedition of 1840–41, *Texas Military History* 6 (1967); Roy L. Swift and Leavitt Corning Jr., *Three Roads to Chihuahua* (Austin: Eakin Press, 1988); J. W. Williams, "The National Road of the Republic of Texas," *Southwestern Historical Quarterly* 47 (1943–44). (b) H. L. Upshur's Sketch Showing the Route of the Military Road from Red River to Austin—Col. Wm. G. Cooke Commanding, Wm. H. Hunt, Engineer (1840). Source: Texas General Land Office.

Map 8. Selected Forts and Military Routes, 1849. Sources: Roger N. Conger et al., *Frontier Forts of Texas* (Waco: Texian Press, 1966); W. Turrentine Jackson, *Wagon Roads West* (Berkeley: University of California Press, 1952); Nathaniel H. Michler, *Bureau of Topographical Engineers Report to U.S. War Department,* July 23, 1850; Waterman L. Ormsby, *The Butterfield Overland Mail* (San Marino: Huntington Library, 1942).

Map 9. Cattle Trails and Indian Nations, 1854–1885. Sources: Wayne Gard, *The Chisholm Trail* (Norman: University of Oklahoma Press, 1954); Julia Kathryn Garrett, *Fort Worth: A Frontier Triumph* (Austin: Encino Press, 1972); Stan Hoig, *Jesse Chisholm* (Niwot, Colo: University of Colorado Press, 1991); U.S. Department of Interior Map of Indian Territory (1876); Donald E. Worcester, *The Chisholm Trail* (Lincoln: University of Nebraska Press, 1980).

Map 10. Selected Railroads at December 31, 1881. Sources: Andrew M. Modelski, "Map of Northern Part of the Mexican National Railway (1881)," *Railroad Maps of North America* (Washington, D.C.: Library of Congress, 1984); Charles S. Potts, *Railroad Transportation in Texas* (Austin: University of Texas, 1909); S. G. Reed, *A History of the Texas Railroads* (New York: Arno Press, 1941).

Map 11. Selected Highways from State Map of June 1917. Sources: Texas Highway Department, *Map Showing Proposed System of State Highways,* June 1917, and *Official Highway Map of 1922.*

Map 12. Pan American Highway, 1936. Sources: *Texas Parade,* August 1941; Samuel Salinas Alvarez, *Historia de los Caminos de Mexico* (Mexico: Banco Nacional de Obras y Servicios Publicos, 1994); Texas Highway Department, *Official Map of Highway System of Texas* (March 1, 1936).

Map 13. PRA Approved Interstate Routes as of August 2, 1947. Source: Public Roads Administration, *National System of Interstate Highways Selected by Joint Action of the Several State*

Highway Departments as Modified and Approved by the Administrator, Federal Works Agency, Public Roads Administration, August 2, 1947.

Map 14. Interstates in Progress, December 31, 1965. Sources: *Dallas Morning News,* September 20, 1965; Enco/Humble Oil and Refining Company, Texas Road Map (March 1966); *Texas Highways,* December 1965.

Map 15. Proposed Texas TGV (1989) and Proposed Loop Roads. Sources: *Austin American Statesman,* November 15, 2000; City of Laredo Planning Department; Executive Summary of Franchise Application to the Texas High Speed Rail Authority, January 16, 1991 (unpublished).

Index

Page numbers in *italics* refer to maps.